TEETH
VOLUME 1
BORN

DONNY CATES co-creator & writer

GARRY BROWN co-creator & artist

MARK ENGLERT colorist

TAYLOR ESPOSITO letterer

GARRY BROWN & MARK ENGLERT front & orginal covers

GARRY BROWN, DYLAN BURNETT, ELIAS CHATZOUDIS, JUAN DOE, FRANCESCO FRANCAVILLA, PHIL HESTER, NAT JONES, CORBYN S. KERN, TOBIAS MORROW, BRENT PEEPLES, SHELBY ROBERTSON, MIKE ROOTH, GEOF SHAW, ELIZABETH TORQUE, ARTURO TORRES, CHRIS VISIONS, KARL WALLER and LARRY WATTS variant covers

JOHN J. HILL logo designer

JOHN J. HILL & COREY BREEN book designers

MIKE MARTS editor

AFTERSHOCK

MIKE MARTS - Editor-in-Chief • JOE PRUETT - Publisher/ Chief Creative Officer • LEE KRAMER - President
JAWAD QURESHI - SVP, Investor Relations • JON KRAMER - Chief Executive Officer • MIKE ZAGARI - SVP, Brand
JAY BEHLING - Chief Financial Officer • STEPHAN NILSON - Publishing Operations Manager
LISA Y. WU - Retailer/Fan Relations Manager • ASHLEY WYATT - Publishing Assistant

AfterShock Trade Dress and Interior Design by JOHN J. HILL • AfterShock Logo Design by COMICRAFT
Original series production (issues 1-5) by CHARLES PRITCHETT • Proofreading by DOCTOR Z.
Publicity: contact AARON MARION (aaron@fifteenminutes.com) & RYAN CROY (ryan@fifteenminutes.com) at 15 MINUTES
Special thanks to TEDDY LEO & LISA MOODY

BABYTEETH VOLUME 1: BORN Published by AfterShock Comics, LLC, 15300 Ventura Boulevard Suite 507, Sherman Oaks, CA 91403. Originally published as Babyteeth #1-5. PRINTED IN KOREA.
First Printing: December 2017. 10 9 8 7 6 5 4 3 2 1

AFTERSHOCKCOMICS.COM Follow us on social media

INTRODUCTION

NEW YORK CITY COMIC-CON
October 2016

After several long months of pitching various project ideas to AfterShock, an exasperated Donny Cates sat down behind our NYCC booth between myself and President Lee Kramer. Looking semi-defeated, Donny turned to each of us and said, "All right, listen...I came up with this new idea last night in my hotel room, but you're probably going to hate it.

"I call it BABYTEETH..."

Donny then proceeded to tell us all about the tumultuous life of young Sadie Ritter. He told us about Sadie's tough-as-nails sister, Heather. He told us about her anchor of a father, Mike. He described the dangers of the Prairie Wolf and the Coyote and Kevin and Darcy and—of course—Marty the demon raccoon.

He went on for close to a half hour describing the intricate would that Sadie lived in, and the crazy adventures she would embark upon. But, you see, he had us from minute one...

"Imagine a sixteen-year-old geek of a girl gets pregnant...and to make matters worse, she gives birth to the Antichrist."

We were hooked.

In those rarest of moments for an editor, I greenlit the project on the spot.

DONNY CATES

GARRY BROWN

BABY✝eeTH

VOLUME

1

BORN

MARK ENGLERT

TAYLOR ESPOSITO

BABY

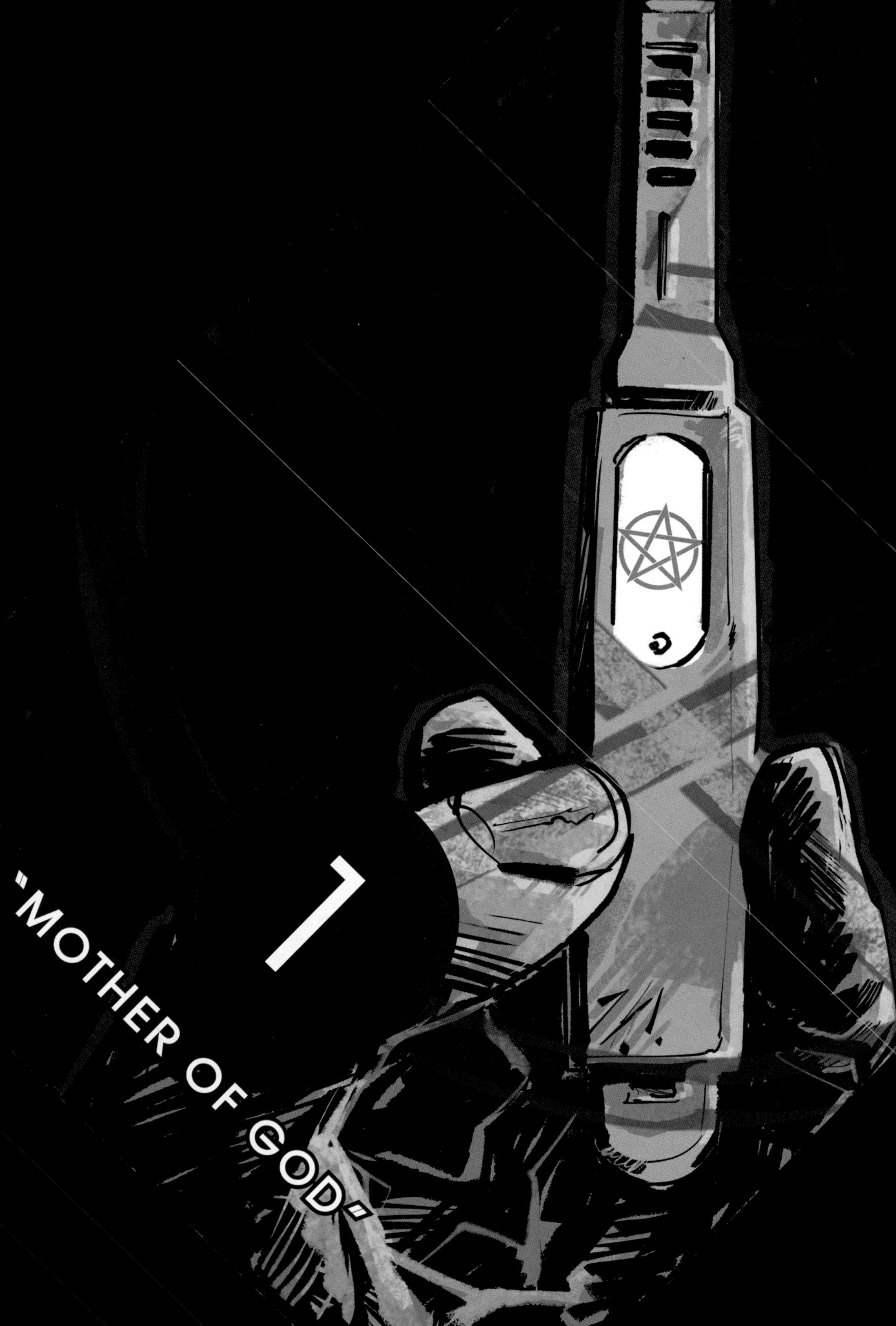
7
"MOTHER OF GOD"

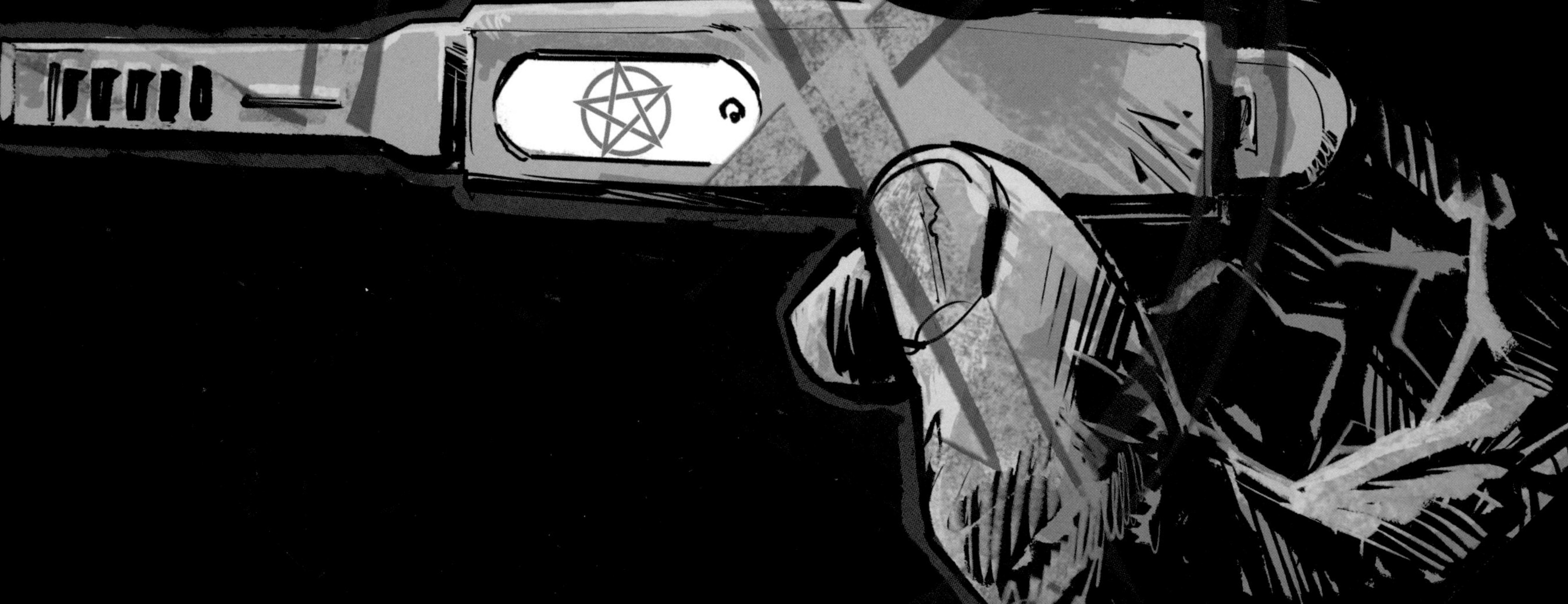

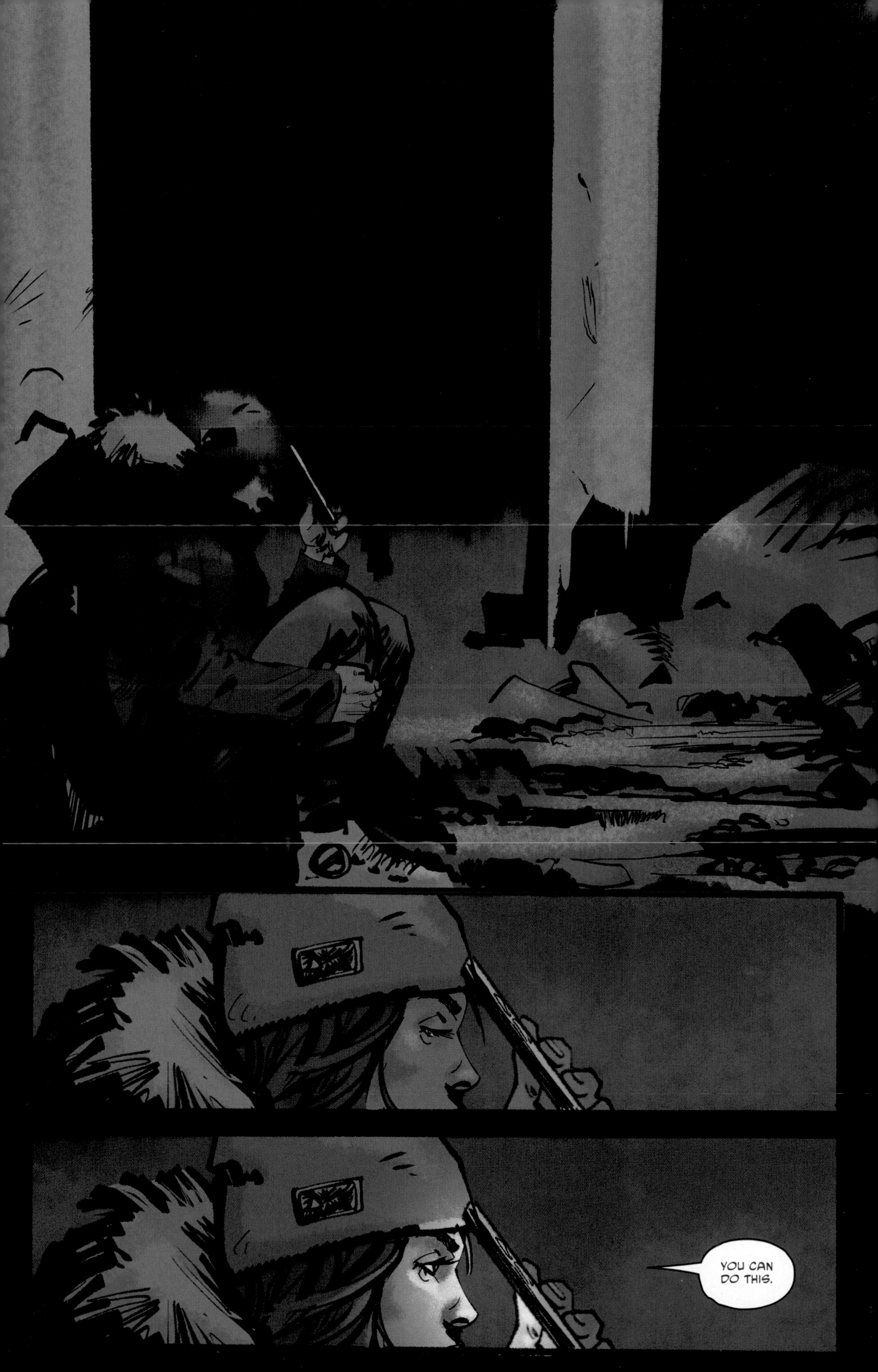
YOU CAN DO THIS.

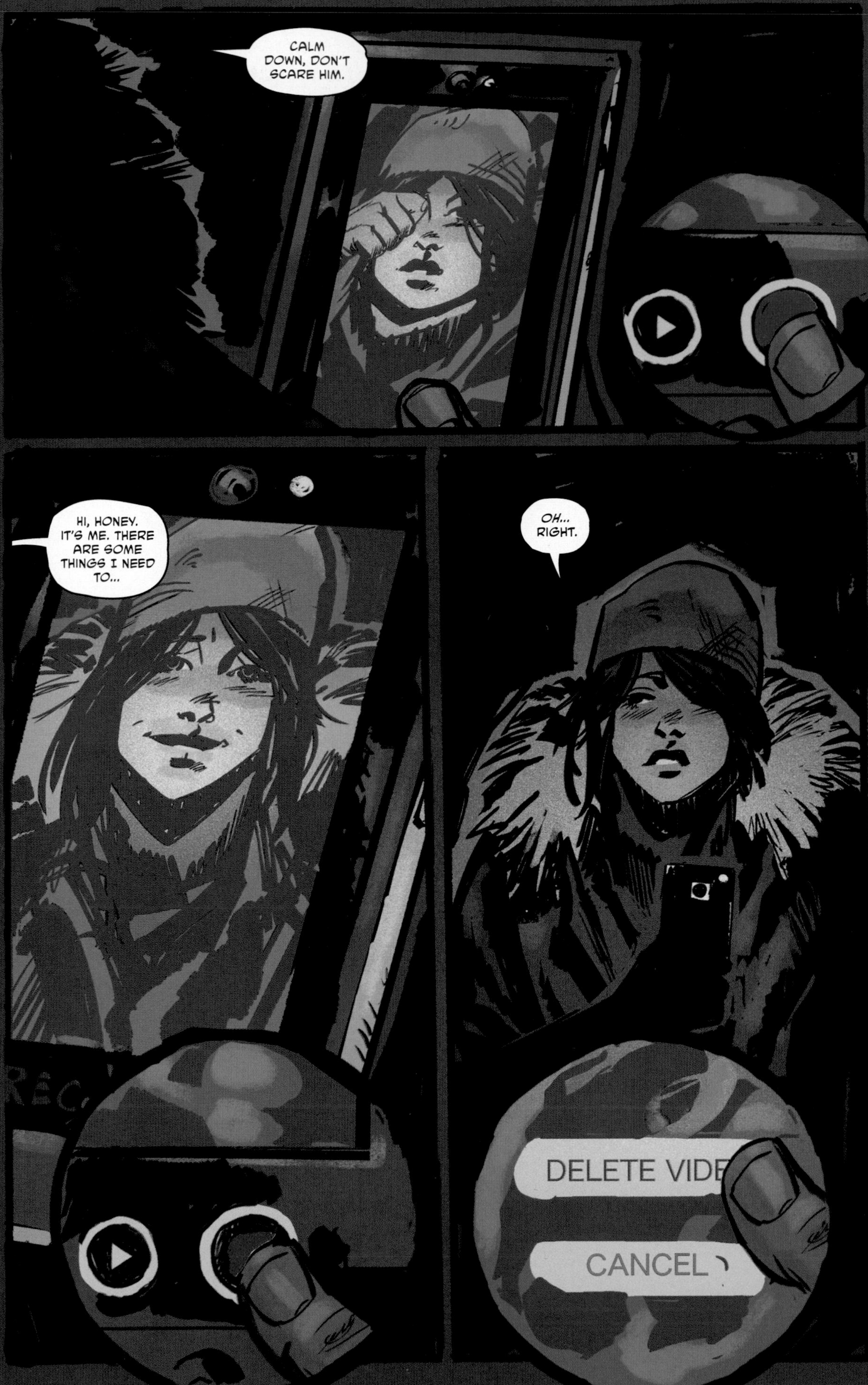
CALM DOWN, DON'T SCARE HIM.
HI, HONEY. IT'S ME. THERE ARE SOME THINGS I NEED TO...
OH... RIGHT.
DELETE VIDE
CANCEL

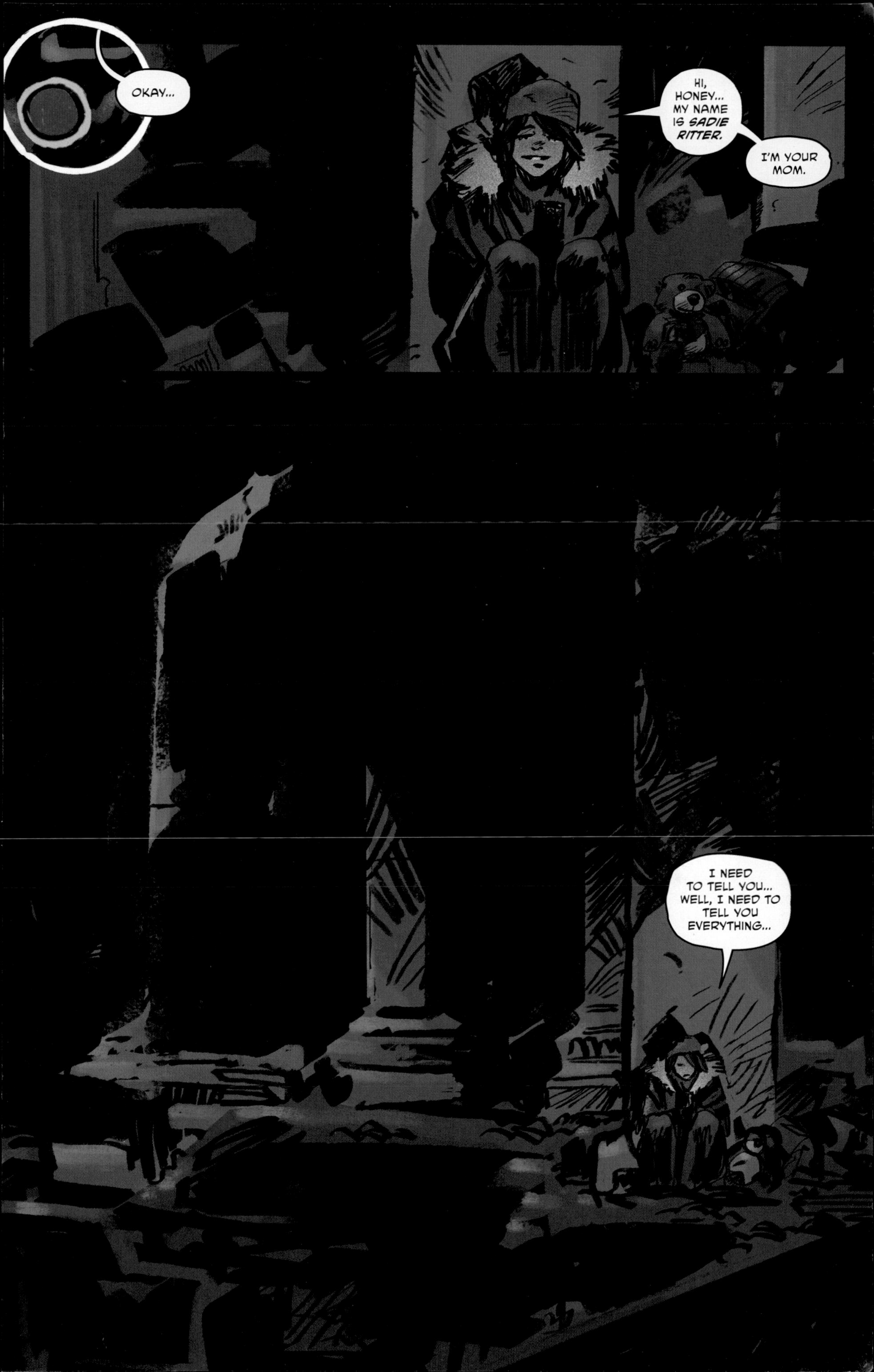
OKAY...
HI, HONEY... MY NAME IS SADIE RITTER.
I'M YOUR MOM.
I NEED TO TELL YOU... WELL, I NEED TO TELL YOU EVERYTHING...

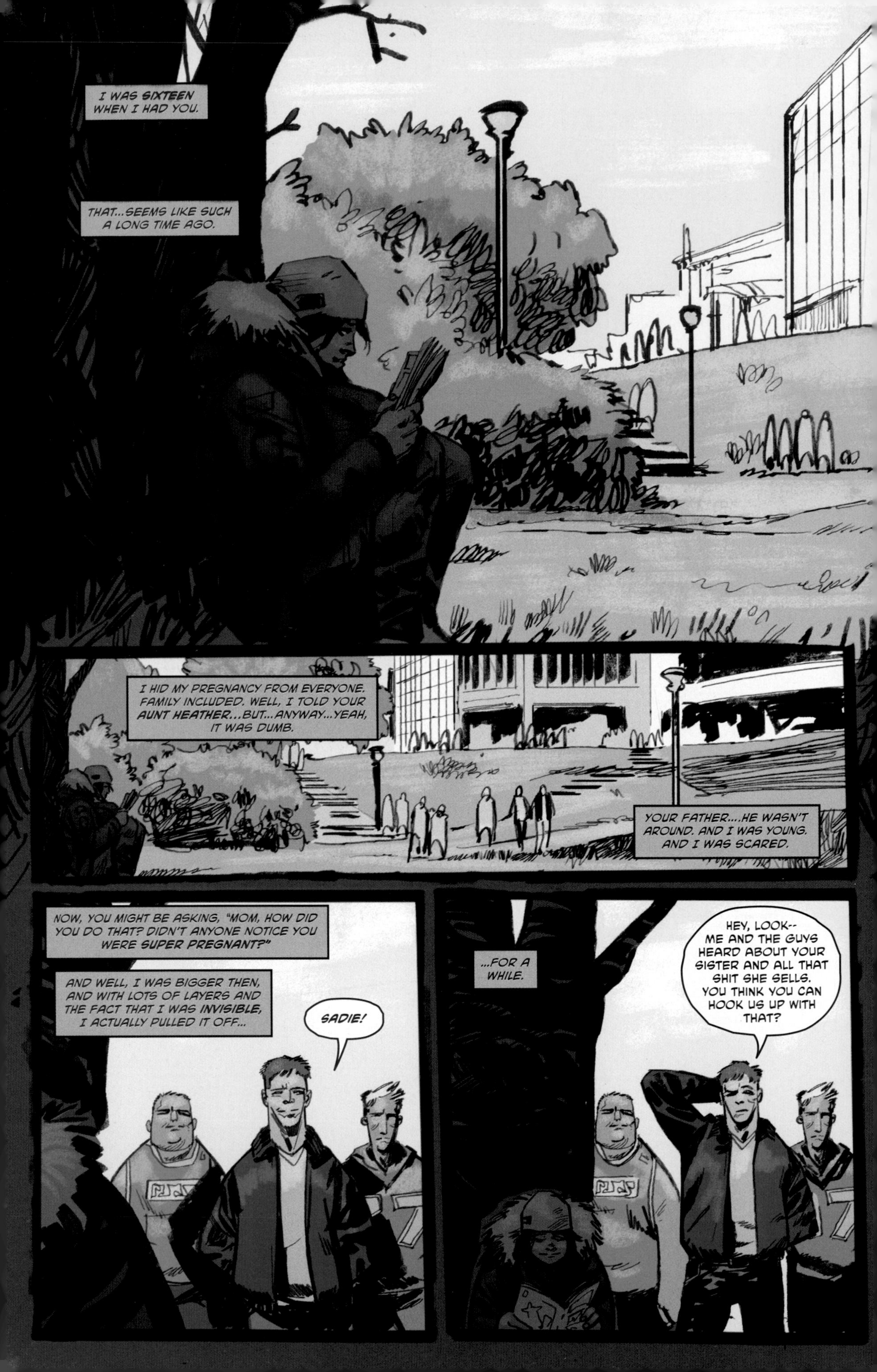

I WAS SIXTEEN WHEN I HAD YOU.
THAT...SEEMS LIKE SUCH A LONG TIME AGO.
I HID MY PREGNANCY FROM EVERYONE. FAMILY INCLUDED. WELL, I TOLD YOUR AUNT HEATHER...BUT...ANYWAY...YEAH, IT WAS DUMB.
YOUR FATHER....HE WASN'T AROUND. AND I WAS YOUNG. AND I WAS SCARED.
NOW, YOU MIGHT BE ASKING, "MOM, HOW DID YOU DO THAT? DIDN'T ANYONE NOTICE YOU WERE SUPER PREGNANT?"
AND WELL, I WAS BIGGER THEN, AND WITH LOTS OF LAYERS AND THE FACT THAT I WAS INVISIBLE, I ACTUALLY PULLED IT OFF...
SADIE!
...FOR A WHILE.
HEY, LOOK-- ME AND THE GUYS HEARD ABOUT YOUR SISTER AND ALL THAT SHIT SHE SELLS. YOU THINK YOU CAN HOOK US UP WITH THAT?

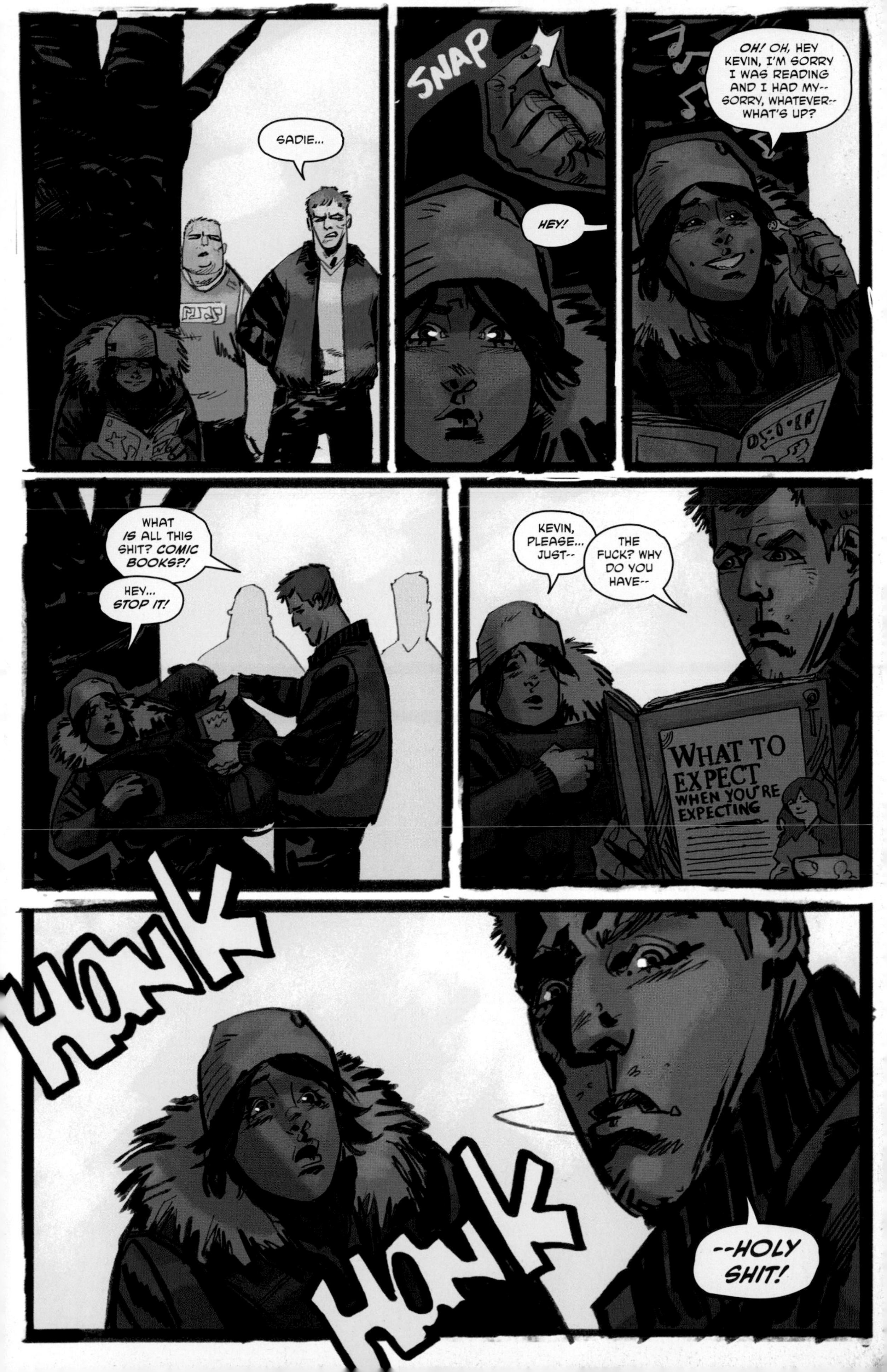
SADIE...
SNAP
HEY!
OH! OH, HEY KEVIN, I'M SORRY I WAS READING AND I HAD MY-- SORRY, WHATEVER-- WHAT'S UP?
WHAT IS ALL THIS SHIT? COMIC BOOKS?!
HEY... STOP IT!
KEVIN, PLEASE... JUST--
THE FUCK? WHY DO YOU HAVE--
WHAT TO EXPECT WHEN YOU'RE EXPECTING
HONK
HONK
--HOLY SHIT!

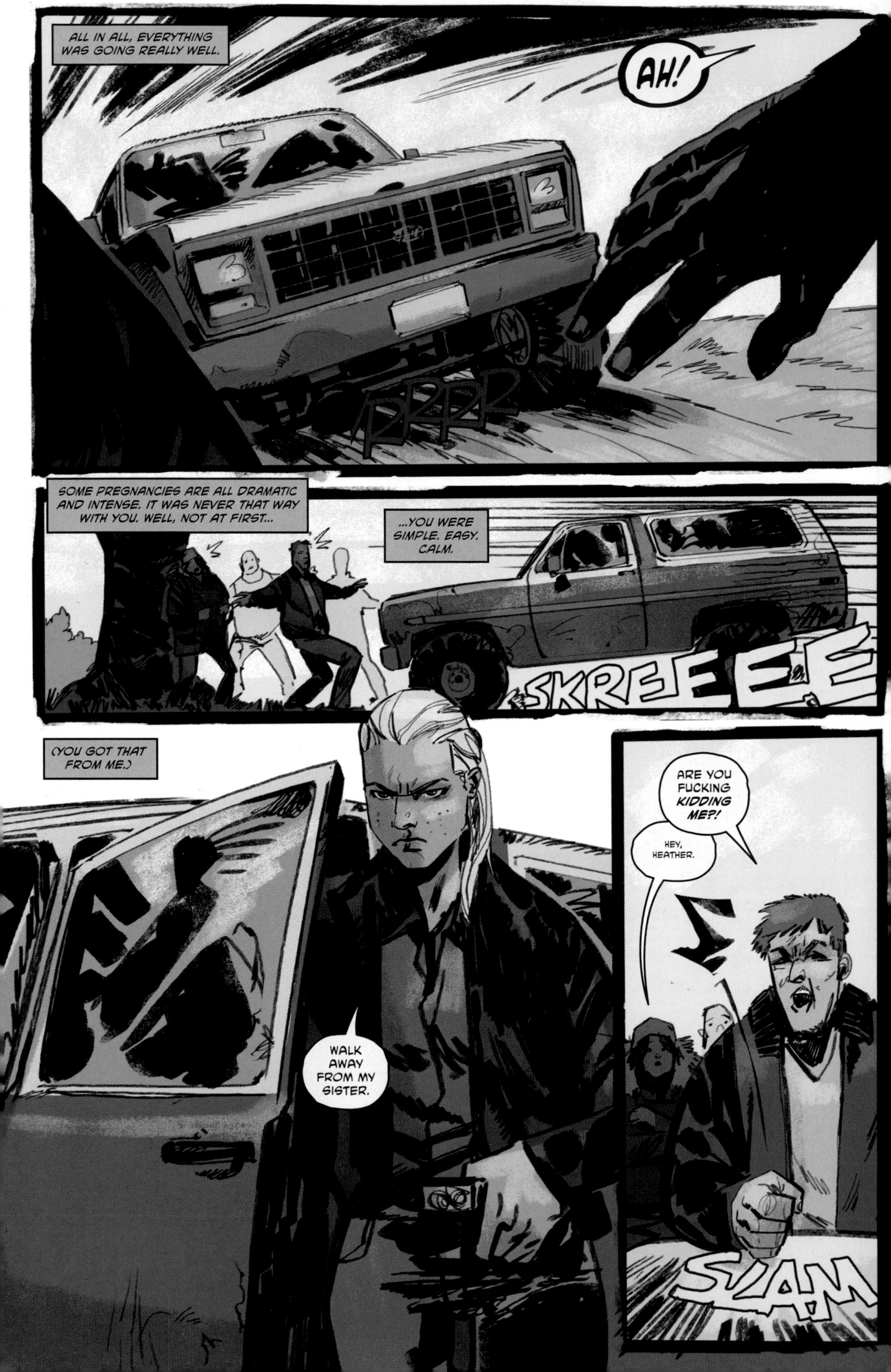
ALL IN ALL, EVERYTHING WAS GOING REALLY WELL.
AH!
SOME PREGNANCIES ARE ALL DRAMATIC AND INTENSE. IT WAS NEVER THAT WAY WITH YOU. WELL, NOT AT FIRST...
...YOU WERE SIMPLE. EASY. CALM.
SKREEEE
(YOU GOT THAT FROM ME.)
WALK AWAY FROM MY SISTER.
ARE YOU FUCKING KIDDING ME?!
HEY, HEATHER.
SLAM

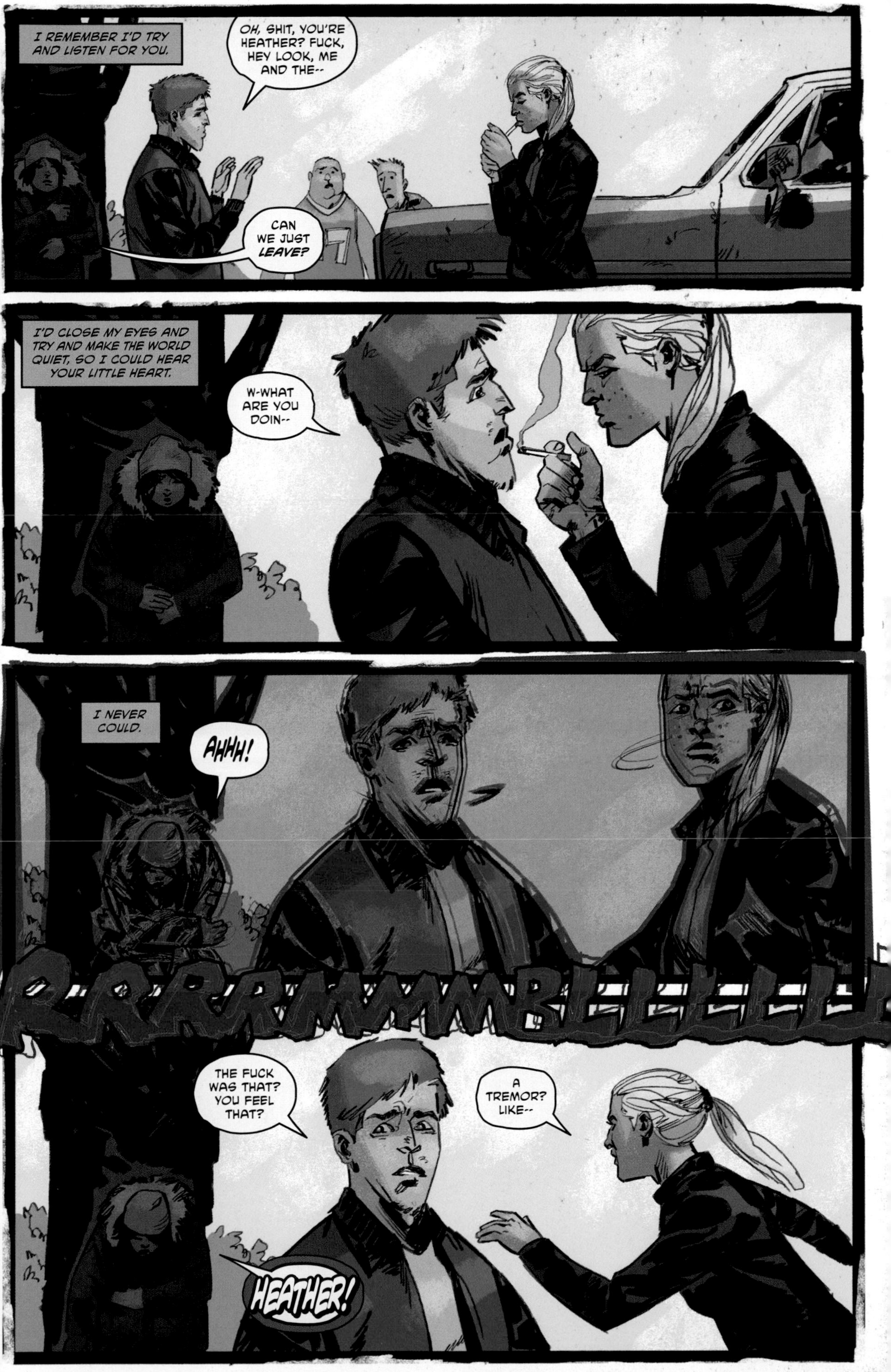
I REMEMBER I'D TRY AND LISTEN FOR YOU.
OH, SHIT, YOU'RE HEATHER? FUCK, HEY LOOK, ME AND THE--
CAN WE JUST LEAVE?
I'D CLOSE MY EYES AND TRY AND MAKE THE WORLD QUIET, SO I COULD HEAR YOUR LITTLE HEART.
W-WHAT ARE YOU DOIN--
I NEVER COULD.
AHHH!
RRRRMMMMBLLLLL
THE FUCK WAS THAT? YOU FEEL THAT?
A TREMOR? LIKE--
HEATHER!

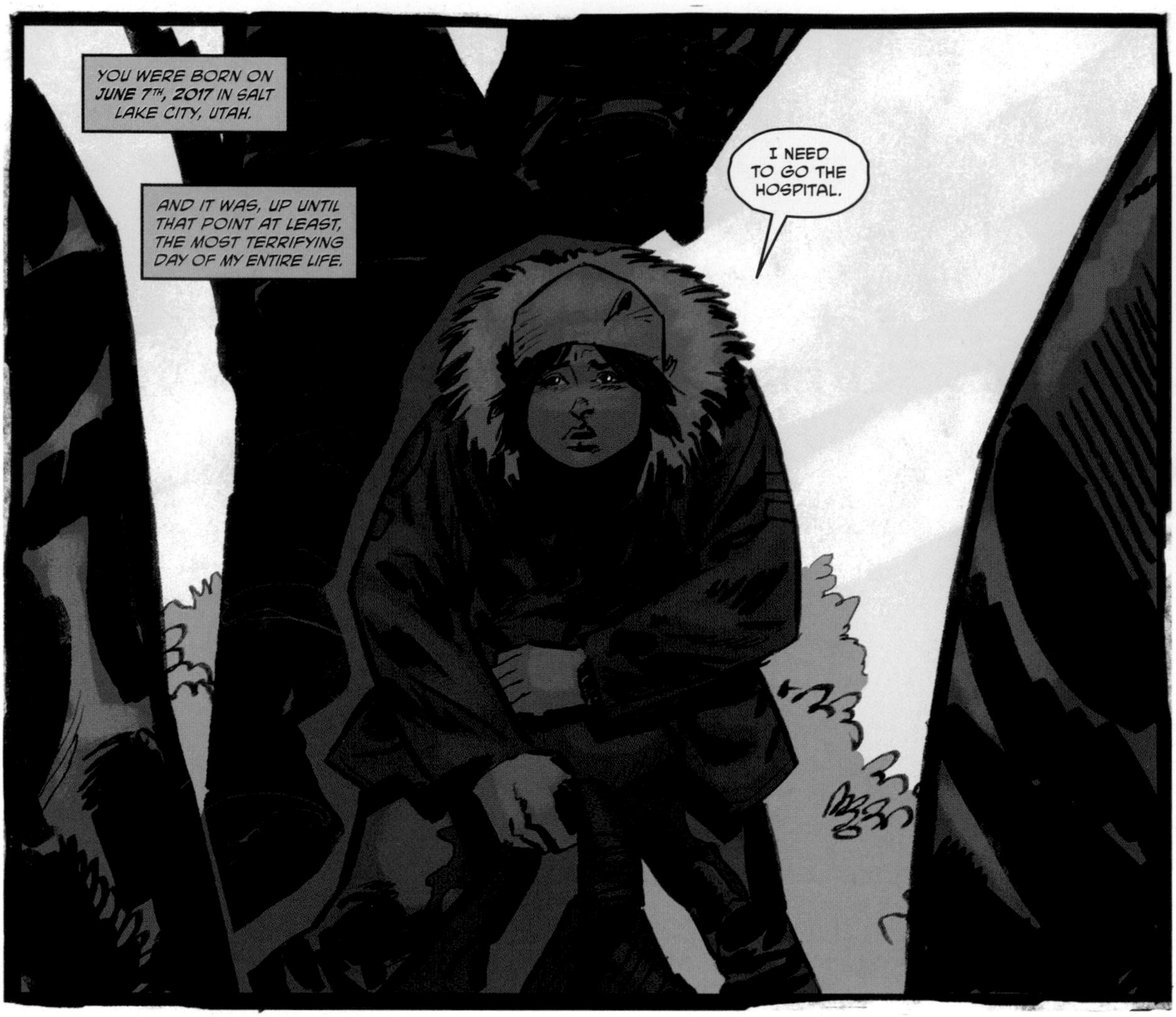
YOU WERE BORN ON JUNE 7TH, 2017 IN SALT LAKE CITY, UTAH.
AND IT WAS, UP UNTIL THAT POINT AT LEAST, THE MOST TERRIFYING DAY OF MY ENTIRE LIFE.
I NEED TO GO THE HOSPITAL.

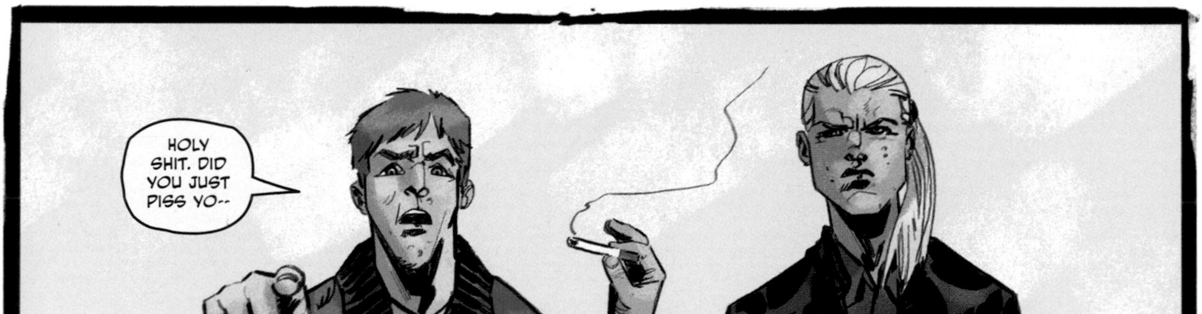
HOLY SHIT. DID YOU JUST PISS YO--

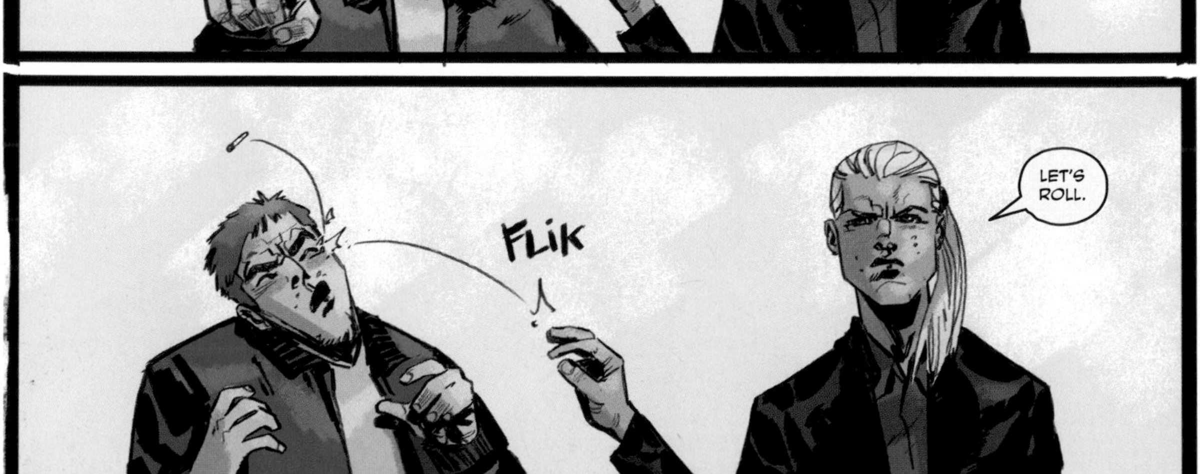
FLIK
LET'S ROLL.

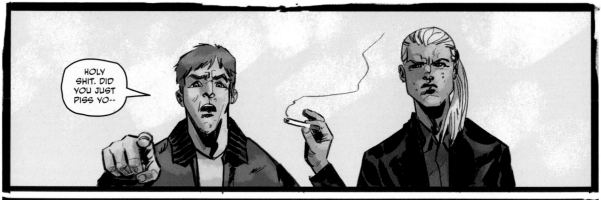

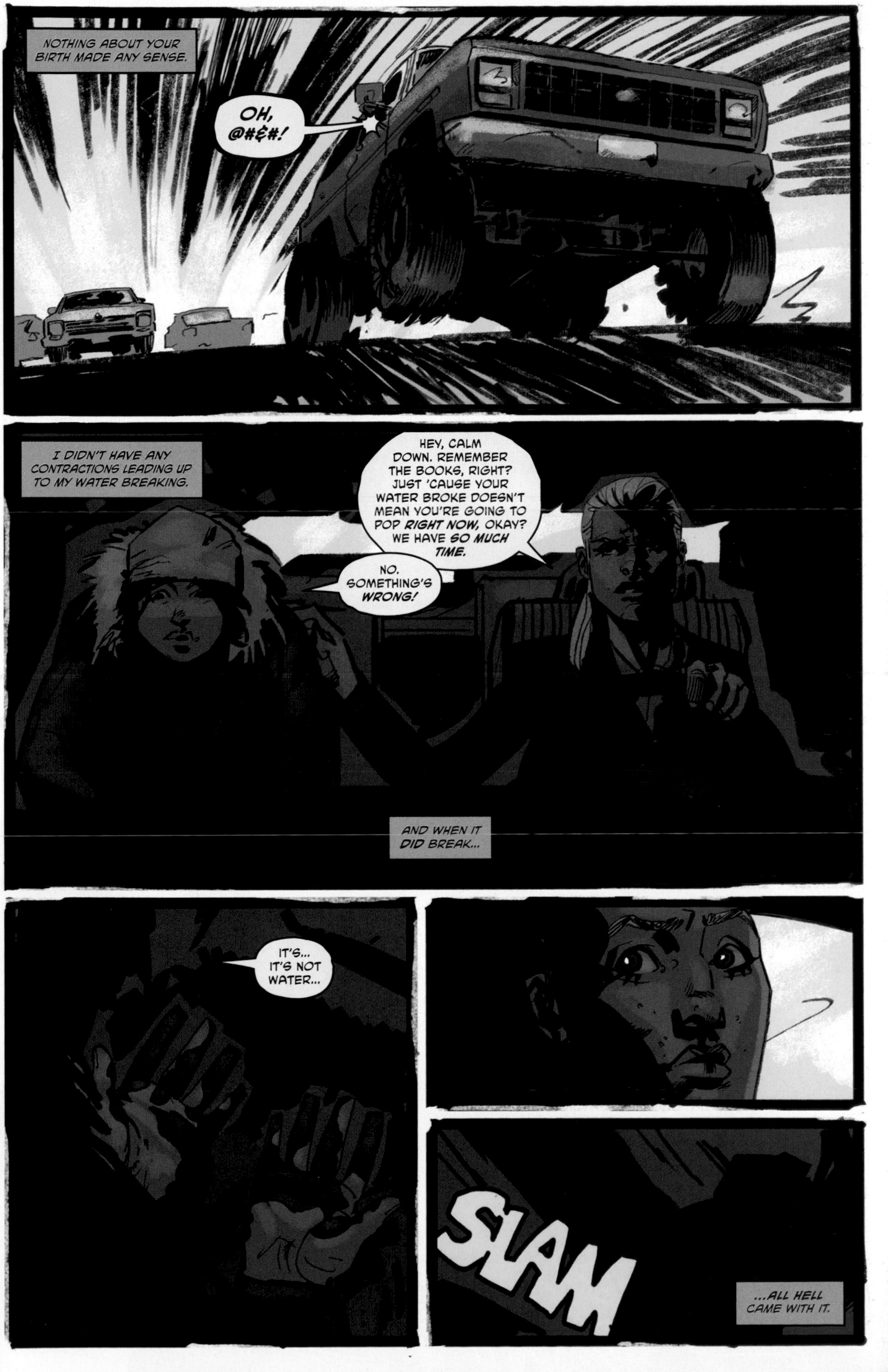
NOTHING ABOUT YOUR BIRTH MADE ANY SENSE.
OH, @#&#!
I DIDN'T HAVE ANY CONTRACTIONS LEADING UP TO MY WATER BREAKING.
HEY, CALM DOWN. REMEMBER THE BOOKS, RIGHT? JUST 'CAUSE YOUR WATER BROKE DOESN'T MEAN YOU'RE GOING TO POP RIGHT NOW, OKAY? WE HAVE SO MUCH TIME.
NO. SOMETHING'S WRONG!
AND WHEN IT DID BREAK...
IT'S... IT'S NOT WATER...
SLAM
...ALL HELL CAME WITH IT.

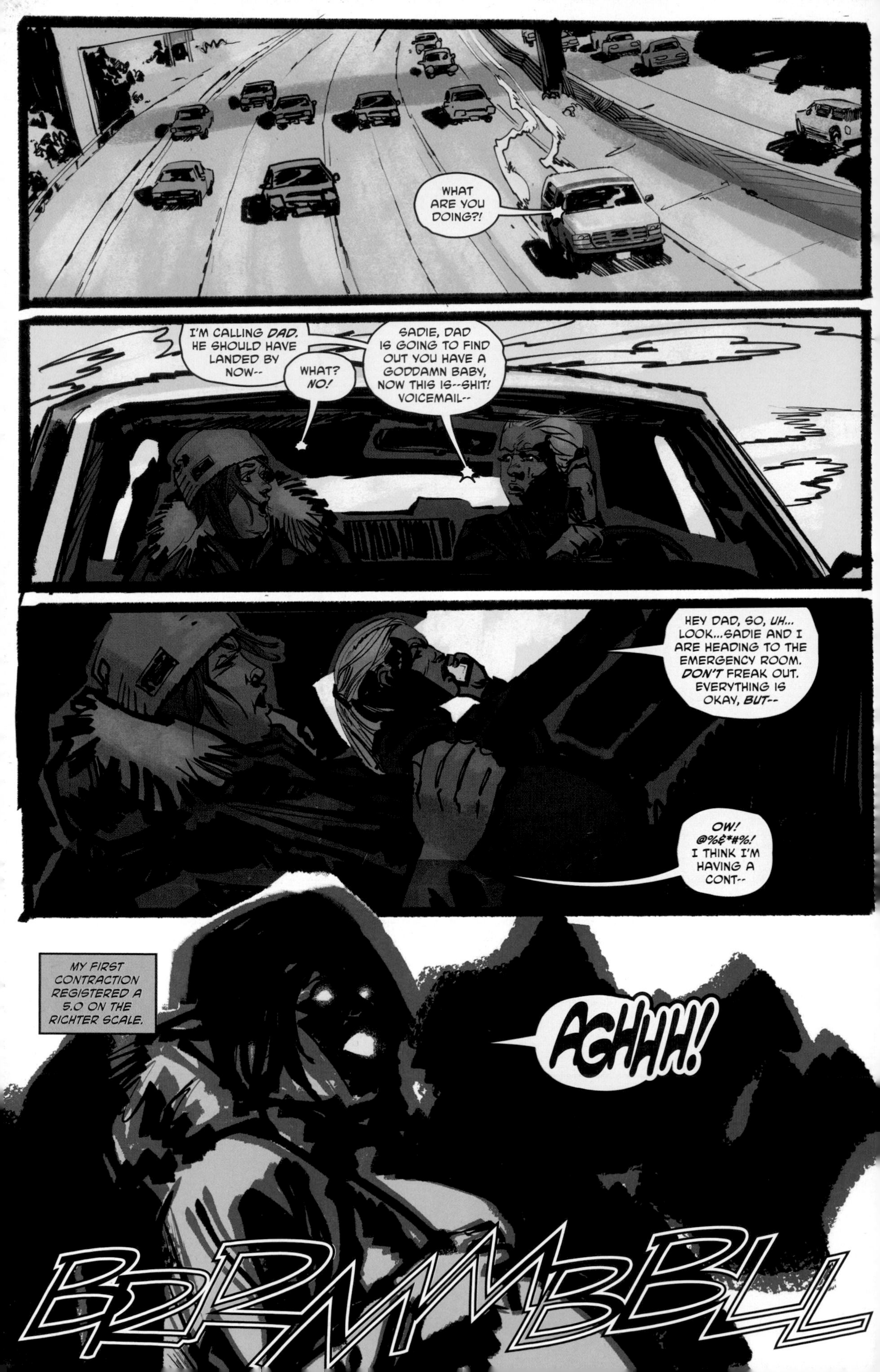
WHAT ARE YOU DOING?!
I'M CALLING DAD. HE SHOULD HAVE LANDED BY NOW--
WHAT? NO!
SADIE, DAD IS GOING TO FIND OUT YOU HAVE A GODDAMN BABY, NOW THIS IS--SHIT! VOICEMAIL--
HEY DAD, SO, UH... LOOK...SADIE AND I ARE HEADING TO THE EMERGENCY ROOM. DON'T FREAK OUT. EVERYTHING IS OKAY, BUT--
OW! @%&*#%! I THINK I'M HAVING A CONT--
MY FIRST CONTRACTION REGISTERED A 5.0 ON THE RICHTER SCALE.
AGHHH!
BRRMMBBLL

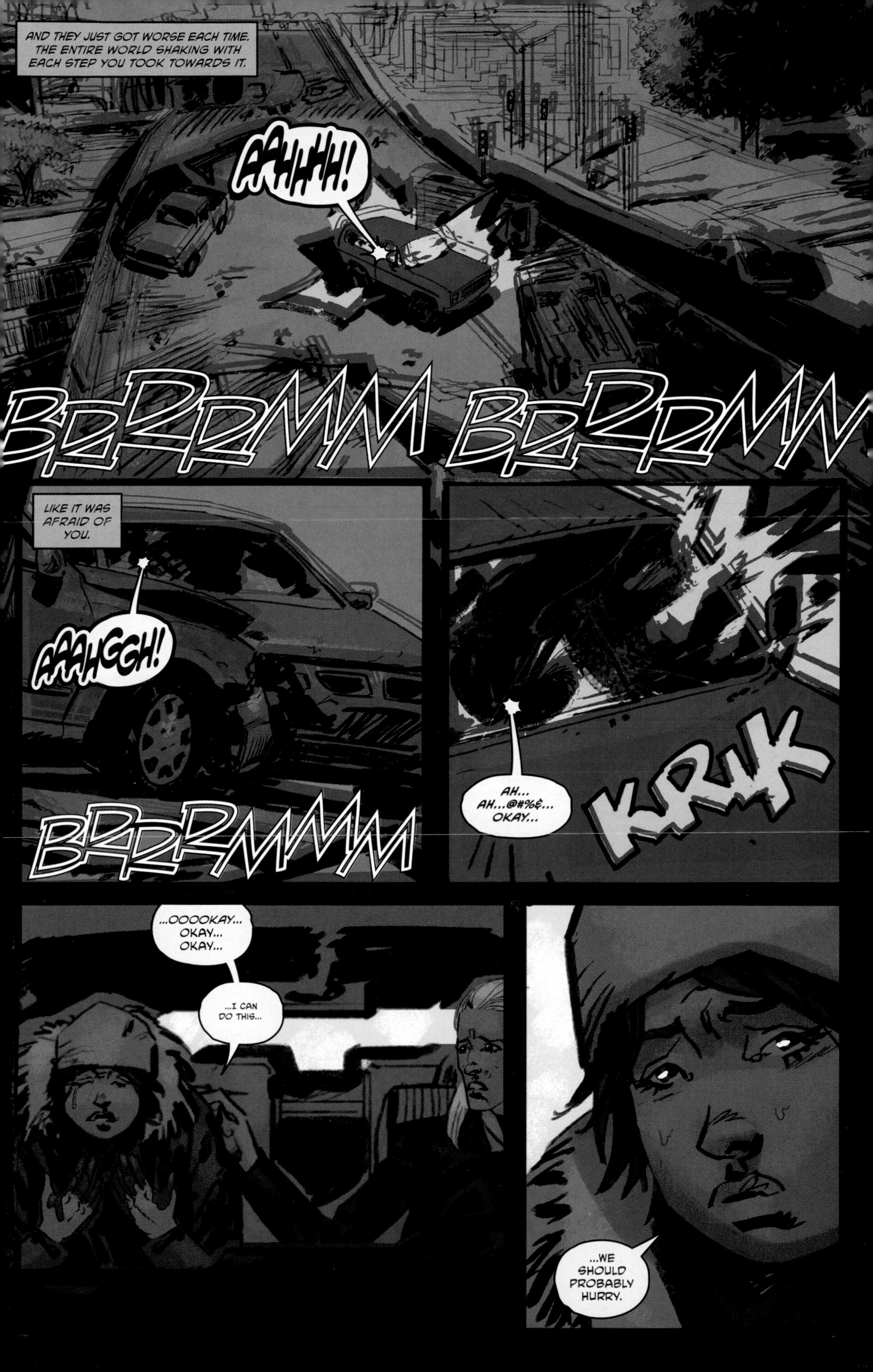
AND THEY JUST GOT WORSE EACH TIME. THE ENTIRE WORLD SHAKING WITH EACH STEP YOU TOOK TOWARDS IT.
AAHHHH!
BRRRMMM BRRRMMN
LIKE IT WAS AFRAID OF YOU.
AAAHGGH!
BRRRRMMMM
AH... AH...@#%&... OKAY...
KRIK
...OOOOKAY... OKAY... OKAY...
...I CAN DO THIS...
...WE SHOULD PROBABLY HURRY.

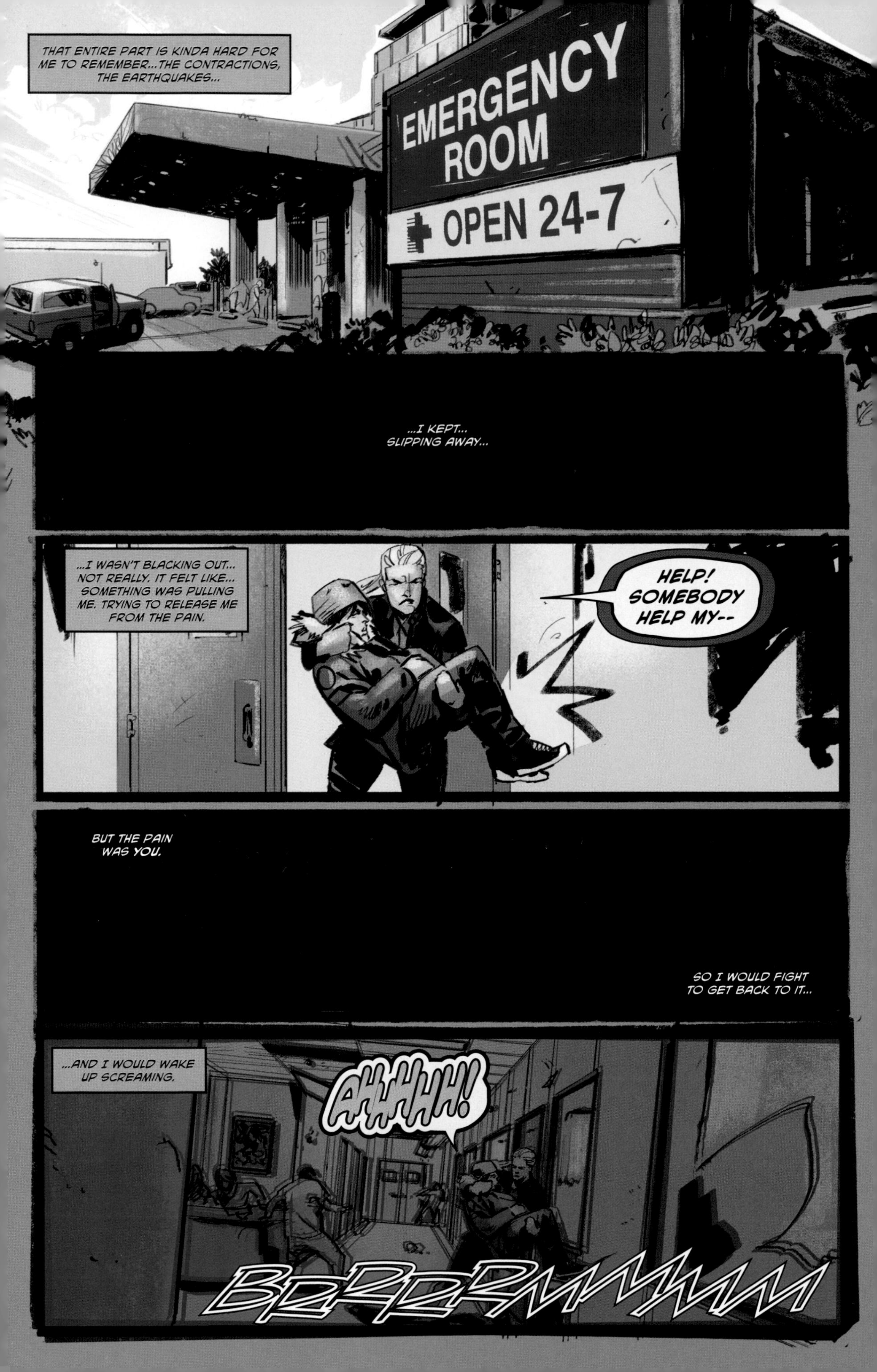
THAT ENTIRE PART IS KINDA HARD FOR ME TO REMEMBER...THE CONTRACTIONS, THE EARTHQUAKES...
EMERGENCY ROOM
OPEN 24-7
...I KEPT... SLIPPING AWAY...
...I WASN'T BLACKING OUT... NOT REALLY. IT FELT LIKE... SOMETHING WAS PULLING ME. TRYING TO RELEASE ME FROM THE PAIN.
HELP! SOMEBODY HELP MY--
BUT THE PAIN WAS YOU.
SO I WOULD FIGHT TO GET BACK TO IT...
...AND I WOULD WAKE UP SCREAMING.
AHHHHH!
BRRRRRMMMMMMM

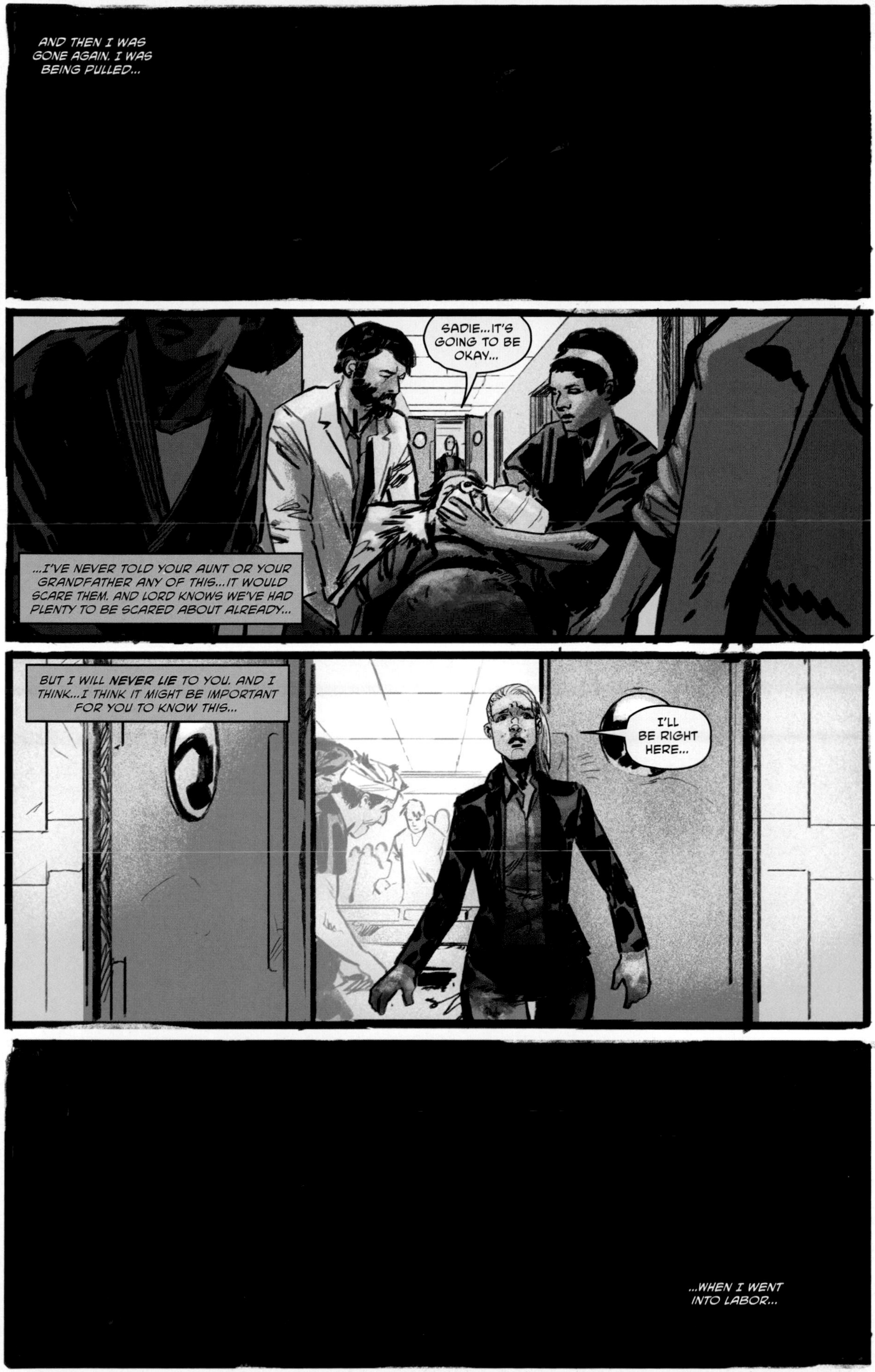
AND THEN I WAS GONE AGAIN. I WAS BEING PULLED...
SADIE...IT'S GOING TO BE OKAY...
...I'VE NEVER TOLD YOUR AUNT OR YOUR GRANDFATHER ANY OF THIS...IT WOULD SCARE THEM. AND LORD KNOWS WE'VE HAD PLENTY TO BE SCARED ABOUT ALREADY...
BUT I WILL **NEVER LIE** TO YOU. AND I THINK...I THINK IT MIGHT BE IMPORTANT FOR YOU TO KNOW THIS...
I'LL BE RIGHT HERE...
...WHEN I WENT INTO LABOR...

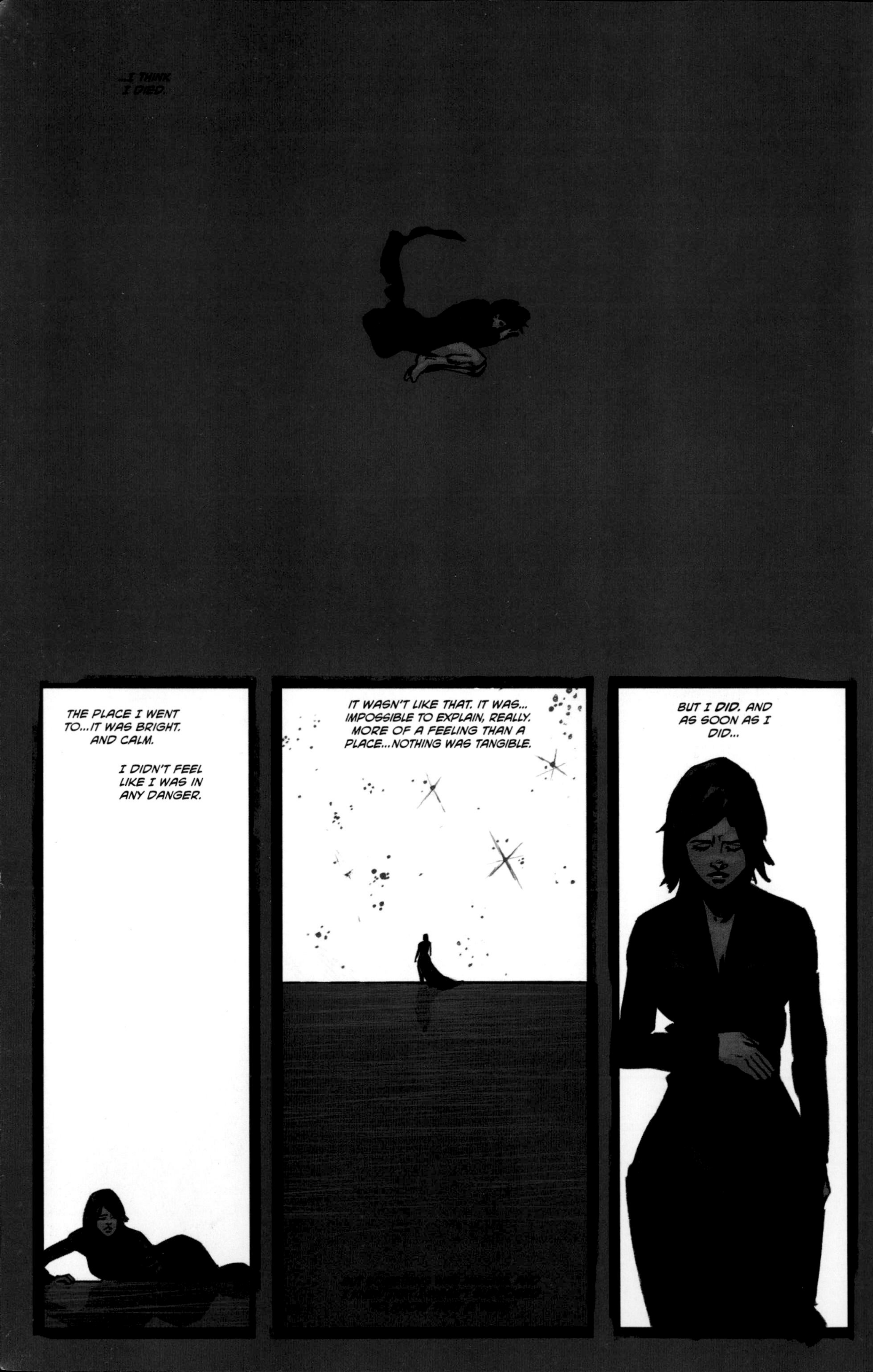
...I THINK I DIED.
THE PLACE I WENT TO...IT WAS BRIGHT. AND CALM.
I DIDN'T FEEL LIKE I WAS IN ANY DANGER.
IT WASN'T LIKE THAT. IT WAS... IMPOSSIBLE TO EXPLAIN, REALLY. MORE OF A FEELING THAN A PLACE...NOTHING WAS TANGIBLE.
BUT I DID. AND AS SOON AS I DID...

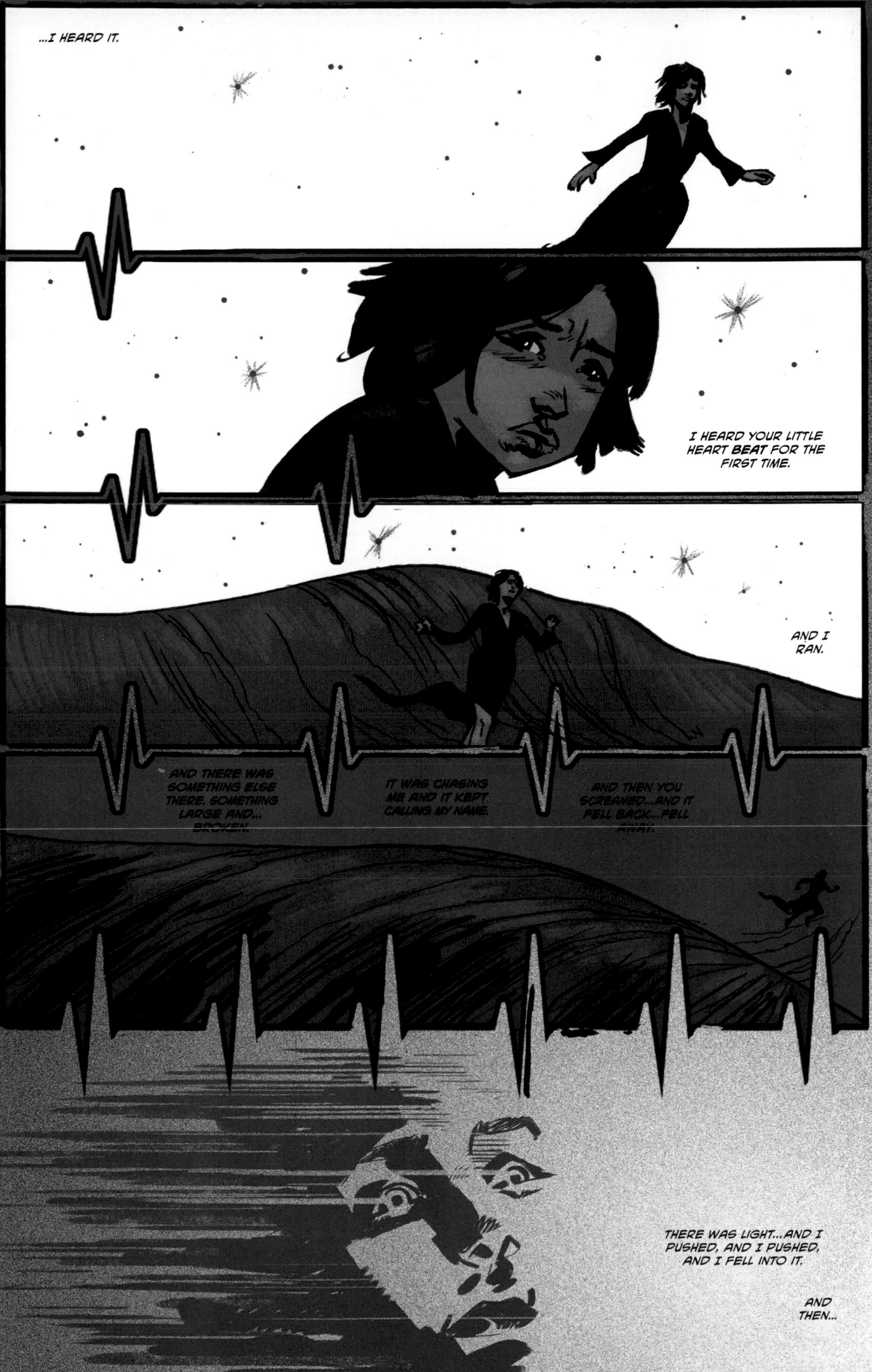
...I HEARD IT.
I HEARD YOUR LITTLE HEART BEAT FOR THE FIRST TIME.
AND I RAN.
AND THERE WAS SOMETHING ELSE THERE. SOMETHING LARGE AND... BROKEN.
IT WAS CHASING ME AND IT KEPT CALLING MY NAME.
AND THEN YOU SCREAMED...AND IT FELL BACK...FELL AWAY.
THERE WAS LIGHT...AND I PUSHED, AND I PUSHED, AND I FELL INTO IT.
AND THEN...

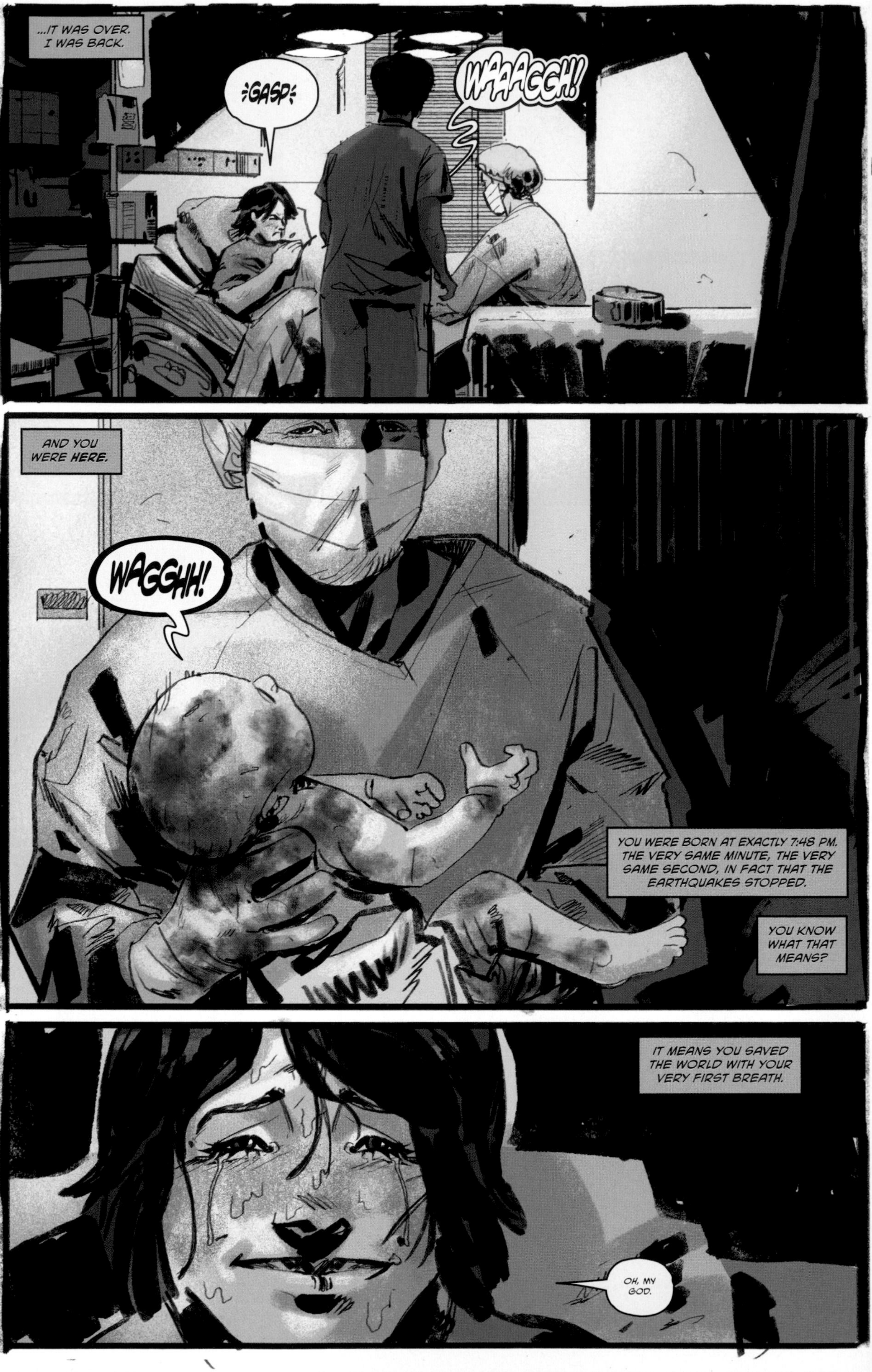
...IT WAS OVER. I WAS BACK.
GASP
WAAAGGH!
AND YOU WERE HERE.
WAGGHH!
YOU WERE BORN AT EXACTLY 7:48 PM. THE VERY SAME MINUTE, THE VERY SAME SECOND, IN FACT THAT THE EARTHQUAKES STOPPED.
YOU KNOW WHAT THAT MEANS?
IT MEANS YOU SAVED THE WORLD WITH YOUR VERY FIRST BREATH.
OH, MY GOD.

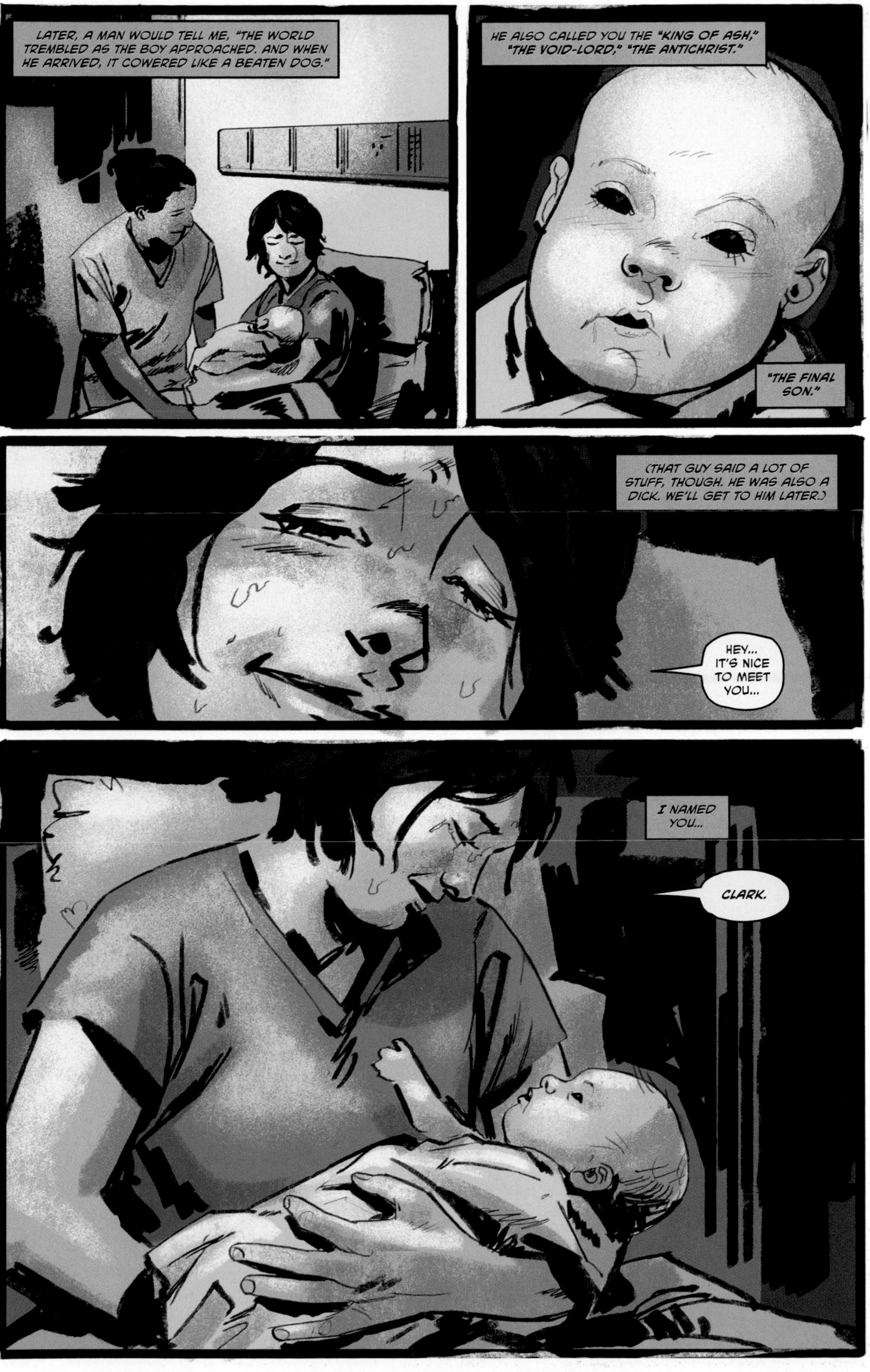
LATER, A MAN WOULD TELL ME, "THE WORLD TREMBLED AS THE BOY APPROACHED. AND WHEN HE ARRIVED, IT COWERED LIKE A BEATEN DOG."
HE ALSO CALLED YOU THE "KING OF ASH," "THE VOID-LORD," "THE ANTICHRIST."
"THE FINAL SON."
(THAT GUY SAID A LOT OF STUFF, THOUGH. HE WAS ALSO A DICK. WE'LL GET TO HIM LATER.)
HEY... IT'S NICE TO MEET YOU...
I NAMED YOU...
CLARK.

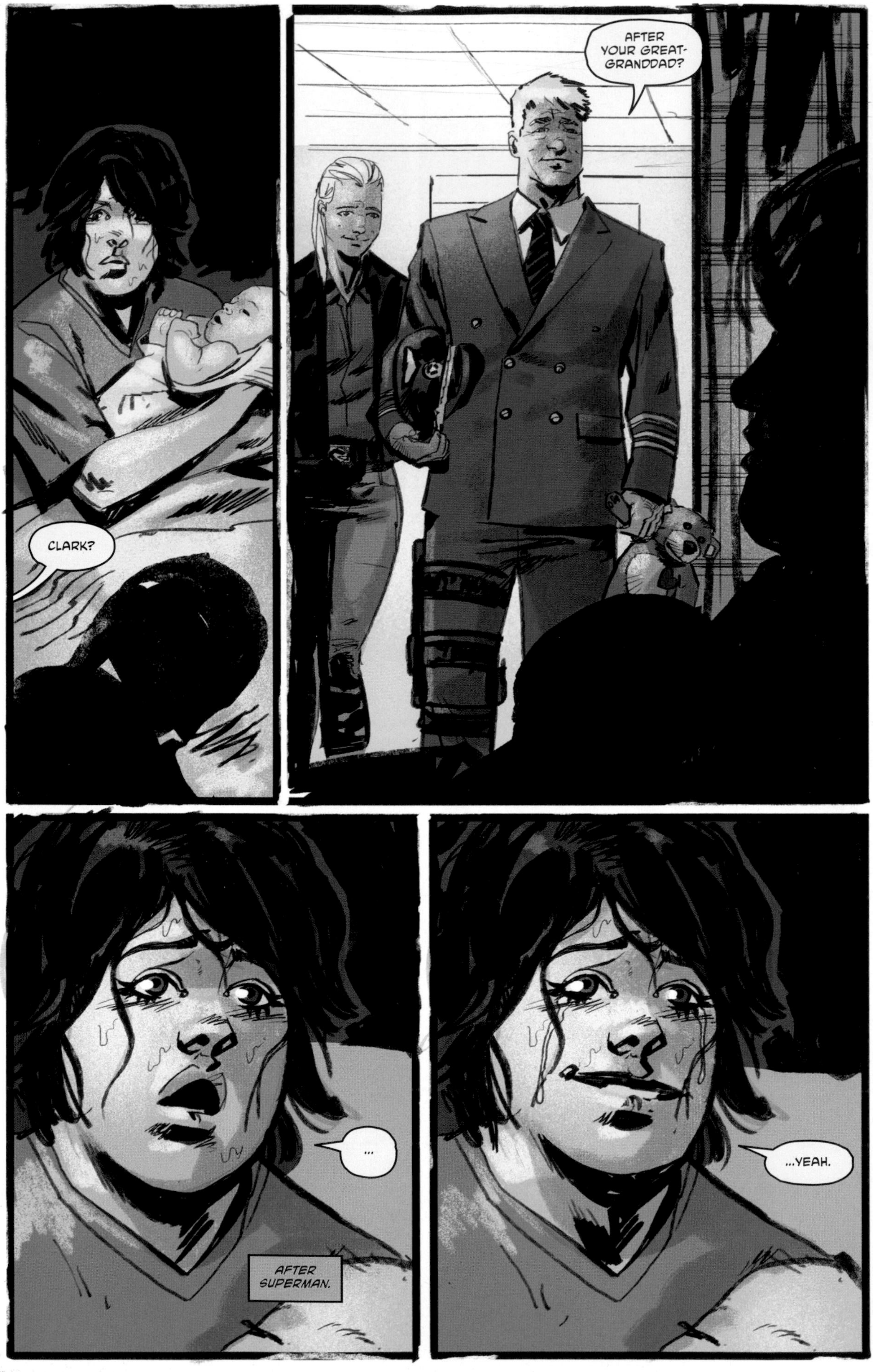
CLARK?
AFTER YOUR GREAT-GRANDDAD?
...
AFTER SUPERMAN.
...YEAH.

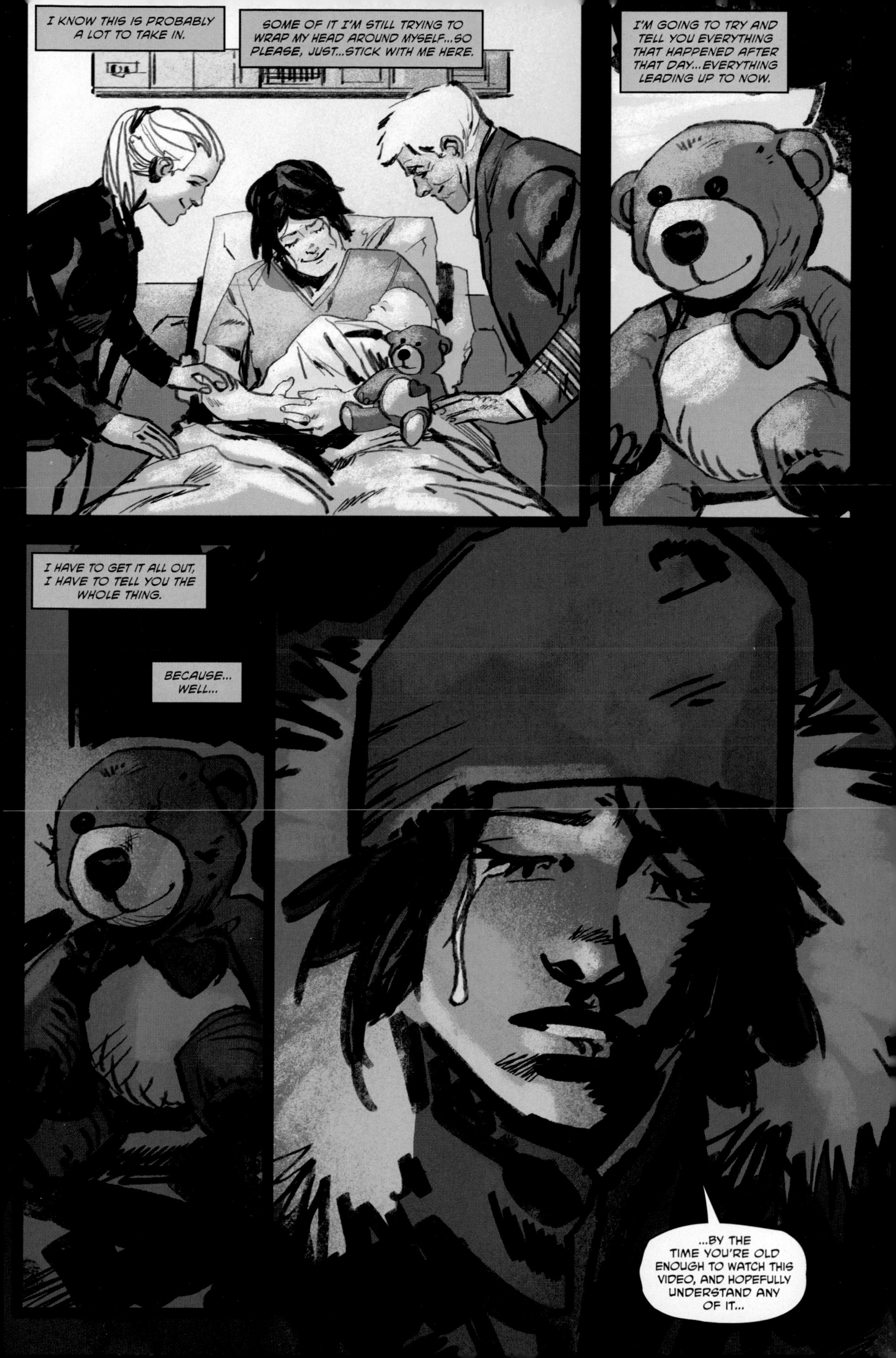
I KNOW THIS IS PROBABLY A LOT TO TAKE IN.
SOME OF IT I'M STILL TRYING TO WRAP MY HEAD AROUND MYSELF...SO PLEASE, JUST...STICK WITH ME HERE.
I'M GOING TO TRY AND TELL YOU EVERYTHING THAT HAPPENED AFTER THAT DAY...EVERYTHING LEADING UP TO NOW.
I HAVE TO GET IT ALL OUT, I HAVE TO TELL YOU THE WHOLE THING.
BECAUSE... WELL...
...BY THE TIME YOU'RE OLD ENOUGH TO WATCH THIS VIDEO, AND HOPEFULLY UNDERSTAND ANY OF IT...

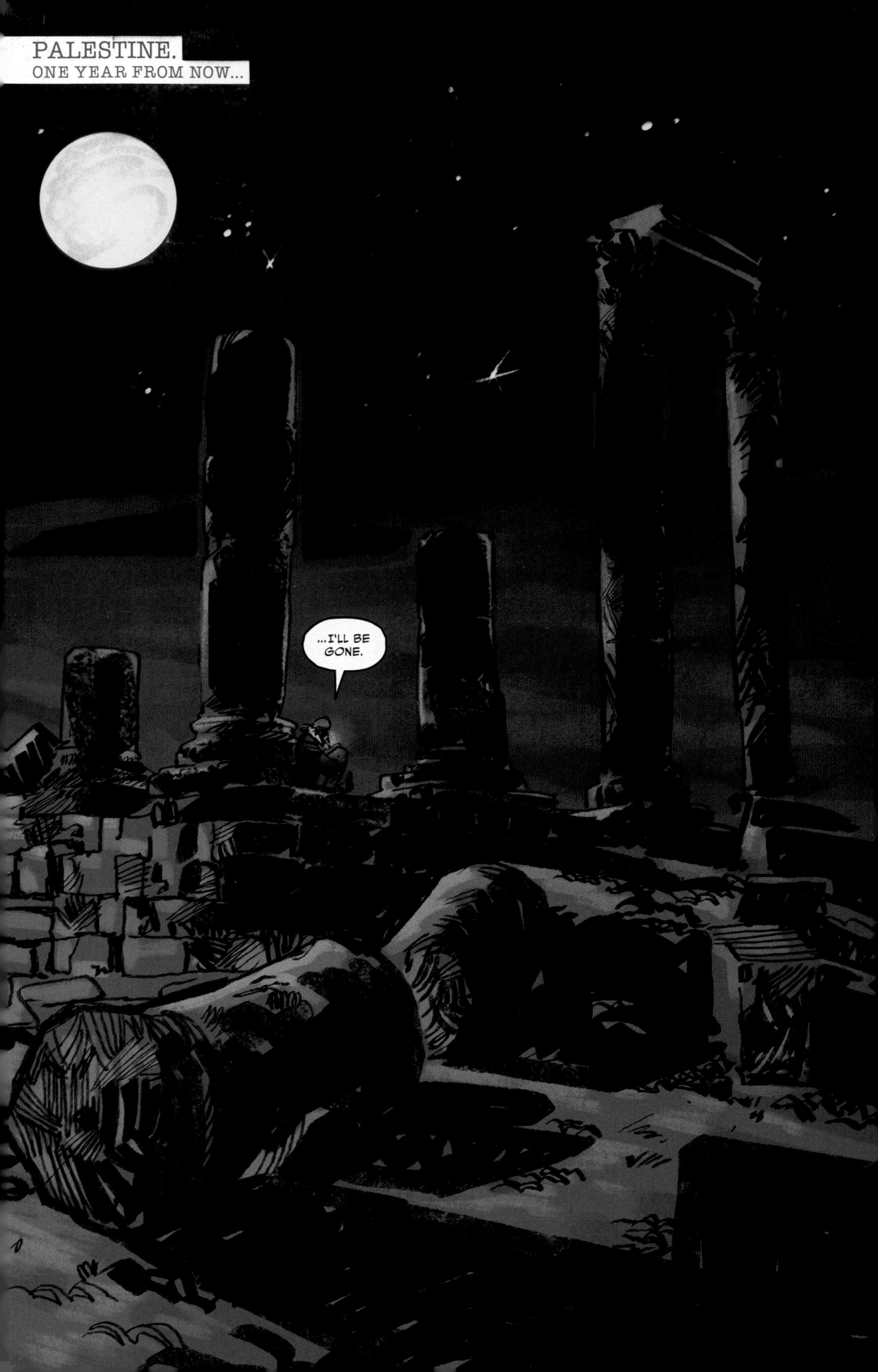
PALESTINE.
ONE YEAR FROM NOW...
...I'LL BE GONE.

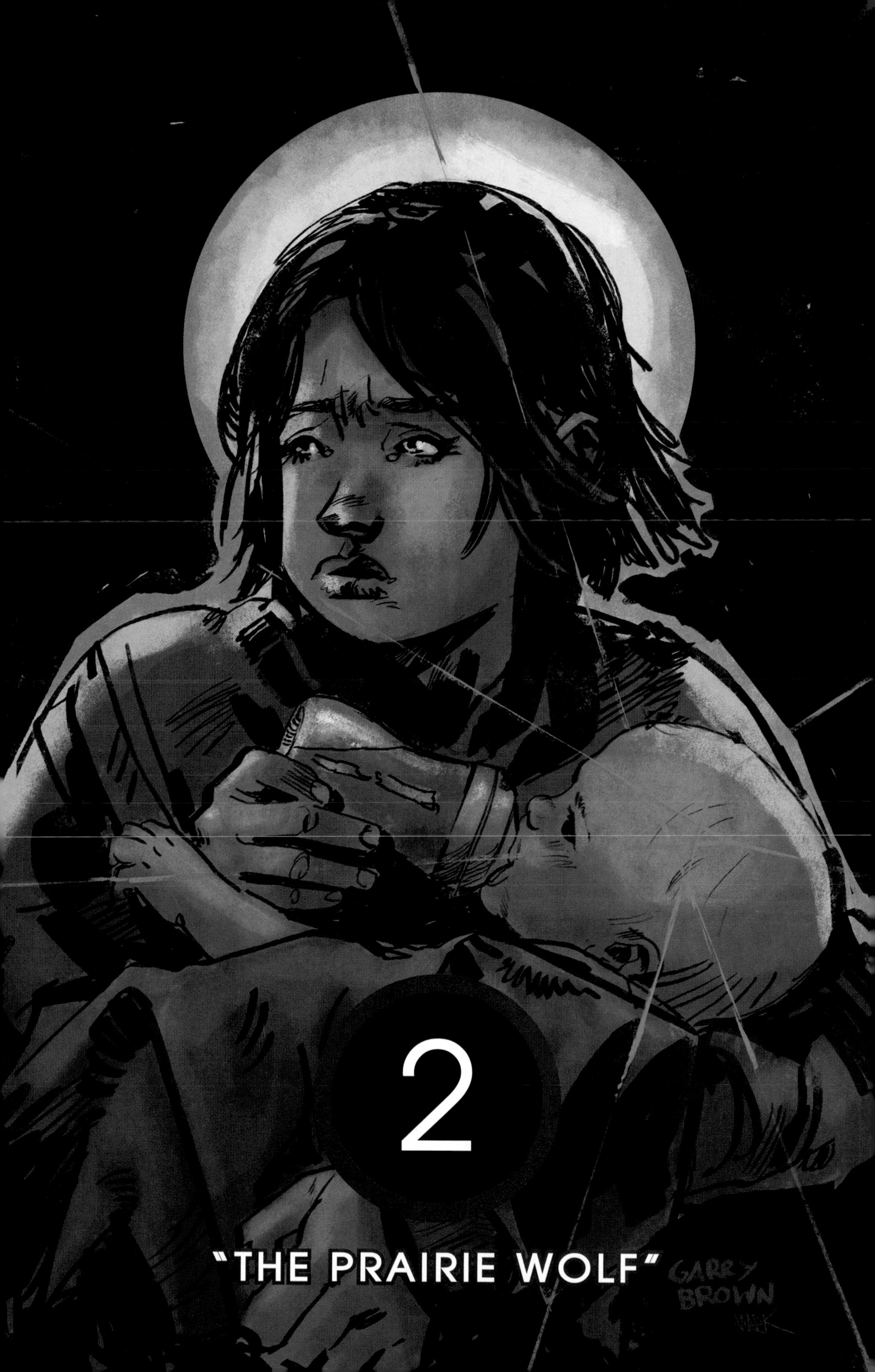
2
"THE PRAIRIE WOLF"
GARRY BROWN

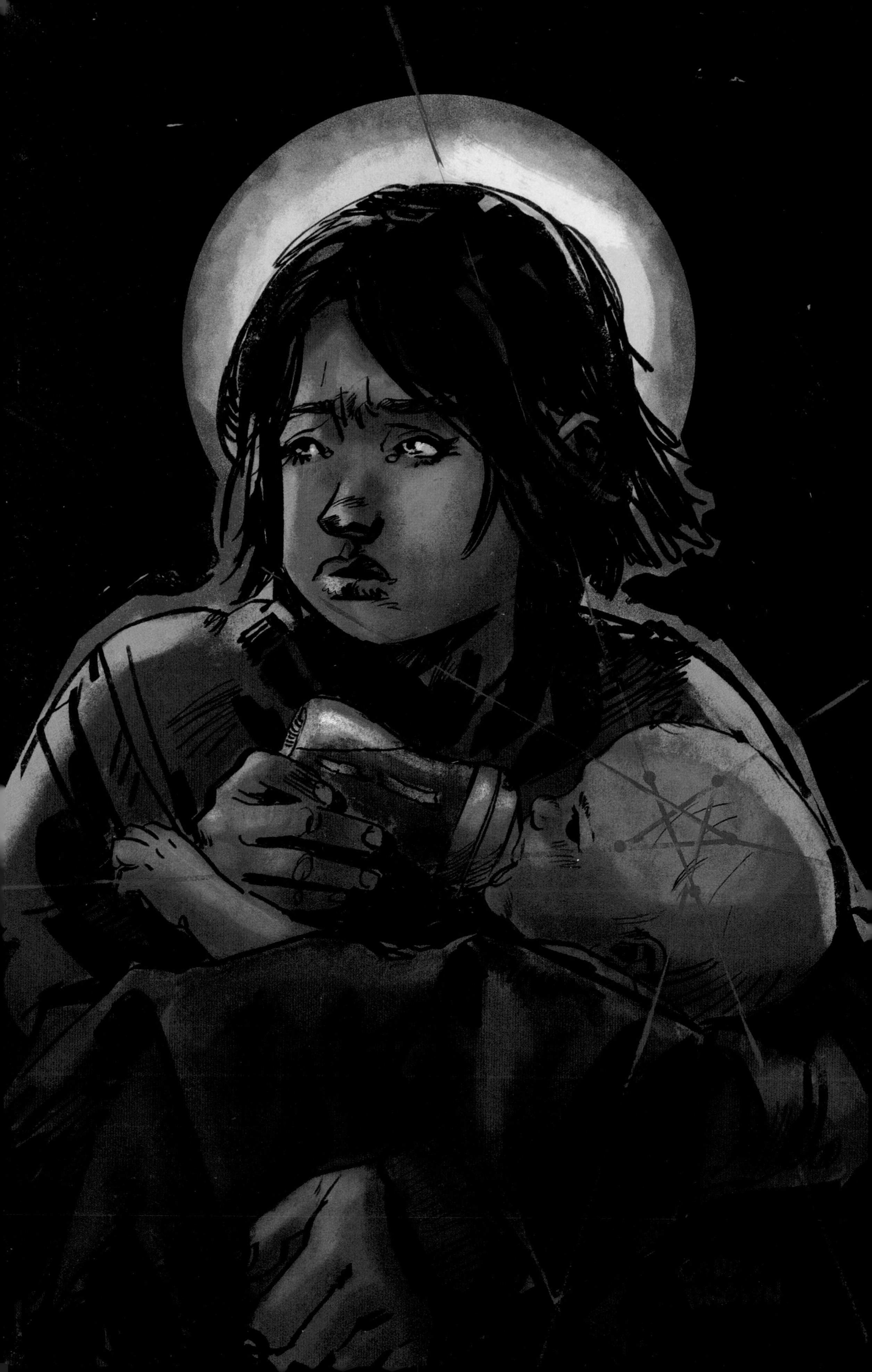

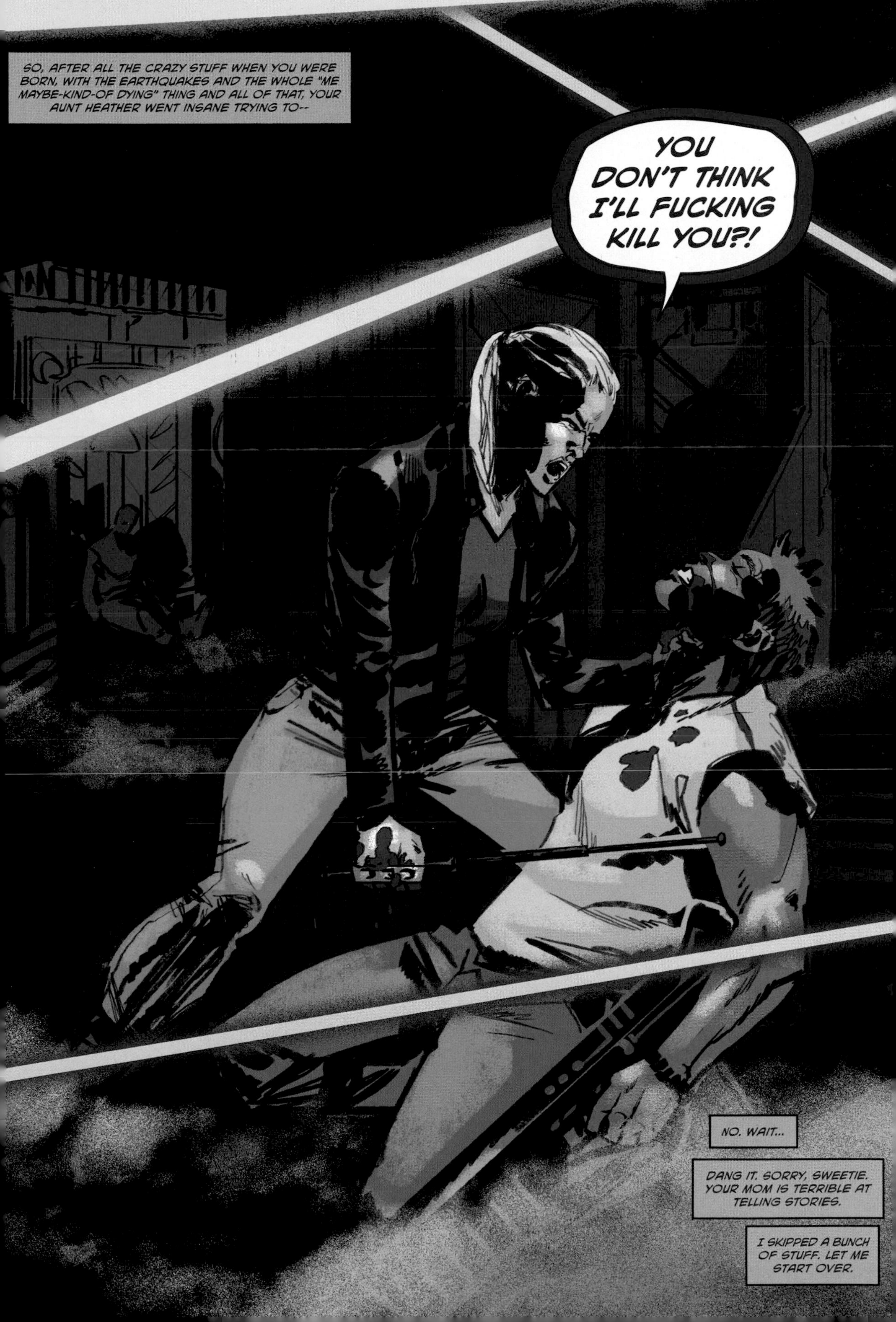
SO, AFTER ALL THE CRAZY STUFF WHEN YOU WERE BORN, WITH THE EARTHQUAKES AND THE WHOLE "ME MAYBE-KIND-OF DYING" THING AND ALL OF THAT, YOUR AUNT HEATHER WENT INSANE TRYING TO--
YOU DON'T THINK I'LL FUCKING KILL YOU?!
NO. WAIT...
DANG IT. SORRY, SWEETIE. YOUR MOM IS TERRIBLE AT TELLING STORIES.
I SKIPPED A BUNCH OF STUFF. LET ME START OVER.

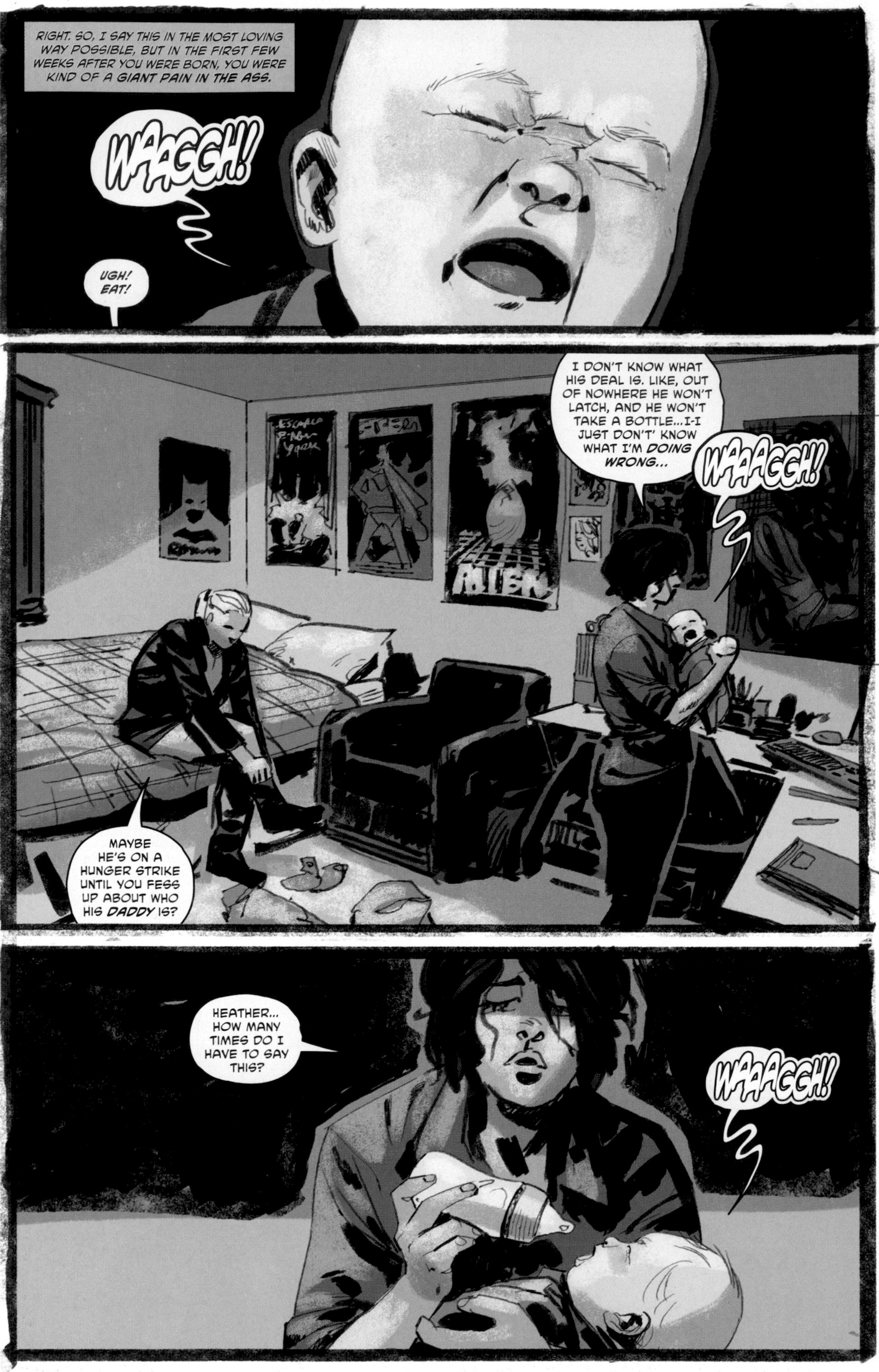
RIGHT. SO, I SAY THIS IN THE MOST LOVING WAY POSSIBLE, BUT IN THE FIRST FEW WEEKS AFTER YOU WERE BORN, YOU WERE KIND OF A GIANT PAIN IN THE ASS.
WAAGGH!
UGH! EAT!
I DON'T KNOW WHAT HIS DEAL IS. LIKE, OUT OF NOWHERE HE WON'T LATCH, AND HE WON'T TAKE A BOTTLE...I-I JUST DON'T' KNOW WHAT I'M DOING WRONG...
WAAAGGH!
MAYBE HE'S ON A HUNGER STRIKE UNTIL YOU FESS UP ABOUT WHO HIS DADDY IS?
HEATHER... HOW MANY TIMES DO I HAVE TO SAY THIS?
WAAAGGH!

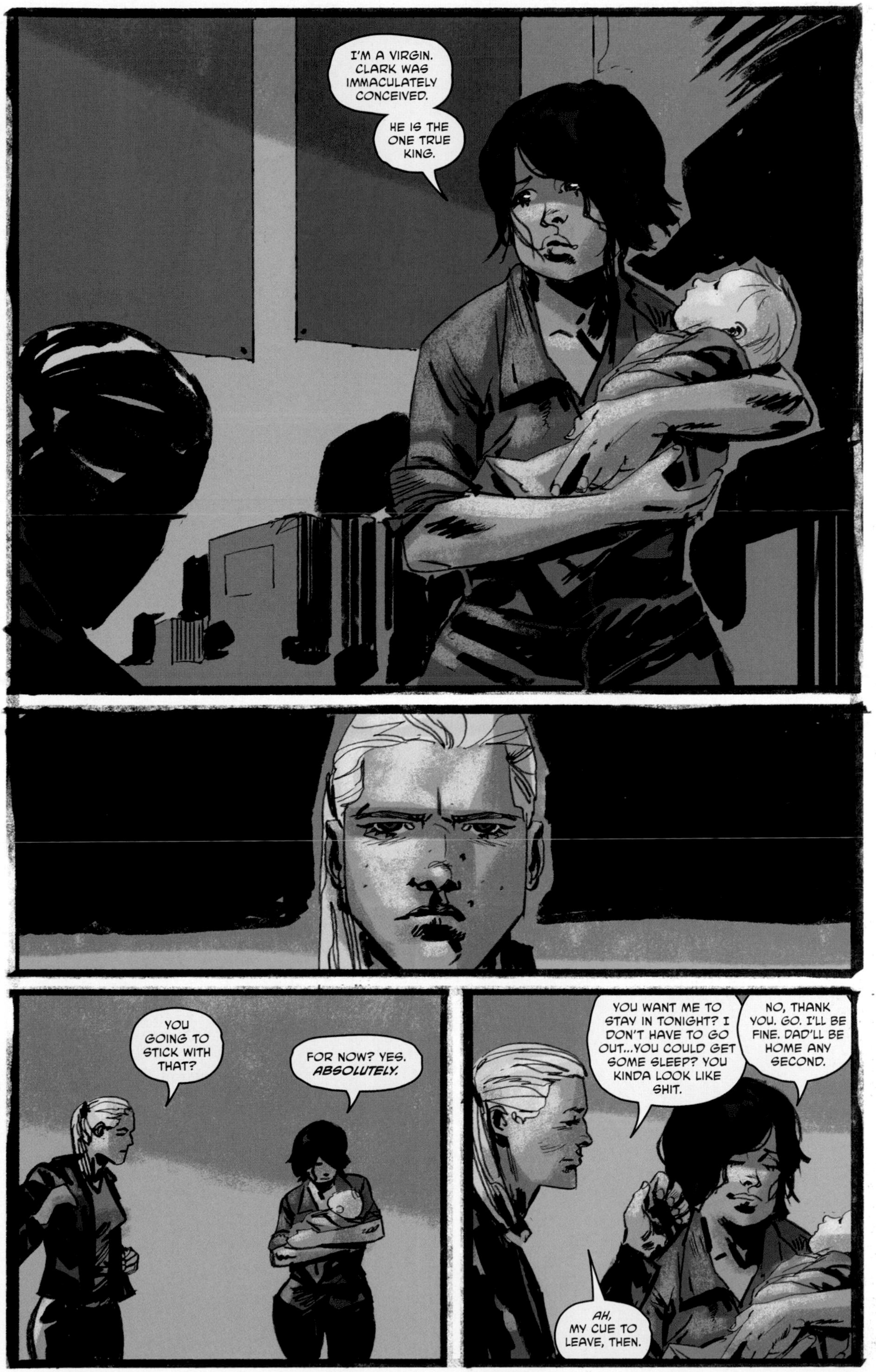
I'M A VIRGIN. CLARK WAS IMMACULATELY CONCEIVED.
HE IS THE ONE TRUE KING.
YOU GOING TO STICK WITH THAT?
FOR NOW? YES. *ABSOLUTELY.*
YOU WANT ME TO STAY IN TONIGHT? I DON'T HAVE TO GO OUT...YOU COULD GET SOME SLEEP? YOU KINDA LOOK LIKE SHIT.
NO, THANK YOU. GO. I'LL BE FINE. DAD'LL BE HOME ANY SECOND.
AH, MY CUE TO LEAVE, THEN.

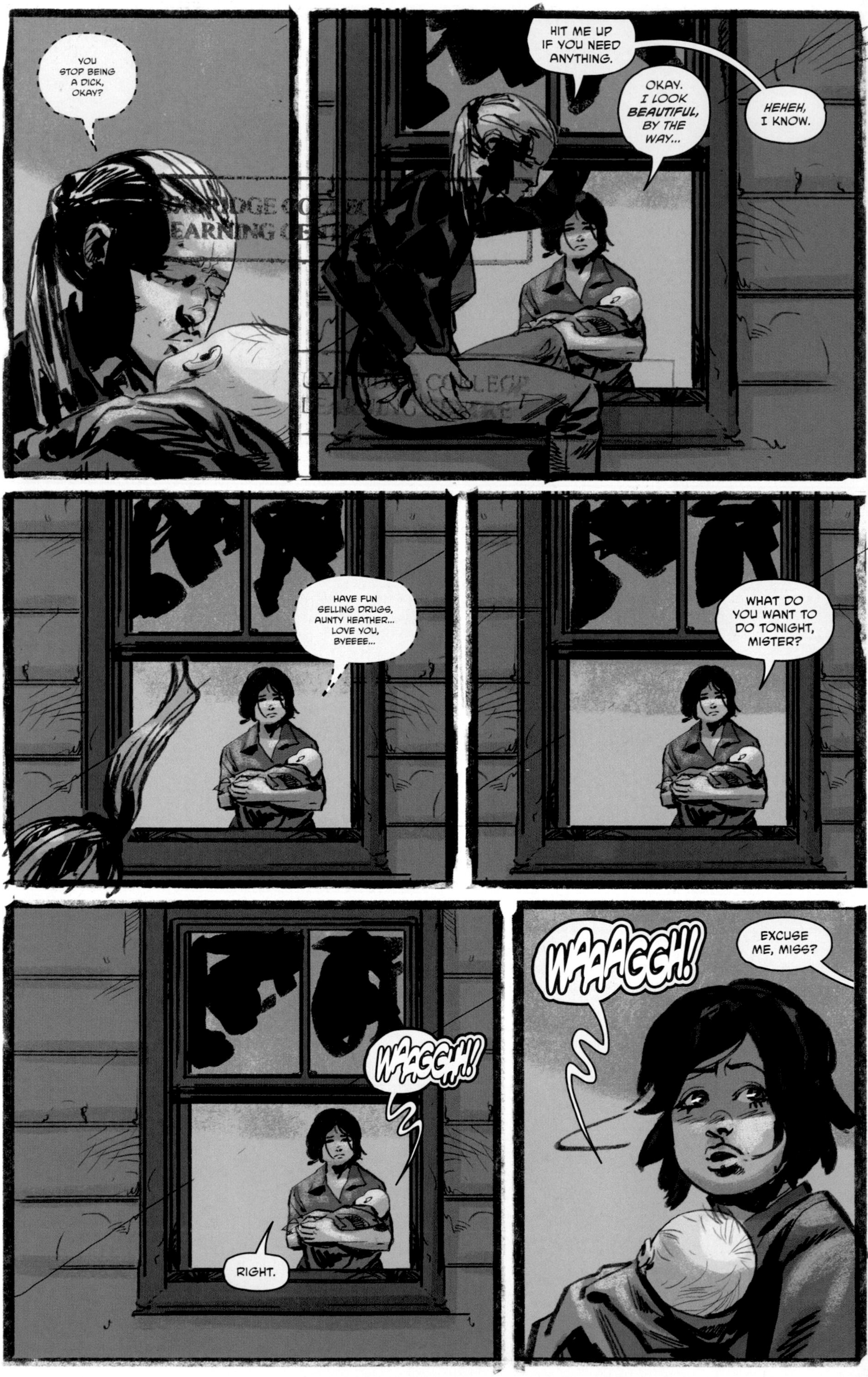
YOU STOP BEING A DICK, OKAY?
HIT ME UP IF YOU NEED ANYTHING.
OKAY. I LOOK BEAUTIFUL, BY THE WAY...
HEHEH, I KNOW.
HAVE FUN SELLING DRUGS, AUNTY HEATHER... LOVE YOU, BYEEEE...
WHAT DO YOU WANT TO DO TONIGHT, MISTER?
WAAGGH!
RIGHT.
WAAAGGH!
EXCUSE ME, MISS?

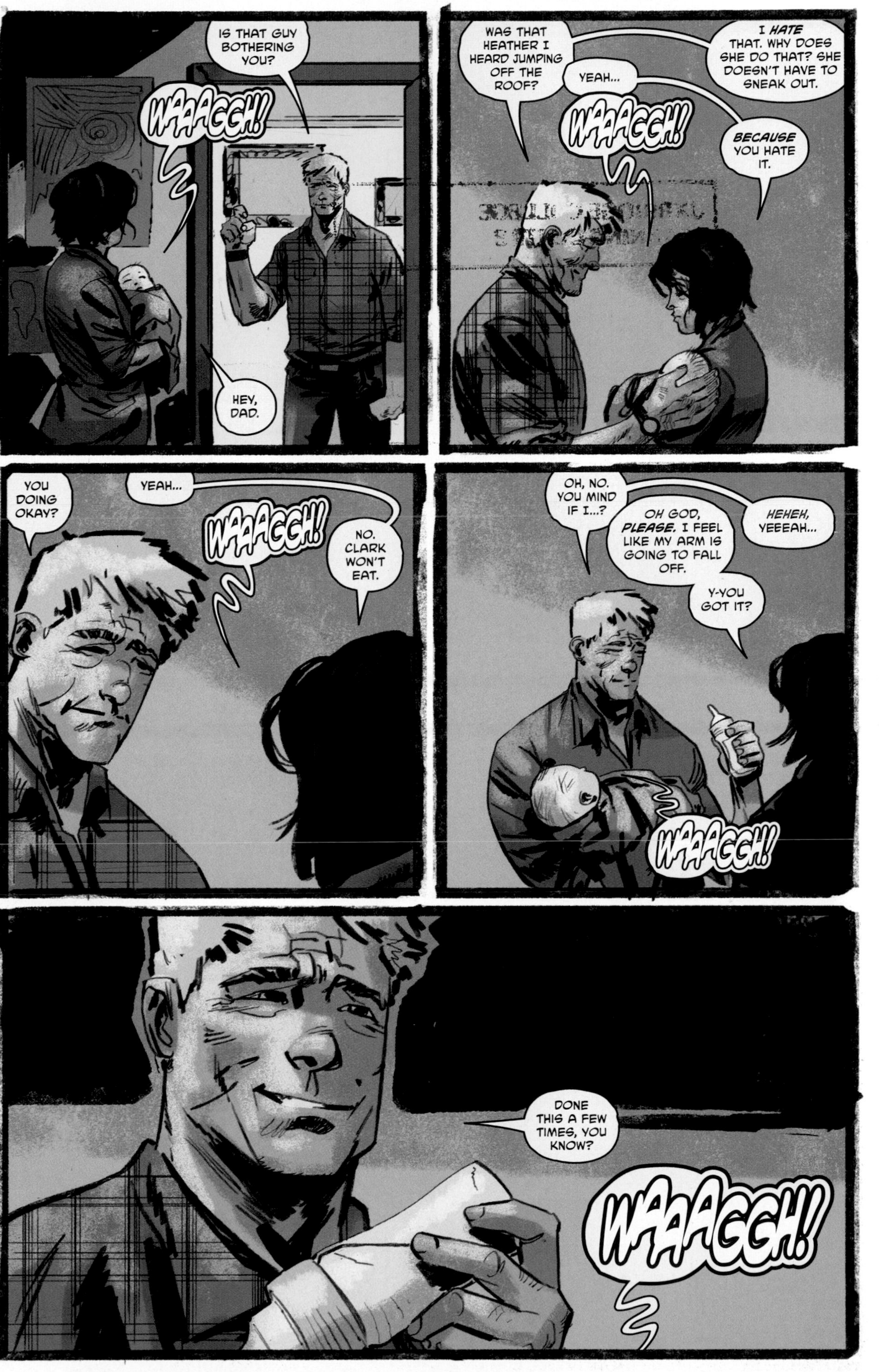
IS THAT GUY BOTHERING YOU?
WAAAGGH!
HEY, DAD.
WAS THAT HEATHER I HEARD JUMPING OFF THE ROOF?
YEAH...
WAAAGGH!
I *HATE* THAT. WHY DOES SHE DO THAT? SHE DOESN'T HAVE TO SNEAK OUT.
BECAUSE YOU HATE IT.
YOU DOING OKAY?
YEAH...
WAAAGGH!
NO. CLARK WON'T EAT.
OH, NO. YOU MIND IF I...?
*OH GOD, **PLEASE.** I FEEL LIKE MY ARM IS GOING TO FALL OFF.*
HEHEH, YEEEAH...
Y-YOU GOT IT?
WAAAGGH!
DONE THIS A FEW TIMES, YOU KNOW?
WAAAGGH!

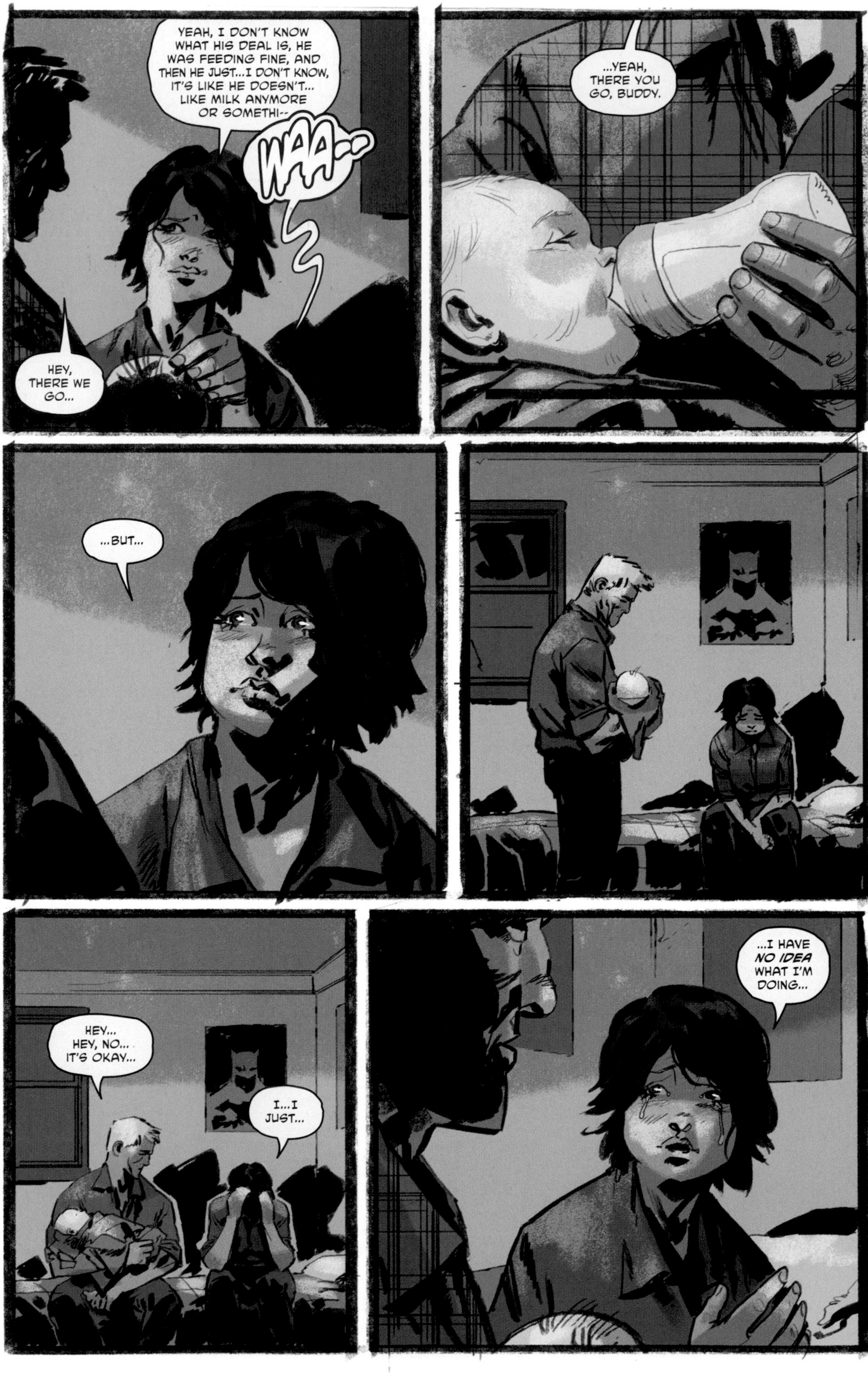
YEAH, I DON'T KNOW WHAT HIS DEAL IS, HE WAS FEEDING FINE, AND THEN HE JUST...I DON'T KNOW, IT'S LIKE HE DOESN'T... LIKE MILK ANYMORE OR SOMETHI--
WAA--
HEY, THERE WE GO...
...YEAH, THERE YOU GO, BUDDY.
...BUT...
HEY... HEY, NO... IT'S OKAY...
I...I JUST...
...I HAVE NO IDEA WHAT I'M DOING...

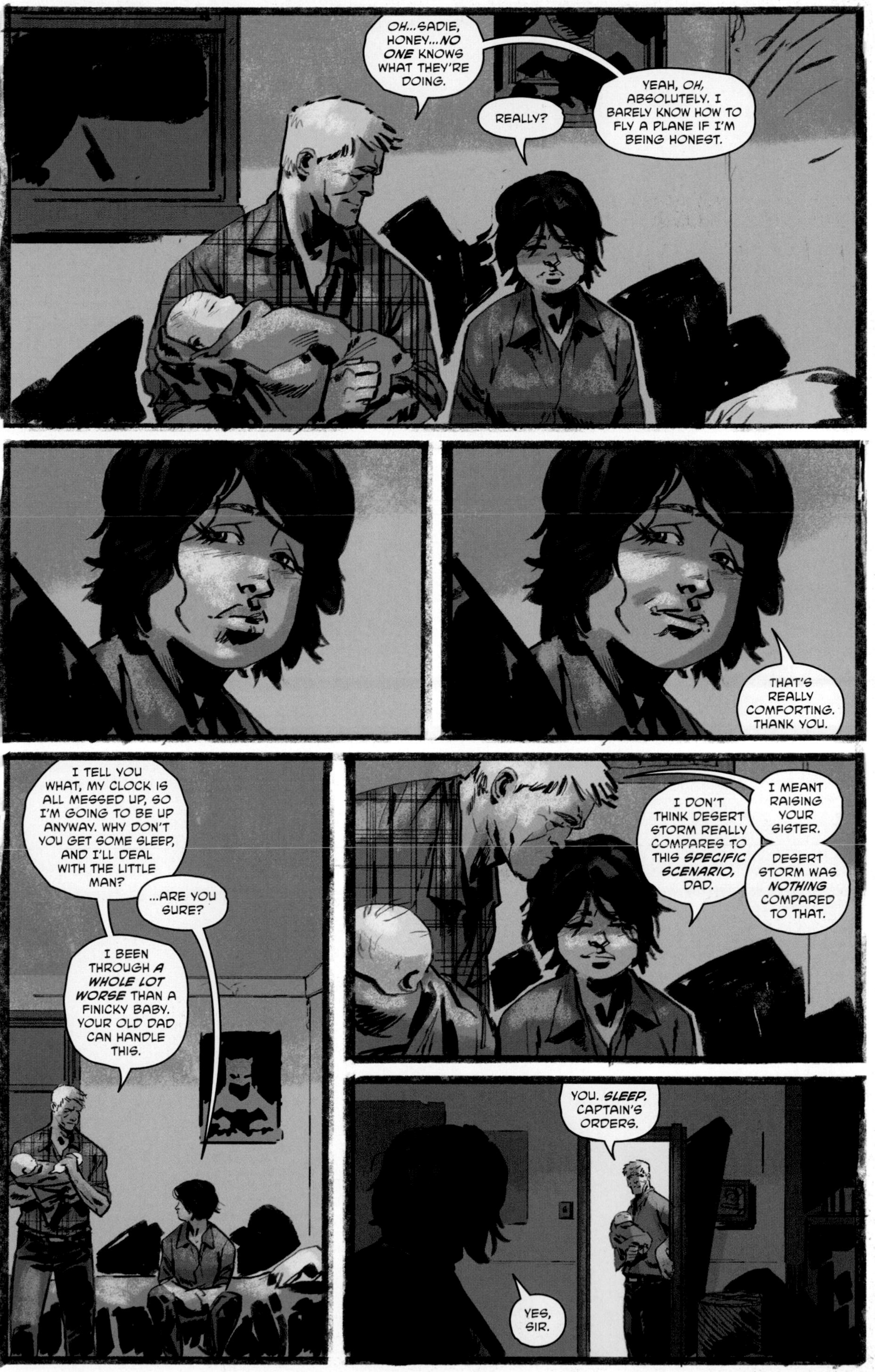
OH...SADIE, HONEY...NO ONE KNOWS WHAT THEY'RE DOING.
REALLY?
YEAH, OH, ABSOLUTELY. I BARELY KNOW HOW TO FLY A PLANE IF I'M BEING HONEST.
THAT'S REALLY COMFORTING. THANK YOU.
I TELL YOU WHAT, MY CLOCK IS ALL MESSED UP, SO I'M GOING TO BE UP ANYWAY. WHY DON'T YOU GET SOME SLEEP, AND I'LL DEAL WITH THE LITTLE MAN?
...ARE YOU SURE?
I BEEN THROUGH A WHOLE LOT WORSE THAN A FINICKY BABY. YOUR OLD DAD CAN HANDLE THIS.
I DON'T THINK DESERT STORM REALLY COMPARES TO THIS SPECIFIC SCENARIO, DAD.
I MEANT RAISING YOUR SISTER.
DESERT STORM WAS NOTHING COMPARED TO THAT.
YOU. SLEEP. CAPTAIN'S ORDERS.
YES, SIR.

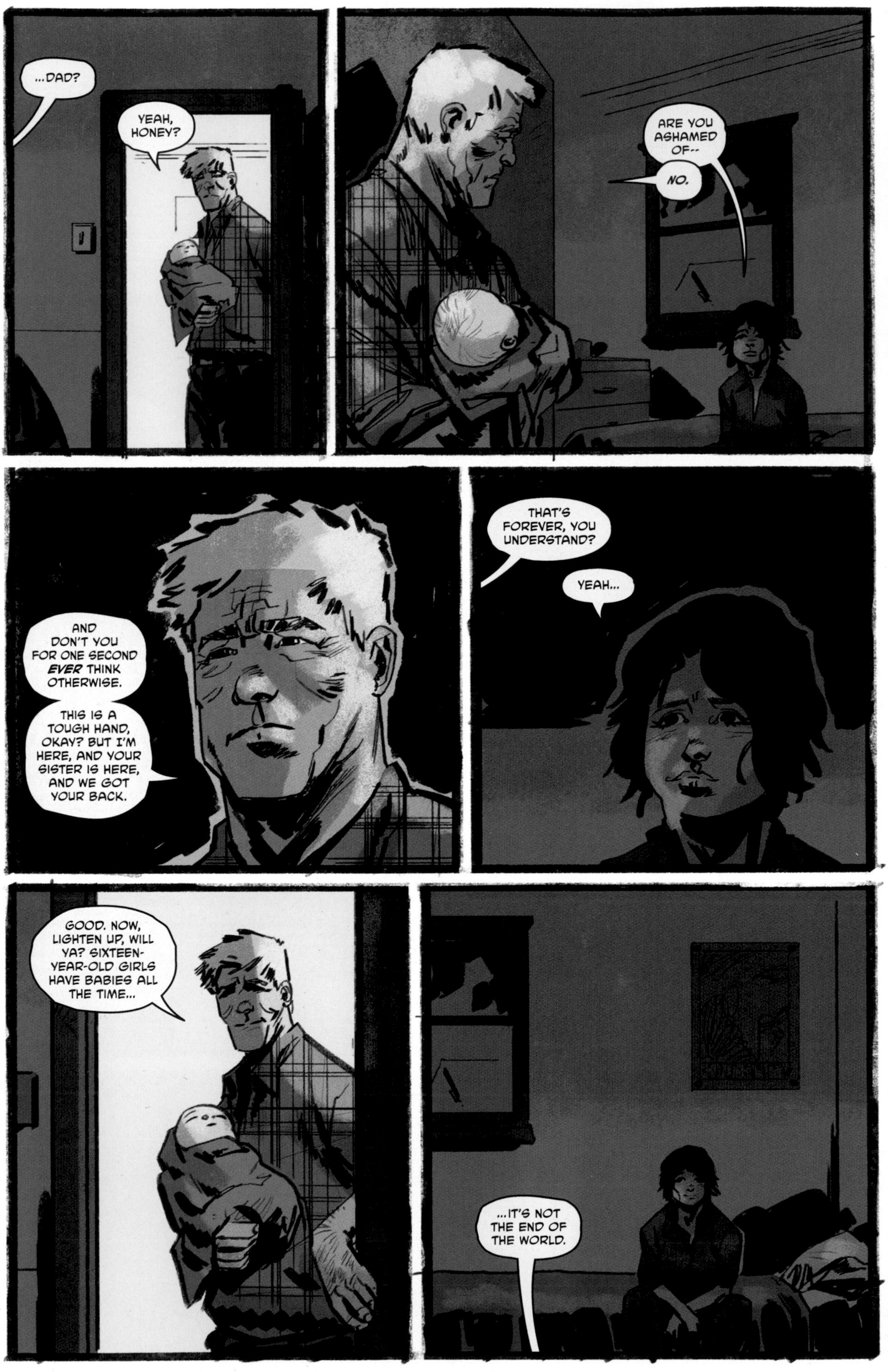
...DAD?
YEAH, HONEY?
ARE YOU ASHAMED OF--
NO.
AND DON'T YOU FOR ONE SECOND *EVER* THINK OTHERWISE.
THIS IS A TOUGH HAND, OKAY? BUT I'M HERE, AND YOUR SISTER IS HERE, AND WE GOT YOUR BACK.
THAT'S FOREVER, YOU UNDERSTAND?
YEAH...
GOOD. NOW, LIGHTEN UP, WILL YA? SIXTEEN-YEAR-OLD GIRLS HAVE BABIES ALL THE TIME...
...IT'S NOT THE END OF THE WORLD.

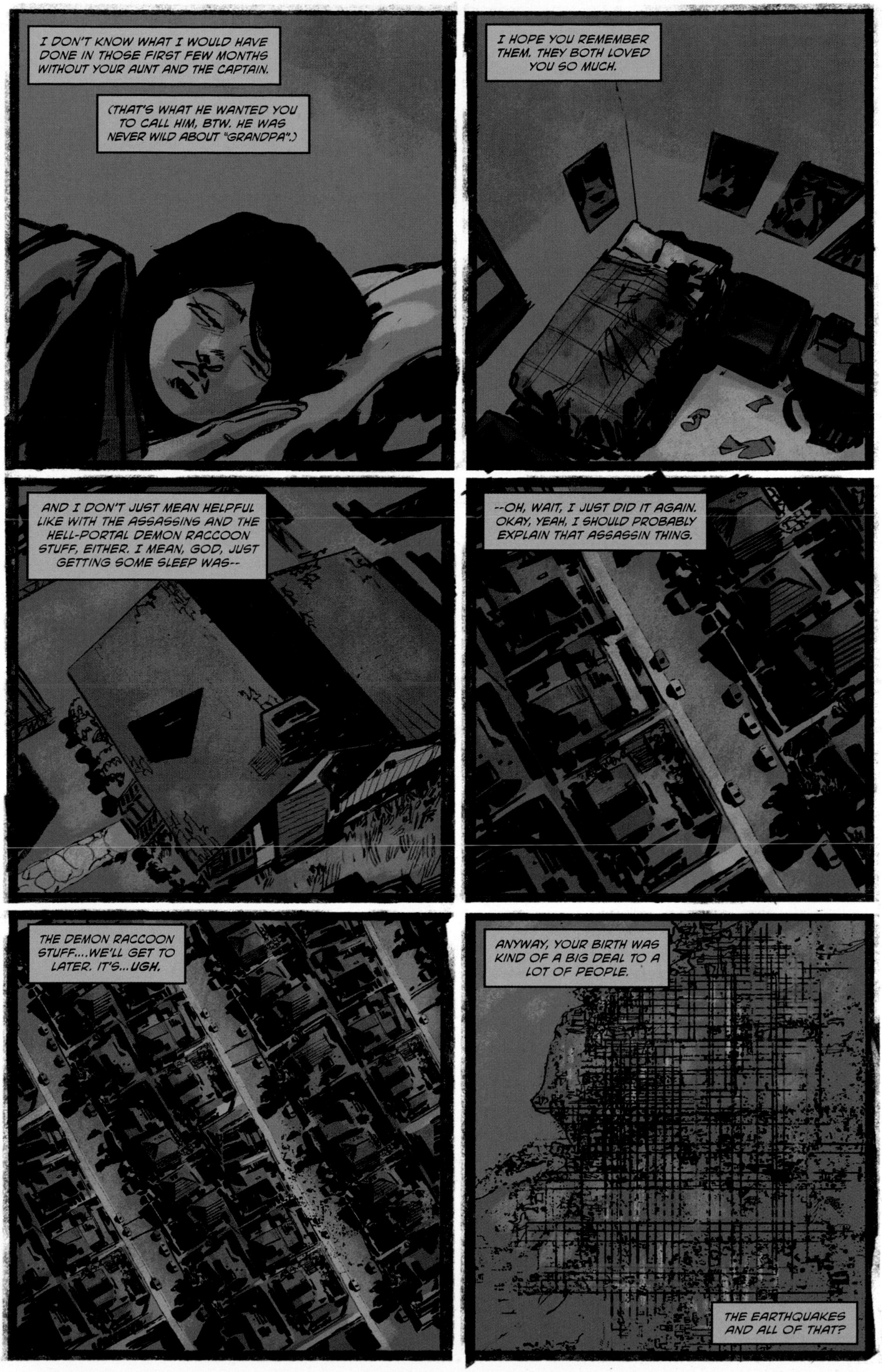
I DON'T KNOW WHAT I WOULD HAVE DONE IN THOSE FIRST FEW MONTHS WITHOUT YOUR AUNT AND THE CAPTAIN.
(THAT'S WHAT HE WANTED YOU TO CALL HIM, BTW. HE WAS NEVER WILD ABOUT "GRANDPA".)
I HOPE YOU REMEMBER THEM. THEY BOTH LOVED YOU SO MUCH.
AND I DON'T JUST MEAN HELPFUL LIKE WITH THE ASSASSINS AND THE HELL-PORTAL DEMON RACCOON STUFF, EITHER. I MEAN, GOD, JUST GETTING SOME SLEEP WAS--
--OH, WAIT, I JUST DID IT AGAIN. OKAY, YEAH, I SHOULD PROBABLY EXPLAIN THAT ASSASSIN THING.
THE DEMON RACCOON STUFF....WE'LL GET TO LATER. IT'S...UGH.
ANYWAY, YOUR BIRTH WAS KIND OF A BIG DEAL TO A LOT OF PEOPLE.
THE EARTHQUAKES AND ALL OF THAT?

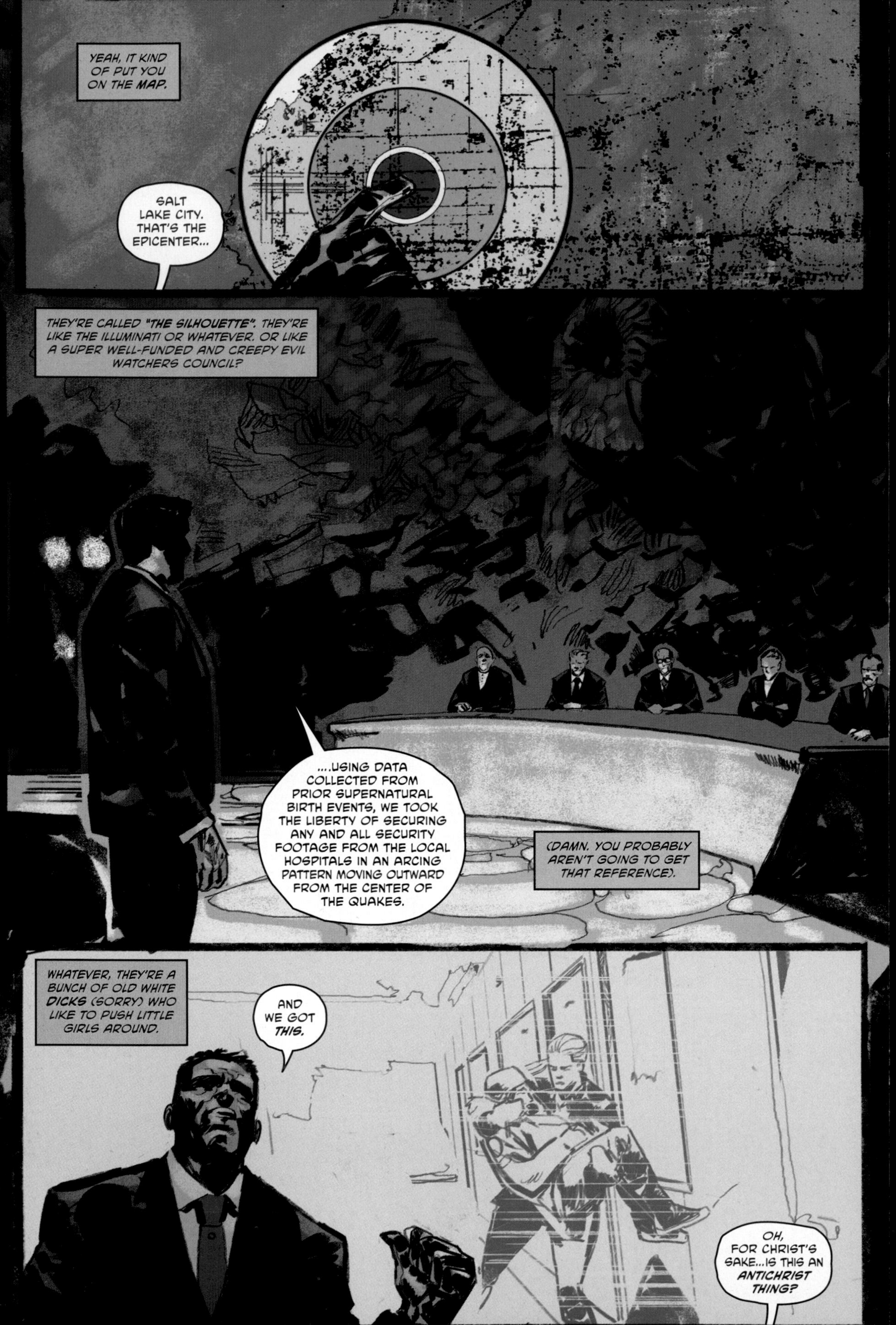

YEAH, IT KIND OF PUT YOU ON THE *MAP*.
SALT LAKE CITY. THAT'S THE EPICENTER...
THEY'RE CALLED "*THE SILHOUETTE*". THEY'RE LIKE THE ILLUMINATI OR WHATEVER. OR LIKE A SUPER WELL-FUNDED AND CREEPY EVIL WATCHERS COUNCIL?
....USING DATA COLLECTED FROM PRIOR SUPERNATURAL BIRTH EVENTS, WE TOOK THE LIBERTY OF SECURING ANY AND ALL SECURITY FOOTAGE FROM THE LOCAL HOSPITALS IN AN ARCING PATTERN MOVING OUTWARD FROM THE CENTER OF THE QUAKES.
(DAMN. YOU PROBABLY AREN'T GOING TO GET THAT REFERENCE).
WHATEVER, THEY'RE A BUNCH OF OLD WHITE *DICKS* (SORRY) WHO LIKE TO PUSH LITTLE GIRLS AROUND.
AND WE GOT *THIS*.
OH, FOR CHRIST'S SAKE...IS THIS AN *ANTICHRIST THING*?

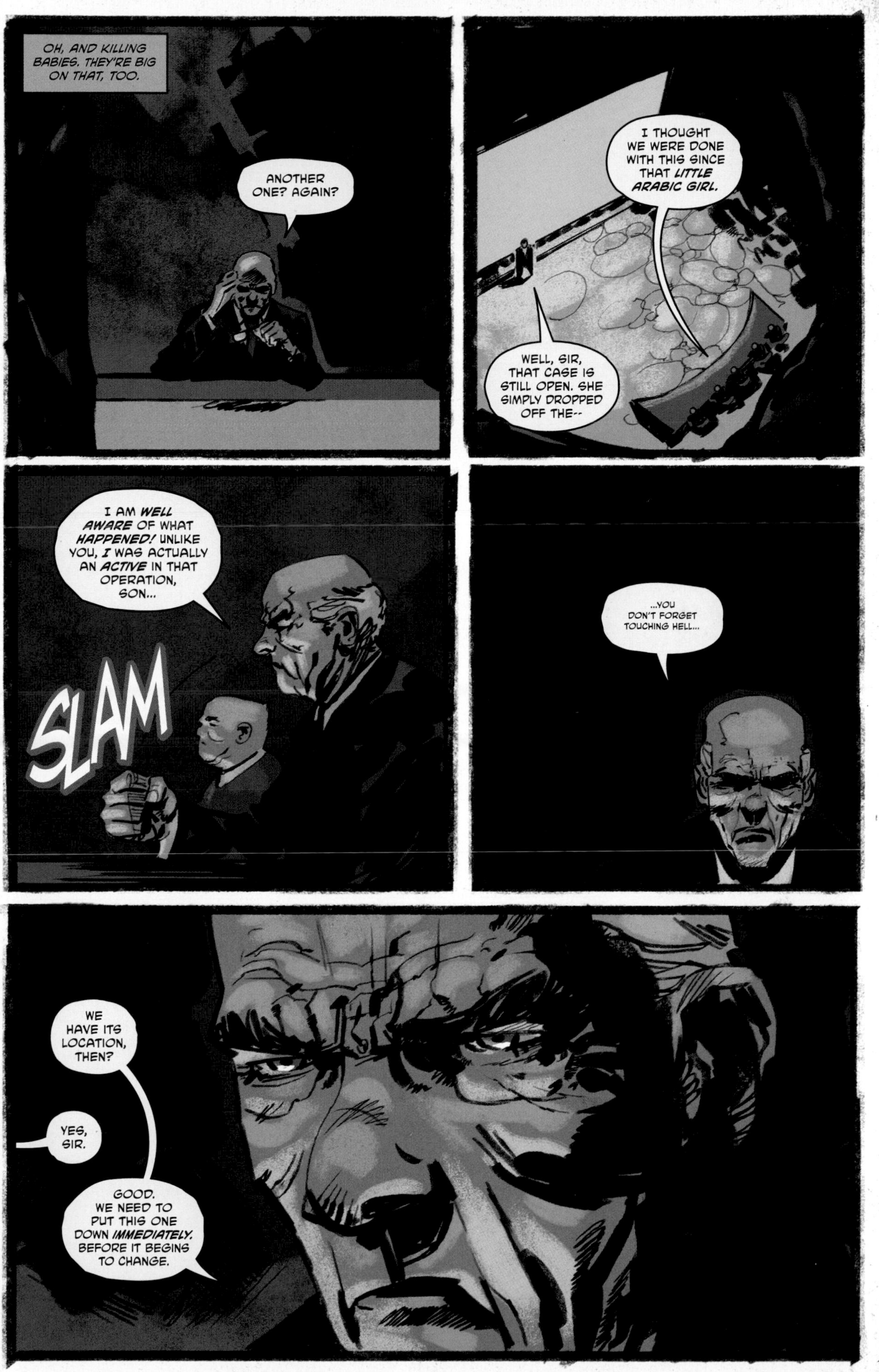
OH, AND KILLING BABIES. THEY'RE BIG ON THAT, TOO.
ANOTHER ONE? AGAIN?
I THOUGHT WE WERE DONE WITH THIS SINCE THAT *LITTLE ARABIC GIRL.*
WELL, SIR, THAT CASE IS STILL OPEN. SHE SIMPLY DROPPED OFF THE--
I AM *WELL AWARE* OF WHAT *HAPPENED!* UNLIKE YOU, *I* WAS ACTUALLY AN *ACTIVE* IN THAT OPERATION, SON...
SLAM
...YOU DON'T FORGET TOUCHING HELL...
WE HAVE ITS LOCATION, THEN?
YES, SIR.
GOOD. WE NEED TO PUT THIS ONE DOWN *IMMEDIATELY.* BEFORE IT BEGINS TO CHANGE.

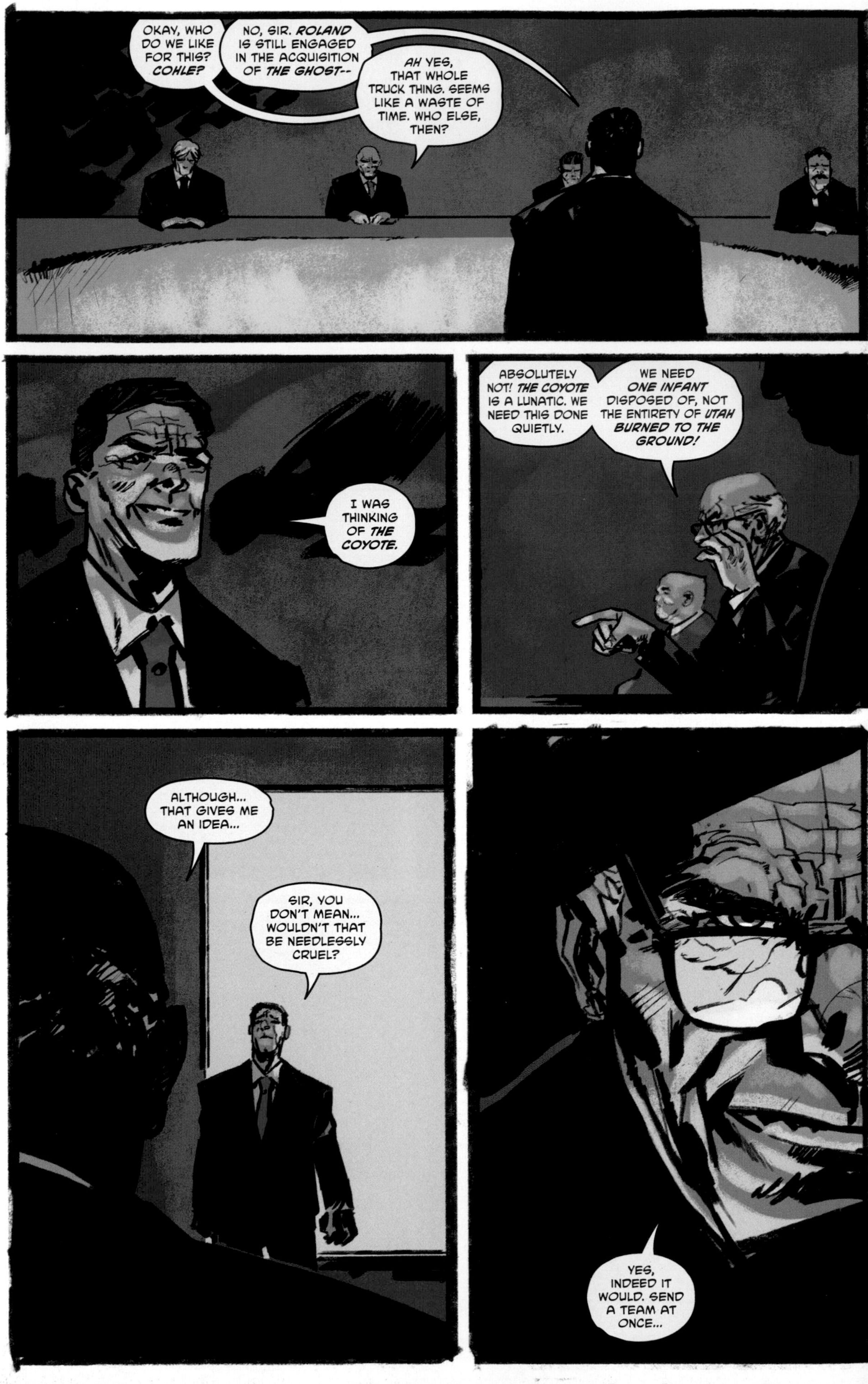
OKAY, WHO DO WE LIKE FOR THIS? COHLE?
NO, SIR. ROLAND IS STILL ENGAGED IN THE ACQUISITION OF THE GHOST--
AH YES, THAT WHOLE TRUCK THING. SEEMS LIKE A WASTE OF TIME. WHO ELSE, THEN?
I WAS THINKING OF THE COYOTE.
ABSOLUTELY NOT! THE COYOTE IS A LUNATIC. WE NEED THIS DONE QUIETLY.
WE NEED ONE INFANT DISPOSED OF, NOT THE ENTIRETY OF UTAH BURNED TO THE GROUND!
ALTHOUGH... THAT GIVES ME AN IDEA...
SIR, YOU DON'T MEAN... WOULDN'T THAT BE NEEDLESSLY CRUEL?
YES, INDEED IT WOULD. SEND A TEAM AT ONCE...

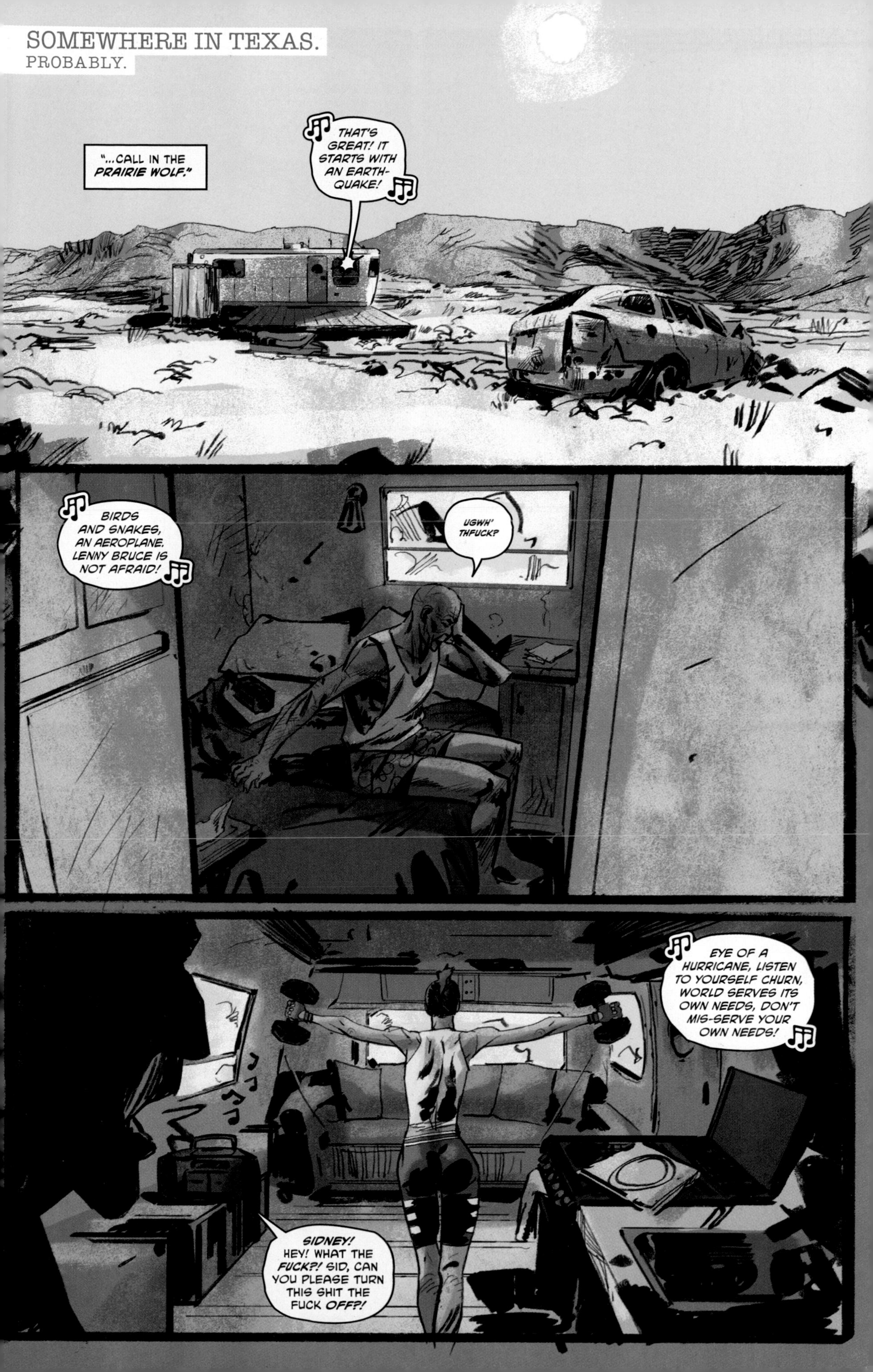
SOMEWHERE IN TEXAS.
PROBABLY.
"...CALL IN THE PRAIRIE WOLF."
THAT'S GREAT! IT STARTS WITH AN EARTH-QUAKE!
BIRDS AND SNAKES, AN AEROPLANE. LENNY BRUCE IS NOT AFRAID!
UGWH' THFUCK?
EYE OF A HURRICANE, LISTEN TO YOURSELF CHURN, WORLD SERVES ITS OWN NEEDS, DON'T MIS-SERVE YOUR OWN NEEDS!
SIDNEY! HEY! WHAT THE FUCK?! SID, CAN YOU PLEASE TURN THIS SHIT THE FUCK OFF?!

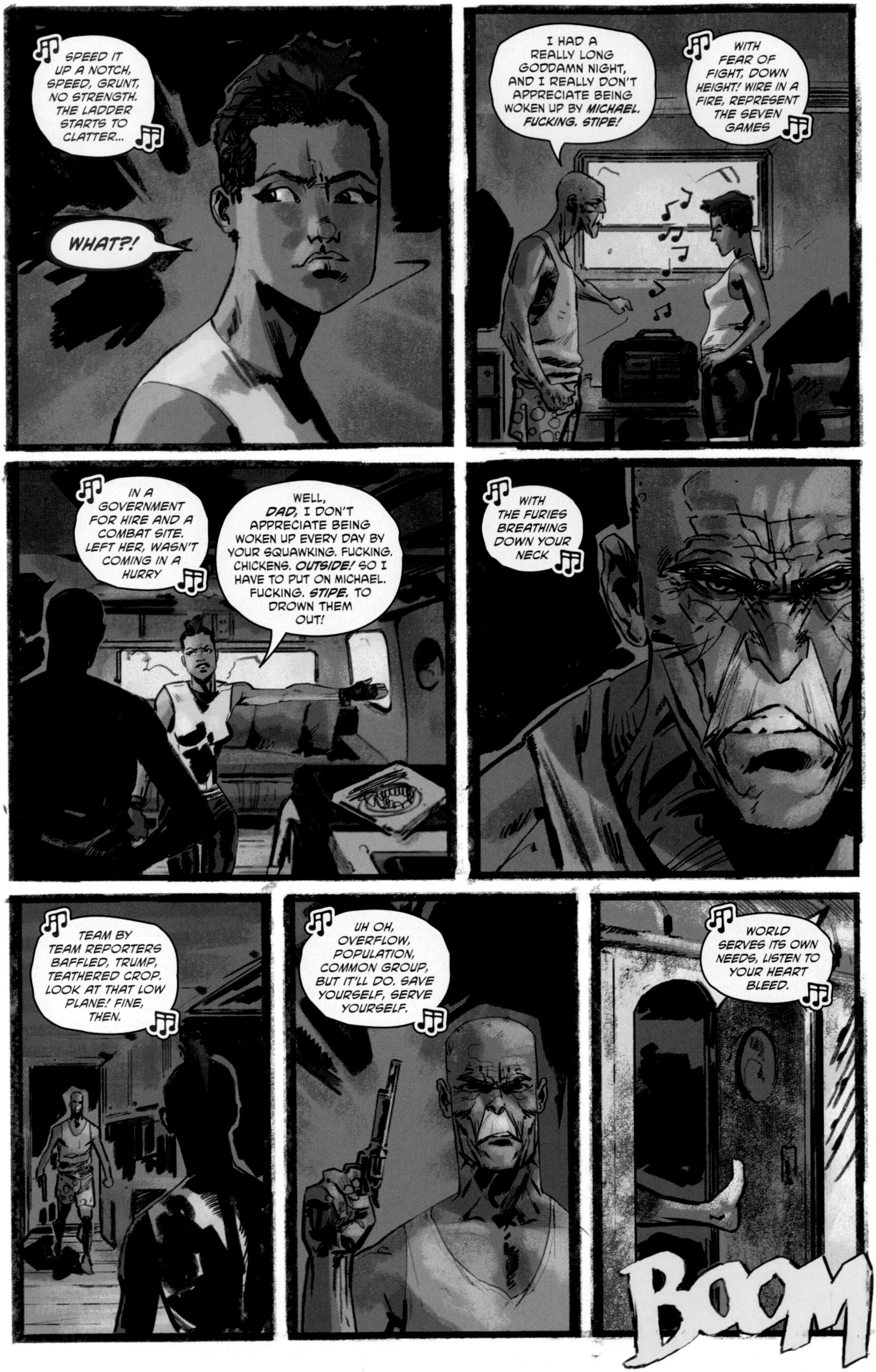
SPEED IT UP A NOTCH, SPEED, GRUNT, NO STRENGTH. THE LADDER STARTS TO CLATTER...
WHAT?!
I HAD A REALLY LONG GODDAMN NIGHT, AND I REALLY DON'T APPRECIATE BEING WOKEN UP BY MICHAEL. FUCKING. STIPE!
WITH FEAR OF FIGHT, DOWN HEIGHT! WIRE IN A FIRE, REPRESENT THE SEVEN GAMES
IN A GOVERNMENT FOR HIRE AND A COMBAT SITE. LEFT HER, WASN'T COMING IN A HURRY
WELL, DAD, I DON'T APPRECIATE BEING WOKEN UP EVERY DAY BY YOUR SQUAWKING. FUCKING. CHICKENS. OUTSIDE! SO I HAVE TO PUT ON MICHAEL. FUCKING. STIPE. TO DROWN THEM OUT!
WITH THE FURIES BREATHING DOWN YOUR NECK
TEAM BY TEAM REPORTERS BAFFLED, TRUMP, TEATHERED CROP. LOOK AT THAT LOW PLANE! FINE, THEN.
UH OH, OVERFLOW, POPULATION, COMMON GROUP, BUT IT'LL DO. SAVE YOURSELF, SERVE YOURSELF.
WORLD SERVES ITS OWN NEEDS, LISTEN TO YOUR HEART BLEED.
BOOM

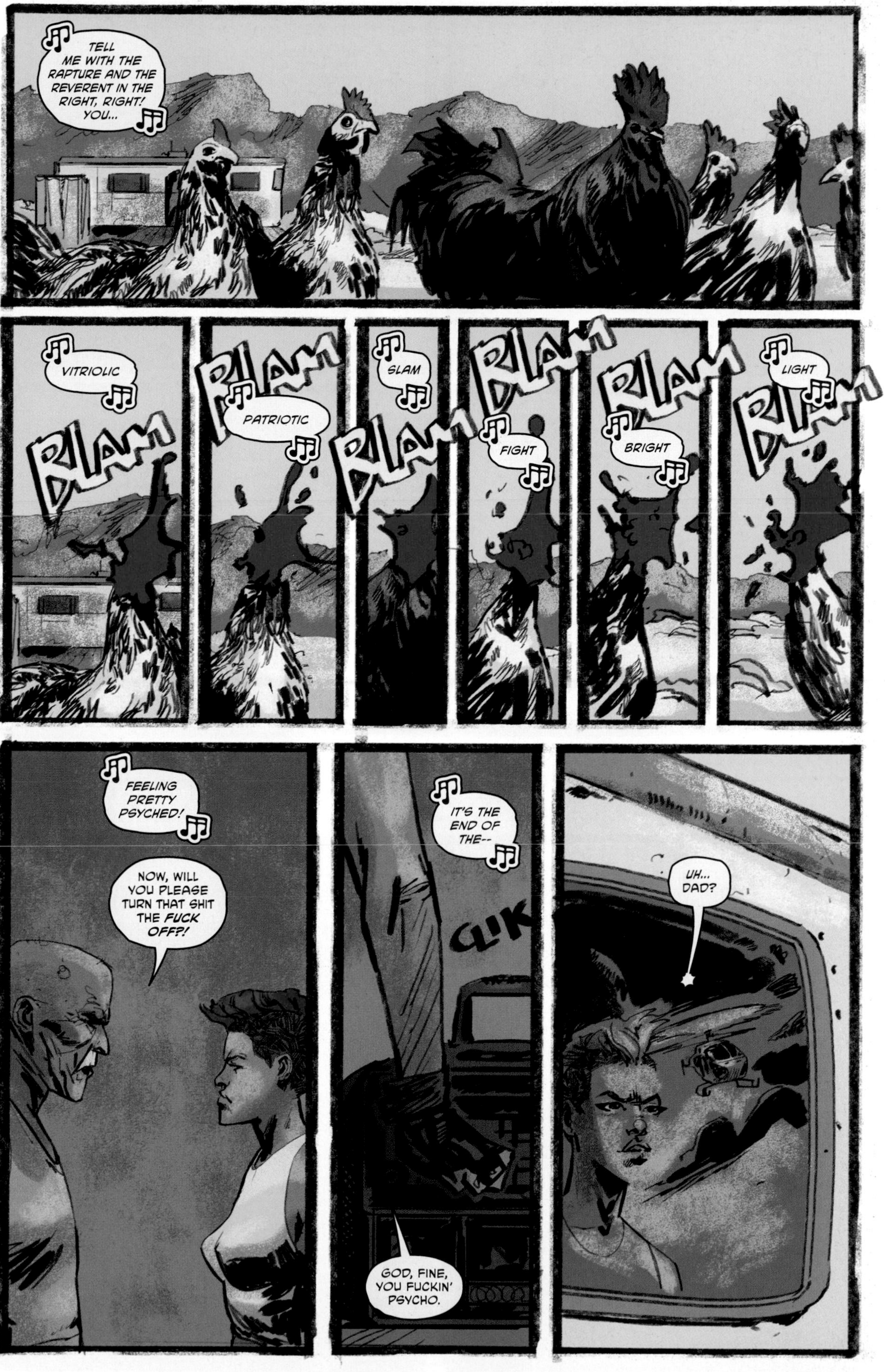
TELL ME WITH THE RAPTURE AND THE REVERENT IN THE RIGHT, RIGHT! YOU...
VITRIOLIC
BLAM
BLAM
PATRIOTIC
SLAM
BLAM
BLAM
FIGHT
BLAM
BRIGHT
LIGHT
BLAM
FEELING PRETTY PSYCHED!
NOW, WILL YOU PLEASE TURN THAT SHIT THE FUCK OFF?!
IT'S THE END OF THE--
CLIK
GOD, FINE, YOU FUCKIN' PSYCHO.
UH... DAD?

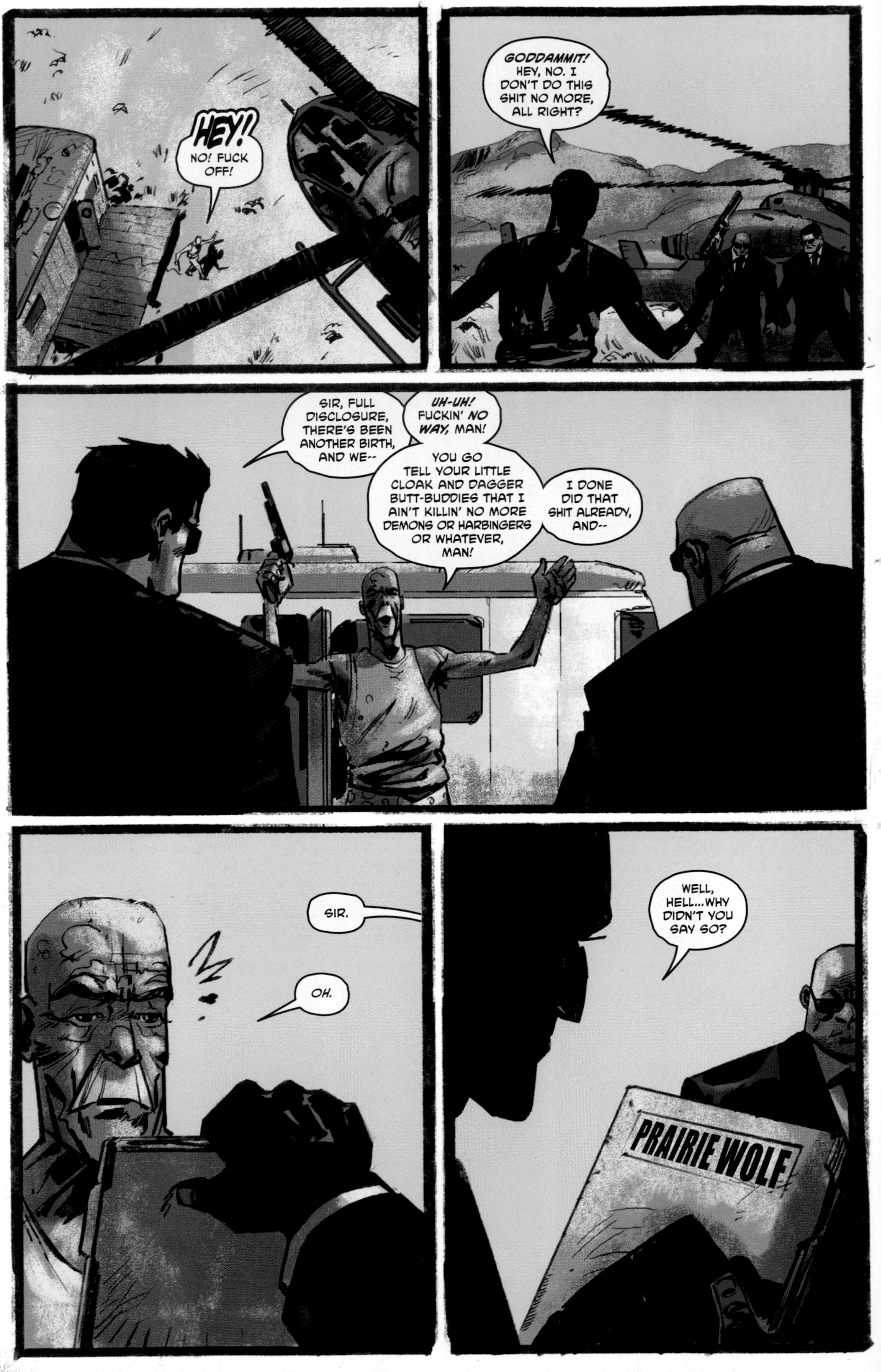
HEY!
NO! FUCK OFF!
GODDAMMIT! HEY, NO. I DON'T DO THIS SHIT NO MORE, ALL RIGHT?
SIR, FULL DISCLOSURE, THERE'S BEEN ANOTHER BIRTH, AND WE--
UH-UH! FUCKIN' NO WAY, MAN!
YOU GO TELL YOUR LITTLE CLOAK AND DAGGER BUTT-BUDDIES THAT I AIN'T KILLIN' NO MORE DEMONS OR HARBINGERS OR WHATEVER, MAN!
I DONE DID THAT SHIT ALREADY, AND--
SIR.
OH.
WELL, HELL...WHY DIDN'T YOU SAY SO?
PRAIRIE WOLF

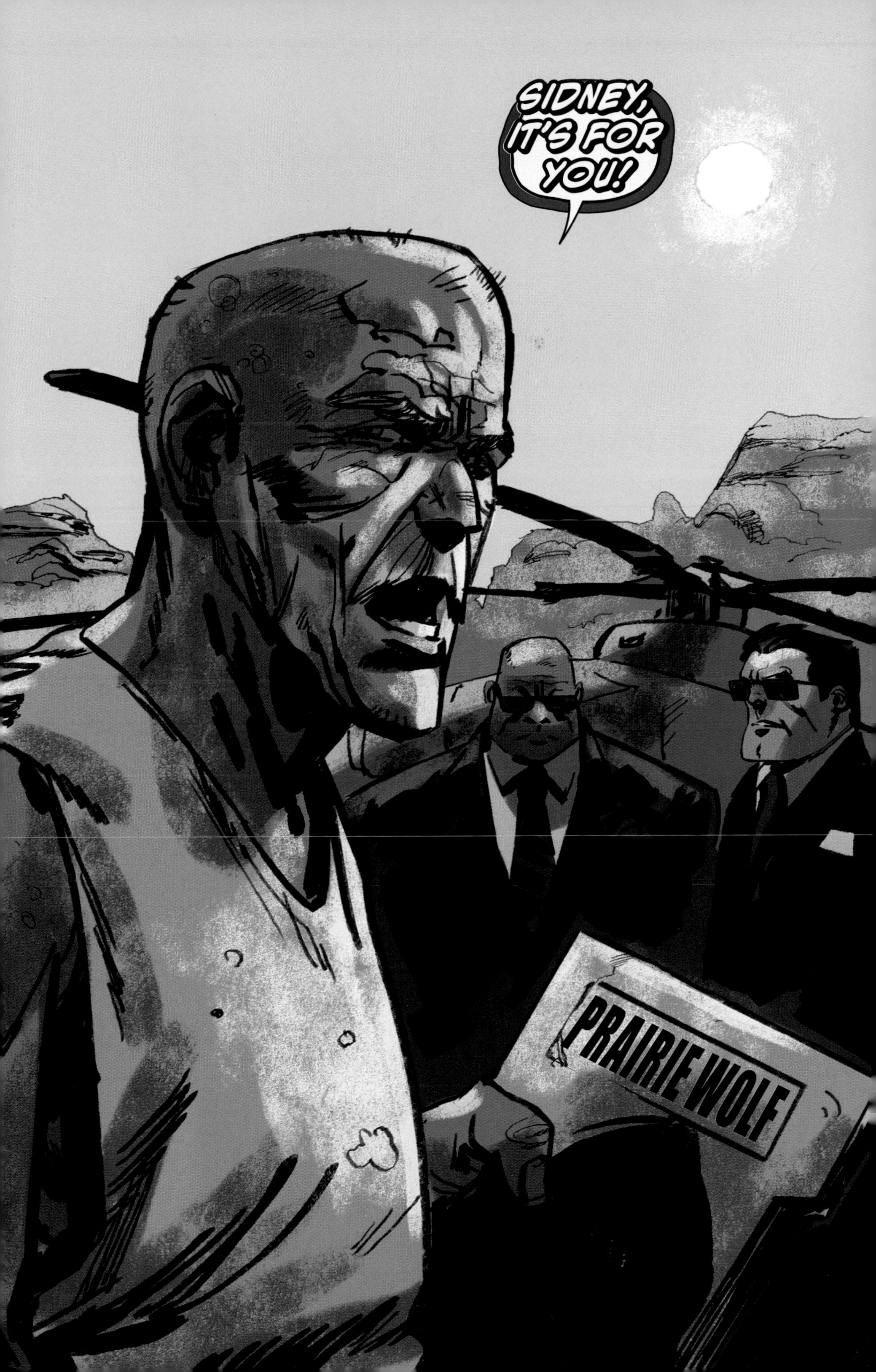
SIDNEY, IT'S FOR YOU!
PRAIRIE WOLF

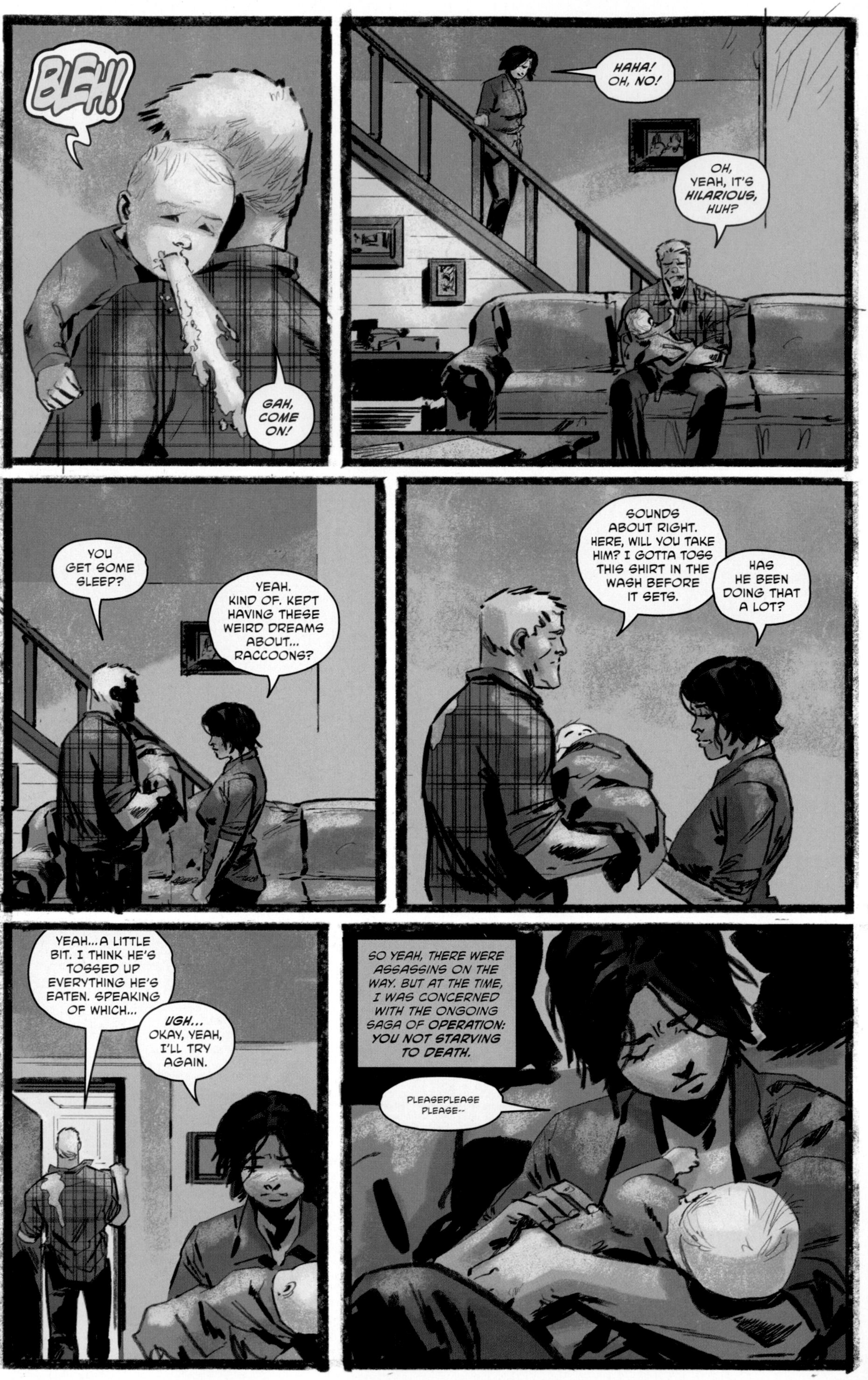
BLEH!!
GAH, COME ON!
HAHA! OH, NO!
OH, YEAH, IT'S HILARIOUS, HUH?
YOU GET SOME SLEEP?
YEAH. KIND OF. KEPT HAVING THESE WEIRD DREAMS ABOUT... RACCOONS?
SOUNDS ABOUT RIGHT. HERE, WILL YOU TAKE HIM? I GOTTA TOSS THIS SHIRT IN THE WASH BEFORE IT SETS.
HAS HE BEEN DOING THAT A LOT?
YEAH...A LITTLE BIT. I THINK HE'S TOSSED UP EVERYTHING HE'S EATEN. SPEAKING OF WHICH...
UGH... OKAY, YEAH, I'LL TRY AGAIN.
SO YEAH, THERE WERE ASSASSINS ON THE WAY. BUT AT THE TIME, I WAS CONCERNED WITH THE ONGOING SAGA OF OPERATION: YOU NOT STARVING TO DEATH.
PLEASEPLEASE PLEASE--

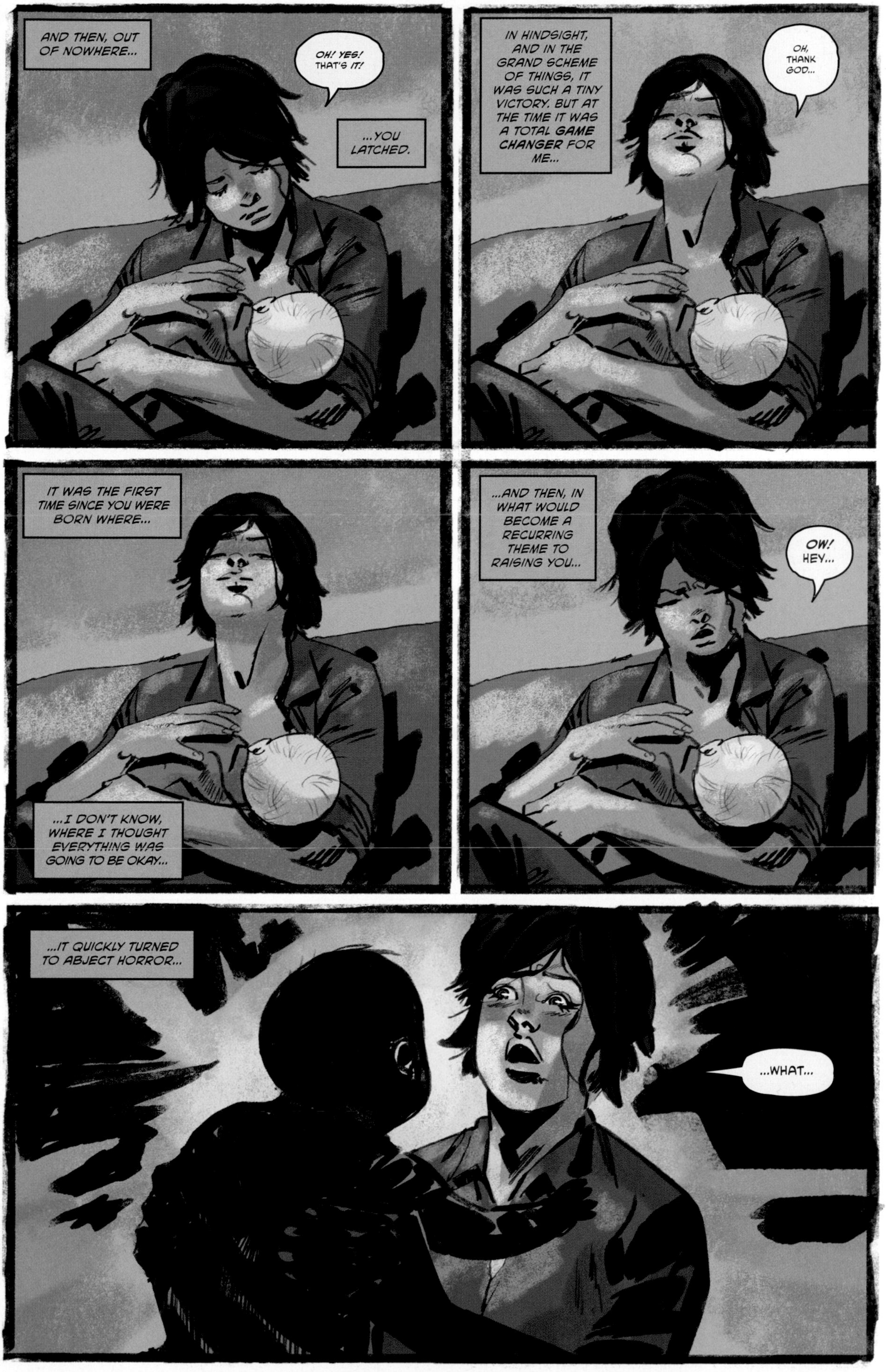
AND THEN, OUT OF NOWHERE...
OH! YES! THAT'S IT!
...YOU LATCHED.
IN HINDSIGHT, AND IN THE GRAND SCHEME OF THINGS, IT WAS SUCH A TINY VICTORY. BUT AT THE TIME IT WAS A TOTAL GAME CHANGER FOR ME...
OH, THANK GOD...
IT WAS THE FIRST TIME SINCE YOU WERE BORN WHERE...
...I DON'T KNOW, WHERE I THOUGHT EVERYTHING WAS GOING TO BE OKAY...
...AND THEN, IN WHAT WOULD BECOME A RECURRING THEME TO RAISING YOU...
OW! HEY...
...IT QUICKLY TURNED TO ABJECT HORROR...
...WHAT...

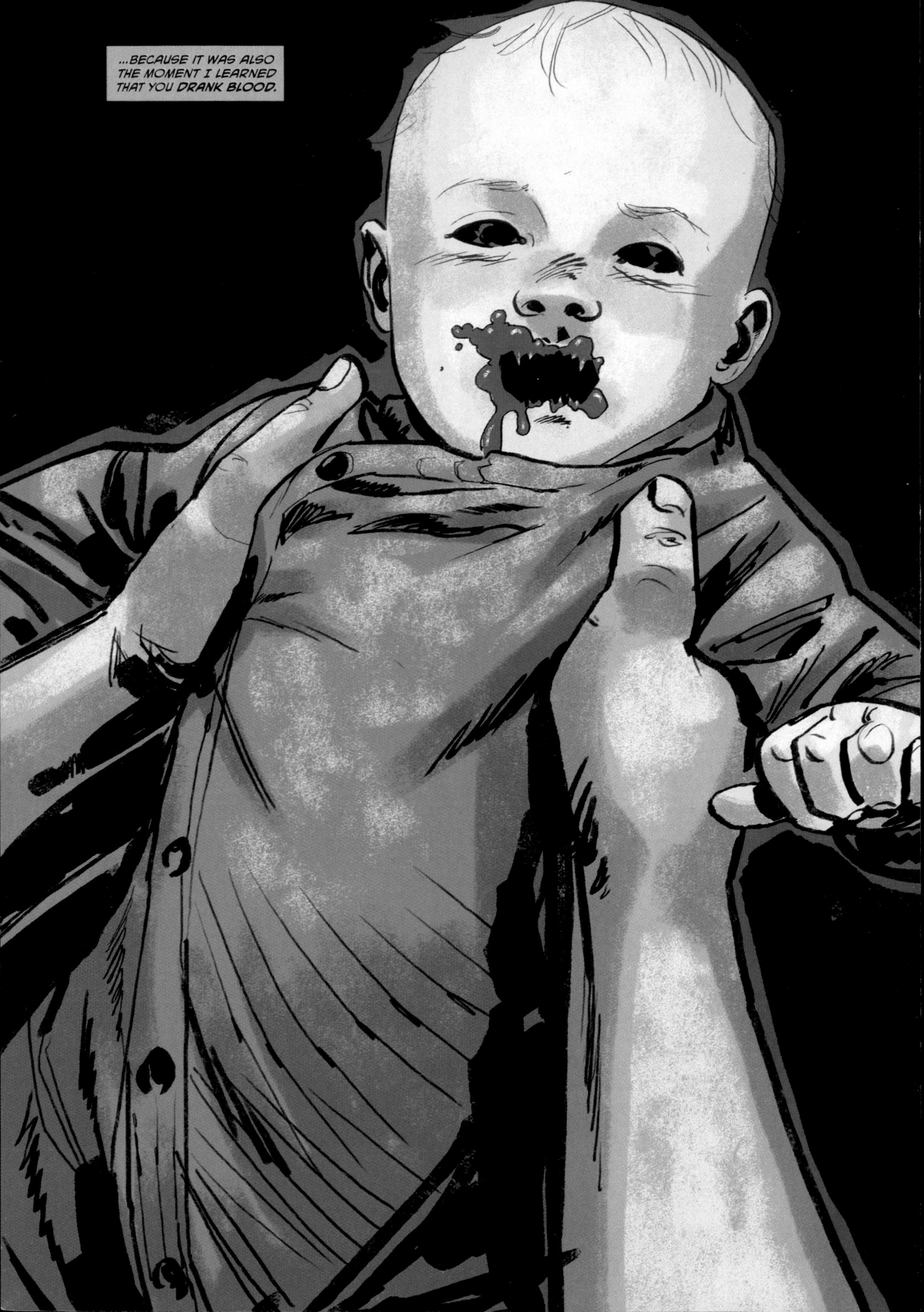
...BECAUSE IT WAS ALSO THE MOMENT I LEARNED THAT YOU DRANK BLOOD.

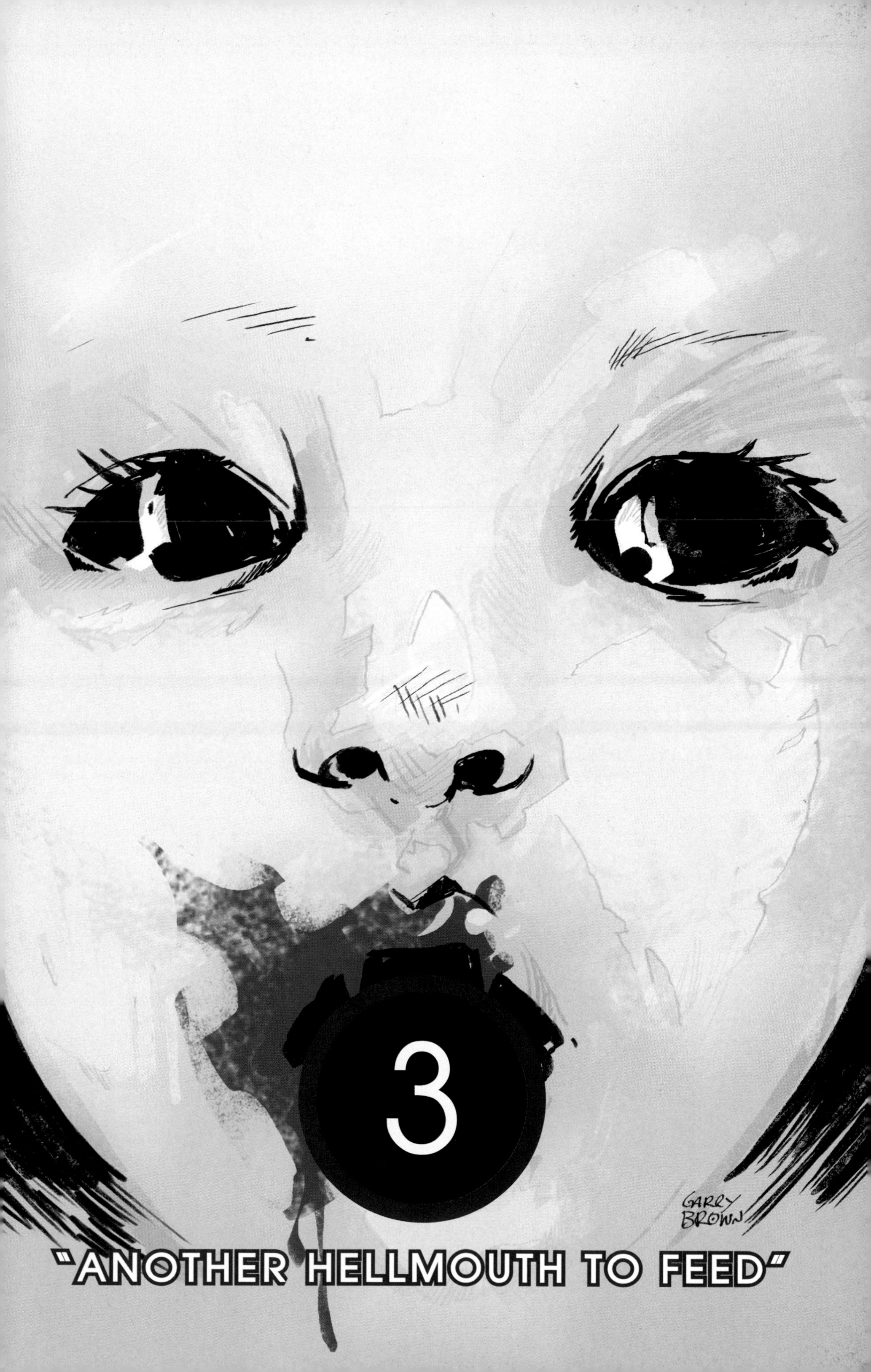
3
GARRY BROWN
"ANOTHER HELLMOUTH TO FEED"

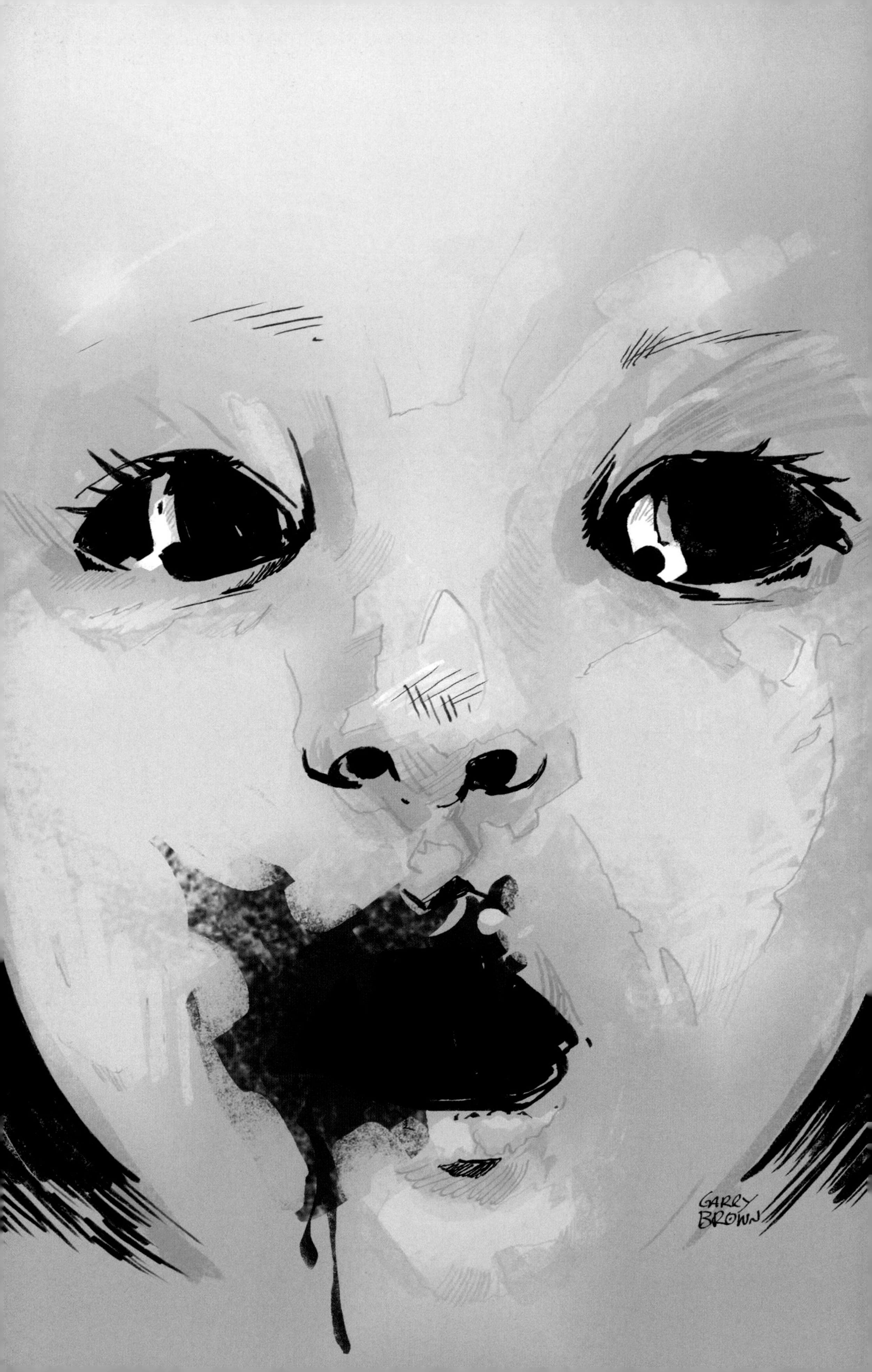
GARRY
BROWN

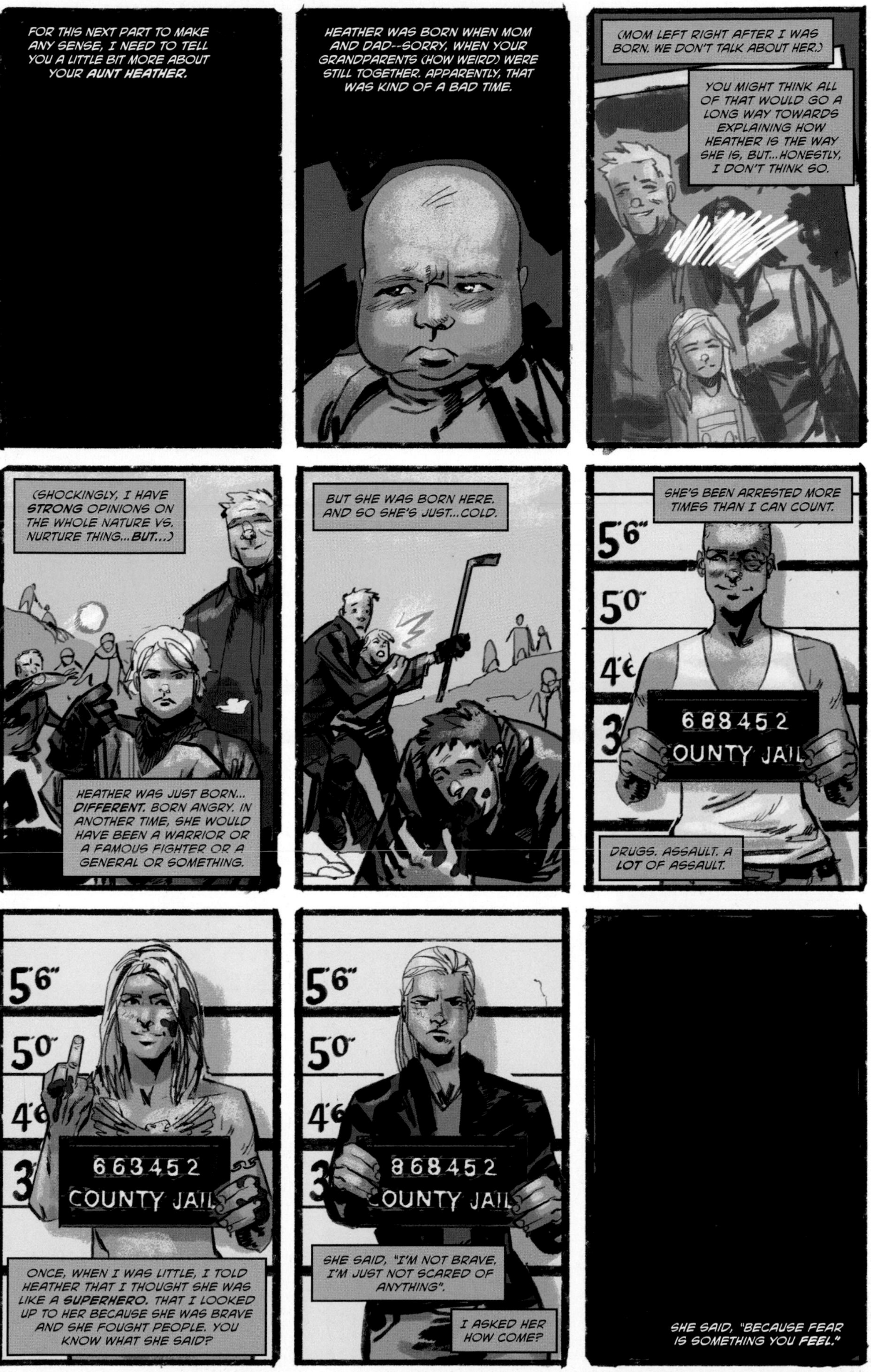
FOR THIS NEXT PART TO MAKE ANY SENSE, I NEED TO TELL YOU A LITTLE BIT MORE ABOUT YOUR AUNT HEATHER.
HEATHER WAS BORN WHEN MOM AND DAD--SORRY, WHEN YOUR GRANDPARENTS (HOW WEIRD) WERE STILL TOGETHER. APPARENTLY, THAT WAS KIND OF A BAD TIME.
(MOM LEFT RIGHT AFTER I WAS BORN. WE DON'T TALK ABOUT HER.)
YOU MIGHT THINK ALL OF THAT WOULD GO A LONG WAY TOWARDS EXPLAINING HOW HEATHER IS THE WAY SHE IS, BUT...HONESTLY, I DON'T THINK SO.
(SHOCKINGLY, I HAVE STRONG OPINIONS ON THE WHOLE NATURE VS. NURTURE THING...BUT...)
HEATHER WAS JUST BORN... DIFFERENT. BORN ANGRY. IN ANOTHER TIME, SHE WOULD HAVE BEEN A WARRIOR OR A FAMOUS FIGHTER OR A GENERAL OR SOMETHING.
BUT SHE WAS BORN HERE. AND SO SHE'S JUST...COLD.
SHE'S BEEN ARRESTED MORE TIMES THAN I CAN COUNT.
688452
COUNTY JAIL
DRUGS. ASSAULT. A LOT OF ASSAULT.
663452
COUNTY JAIL
ONCE, WHEN I WAS LITTLE, I TOLD HEATHER THAT I THOUGHT SHE WAS LIKE A SUPERHERO. THAT I LOOKED UP TO HER BECAUSE SHE WAS BRAVE AND SHE FOUGHT PEOPLE. YOU KNOW WHAT SHE SAID?
868452
COUNTY JAIL
SHE SAID, "I'M NOT BRAVE. I'M JUST NOT SCARED OF ANYTHING".
I ASKED HER HOW COME?
SHE SAID, "BECAUSE FEAR IS SOMETHING YOU FEEL."

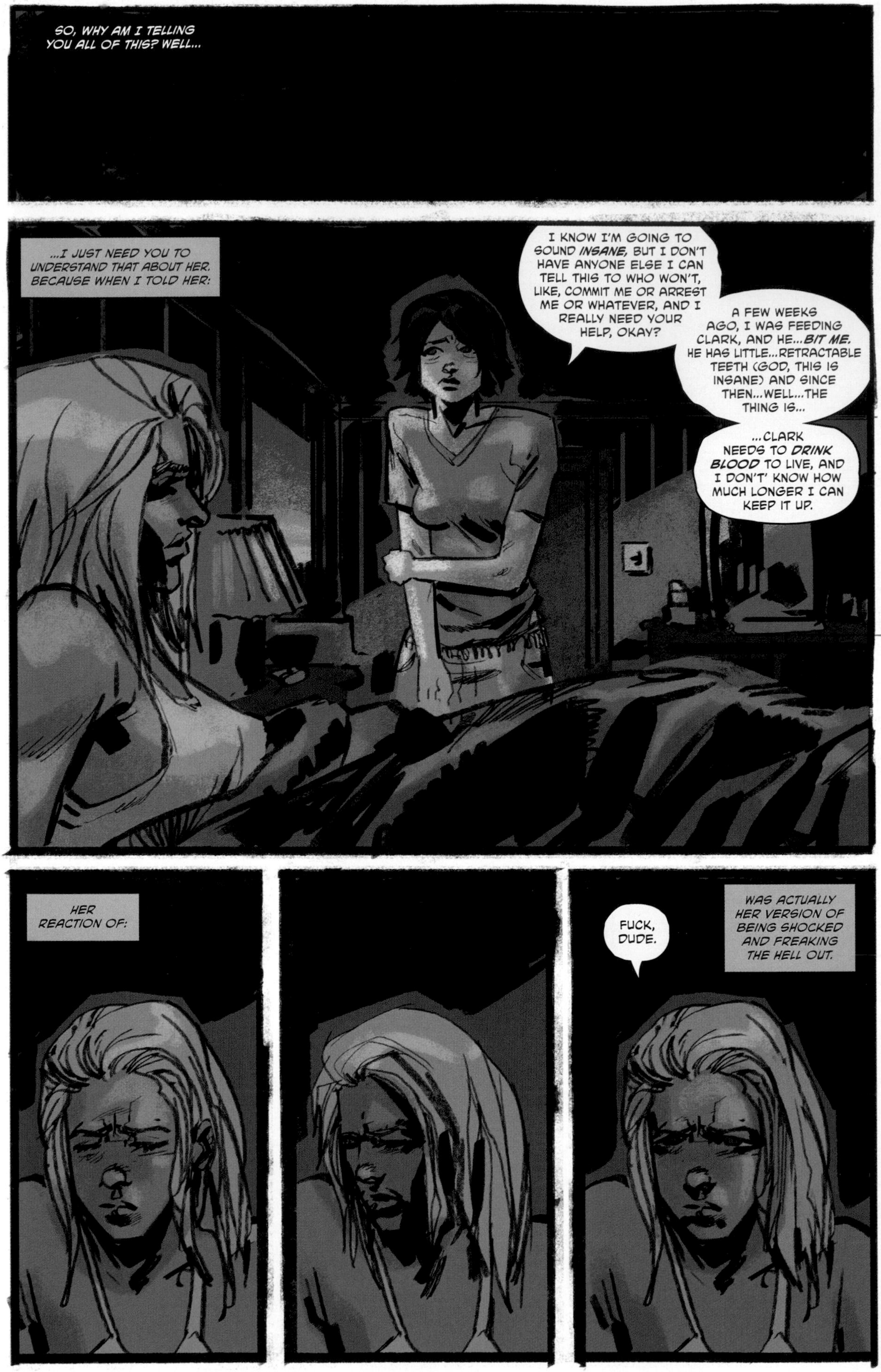
SO, WHY AM I TELLING YOU ALL OF THIS? WELL...
...I JUST NEED YOU TO UNDERSTAND THAT ABOUT HER. BECAUSE WHEN I TOLD HER:
I KNOW I'M GOING TO SOUND INSANE, BUT I DON'T HAVE ANYONE ELSE I CAN TELL THIS TO WHO WON'T, LIKE, COMMIT ME OR ARREST ME OR WHATEVER, AND I REALLY NEED YOUR HELP, OKAY?
A FEW WEEKS AGO, I WAS FEEDING CLARK, AND HE...BIT ME. HE HAS LITTLE...RETRACTABLE TEETH (GOD, THIS IS INSANE) AND SINCE THEN...WELL...THE THING IS...
...CLARK NEEDS TO DRINK BLOOD TO LIVE, AND I DON'T' KNOW HOW MUCH LONGER I CAN KEEP IT UP.
HER REACTION OF:
FUCK, DUDE.
WAS ACTUALLY HER VERSION OF BEING SHOCKED AND FREAKING THE HELL OUT.

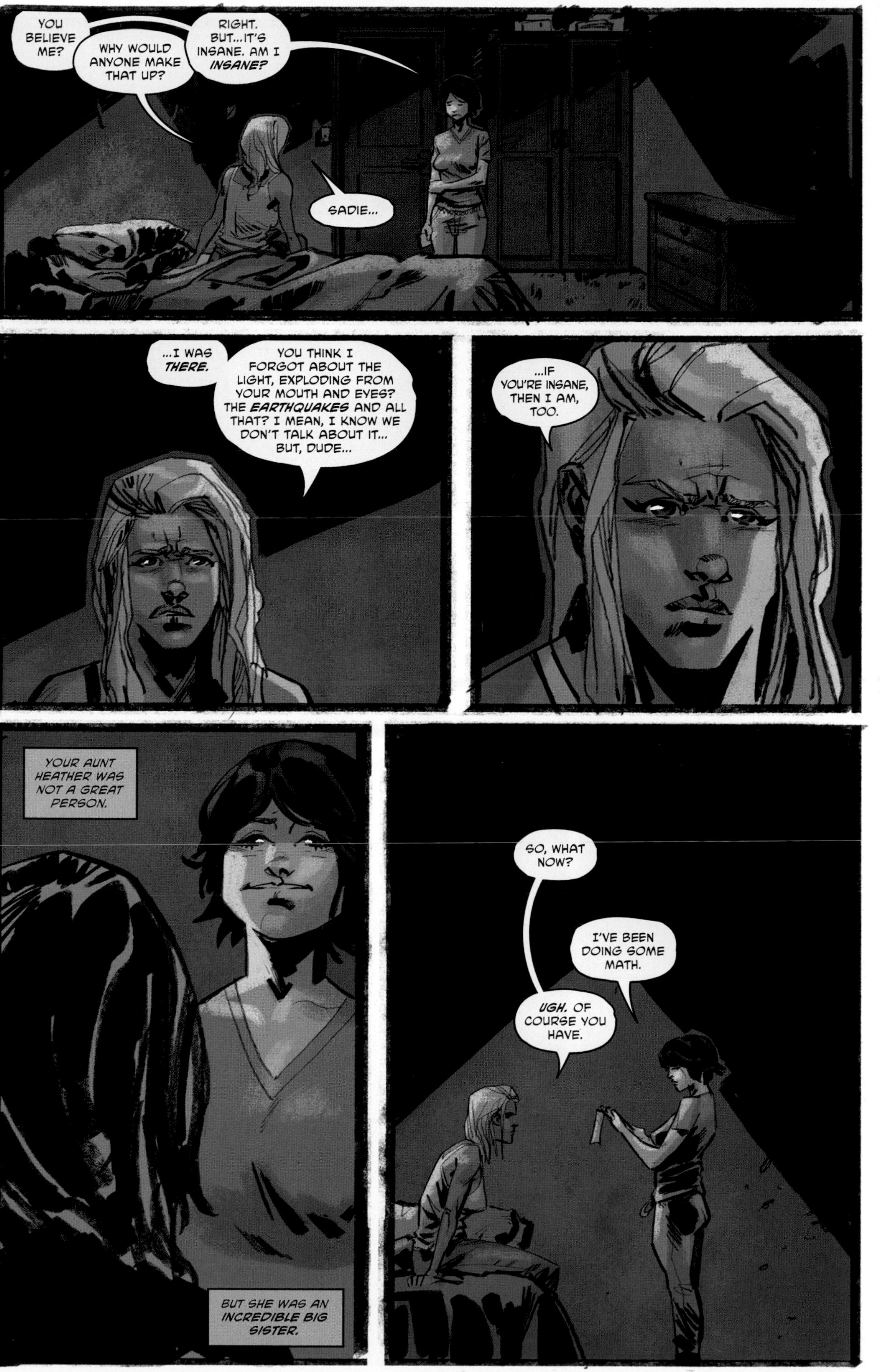
YOU BELIEVE ME?
WHY WOULD ANYONE MAKE THAT UP?
RIGHT. BUT...IT'S INSANE. AM I *INSANE?*
SADIE...
...I WAS *THERE.*
YOU THINK I FORGOT ABOUT THE LIGHT, EXPLODING FROM YOUR MOUTH AND EYES? THE *EARTHQUAKES* AND ALL THAT? I MEAN, I KNOW WE DON'T TALK ABOUT IT... BUT, DUDE...
...IF YOU'RE INSANE, THEN I AM, TOO.
YOUR AUNT HEATHER WAS NOT A GREAT PERSON.
BUT SHE WAS AN INCREDIBLE BIG SISTER.
SO, WHAT NOW?
I'VE BEEN DOING SOME MATH.
UGH. OF COURSE YOU HAVE.

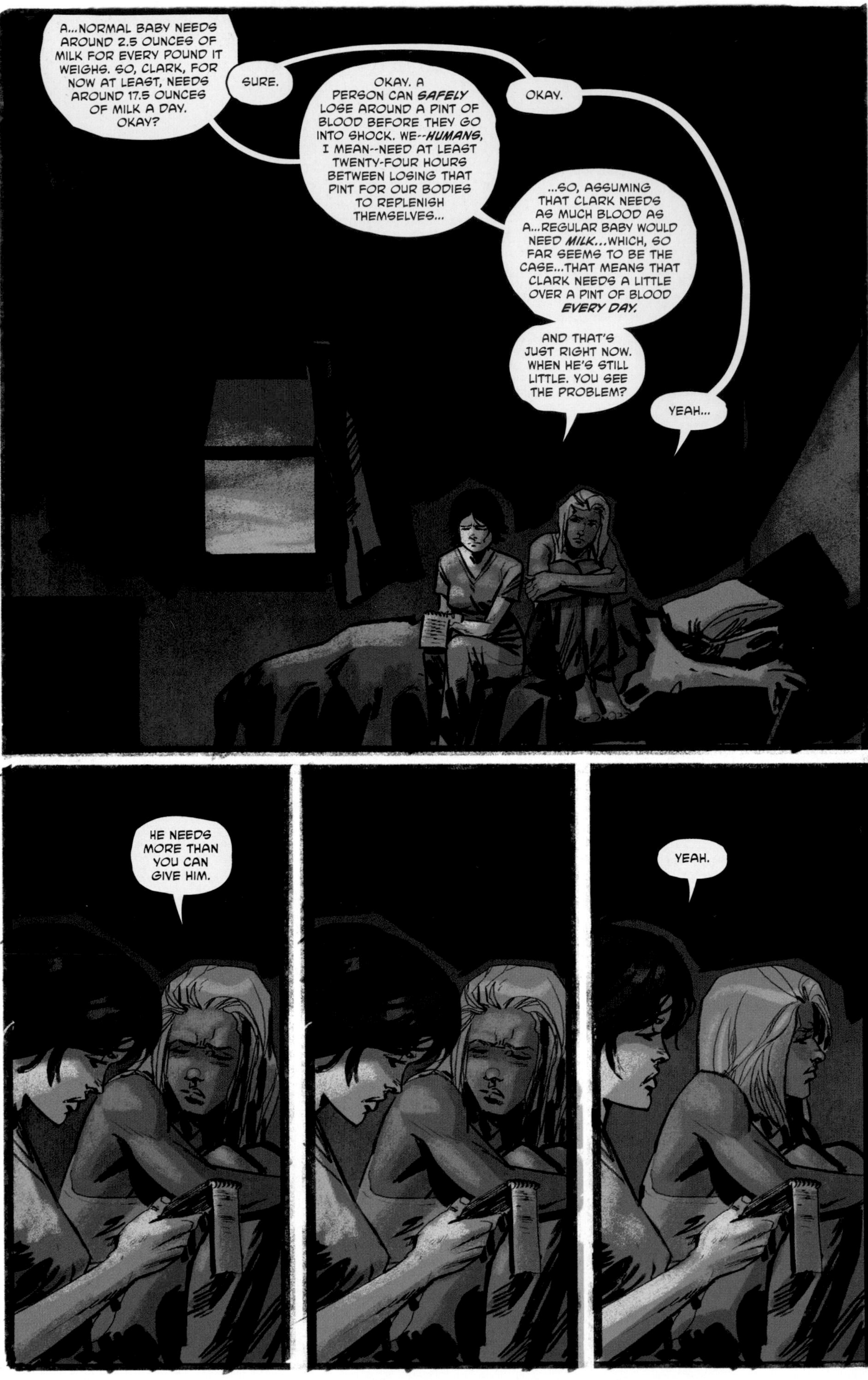
A...NORMAL BABY NEEDS AROUND 2.5 OUNCES OF MILK FOR EVERY POUND IT WEIGHS. SO, CLARK, FOR NOW AT LEAST, NEEDS AROUND 17.5 OUNCES OF MILK A DAY. OKAY?
SURE.
OKAY. A PERSON CAN SAFELY LOSE AROUND A PINT OF BLOOD BEFORE THEY GO INTO SHOCK. WE--HUMANS, I MEAN--NEED AT LEAST TWENTY-FOUR HOURS BETWEEN LOSING THAT PINT FOR OUR BODIES TO REPLENISH THEMSELVES...
OKAY.
...SO, ASSUMING THAT CLARK NEEDS AS MUCH BLOOD AS A...REGULAR BABY WOULD NEED MILK...WHICH, SO FAR SEEMS TO BE THE CASE...THAT MEANS THAT CLARK NEEDS A LITTLE OVER A PINT OF BLOOD EVERY DAY.
AND THAT'S JUST RIGHT NOW. WHEN HE'S STILL LITTLE. YOU SEE THE PROBLEM?
YEAH...
HE NEEDS MORE THAN YOU CAN GIVE HIM.
YEAH.

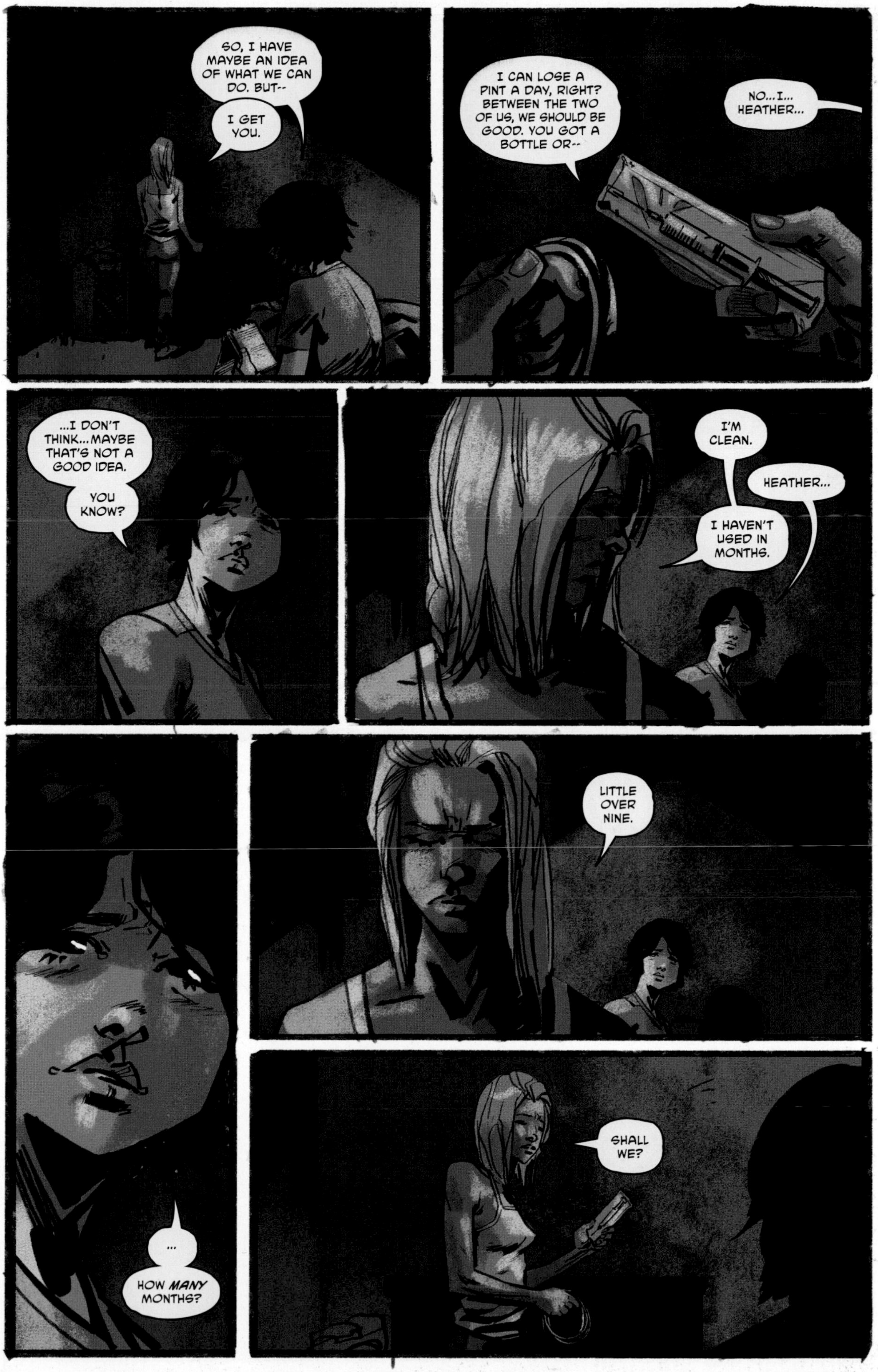
SO, I HAVE MAYBE AN IDEA OF WHAT WE CAN DO. BUT--
I GET YOU.
I CAN LOSE A PINT A DAY, RIGHT? BETWEEN THE TWO OF US, WE SHOULD BE GOOD. YOU GOT A BOTTLE OR--
NO... I... HEATHER...
...I DON'T THINK... MAYBE THAT'S NOT A GOOD IDEA.
YOU KNOW?
I'M CLEAN.
HEATHER...
I HAVEN'T USED IN MONTHS.
...
HOW *MANY* MONTHS?
LITTLE OVER NINE.
SHALL WE?

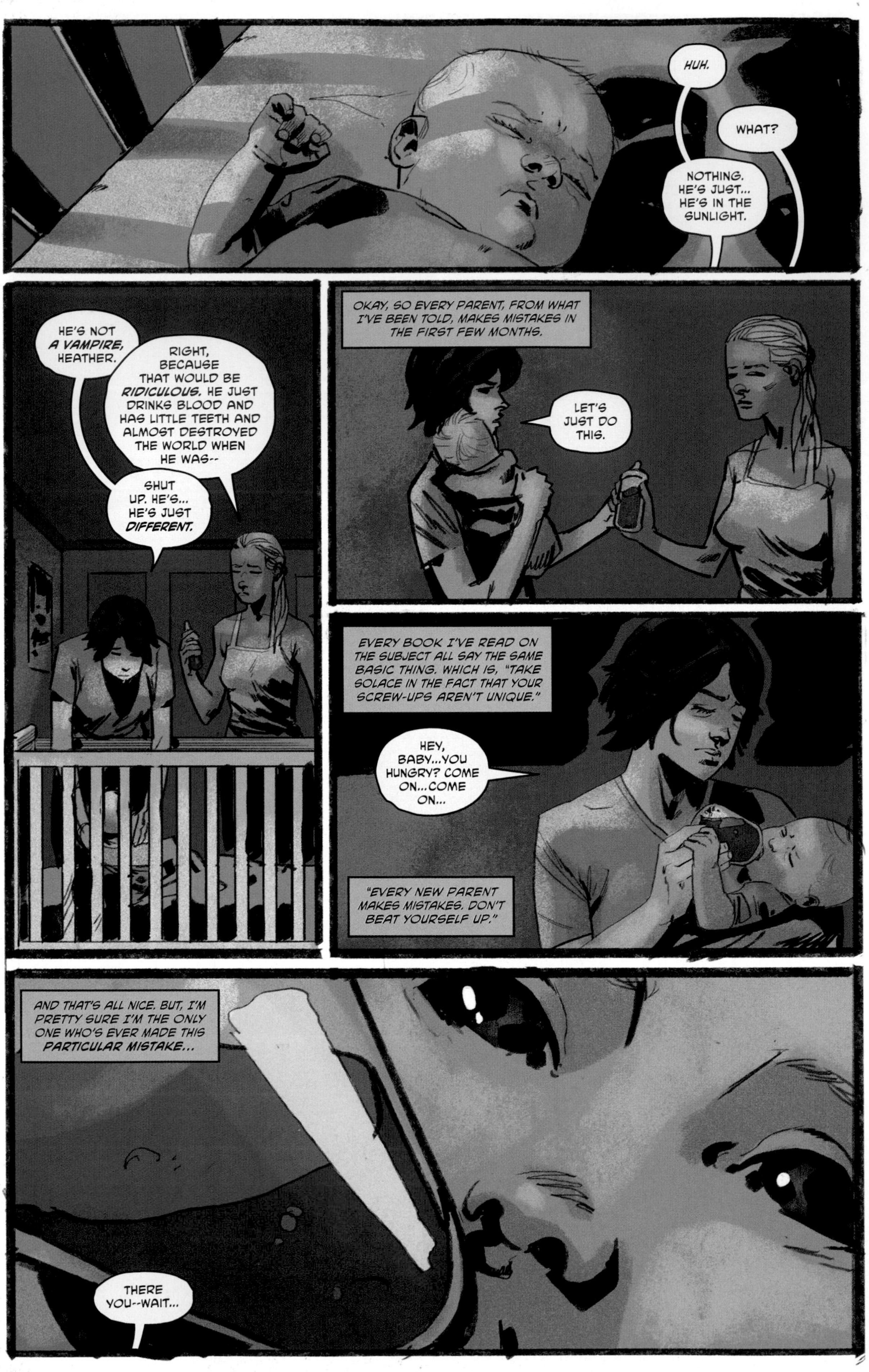
HUH.
WHAT?
NOTHING. HE'S JUST... HE'S IN THE SUNLIGHT.
HE'S NOT *A VAMPIRE,* HEATHER.
RIGHT, BECAUSE THAT WOULD BE *RIDICULOUS.* HE JUST DRINKS BLOOD AND HAS LITTLE TEETH AND ALMOST DESTROYED THE WORLD WHEN HE WAS--
SHUT UP. HE'S... HE'S JUST *DIFFERENT.*
OKAY, SO EVERY PARENT, FROM WHAT I'VE BEEN TOLD, MAKES MISTAKES IN THE FIRST FEW MONTHS.
LET'S JUST DO THIS.
EVERY BOOK I'VE READ ON THE SUBJECT ALL SAY THE SAME BASIC THING. WHICH IS, "TAKE SOLACE IN THE FACT THAT YOUR SCREW-UPS AREN'T UNIQUE."
HEY, BABY...YOU HUNGRY? COME ON...COME ON...
"EVERY NEW PARENT MAKES MISTAKES. DON'T BEAT YOURSELF UP."
AND THAT'S ALL NICE. BUT, I'M PRETTY SURE I'M THE ONLY ONE WHO'S EVER MADE THIS *PARTICULAR MISTAKE...*
THERE YOU--WAIT...

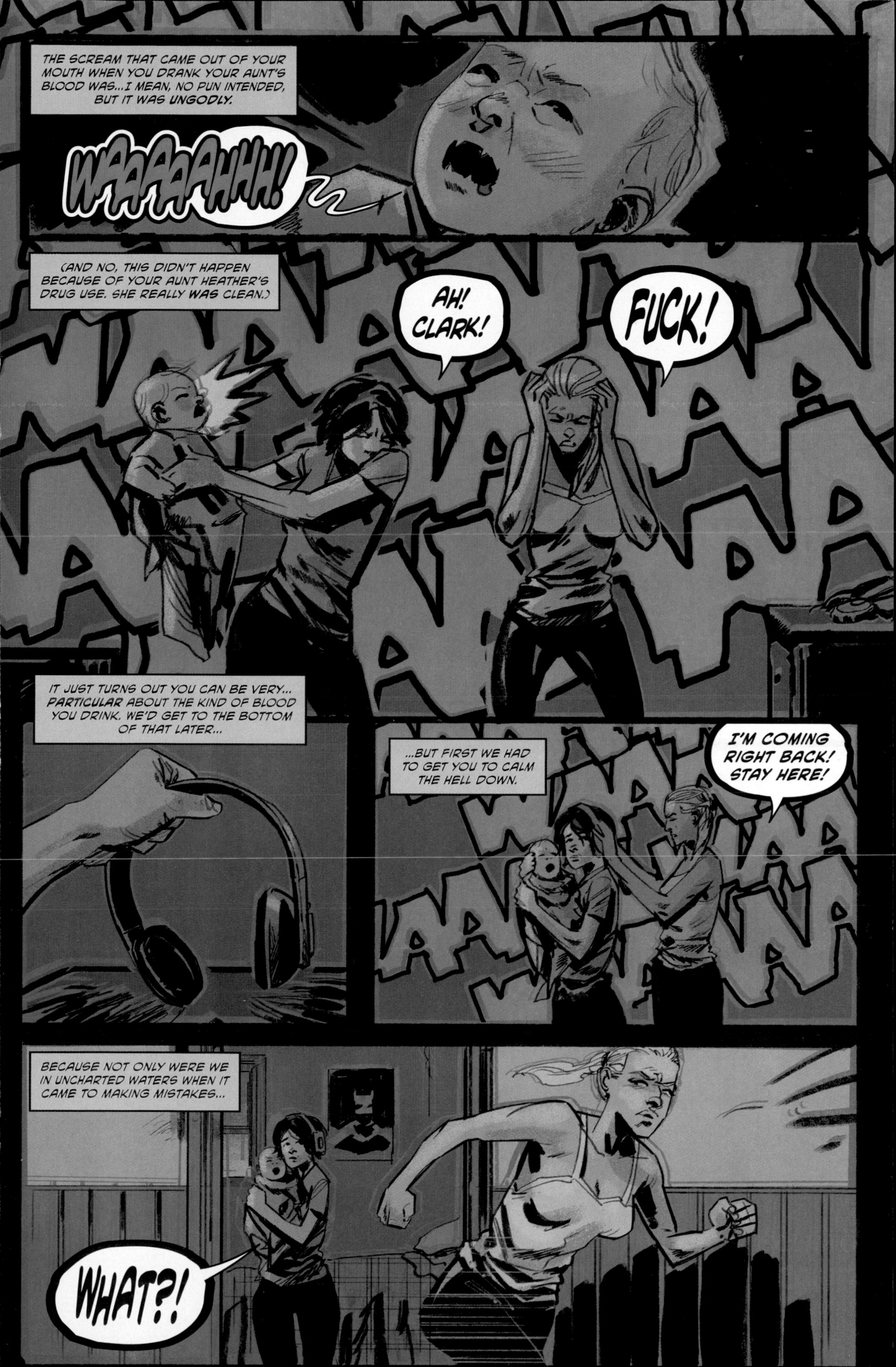
THE SCREAM THAT CAME OUT OF YOUR MOUTH WHEN YOU DRANK YOUR AUNT'S BLOOD WAS...I MEAN, NO PUN INTENDED, BUT IT WAS UNGODLY.
WAAAAAHHH!
(AND NO, THIS DIDN'T HAPPEN BECAUSE OF YOUR AUNT HEATHER'S DRUG USE. SHE REALLY WAS CLEAN.)
AH! CLARK!
FUCK!
IT JUST TURNS OUT YOU CAN BE VERY... PARTICULAR ABOUT THE KIND OF BLOOD YOU DRINK. WE'D GET TO THE BOTTOM OF THAT LATER...
...BUT FIRST WE HAD TO GET YOU TO CALM THE HELL DOWN.
I'M COMING RIGHT BACK! STAY HERE!
BECAUSE NOT ONLY WERE WE IN UNCHARTED WATERS WHEN IT CAME TO MAKING MISTAKES...
WHAT?!

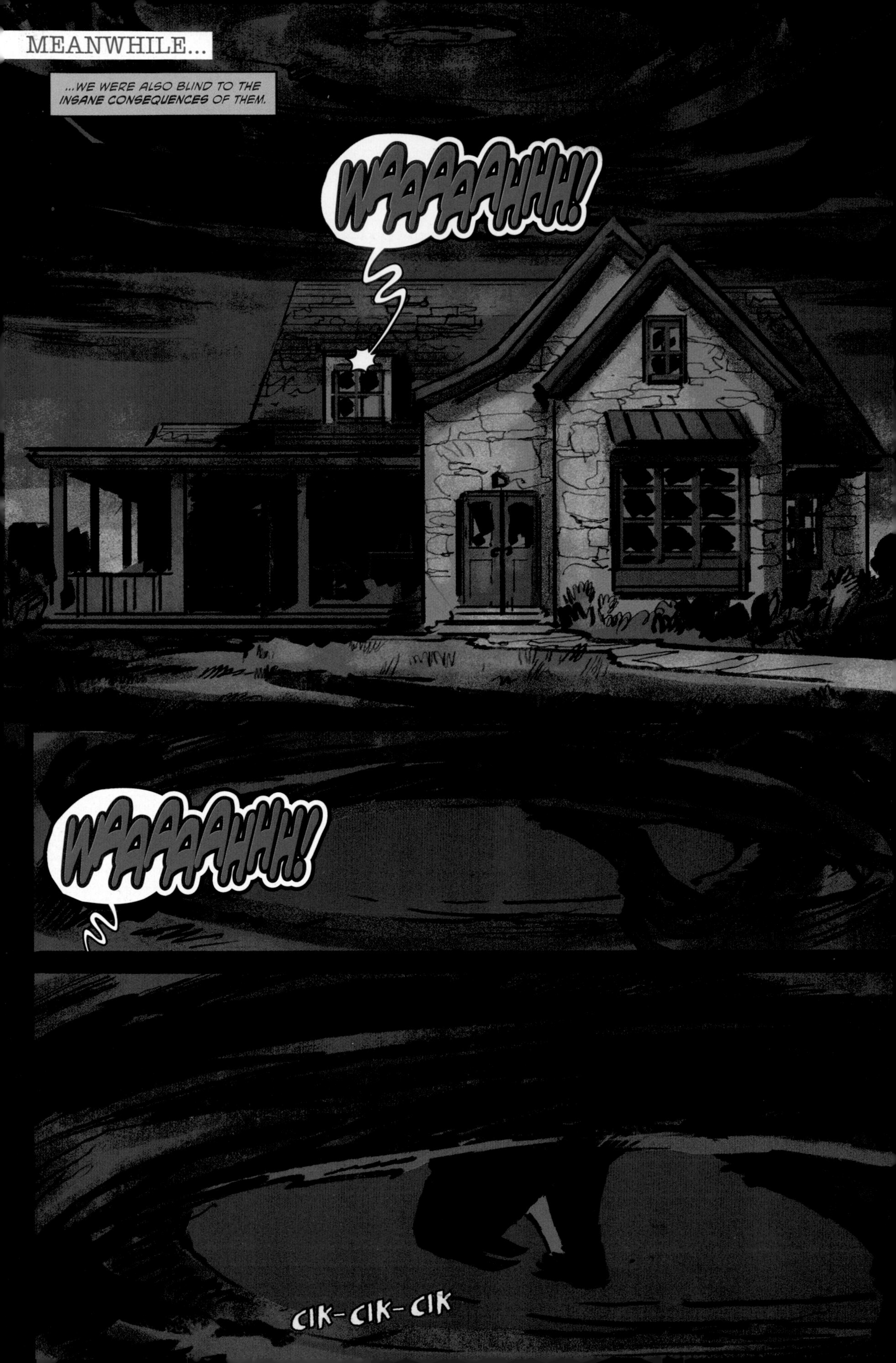
MEANWHILE...
...WE WERE ALSO BLIND TO THE INSANE CONSEQUENCES OF THEM.
WAAAAAHHH!
WAAAAAHHH!
CIK-CIK-CIK

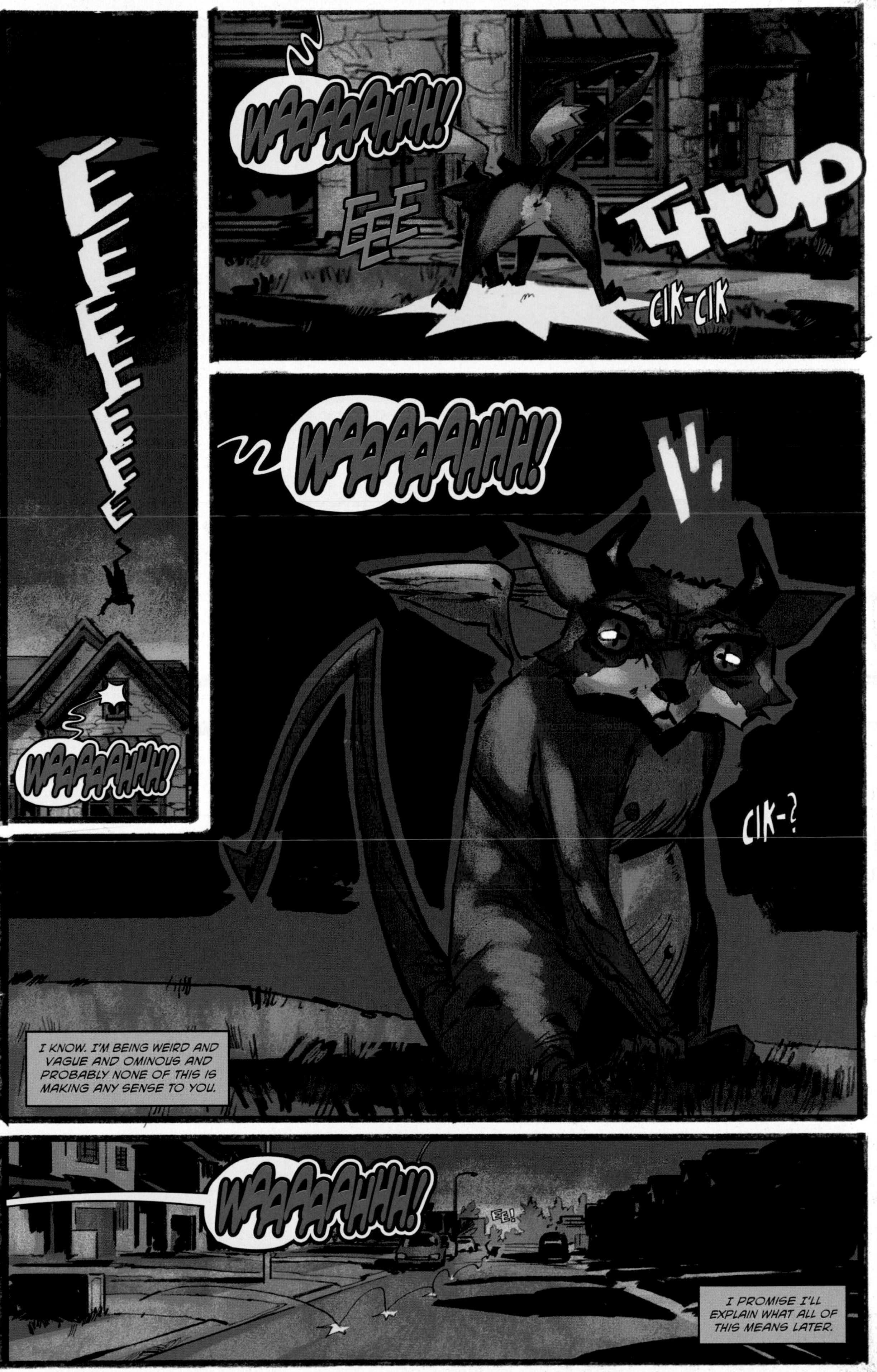
EEEEEEEEE
WAAAAAHHH!
WAAAAAHHH!
EEE
THUP
CIK-CIK
WAAAAAHHH!
!!
CIK-?
I KNOW. I'M BEING WEIRD AND VAGUE AND OMINOUS AND PROBABLY NONE OF THIS IS MAKING ANY SENSE TO YOU.
WAAAAAHHH!
EE!
I PROMISE I'LL EXPLAIN WHAT ALL OF THIS MEANS LATER.

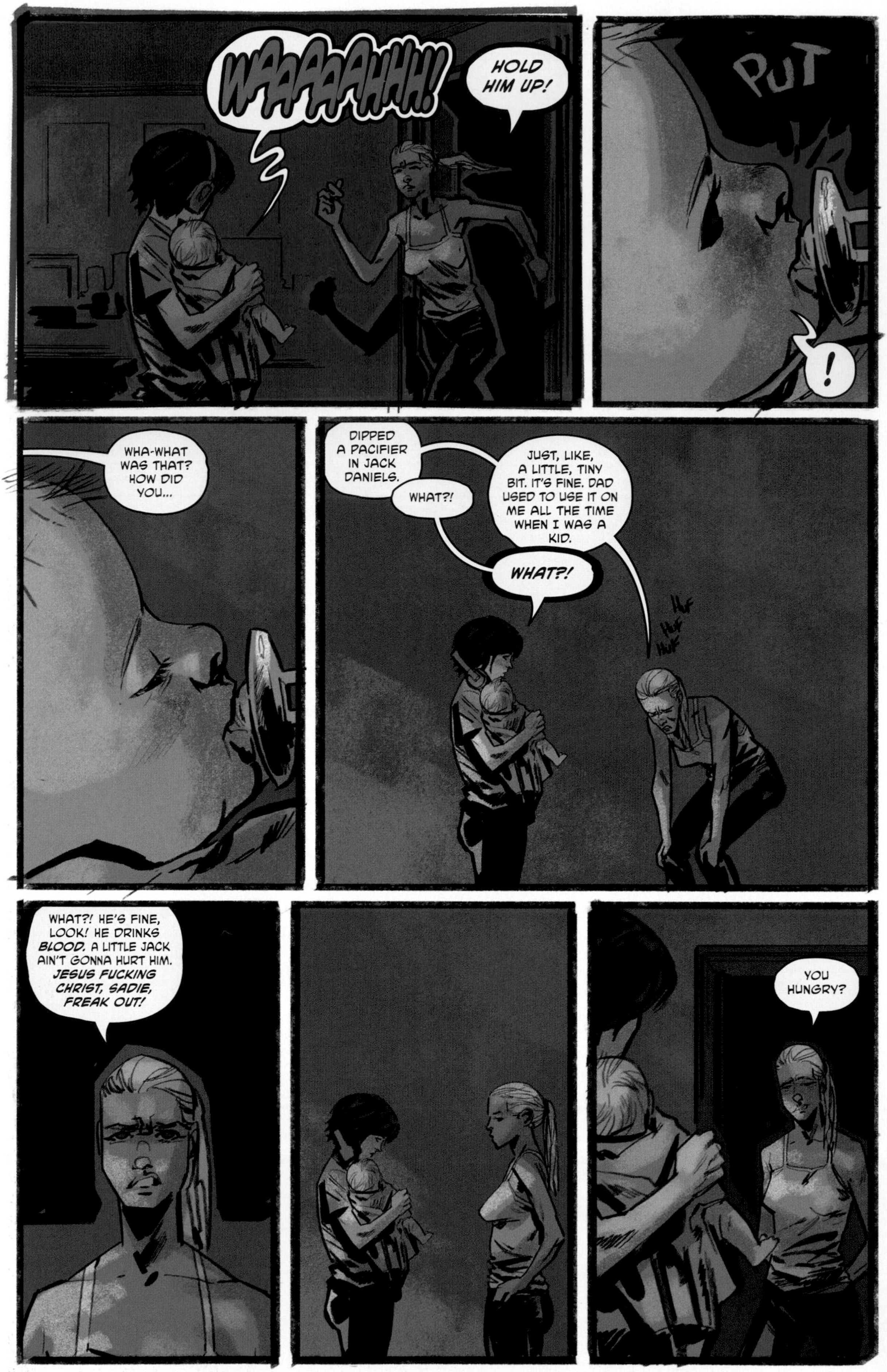
WAAAAAHHH!
HOLD HIM UP!
PUT
!
WHA-WHAT WAS THAT? HOW DID YOU...
DIPPED A PACIFIER IN JACK DANIELS.
WHAT?!
JUST, LIKE, A LITTLE, TINY BIT. IT'S FINE. DAD USED TO USE IT ON ME ALL THE TIME WHEN I WAS A KID.
WHAT?!
HUF HUF HUF
WHAT?! HE'S FINE, LOOK! HE DRINKS BLOOD. A LITTLE JACK AIN'T GONNA HURT HIM. JESUS FUCKING CHRIST, SADIE, FREAK OUT!
YOU HUNGRY?

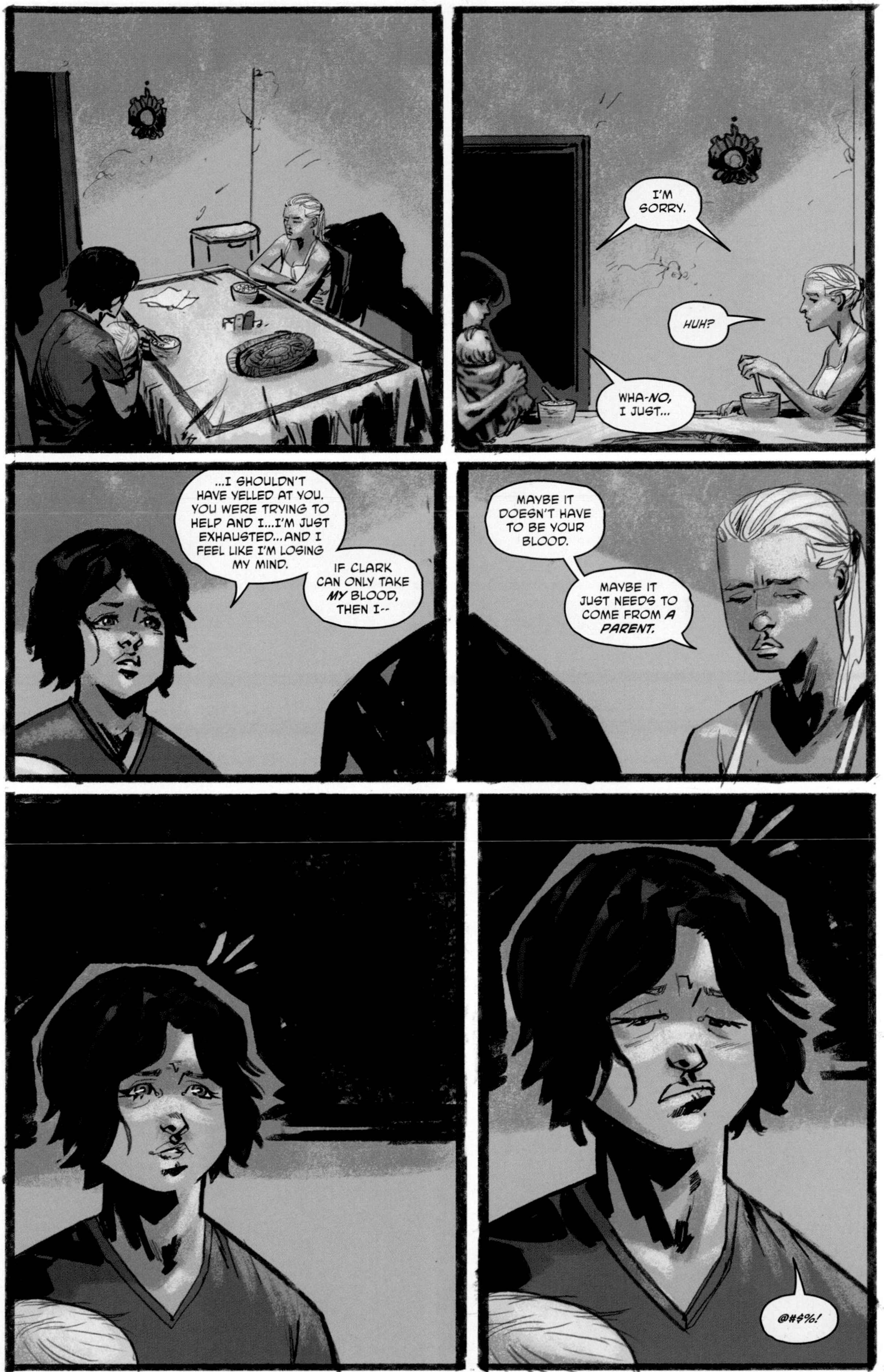
I'M SORRY.
HUH?
WHA-*NO*, I JUST...
...I SHOULDN'T HAVE YELLED AT YOU. YOU WERE TRYING TO HELP AND I...I'M JUST EXHAUSTED...AND I FEEL LIKE I'M LOSING MY MIND.
IF CLARK CAN ONLY TAKE *MY* BLOOD, THEN I--
MAYBE IT DOESN'T HAVE TO BE YOUR BLOOD.
MAYBE IT JUST NEEDS TO COME FROM *A PARENT.*
@#$%!

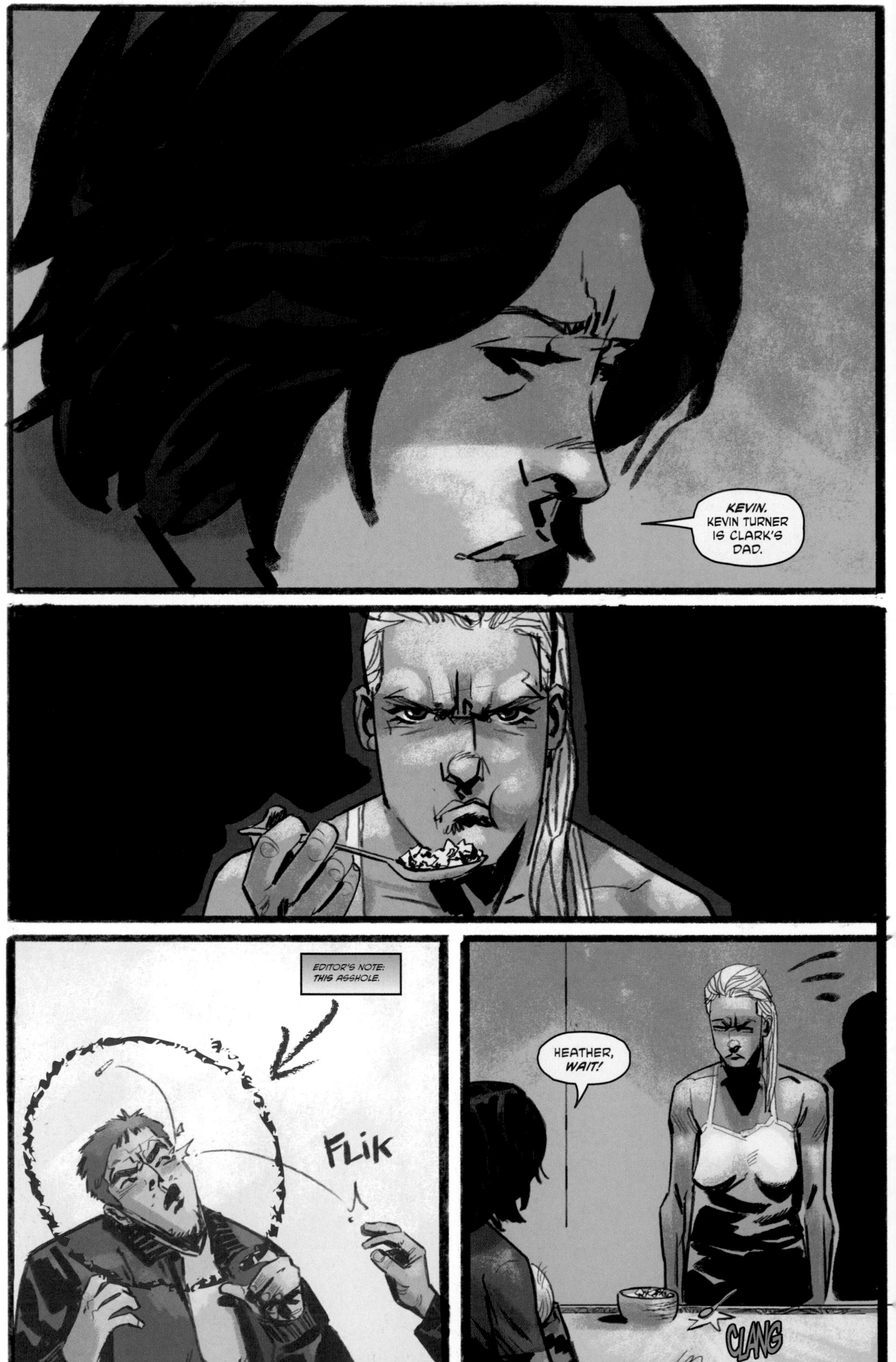
KEVIN. KEVIN TURNER IS CLARK'S DAD.
EDITOR'S NOTE: THIS ASSHOLE.
FLIK
HEATHER, WAIT!
CLANG

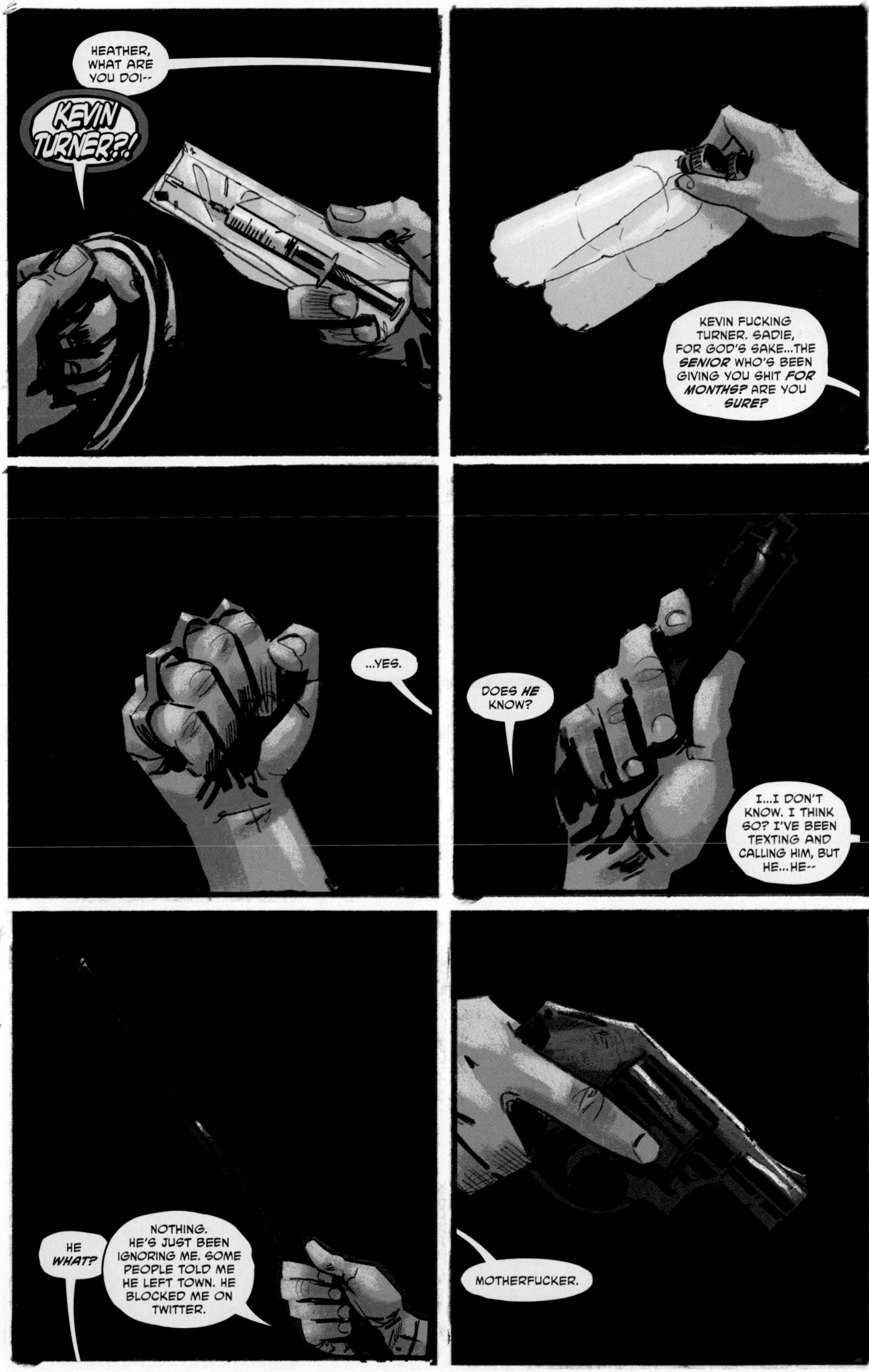
HEATHER, WHAT ARE YOU DOI--
KEVIN TURNER?!
KEVIN FUCKING TURNER. SADIE, FOR GOD'S SAKE...THE SENIOR WHO'S BEEN GIVING YOU SHIT FOR MONTHS? ARE YOU SURE?
...YES.
DOES HE KNOW?
I...I DON'T KNOW. I THINK SO? I'VE BEEN TEXTING AND CALLING HIM, BUT HE...HE--
HE WHAT?
NOTHING. HE'S JUST BEEN IGNORING ME. SOME PEOPLE TOLD ME HE LEFT TOWN. HE BLOCKED ME ON TWITTER.
MOTHERFUCKER.

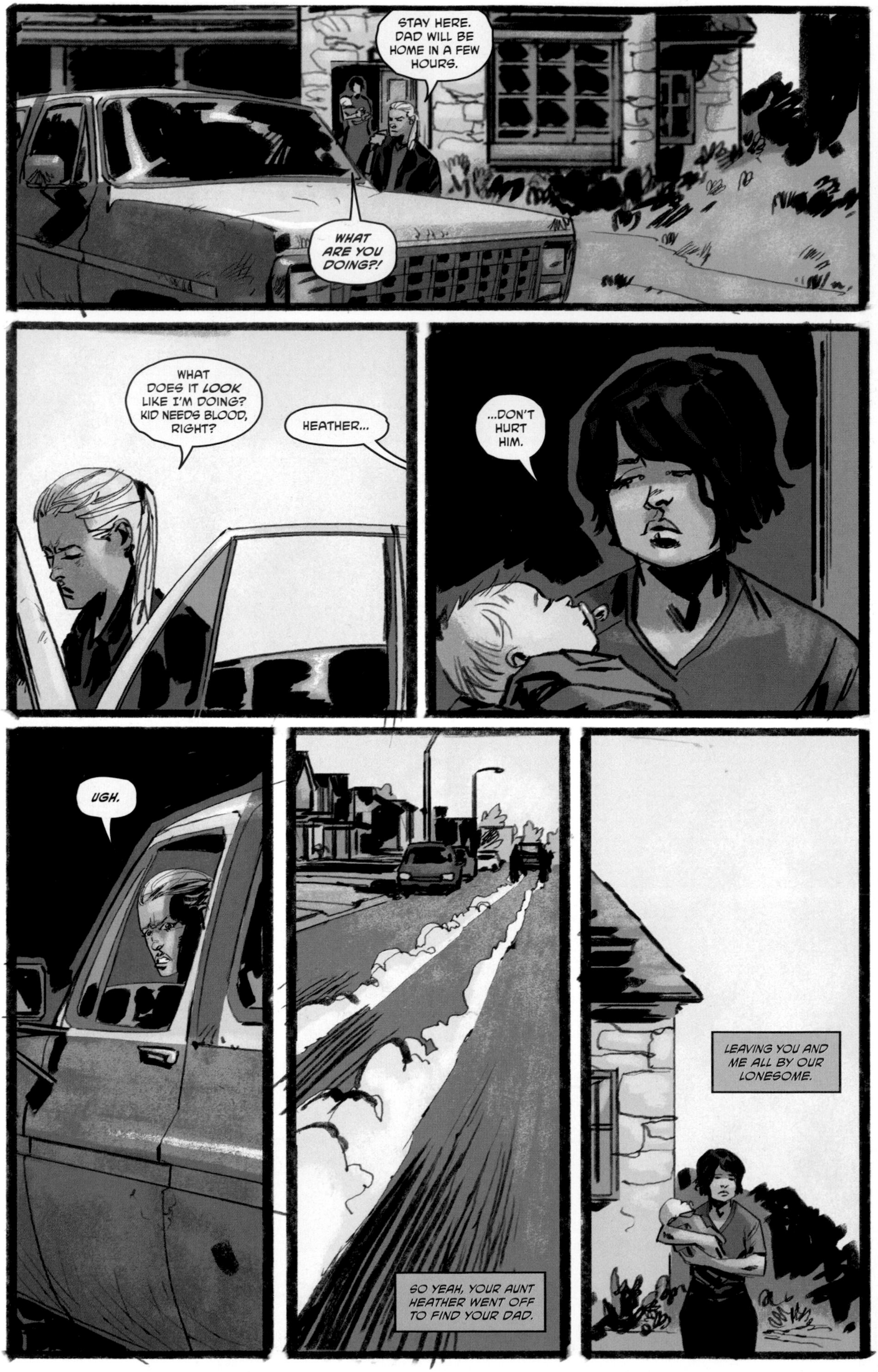
STAY HERE. DAD WILL BE HOME IN A FEW HOURS.
WHAT ARE YOU DOING?!
WHAT DOES IT LOOK LIKE I'M DOING? KID NEEDS BLOOD, RIGHT?
HEATHER...
...DON'T HURT HIM.
UGH.
SO YEAH, YOUR AUNT HEATHER WENT OFF TO FIND YOUR DAD.
LEAVING YOU AND ME ALL BY OUR LONESOME.

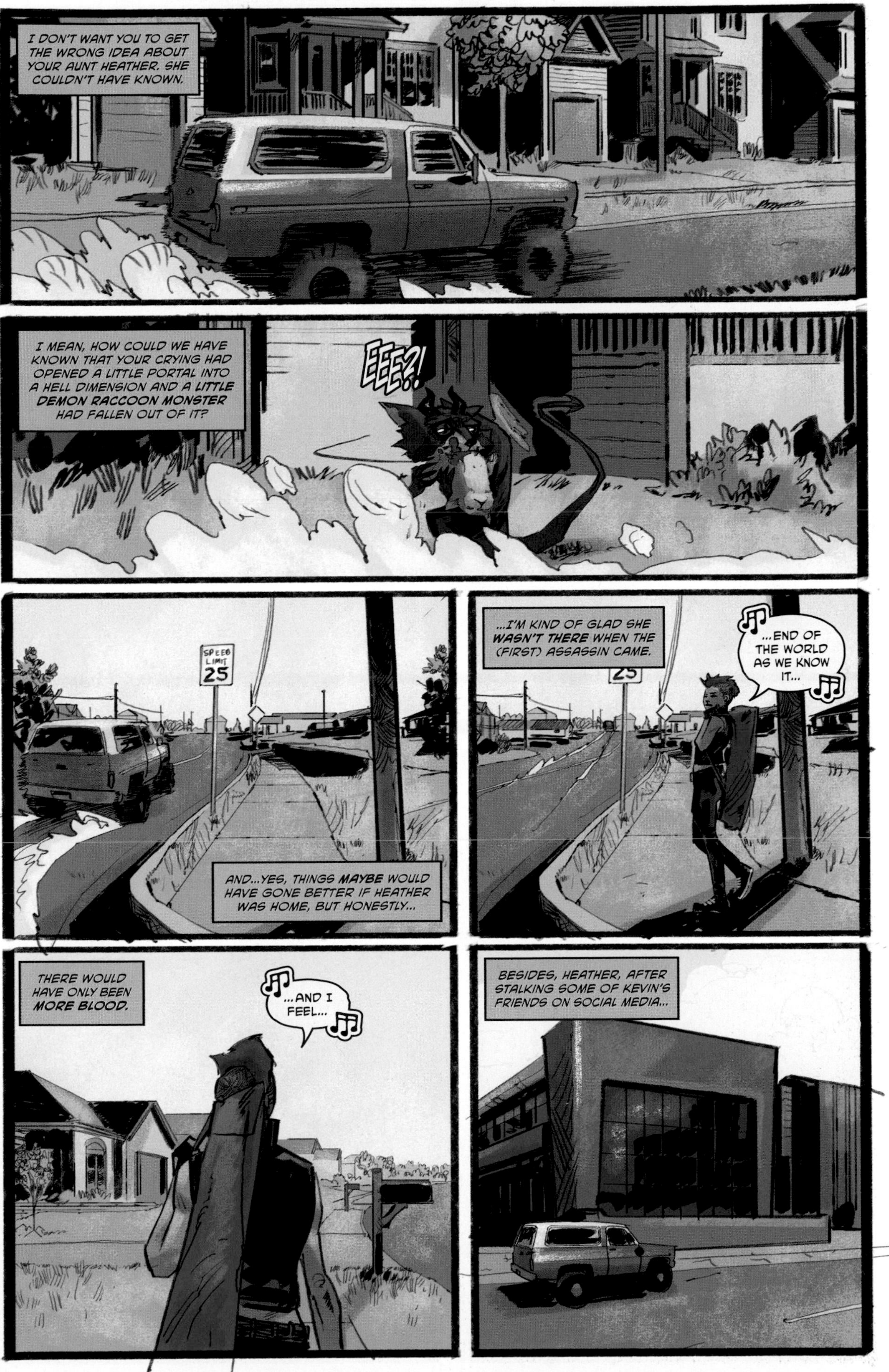
I DON'T WANT YOU TO GET THE WRONG IDEA ABOUT YOUR AUNT HEATHER. SHE COULDN'T HAVE KNOWN.
I MEAN, HOW COULD WE HAVE KNOWN THAT YOUR CRYING HAD OPENED A LITTLE PORTAL INTO A HELL DIMENSION AND A LITTLE DEMON RACCOON MONSTER HAD FALLEN OUT OF IT?
EEE?!
SPEED LIMIT 25
AND...YES, THINGS MAYBE WOULD HAVE GONE BETTER IF HEATHER WAS HOME, BUT HONESTLY...
...I'M KIND OF GLAD SHE WASN'T THERE WHEN THE (FIRST) ASSASSIN CAME.
...END OF THE WORLD AS WE KNOW IT...
THERE WOULD HAVE ONLY BEEN MORE BLOOD.
...AND I FEEL...
BESIDES, HEATHER, AFTER STALKING SOME OF KEVIN'S FRIENDS ON SOCIAL MEDIA...

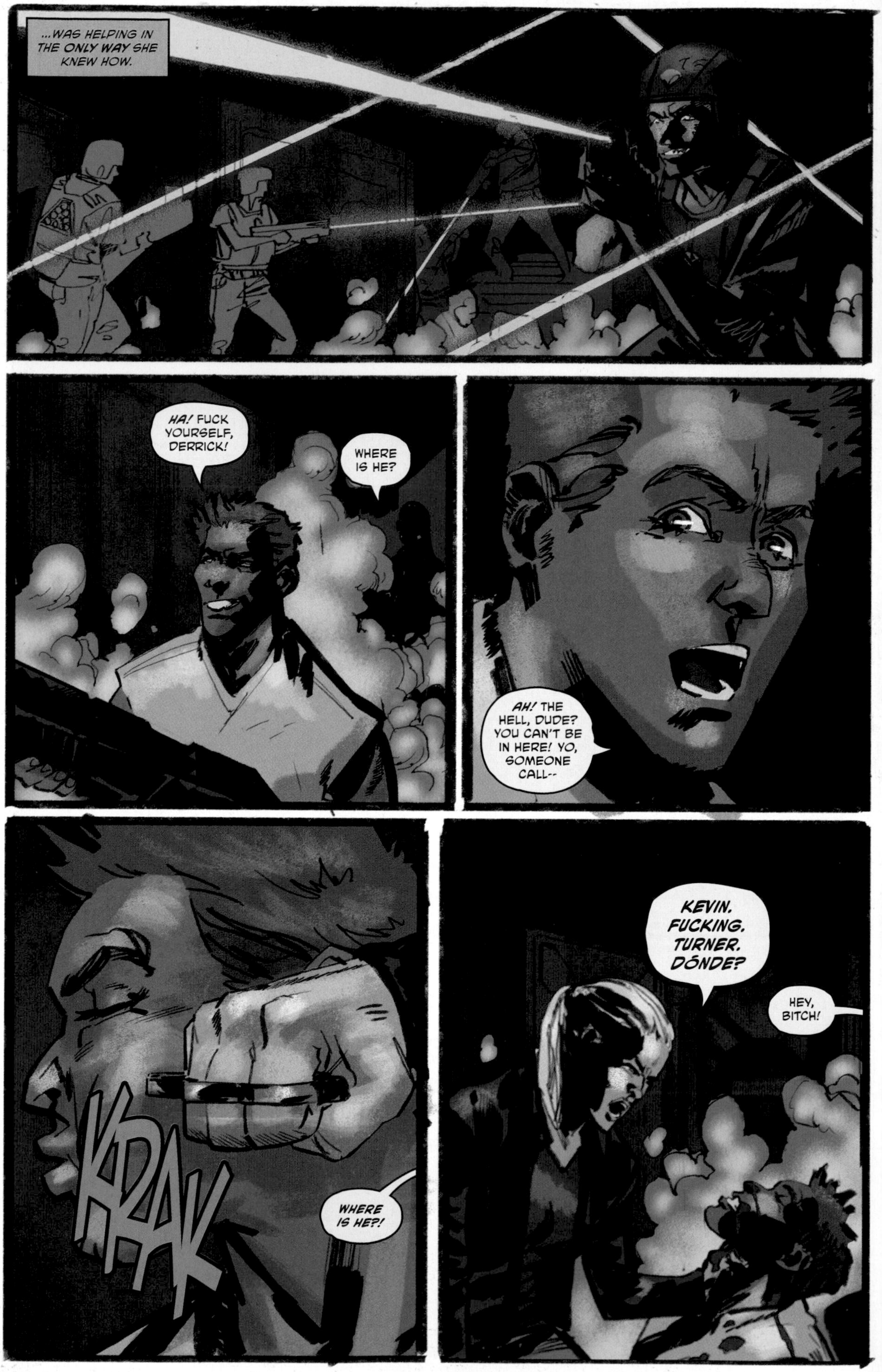
...WAS HELPING IN THE ONLY WAY SHE KNEW HOW.
HA! FUCK YOURSELF, DERRICK!
WHERE IS HE?
AH! THE HELL, DUDE? YOU CAN'T BE IN HERE! YO, SOMEONE CALL--
KRAK
WHERE IS HE?!
KEVIN. FUCKING. TURNER. DÓNDE?
HEY, BITCH!

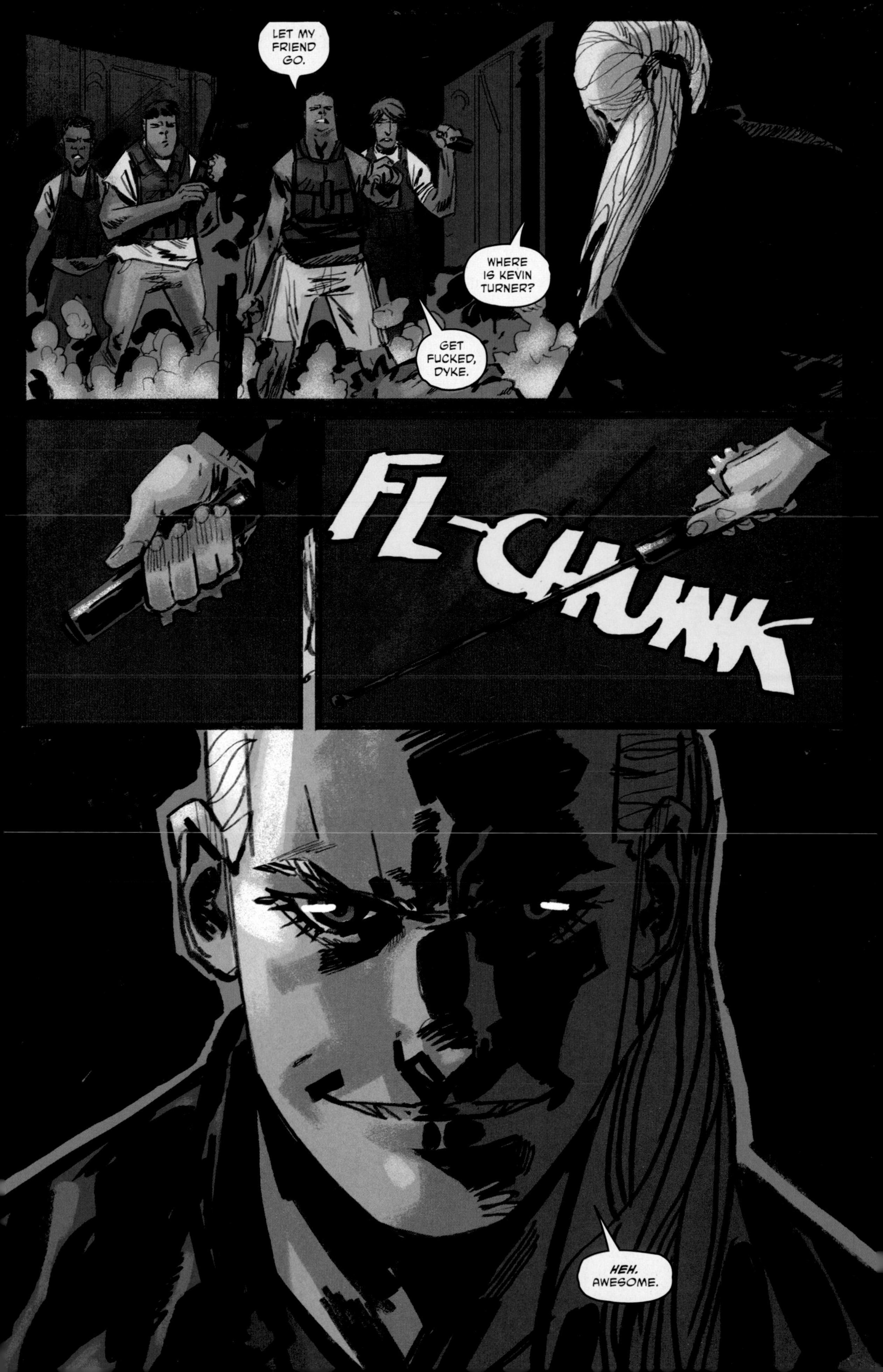
LET MY FRIEND GO.
WHERE IS KEVIN TURNER?
GET FUCKED, DYKE.
FL-CHUNK
HEH. AWESOME.

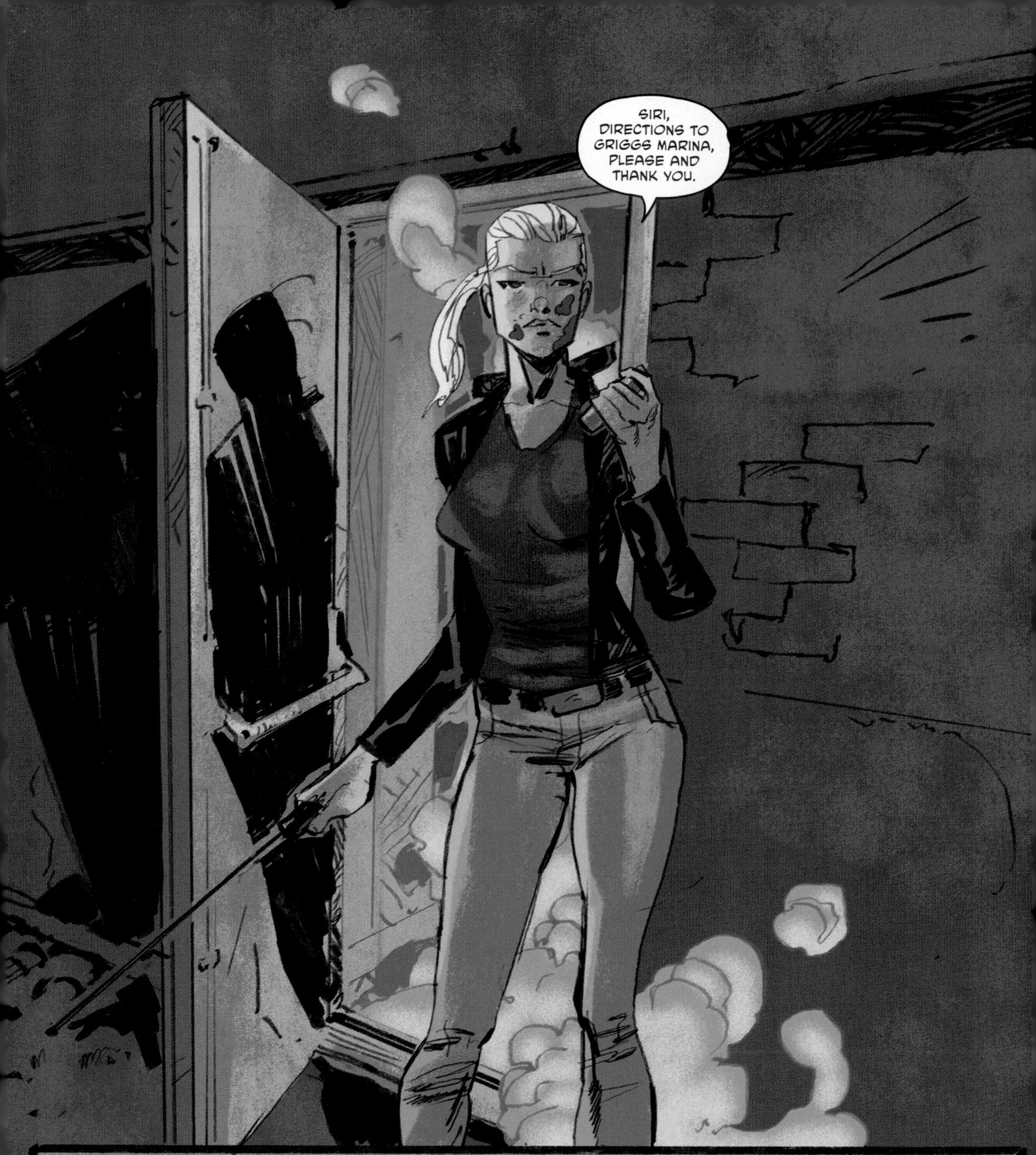
SIRI, DIRECTIONS TO GRIGGS MARINA, PLEASE AND THANK YOU.

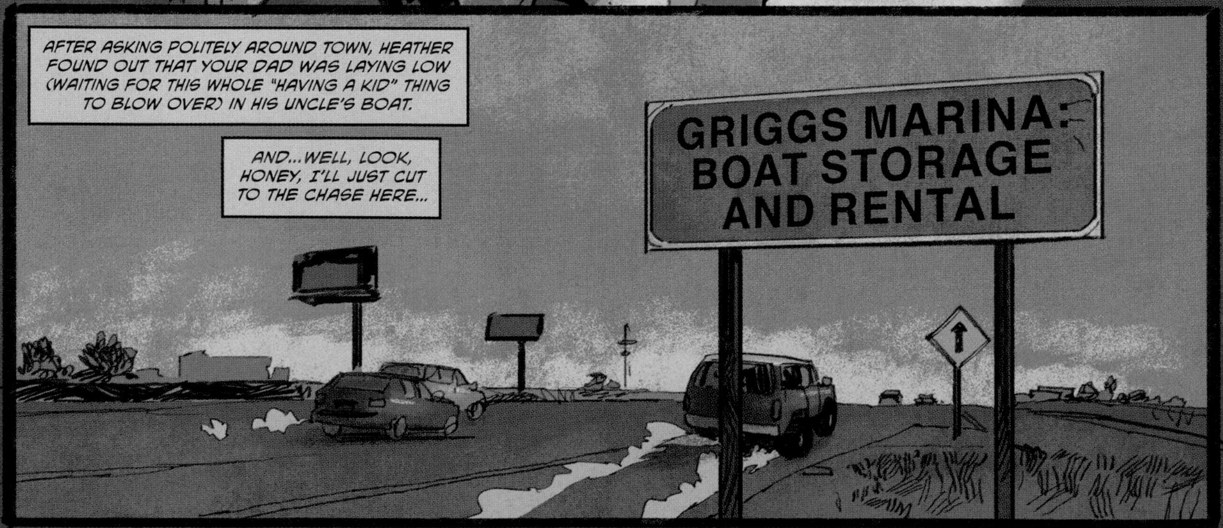
AFTER ASKING POLITELY AROUND TOWN, HEATHER FOUND OUT THAT YOUR DAD WAS LAYING LOW (WAITING FOR THIS WHOLE "HAVING A KID" THING TO BLOW OVER) IN HIS UNCLE'S BOAT.
AND...WELL, LOOK, HONEY, I'LL JUST CUT TO THE CHASE HERE...
GRIGGS MARINA: BOAT STORAGE AND RENTAL

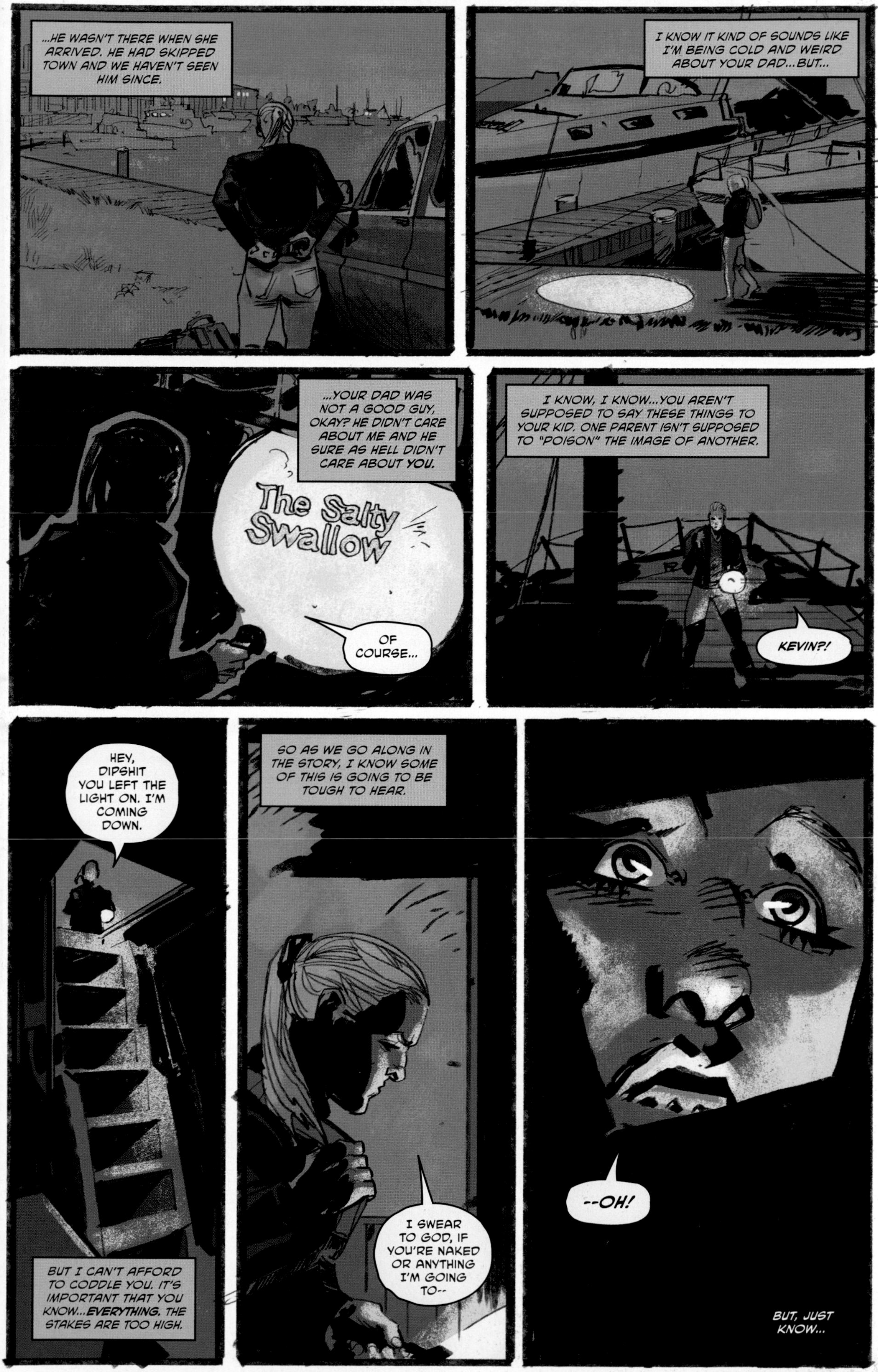
...HE WASN'T THERE WHEN SHE ARRIVED. HE HAD SKIPPED TOWN AND WE HAVEN'T SEEN HIM SINCE.
I KNOW IT KIND OF SOUNDS LIKE I'M BEING COLD AND WEIRD ABOUT YOUR DAD...BUT...
...YOUR DAD WAS NOT A GOOD GUY, OKAY? HE DIDN'T CARE ABOUT ME AND HE SURE AS HELL DIDN'T CARE ABOUT YOU.
The Salty Swallow
OF COURSE...
I KNOW, I KNOW...YOU AREN'T SUPPOSED TO SAY THESE THINGS TO YOUR KID. ONE PARENT ISN'T SUPPOSED TO "POISON" THE IMAGE OF ANOTHER.
KEVIN?!
HEY, DIPSHIT YOU LEFT THE LIGHT ON. I'M COMING DOWN.
BUT I CAN'T AFFORD TO CODDLE YOU. IT'S IMPORTANT THAT YOU KNOW...EVERYTHING. THE STAKES ARE TOO HIGH.
SO AS WE GO ALONG IN THE STORY, I KNOW SOME OF THIS IS GOING TO BE TOUGH TO HEAR.
I SWEAR TO GOD, IF YOU'RE NAKED OR ANYTHING I'M GOING TO--
--OH!
BUT, JUST KNOW...

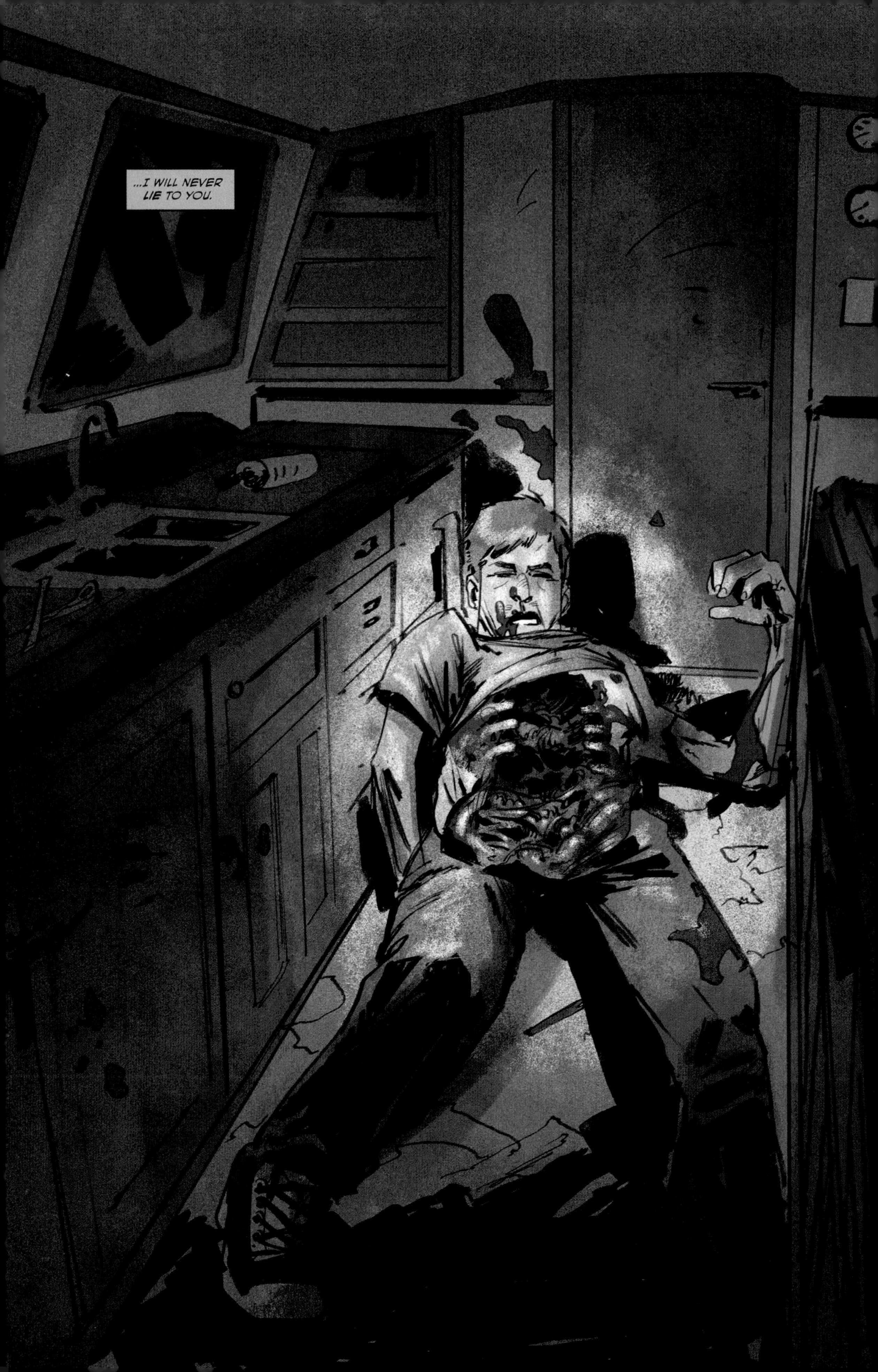
...I WILL NEVER LIE TO YOU.

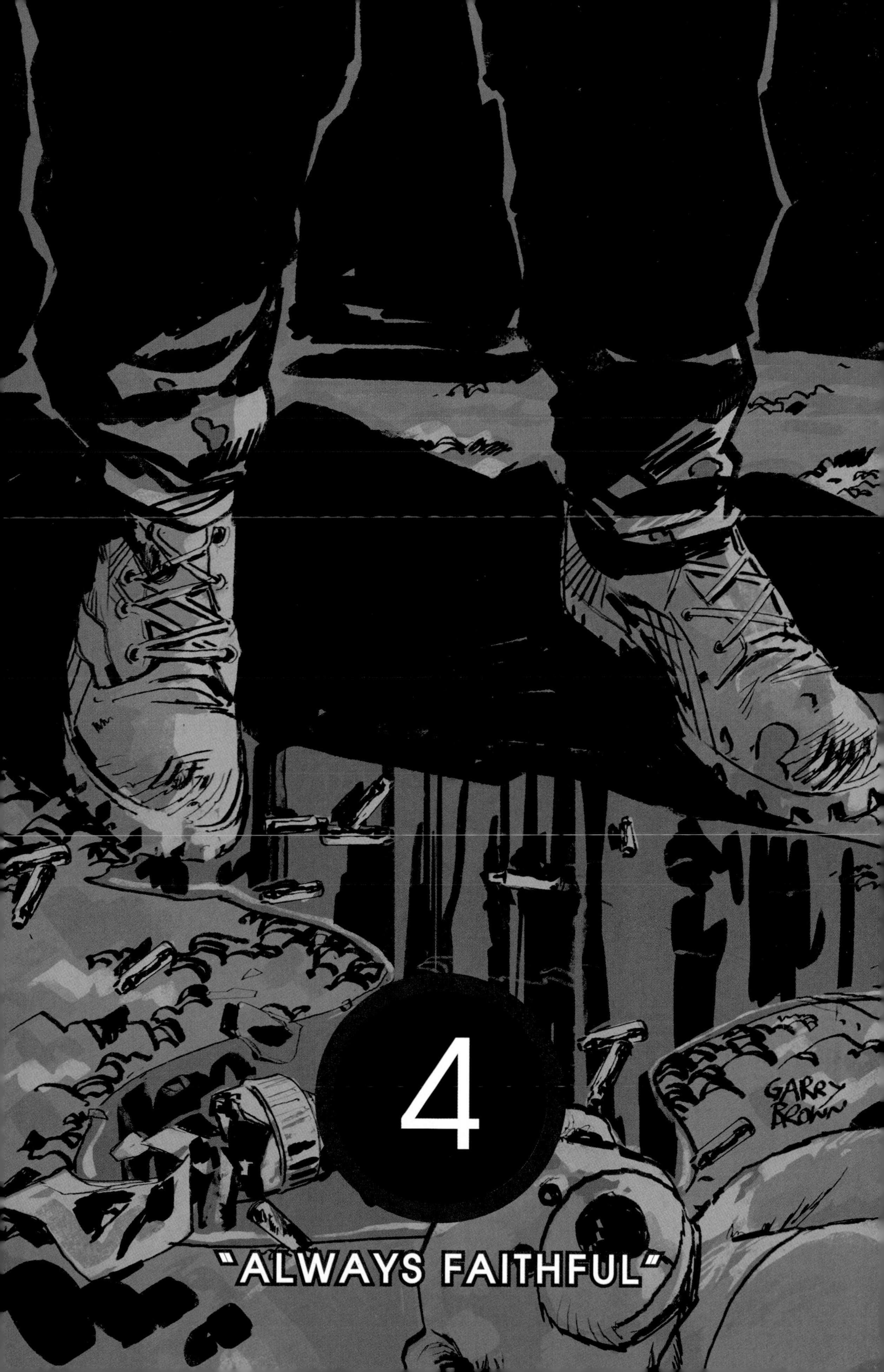
4
"ALWAYS FAITHFUL"
GARRY BROWN

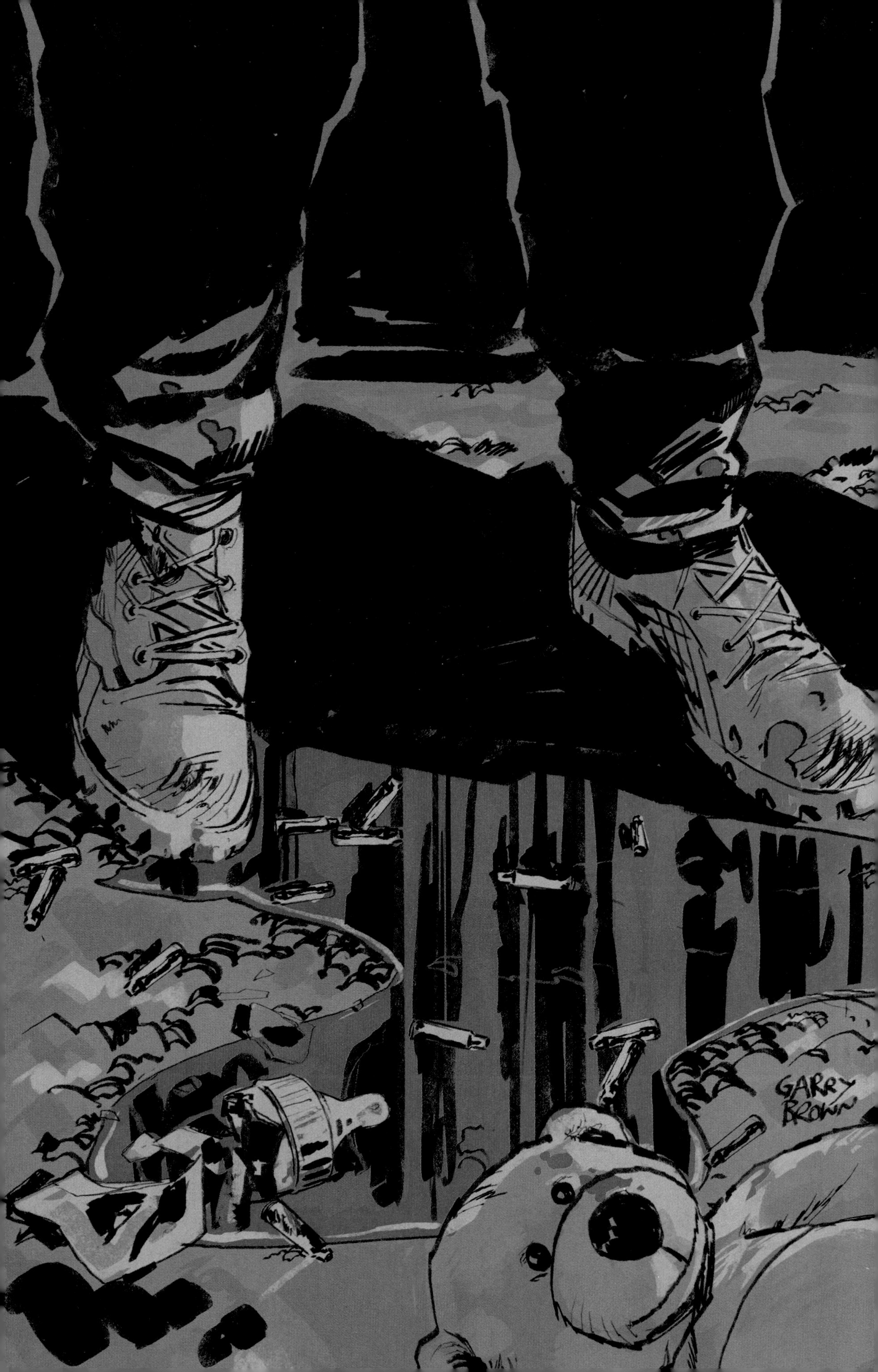
GARRY
BROWN

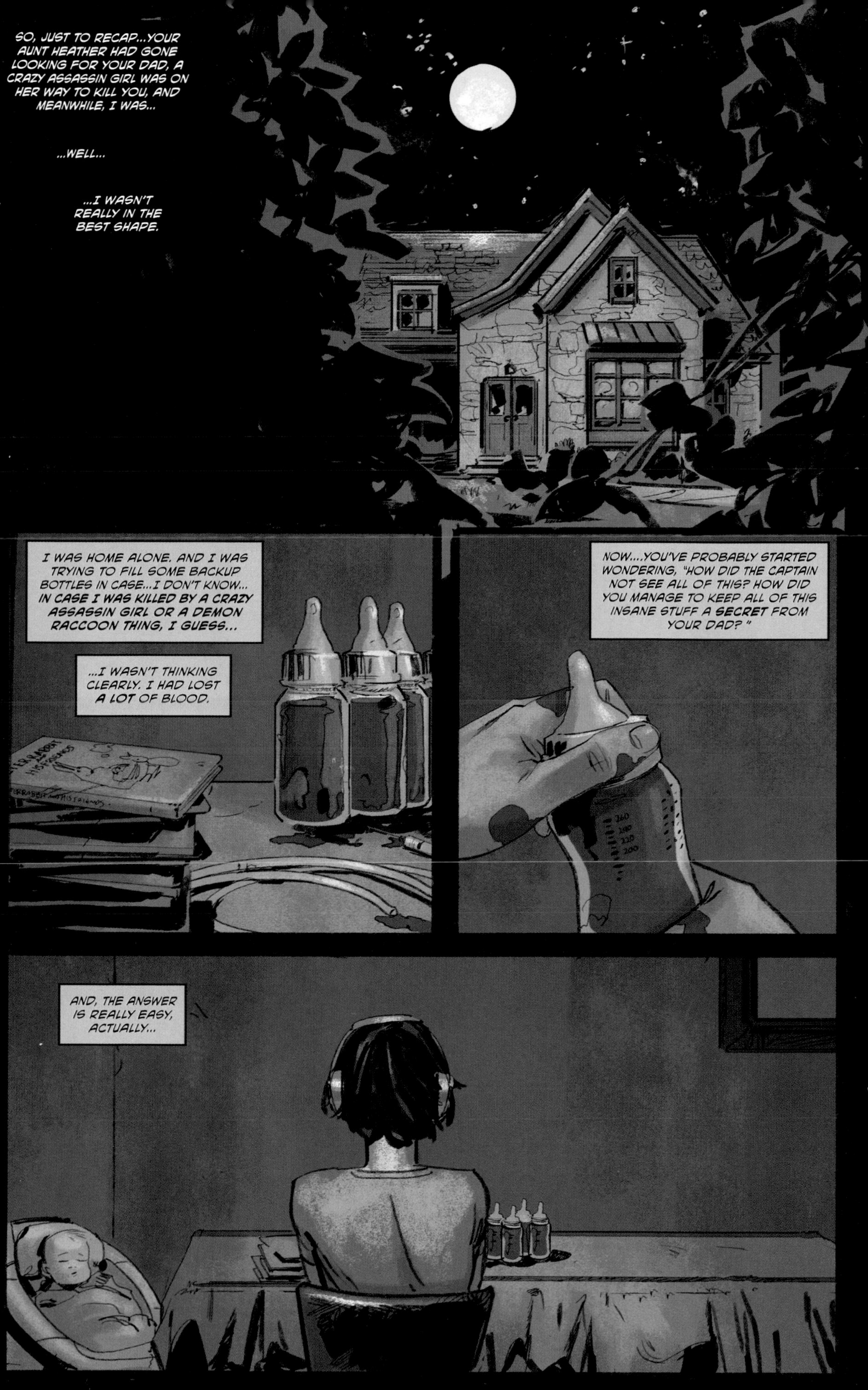

SO, JUST TO RECAP...YOUR AUNT HEATHER HAD GONE LOOKING FOR YOUR DAD, A CRAZY ASSASSIN GIRL WAS ON HER WAY TO KILL YOU, AND MEANWHILE, I WAS...
...WELL...
...I WASN'T REALLY IN THE BEST SHAPE.
I WAS HOME ALONE. AND I WAS TRYING TO FILL SOME BACKUP BOTTLES IN CASE...I DON'T KNOW... IN CASE I WAS KILLED BY A CRAZY ASSASSIN GIRL OR A DEMON RACCOON THING, I GUESS...
...I WASN'T THINKING CLEARLY. I HAD LOST A LOT OF BLOOD.
NOW....YOU'VE PROBABLY STARTED WONDERING, "HOW DID THE CAPTAIN NOT SEE ALL OF THIS? HOW DID YOU MANAGE TO KEEP ALL OF THIS INSANE STUFF A SECRET FROM YOUR DAD?"
AND, THE ANSWER IS REALLY EASY, ACTUALLY...

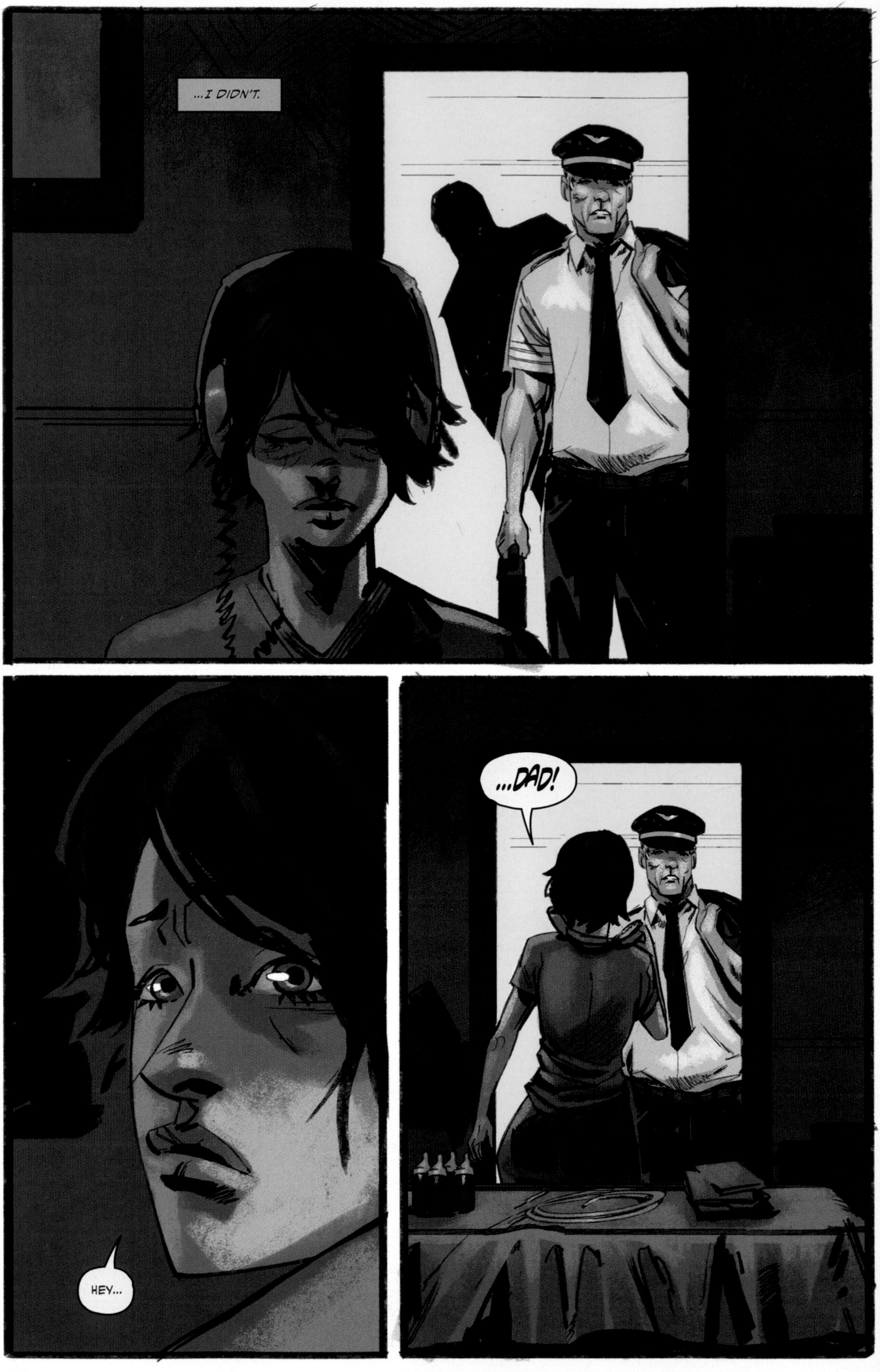
...I DIDN'T.
HEY...
...DAD!

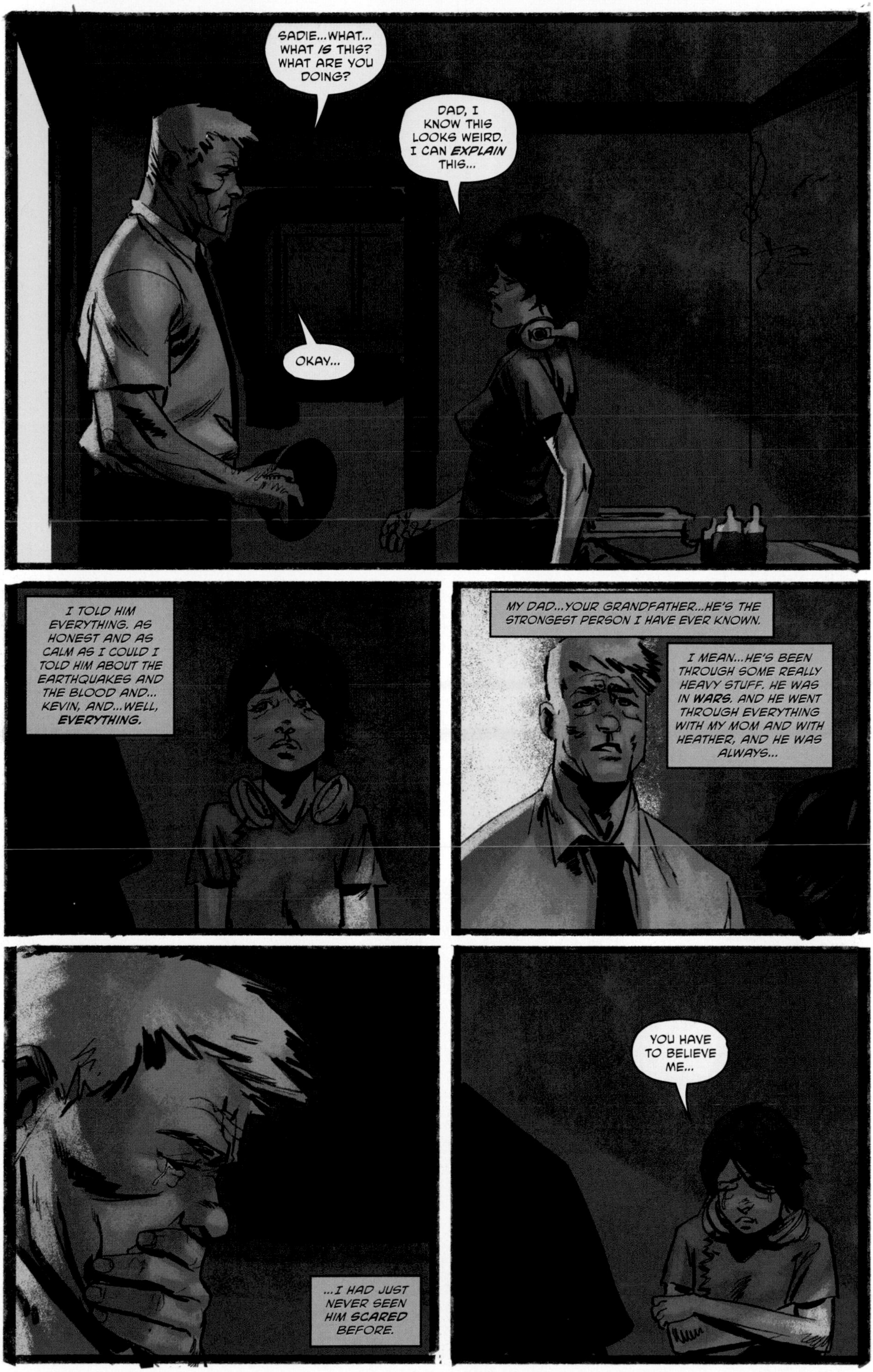
SADIE...WHAT... WHAT IS THIS? WHAT ARE YOU DOING?
DAD, I KNOW THIS LOOKS WEIRD. I CAN EXPLAIN THIS...
OKAY...
I TOLD HIM EVERYTHING. AS HONEST AND AS CALM AS I COULD I TOLD HIM ABOUT THE EARTHQUAKES AND THE BLOOD AND... KEVIN, AND...WELL, EVERYTHING.
MY DAD...YOUR GRANDFATHER...HE'S THE STRONGEST PERSON I HAVE EVER KNOWN.
I MEAN...HE'S BEEN THROUGH SOME REALLY HEAVY STUFF. HE WAS IN WARS, AND HE WENT THROUGH EVERYTHING WITH MY MOM AND WITH HEATHER, AND HE WAS ALWAYS...
...I HAD JUST NEVER SEEN HIM SCARED BEFORE.
YOU HAVE TO BELIEVE ME...

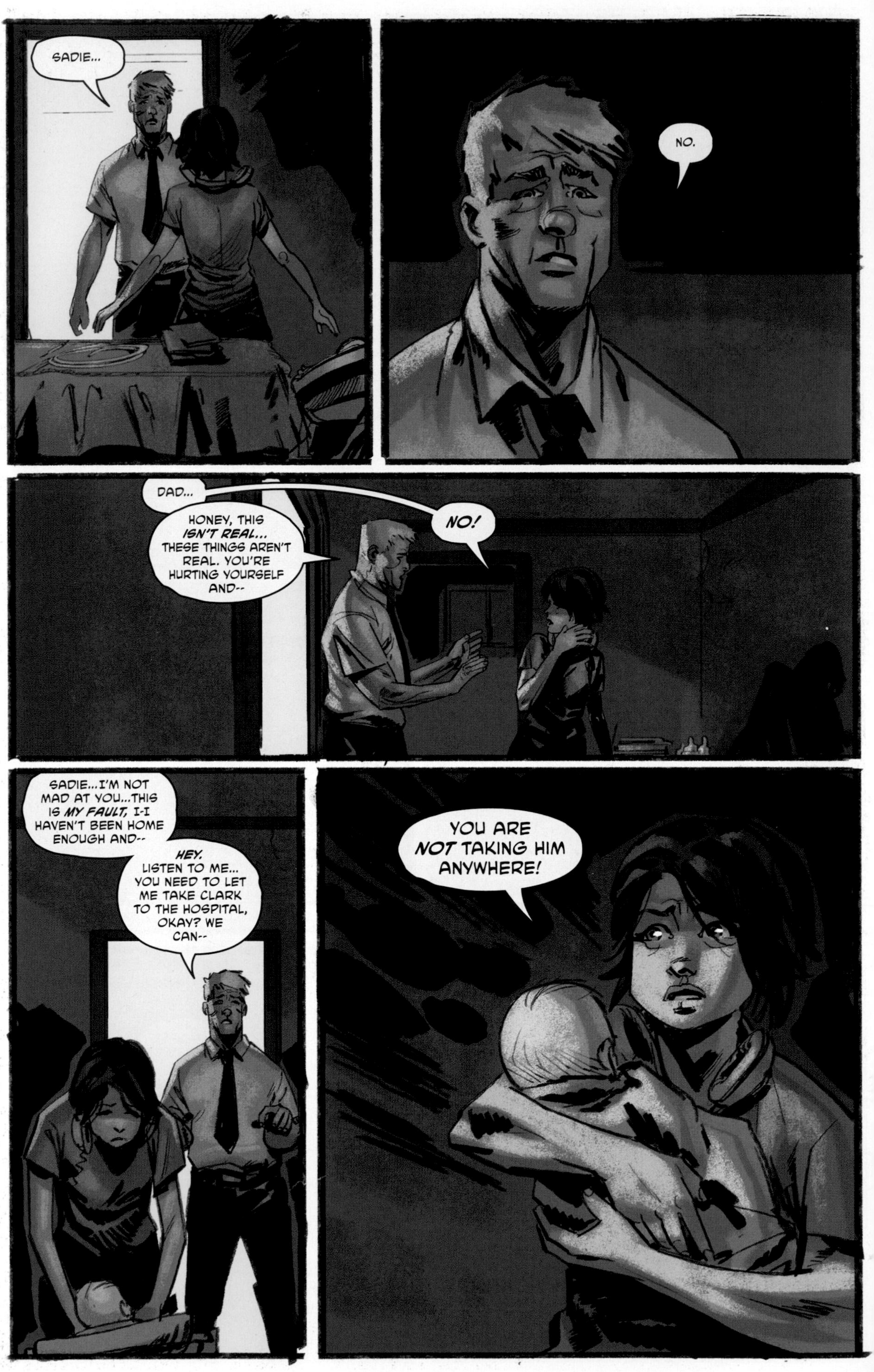
SADIE...
NO.
DAD...
HONEY, THIS *ISN'T REAL...* THESE THINGS AREN'T REAL. YOU'RE HURTING YOURSELF AND--
NO!
SADIE...I'M NOT MAD AT YOU...THIS IS *MY FAULT,* I-I HAVEN'T BEEN HOME ENOUGH AND--
HEY. LISTEN TO ME... YOU NEED TO LET ME TAKE CLARK TO THE HOSPITAL, OKAY? WE CAN--
YOU ARE *NOT* TAKING HIM ANYWHERE!

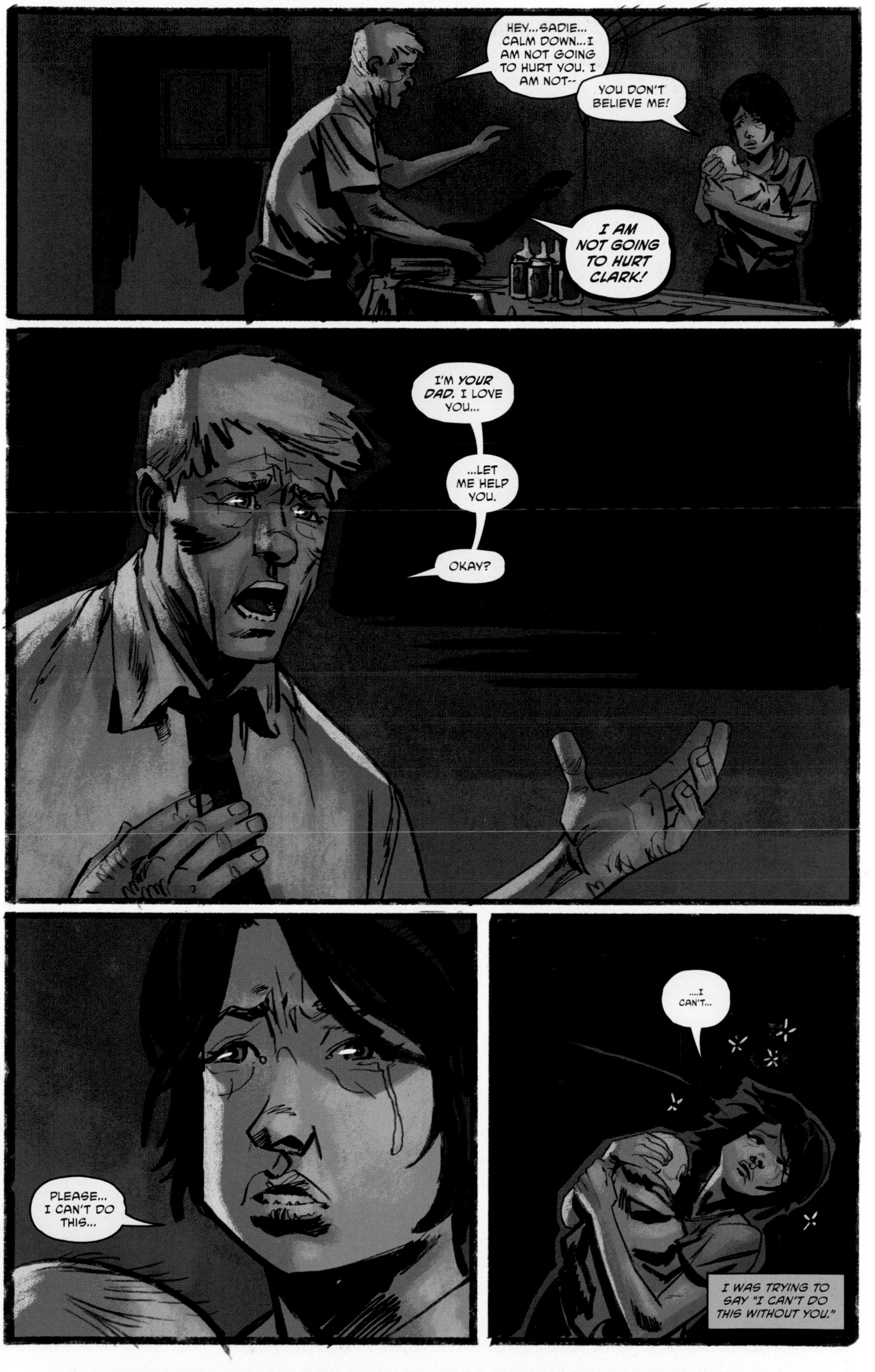
HEY...SADIE... CALM DOWN...I AM NOT GOING TO HURT YOU. I AM NOT--
YOU DON'T BELIEVE ME!
I AM NOT GOING TO HURT CLARK!
I'M *YOUR DAD.* I LOVE YOU...
...LET ME HELP YOU.
OKAY?
PLEASE... I CAN'T DO THIS...
....I CAN'T...
I WAS TRYING TO SAY "I CAN'T DO THIS WITHOUT YOU."

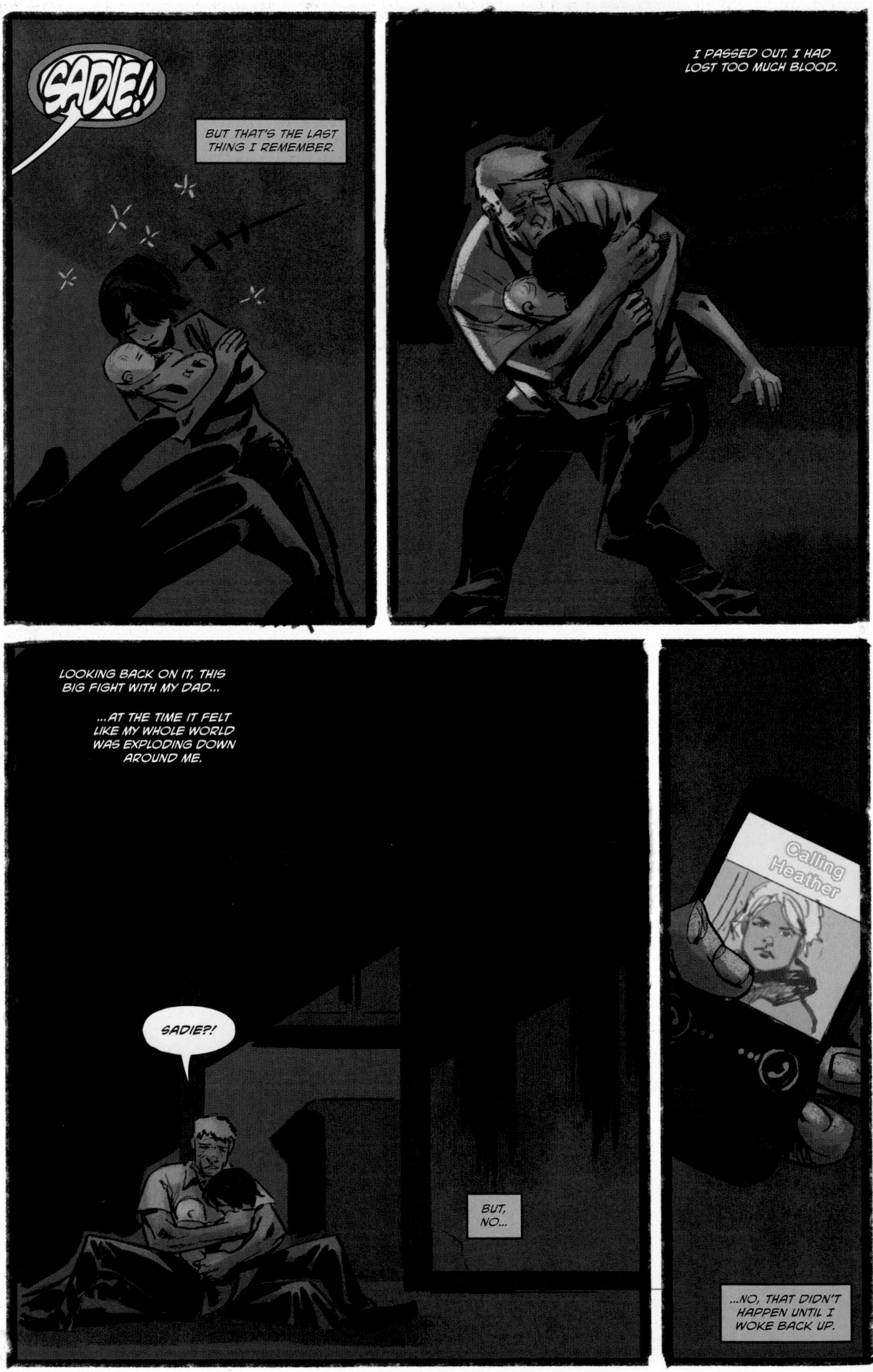
SADIE!
BUT THAT'S THE LAST THING I REMEMBER.
I PASSED OUT. I HAD LOST TOO MUCH BLOOD.
LOOKING BACK ON IT, THIS BIG FIGHT WITH MY DAD...
...AT THE TIME IT FELT LIKE MY WHOLE WORLD WAS EXPLODING DOWN AROUND ME.
SADIE?!
BUT, NO...
Calling Heather
...NO, THAT DIDN'T HAPPEN UNTIL I WOKE BACK UP.

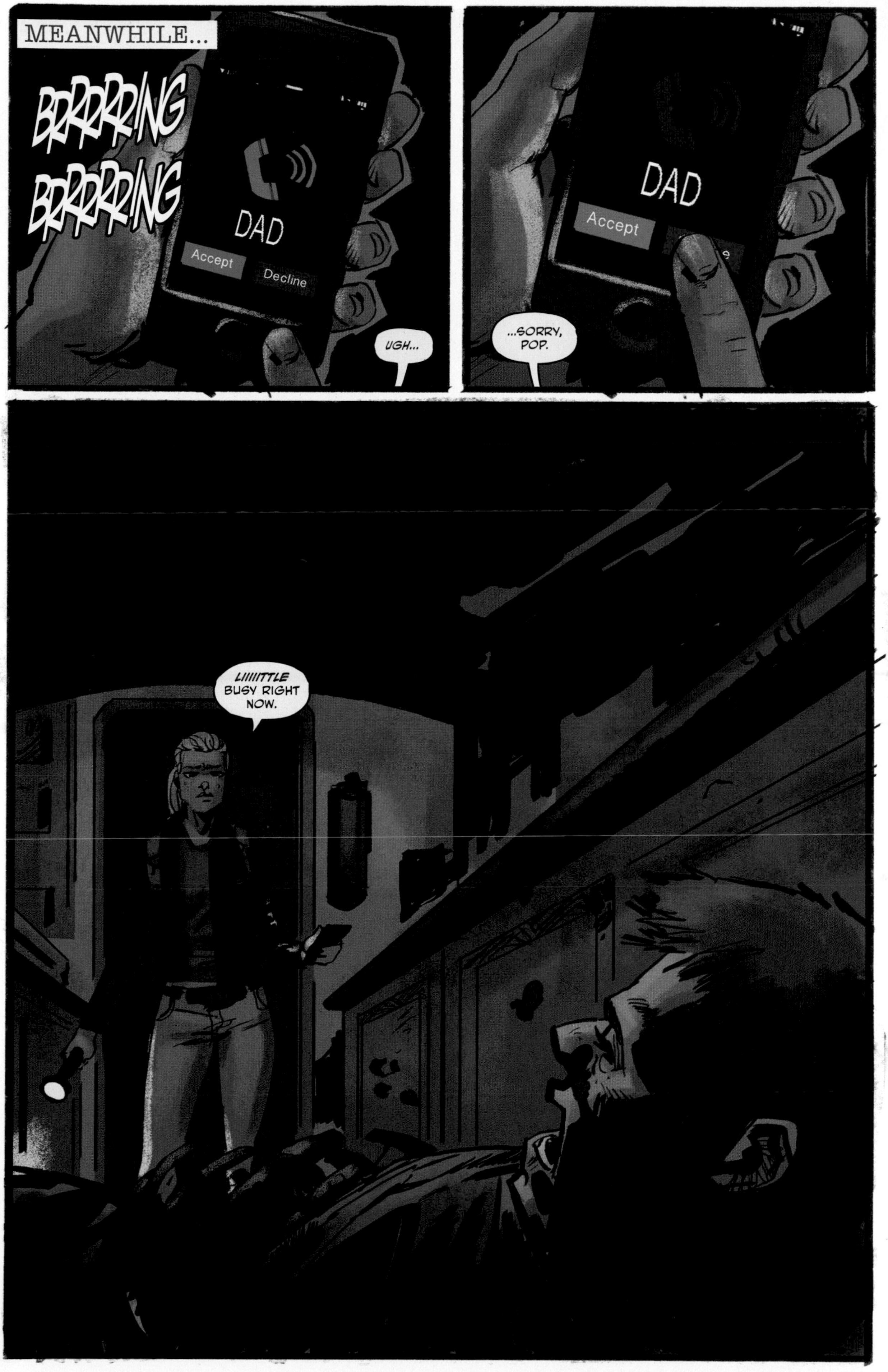
MEANWHILE...
BRRRRRING
BRRRRRING
DAD
Accept
Decline
UGH...
DAD
Accept
...SORRY, POP.
LIIIIITTLE BUSY RIGHT NOW.

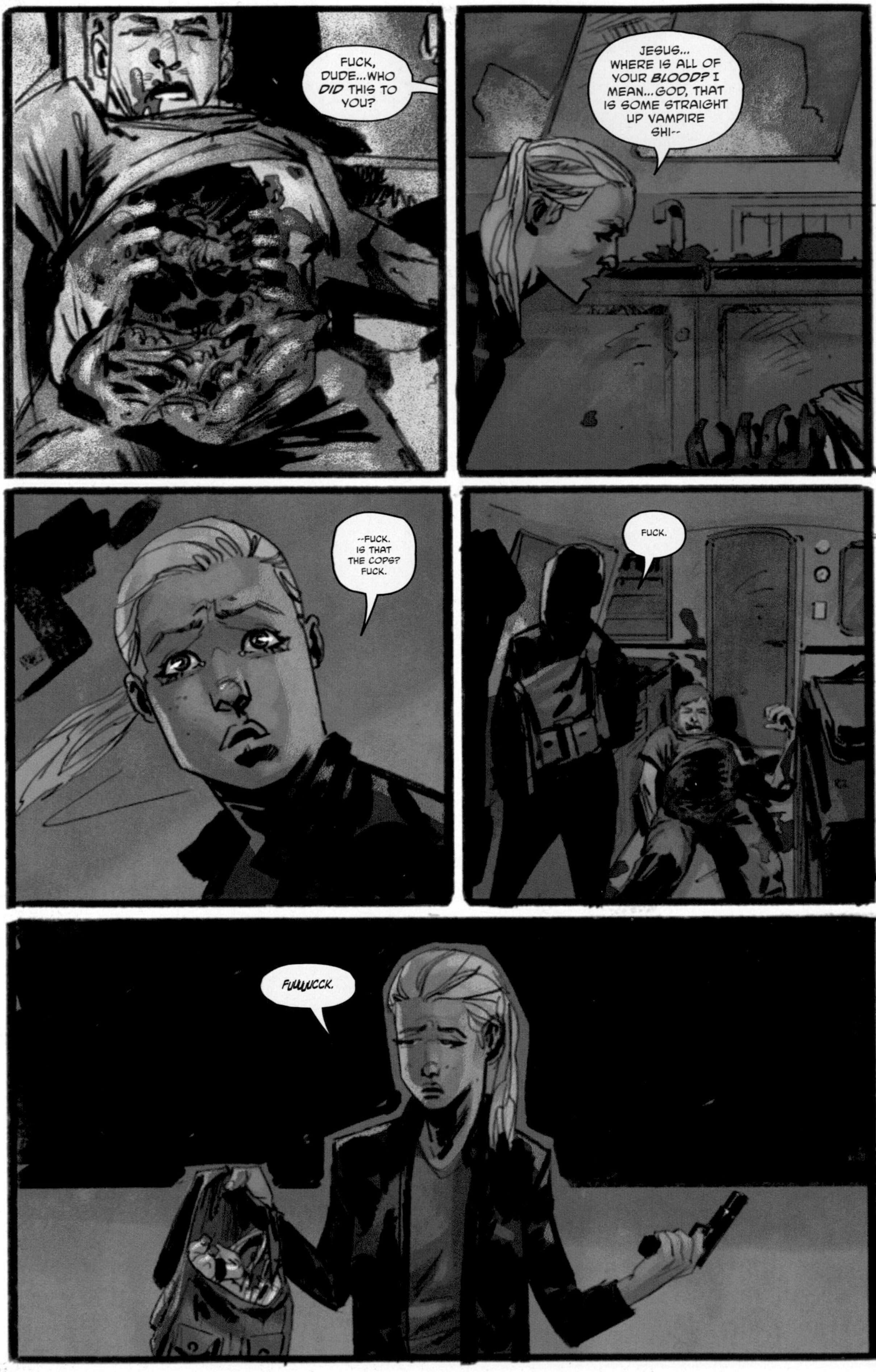
FUCK, DUDE...WHO DID THIS TO YOU?
JESUS... WHERE IS ALL OF YOUR BLOOD? I MEAN...GOD, THAT IS SOME STRAIGHT UP VAMPIRE SHI--
--FUCK. IS THAT THE COPS? FUCK.
FUCK.
FUUUUCCK.

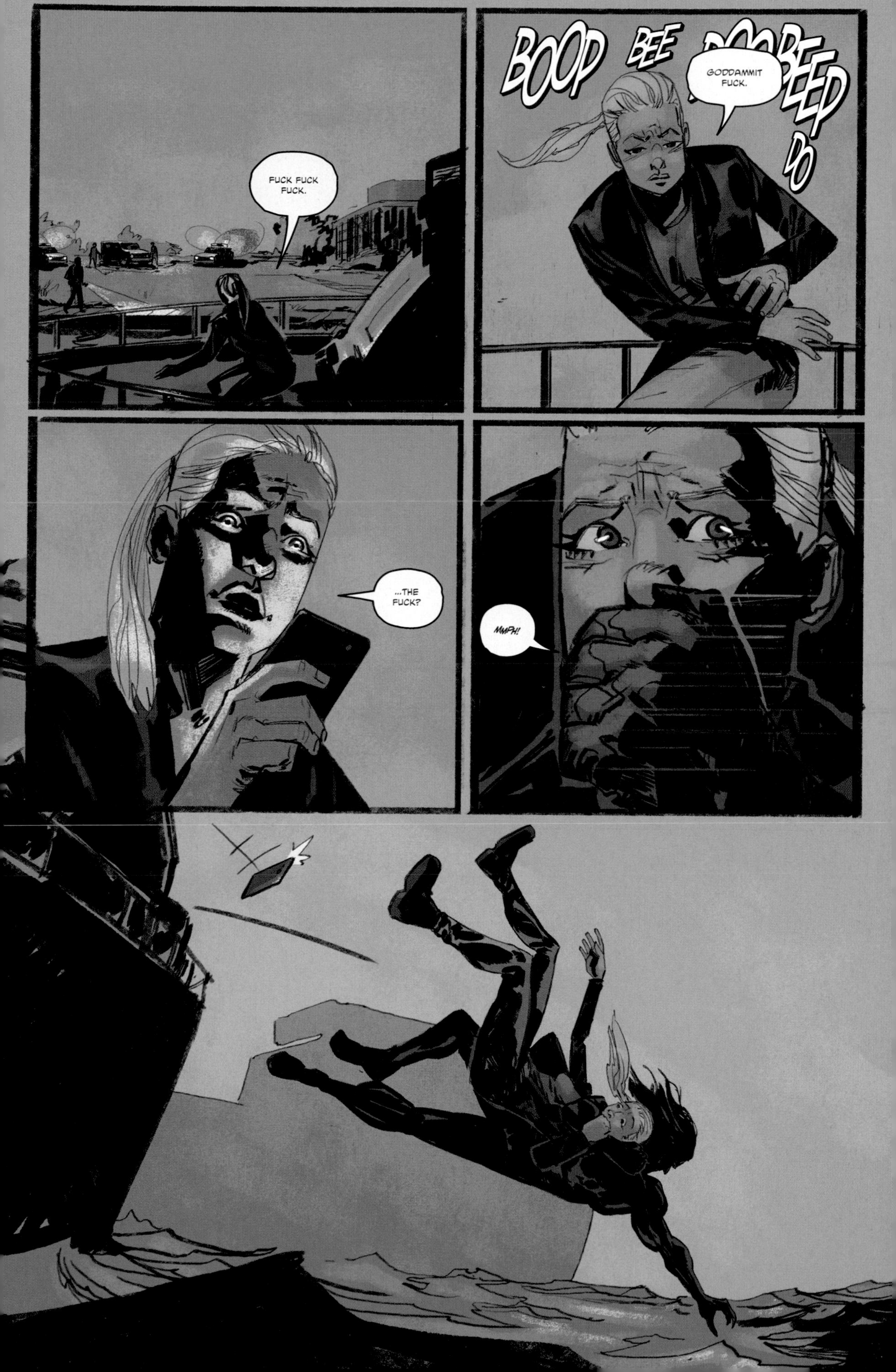
FUCK FUCK FUCK.
BOOP BEE DOO BEEP DO
GODDAMMIT FUCK.
...THE FUCK?
MMPH!

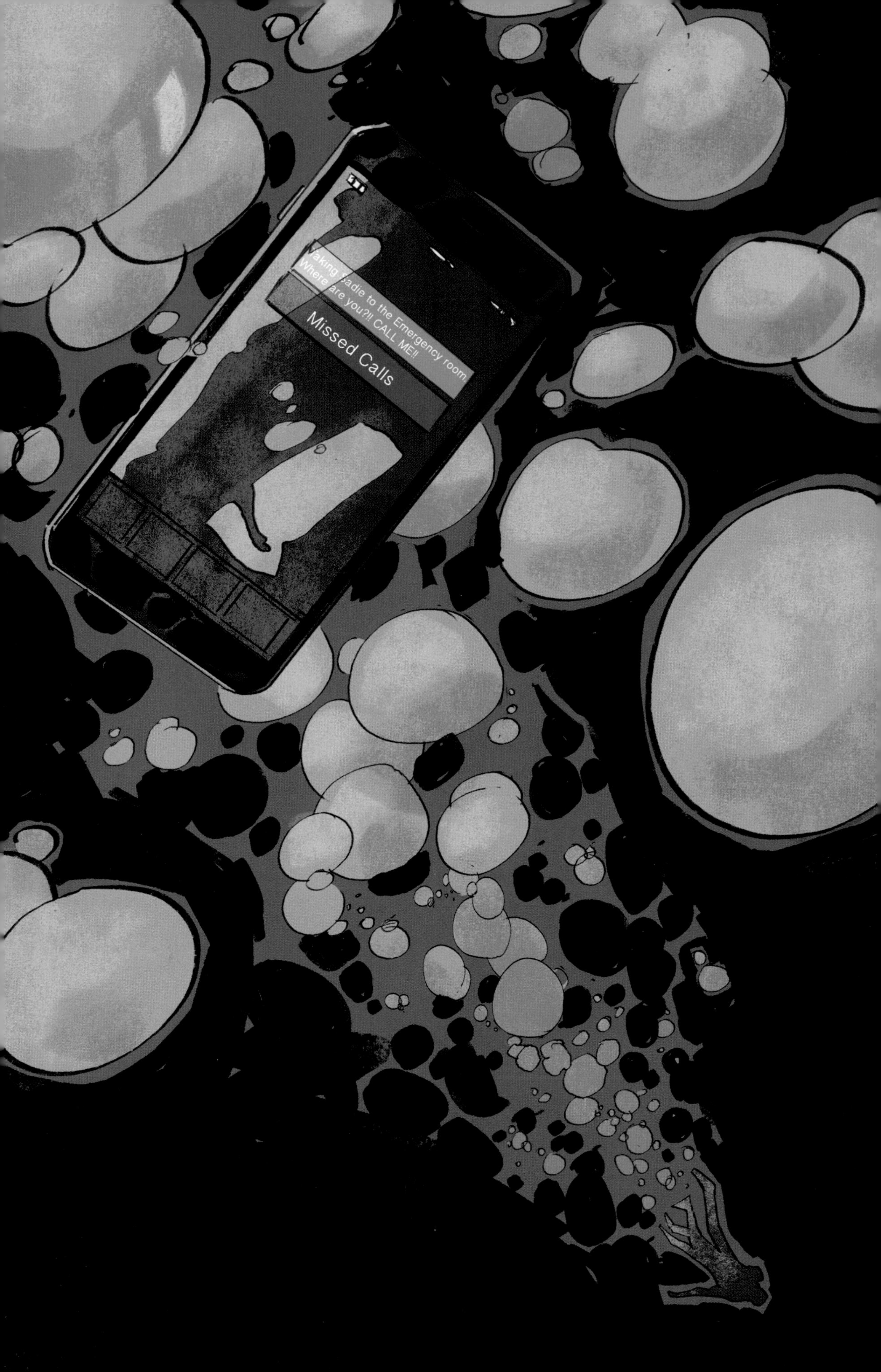
Taking Sadie to the Emergency room.
Where are you?!! CALL ME!!
Missed Calls

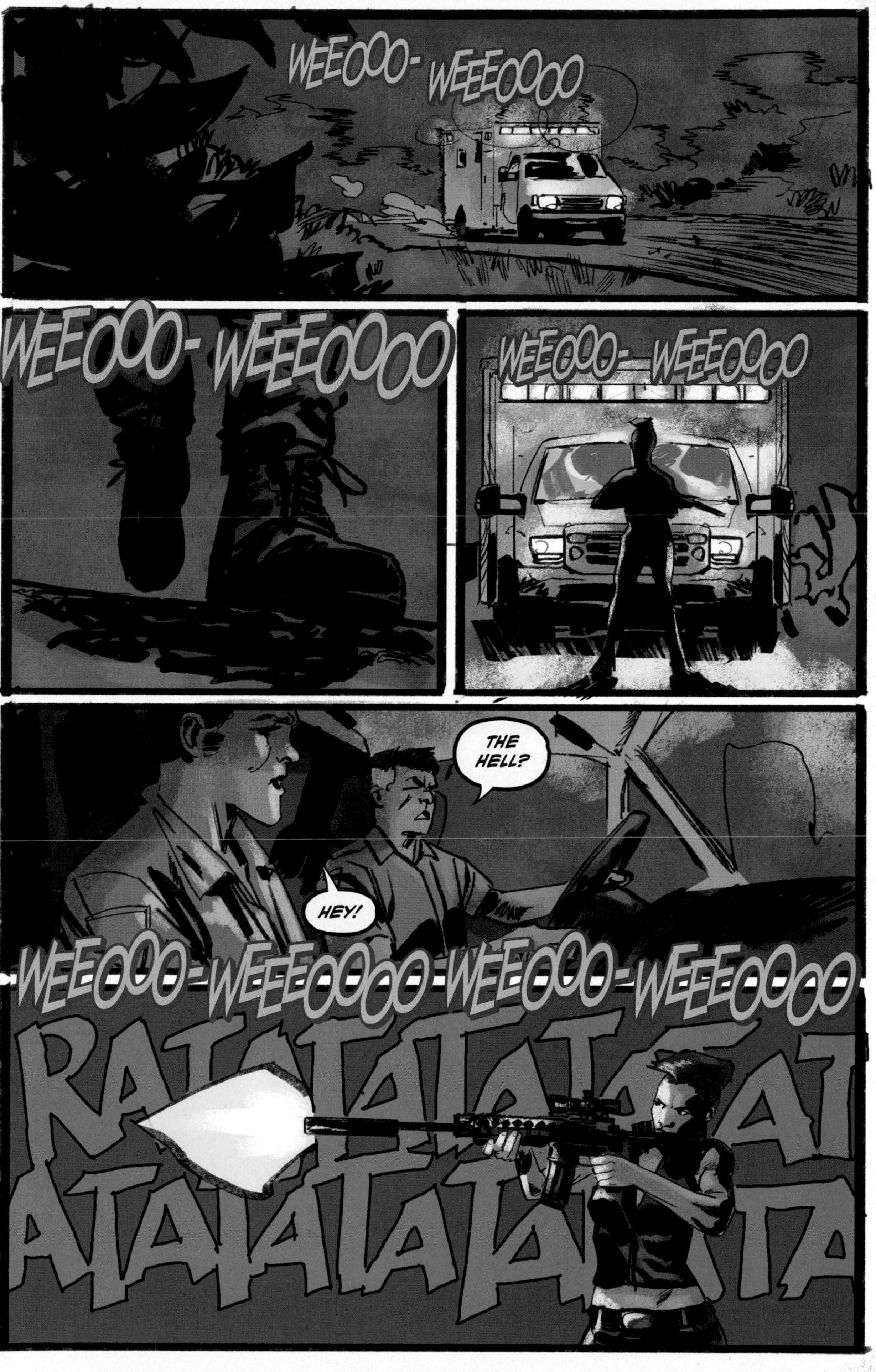
WEEOOO- WEEEOOOO
WEEOOO- WEEEOOOO
WEEOOO- WEEEOOOO
THE HELL?
HEY!
WEEOOO-WEEEOOOO-WEEOOO-WEEEOOOO
RATATATATATATATATATATATATA

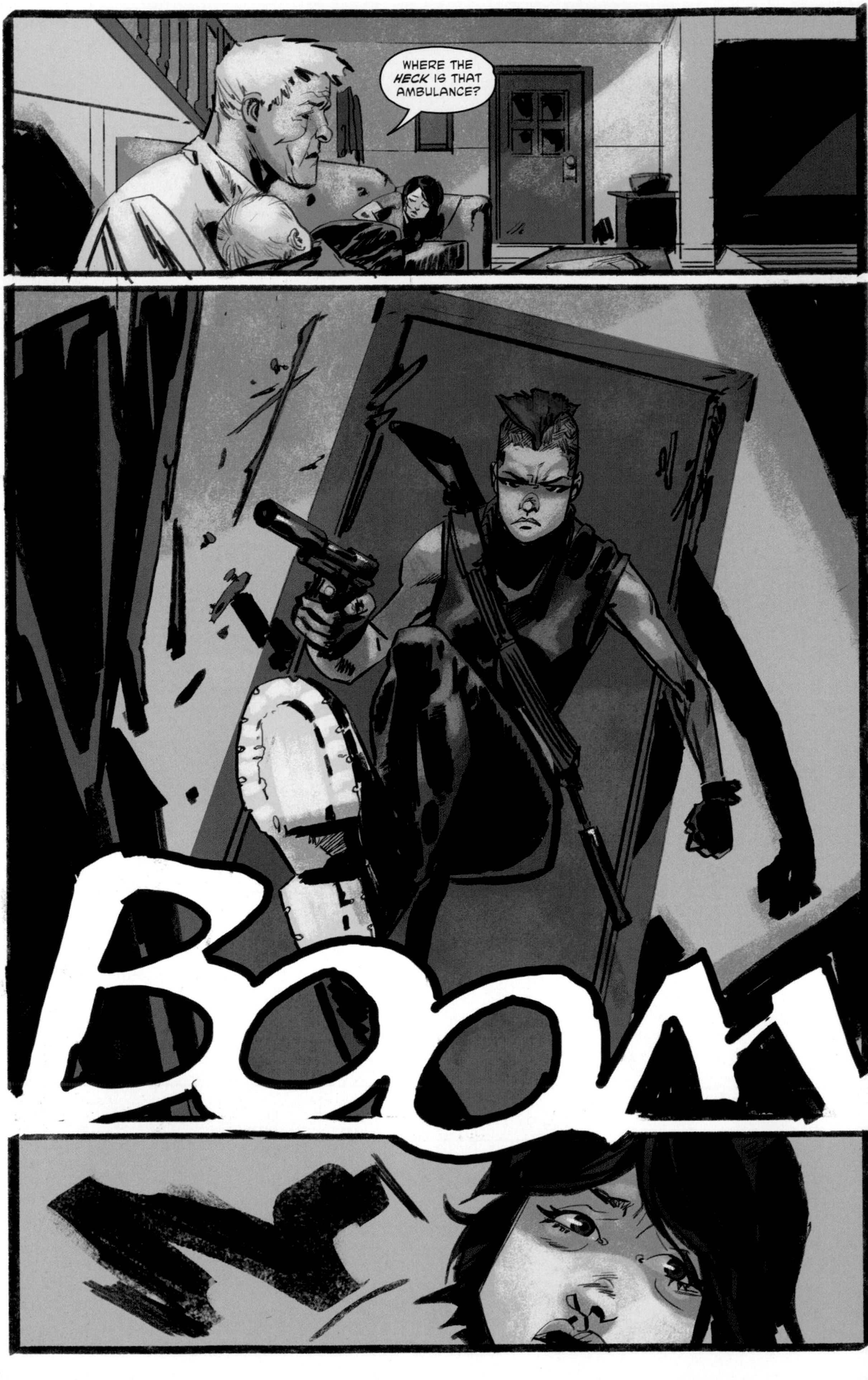

WHERE THE HECK IS THAT AMBULANCE?
BOOM

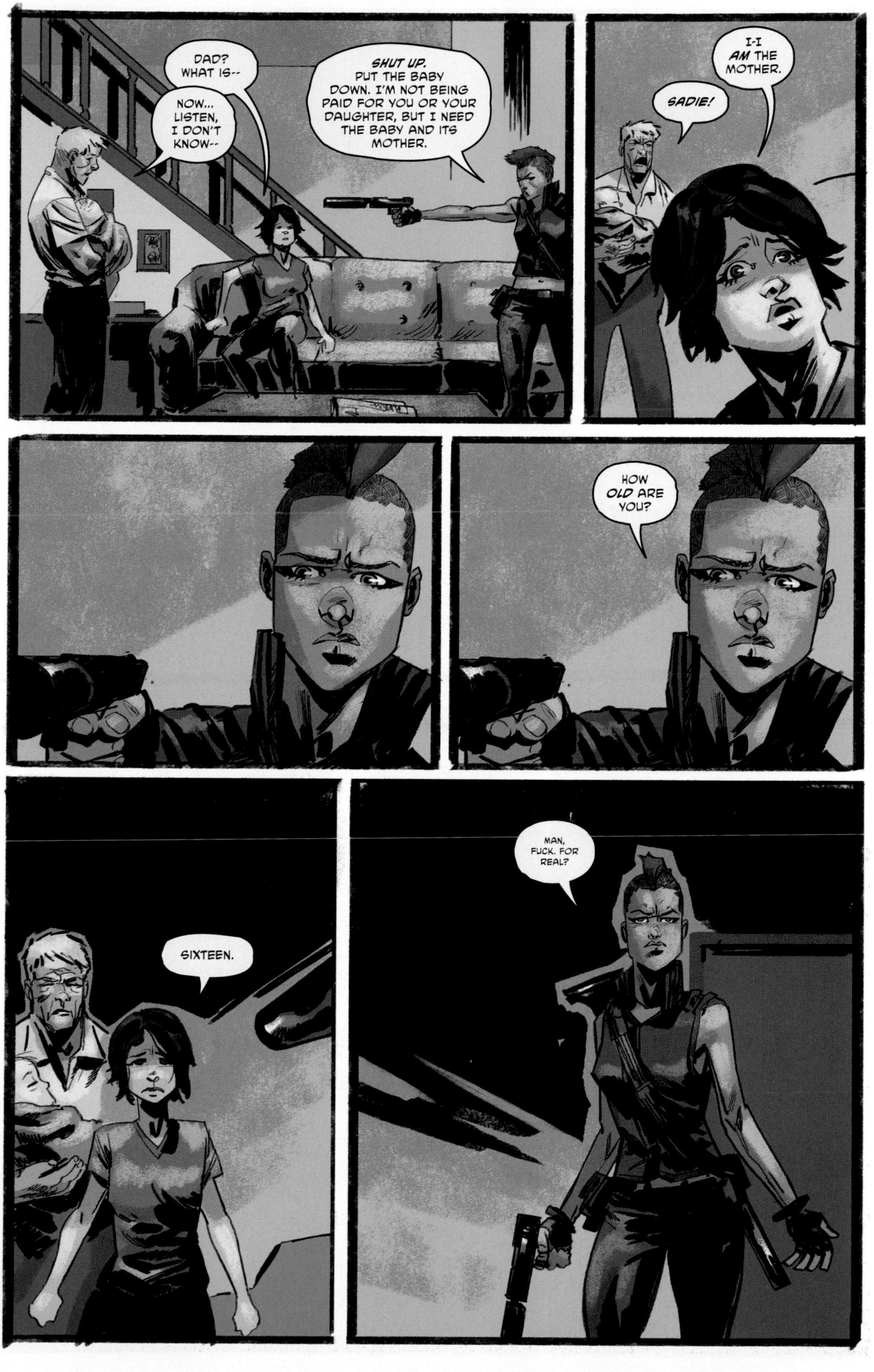

DAD? WHAT IS--
NOW... LISTEN, I DON'T KNOW--
SHUT UP. PUT THE BABY DOWN. I'M NOT BEING PAID FOR YOU OR YOUR DAUGHTER, BUT I NEED THE BABY AND ITS MOTHER.
SADIE!
I-I AM THE MOTHER.
HOW OLD ARE YOU?
SIXTEEN.
MAN, FUCK. FOR REAL?

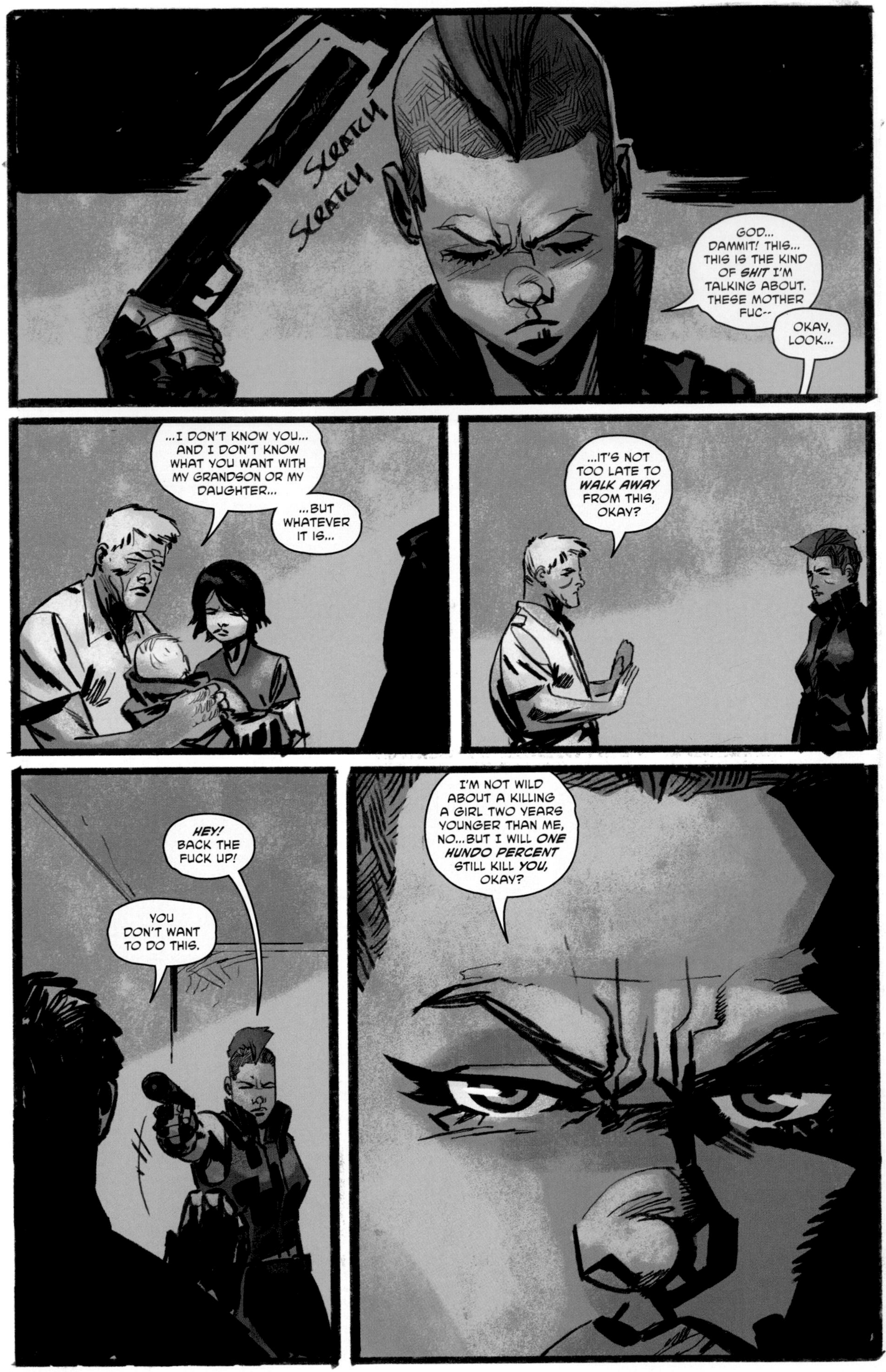
SCRATCH
SCRATCH
GOD... DAMMIT! THIS... THIS IS THE KIND OF SHIT I'M TALKING ABOUT. THESE MOTHER FUC--
OKAY, LOOK...
...I DON'T KNOW YOU... AND I DON'T KNOW WHAT YOU WANT WITH MY GRANDSON OR MY DAUGHTER...
...BUT WHATEVER IT IS...
...IT'S NOT TOO LATE TO WALK AWAY FROM THIS, OKAY?
HEY! BACK THE FUCK UP!
YOU DON'T WANT TO DO THIS.
I'M NOT WILD ABOUT A KILLING A GIRL TWO YEARS YOUNGER THAN ME, NO...BUT I WILL ONE HUNDO PERCENT STILL KILL YOU, OKAY?

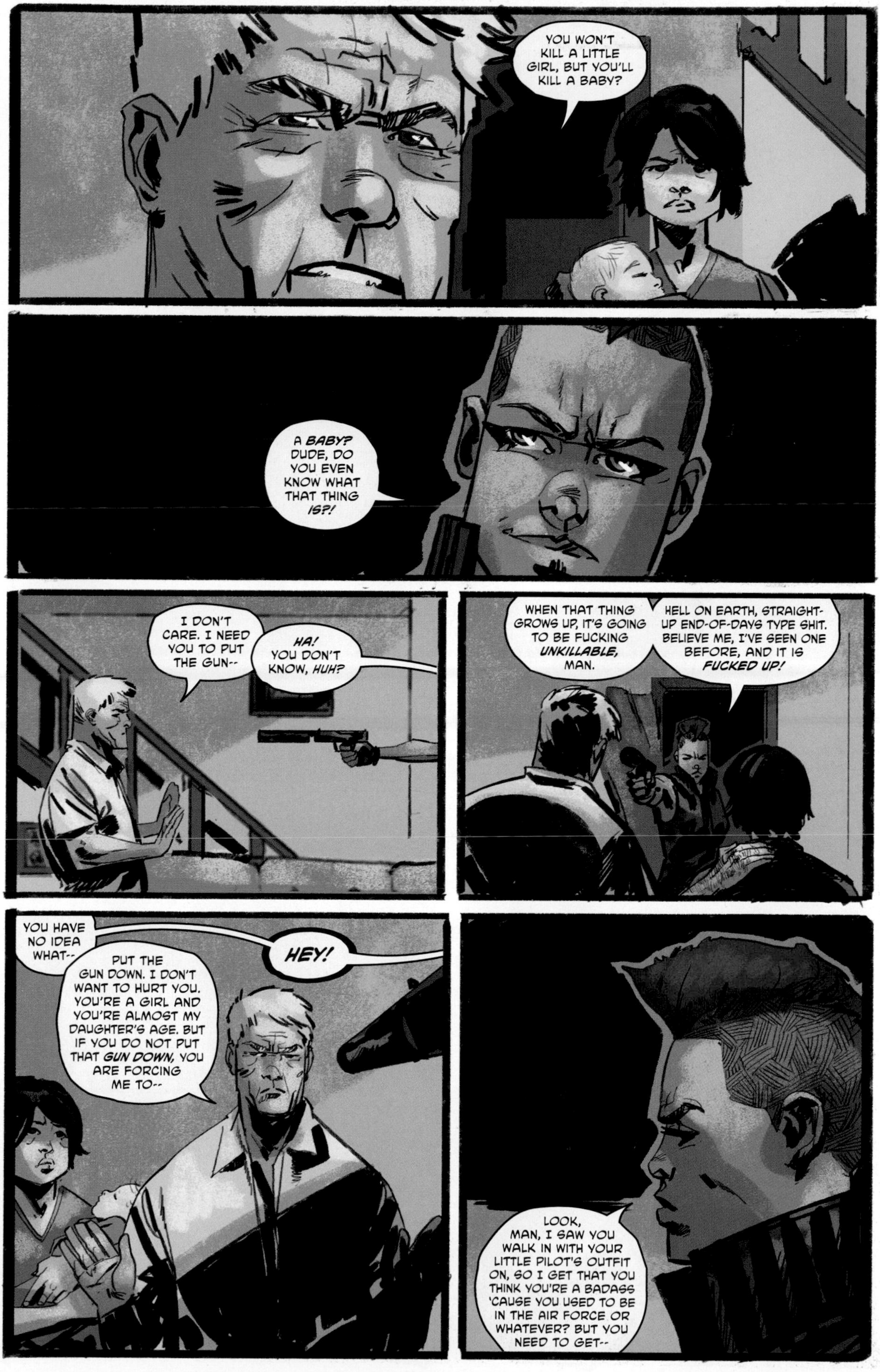
YOU WON'T KILL A LITTLE GIRL, BUT YOU'LL KILL A BABY?
A BABY? DUDE, DO YOU EVEN KNOW WHAT THAT THING IS?!
I DON'T CARE. I NEED YOU TO PUT THE GUN--
HA! YOU DON'T KNOW, HUH?
WHEN THAT THING GROWS UP, IT'S GOING TO BE FUCKING UNKILLABLE, MAN.
HELL ON EARTH, STRAIGHT-UP END-OF-DAYS TYPE SHIT. BELIEVE ME, I'VE SEEN ONE BEFORE, AND IT IS FUCKED UP!
YOU HAVE NO IDEA WHAT--
HEY!
PUT THE GUN DOWN. I DON'T WANT TO HURT YOU. YOU'RE A GIRL AND YOU'RE ALMOST MY DAUGHTER'S AGE. BUT IF YOU DO NOT PUT THAT GUN DOWN, YOU ARE FORCING ME TO--
LOOK, MAN, I SAW YOU WALK IN WITH YOUR LITTLE PILOT'S OUTFIT ON, SO I GET THAT YOU THINK YOU'RE A BADASS 'CAUSE YOU USED TO BE IN THE AIR FORCE OR WHATEVER? BUT YOU NEED TO GET--

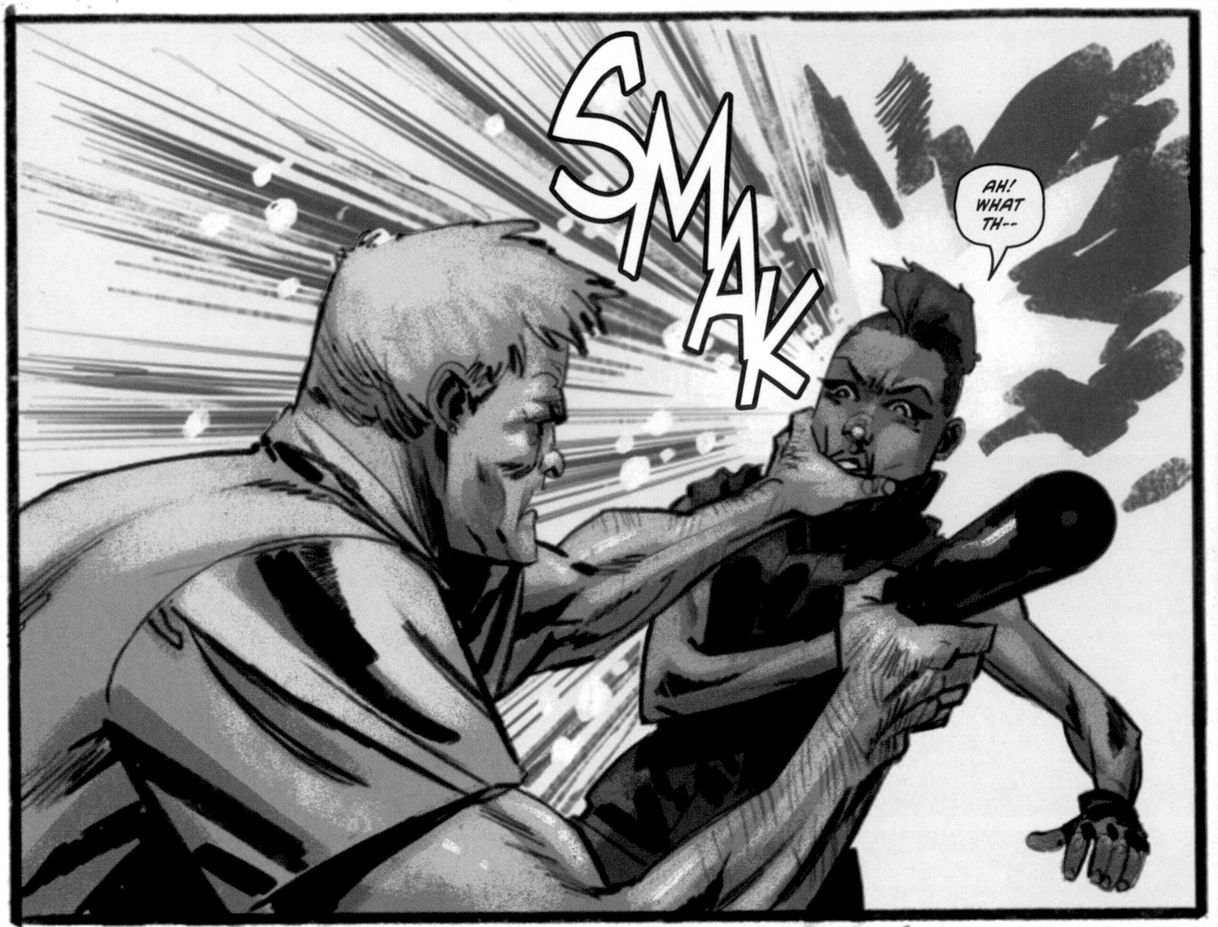
SMAK
AH! WHAT TH--

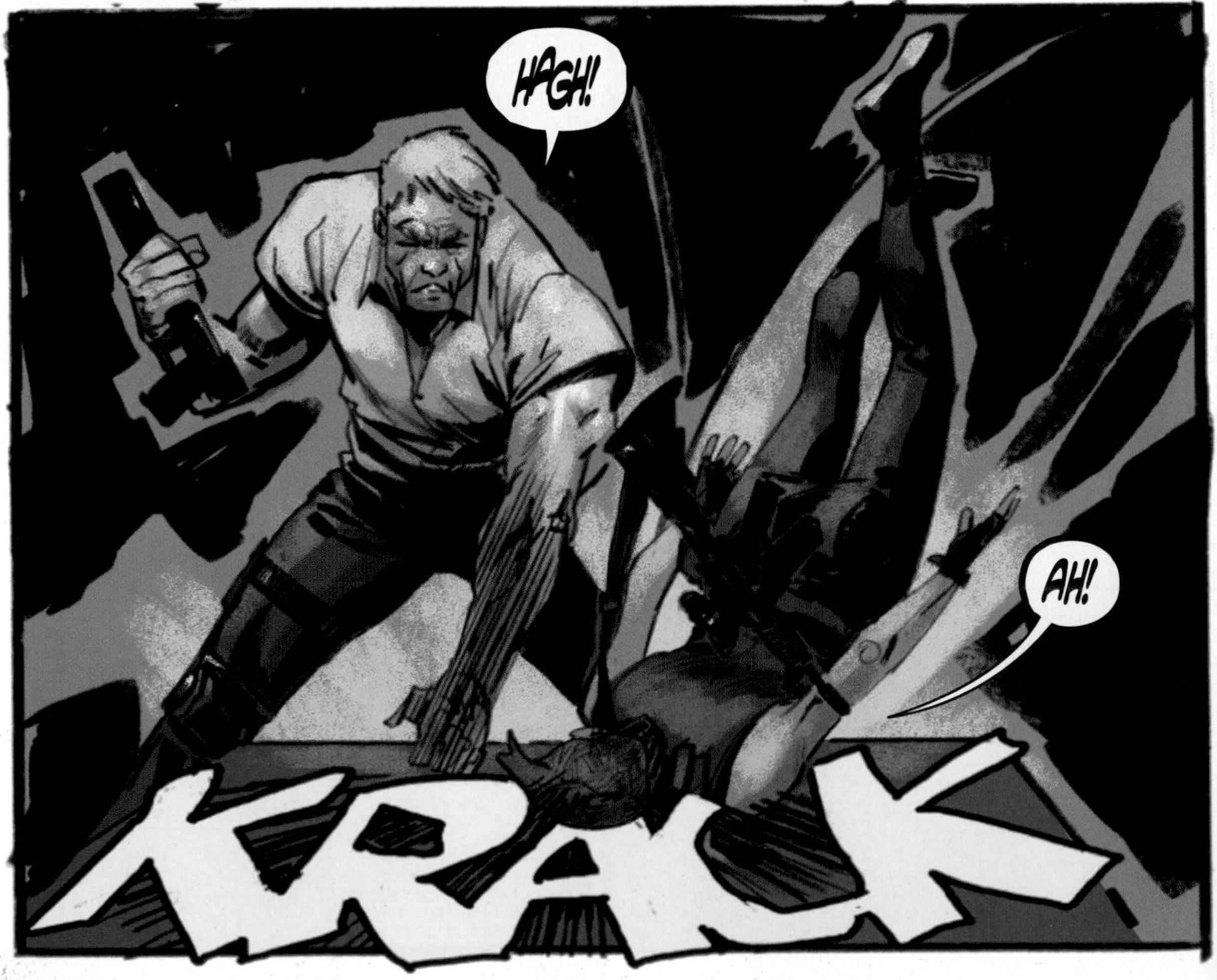
HAGH!
AH!
KRAK

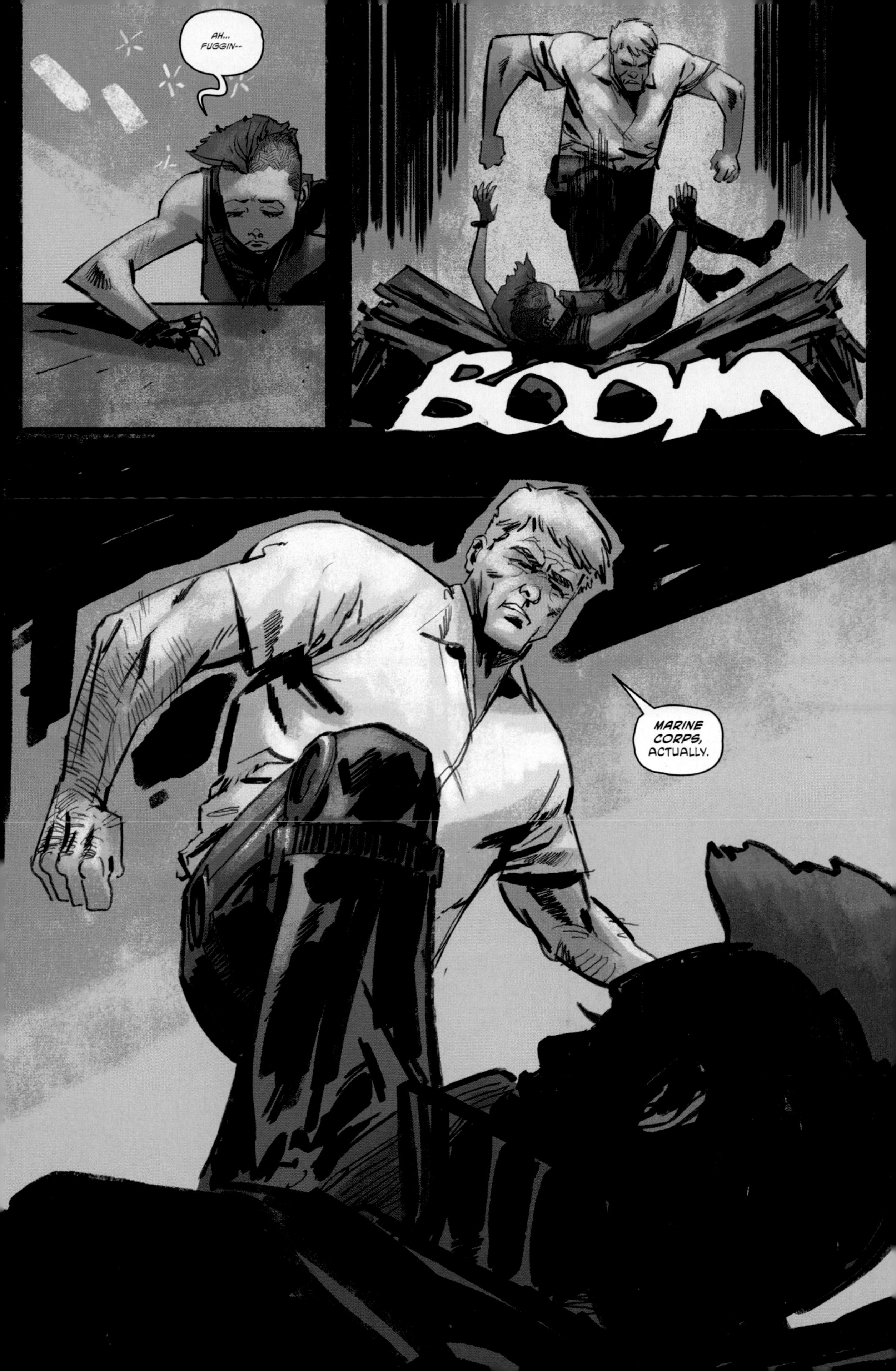
AH... FUGGIN--
BOOM
MARINE CORPS, ACTUALLY.

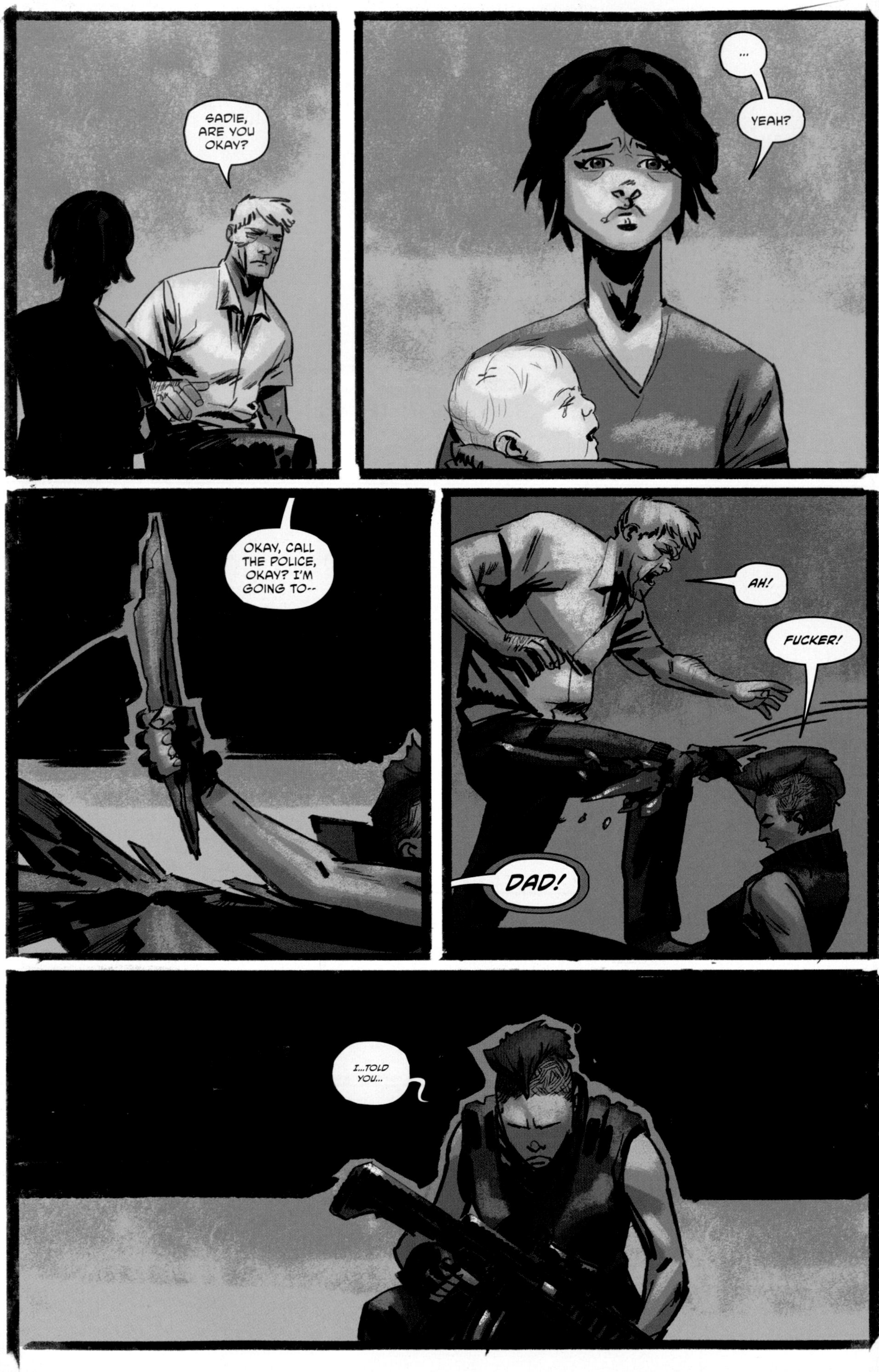
SADIE, ARE YOU OKAY?
...
YEAH?
OKAY, CALL THE POLICE, OKAY? I'M GOING TO--
AH!
FUCKER!
DAD!
I...TOLD YOU...

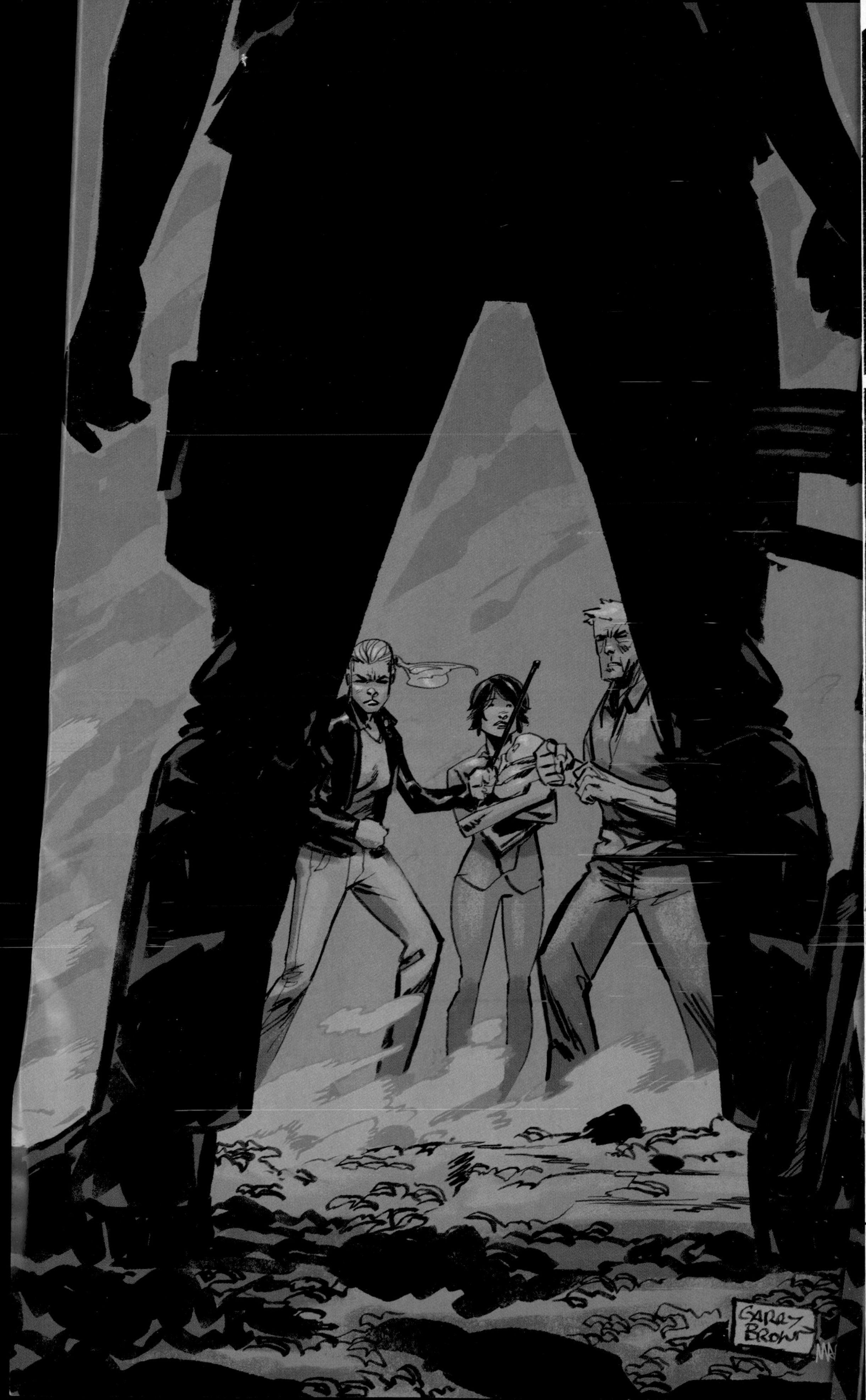

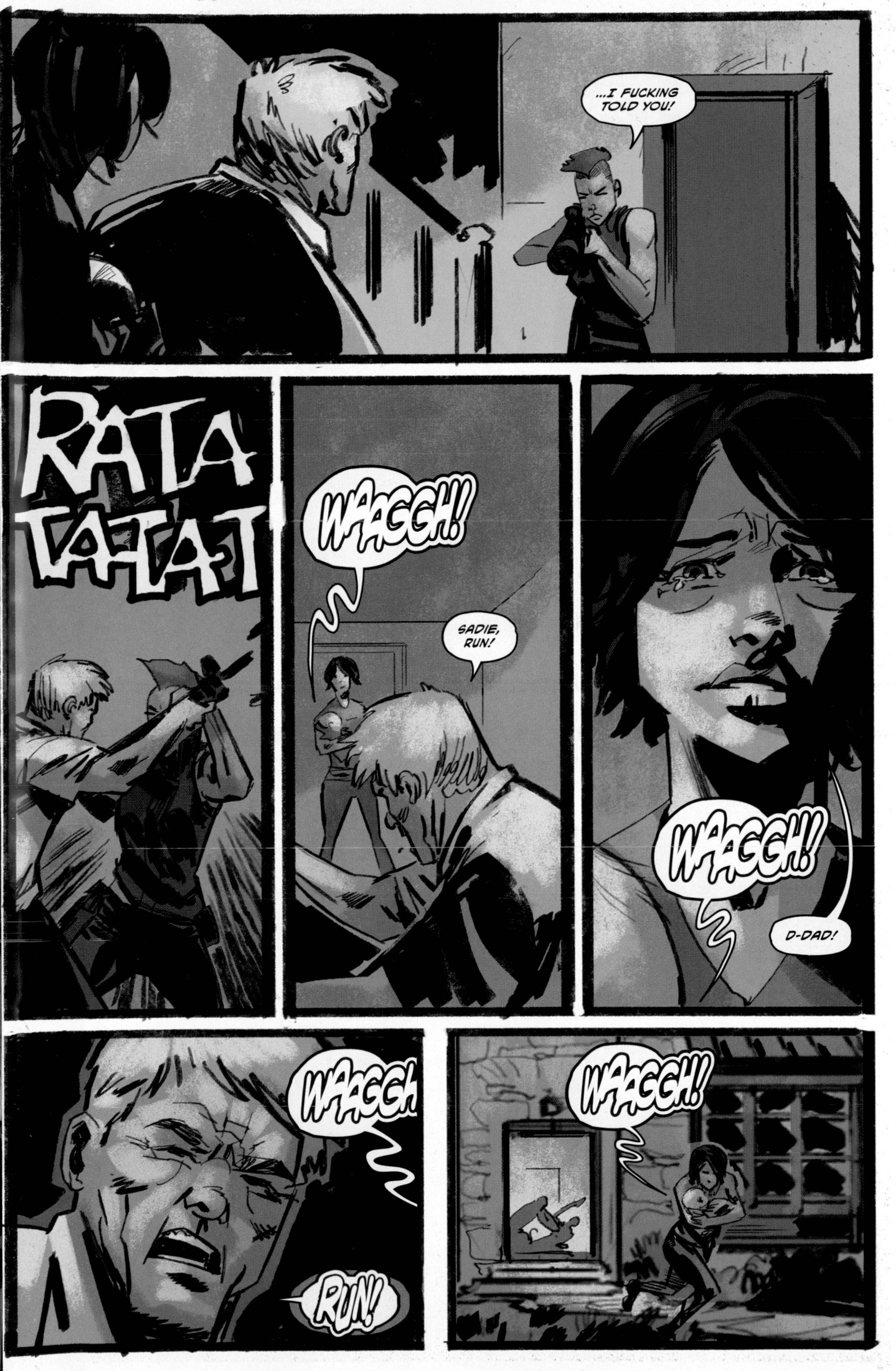
...I FUCKING TOLD YOU!
RATA TATAT
WAAGGH!
SADIE, RUN!
WAAGGH!
D-DAD!
WAAGGH
RUN!
WAAGGH!

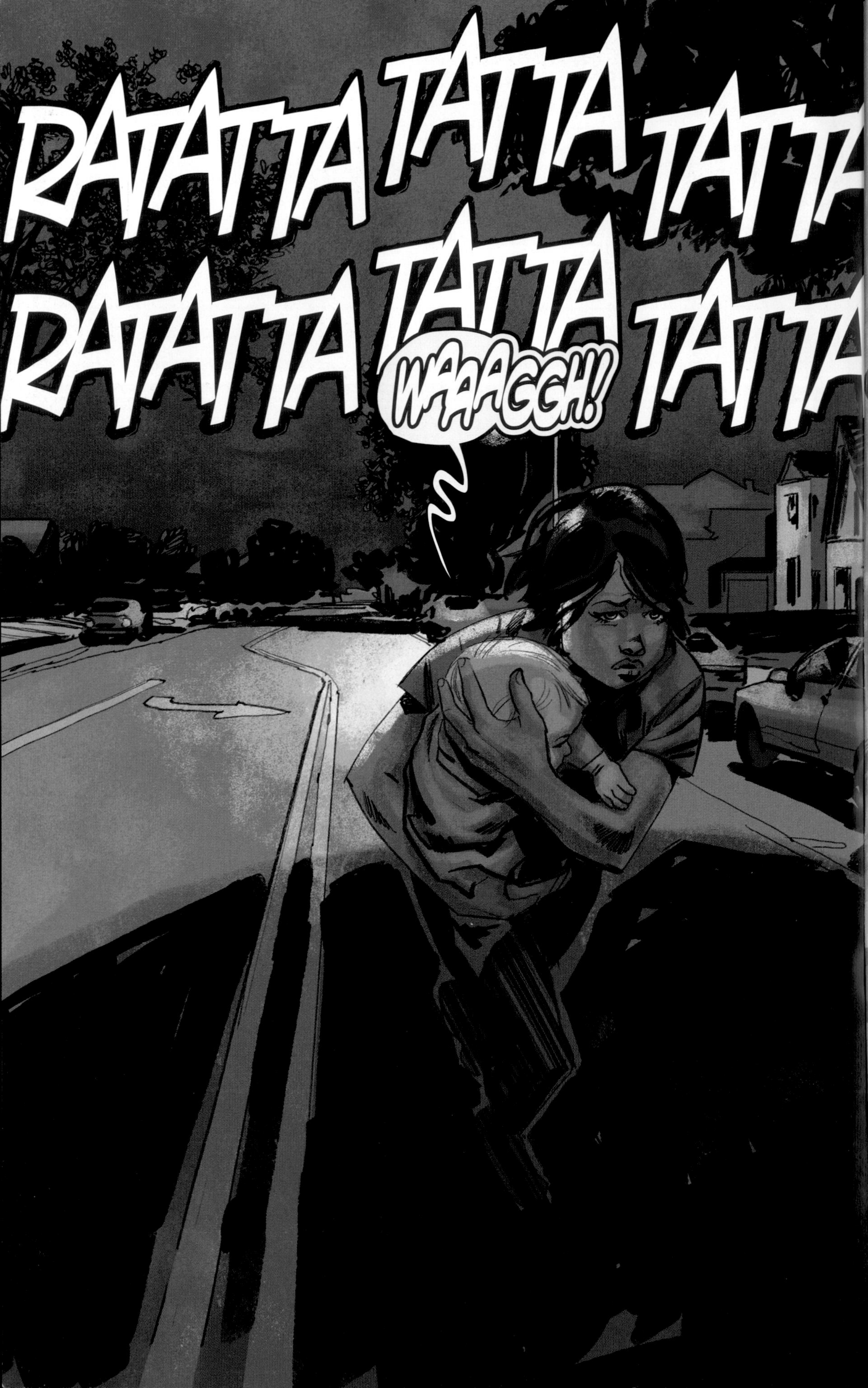
RATATTA TATTA TATTA
RATATTA TATTA TATTA
WAAAGGH!

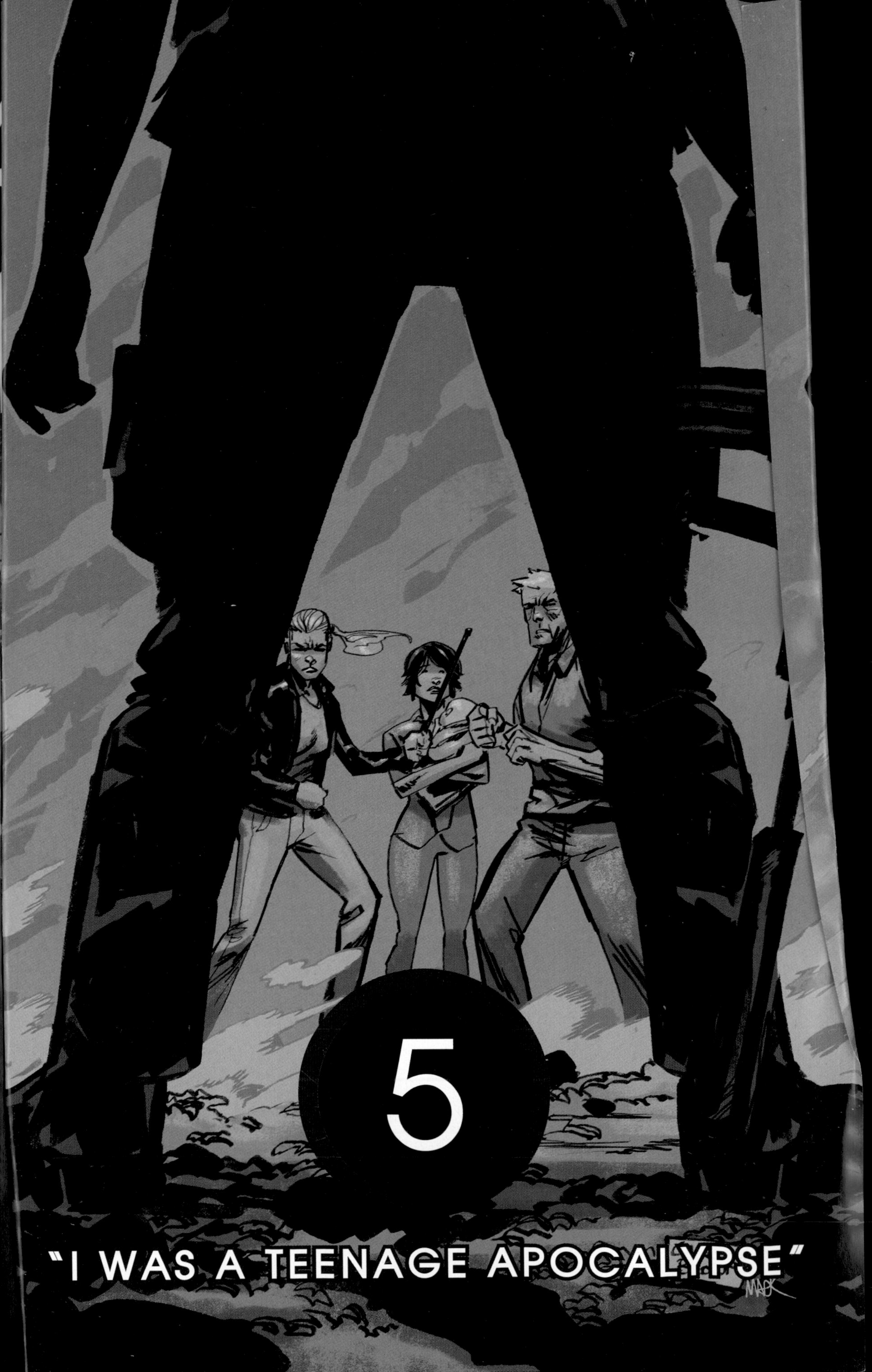
5
"I WAS A TEENAGE APOCALYPSE"
MACK

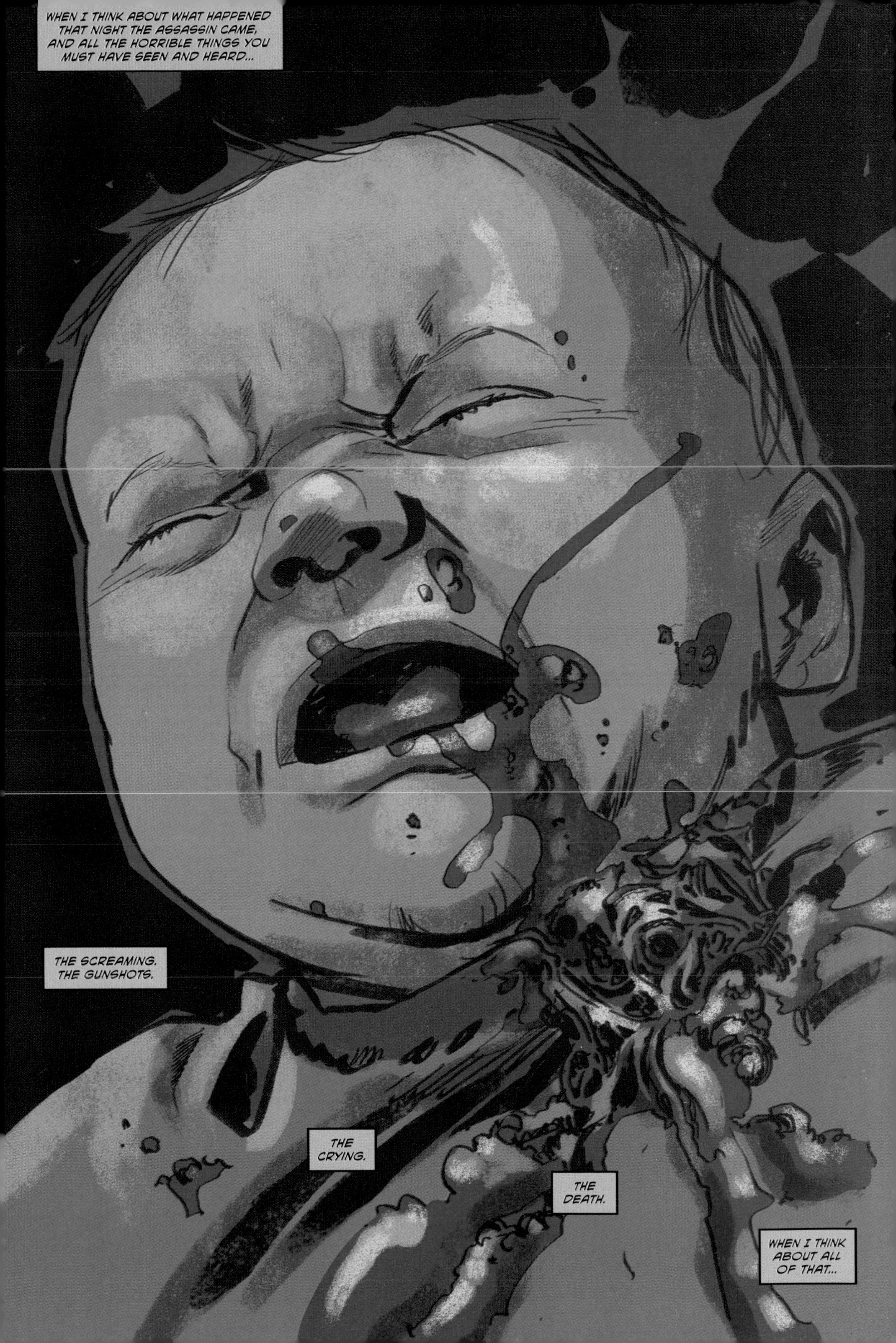
WHEN I THINK ABOUT WHAT HAPPENED THAT NIGHT THE ASSASSIN CAME, AND ALL THE HORRIBLE THINGS YOU MUST HAVE SEEN AND HEARD...
THE SCREAMING. THE GUNSHOTS.
THE CRYING.
THE DEATH.
WHEN I THINK ABOUT ALL OF THAT...

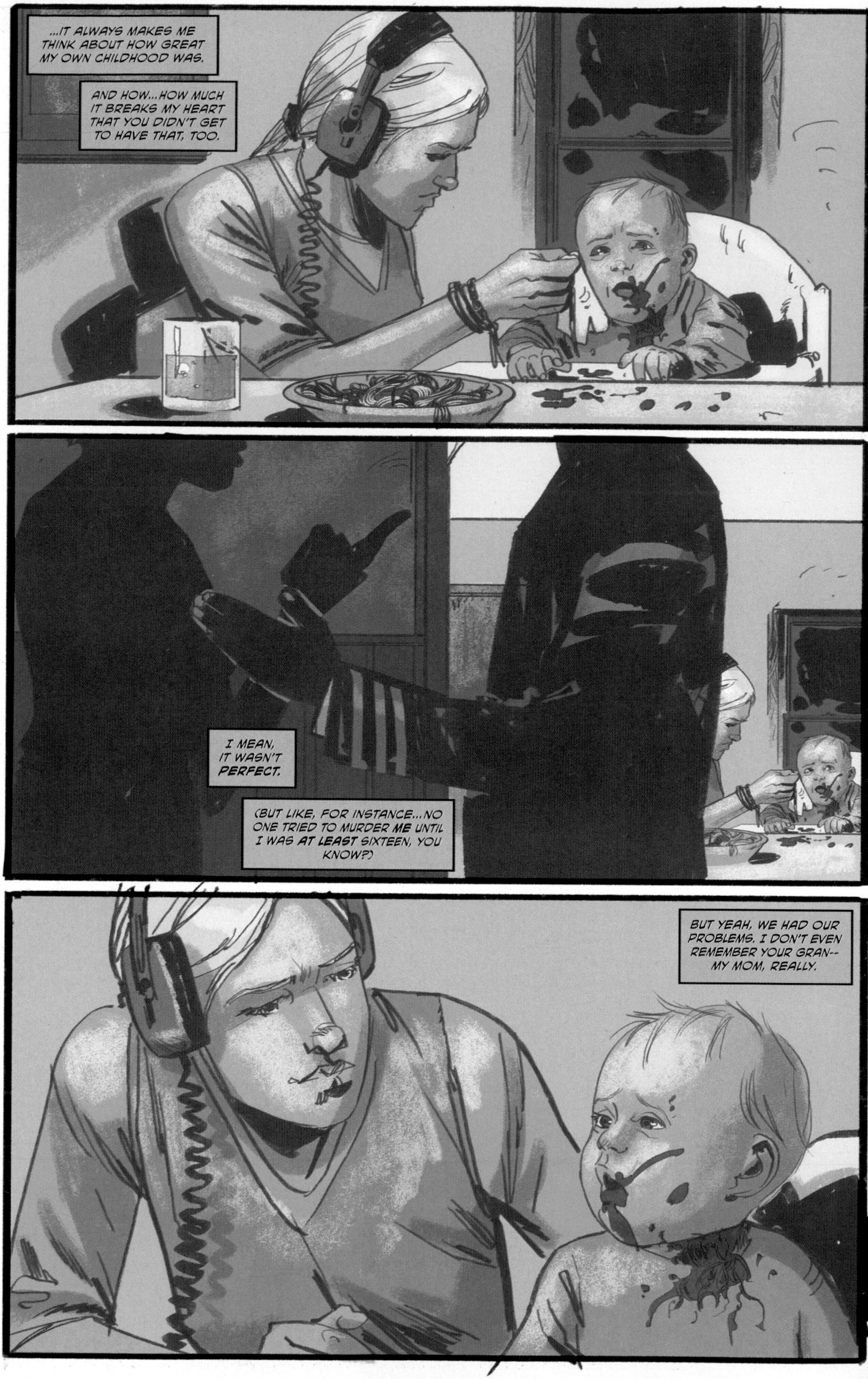
...IT ALWAYS MAKES ME THINK ABOUT HOW GREAT MY OWN CHILDHOOD WAS.
AND HOW...HOW MUCH IT BREAKS MY HEART THAT YOU DIDN'T GET TO HAVE THAT, TOO.
I MEAN, IT WASN'T PERFECT.
(BUT LIKE, FOR INSTANCE...NO ONE TRIED TO MURDER ME UNTIL I WAS AT LEAST SIXTEEN, YOU KNOW?)
BUT YEAH, WE HAD OUR PROBLEMS. I DON'T EVEN REMEMBER YOUR GRAN-- MY MOM, REALLY.

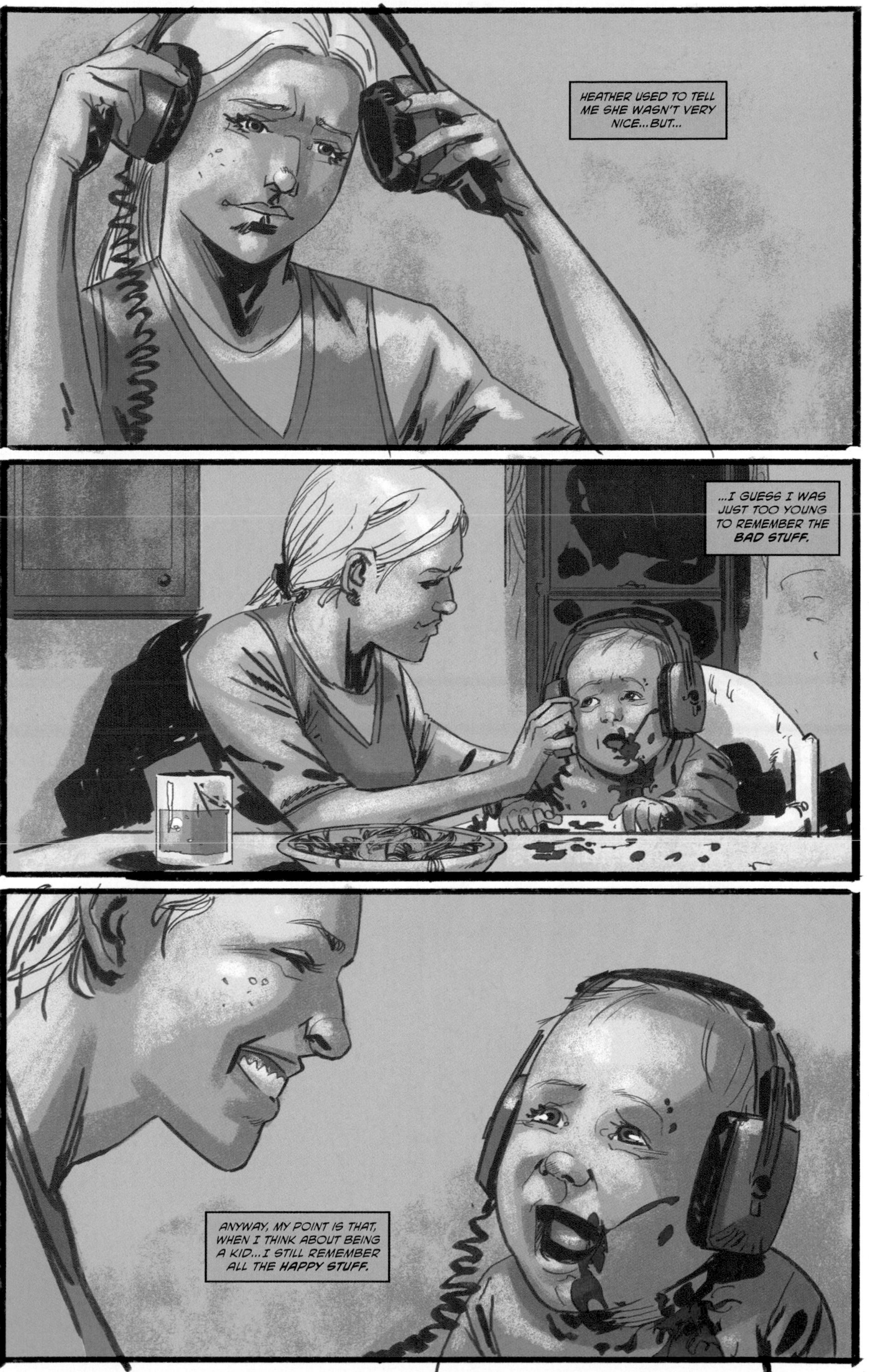
HEATHER USED TO TELL ME SHE WASN'T VERY NICE...BUT...
...I GUESS I WAS JUST TOO YOUNG TO REMEMBER THE BAD STUFF.
ANYWAY, MY POINT IS THAT, WHEN I THINK ABOUT BEING A KID...I STILL REMEMBER ALL THE HAPPY STUFF.

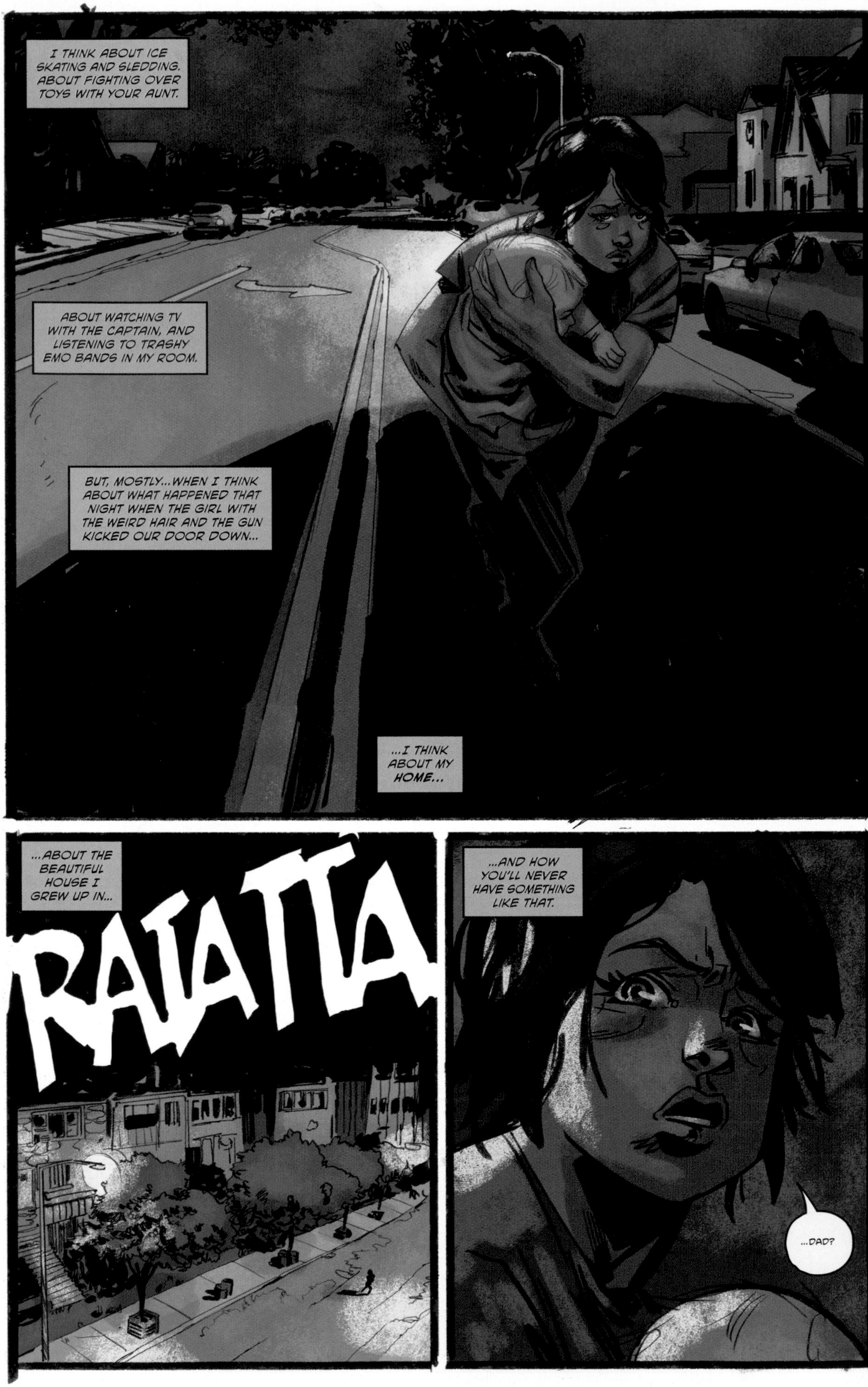
I THINK ABOUT ICE SKATING AND SLEDDING. ABOUT FIGHTING OVER TOYS WITH YOUR AUNT.
ABOUT WATCHING TV WITH THE CAPTAIN, AND LISTENING TO TRASHY EMO BANDS IN MY ROOM.
BUT, MOSTLY...WHEN I THINK ABOUT WHAT HAPPENED THAT NIGHT WHEN THE GIRL WITH THE WEIRD HAIR AND THE GUN KICKED OUR DOOR DOWN...
...I THINK ABOUT MY HOME...
...ABOUT THE BEAUTIFUL HOUSE I GREW UP IN...
RATATTA
...AND HOW YOU'LL NEVER HAVE SOMETHING LIKE THAT.
...DAD?

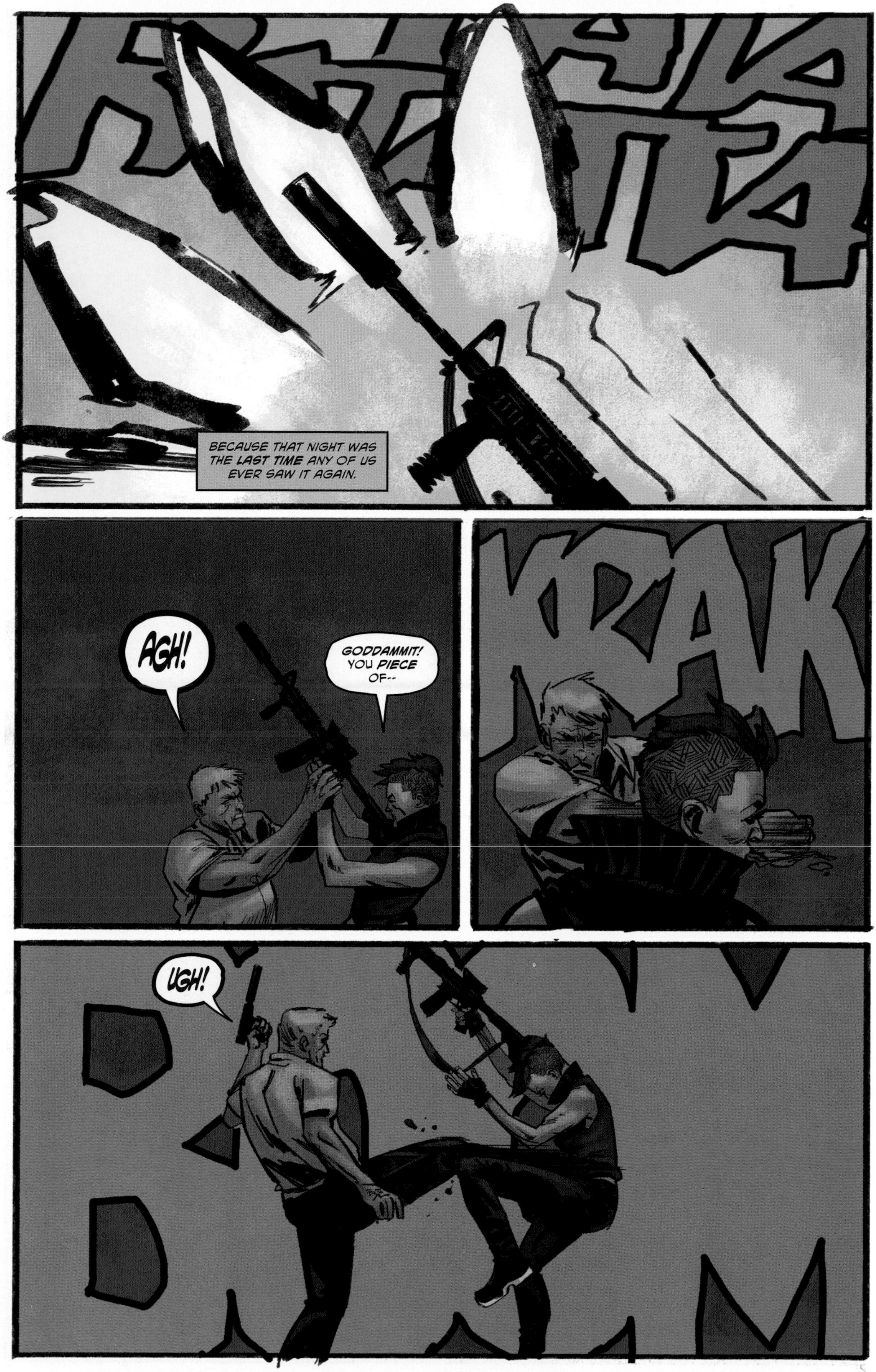
BECAUSE THAT NIGHT WAS THE LAST TIME ANY OF US EVER SAW IT AGAIN.
AGH!
GODDAMMIT! YOU PIECE OF--
KRAK
UGH!

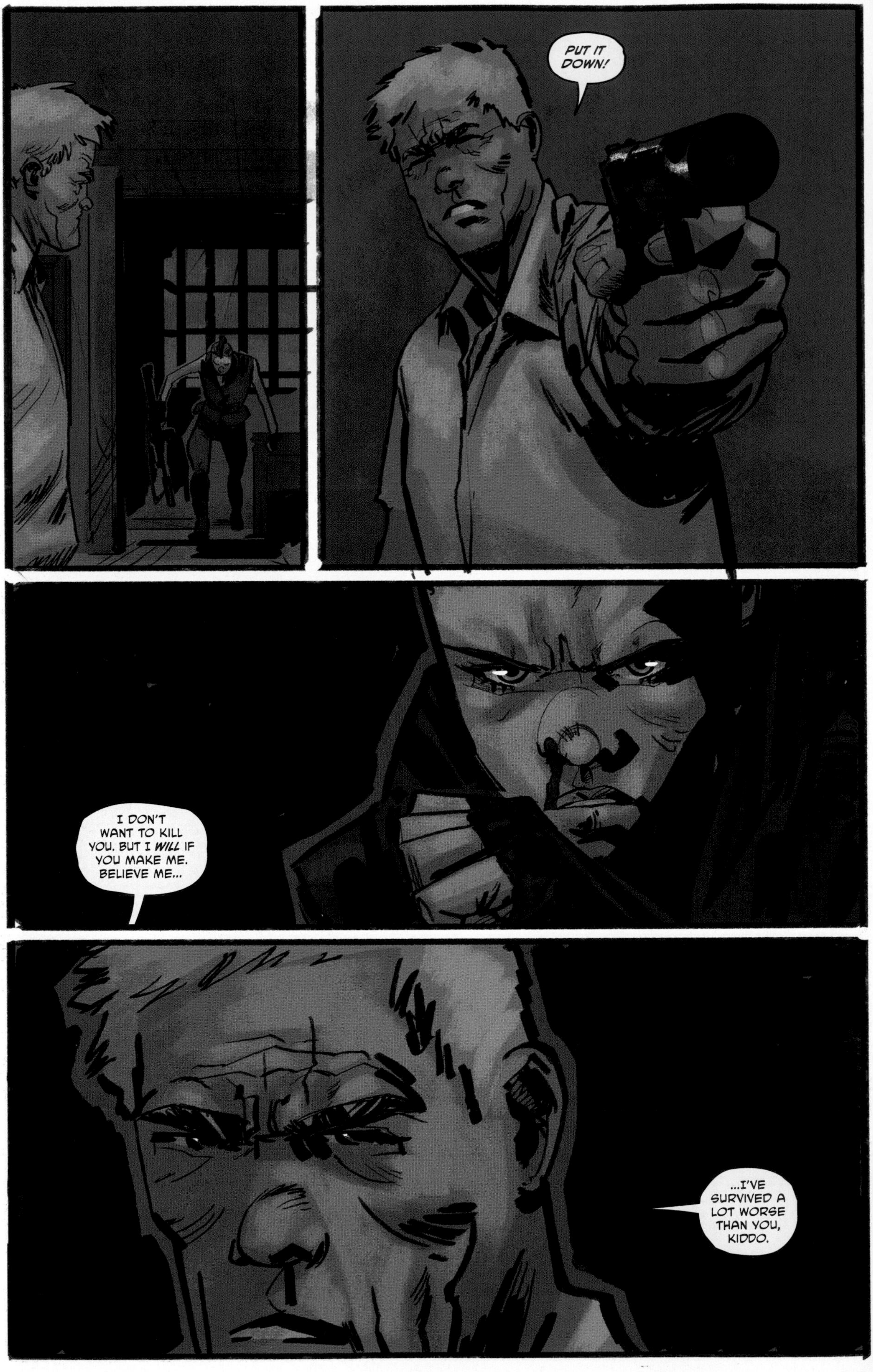
PUT IT DOWN!
I DON'T WANT TO KILL YOU. BUT I *WILL* IF YOU MAKE ME. BELIEVE ME...
...I'VE SURVIVED A LOT WORSE THAN YOU, KIDDO.

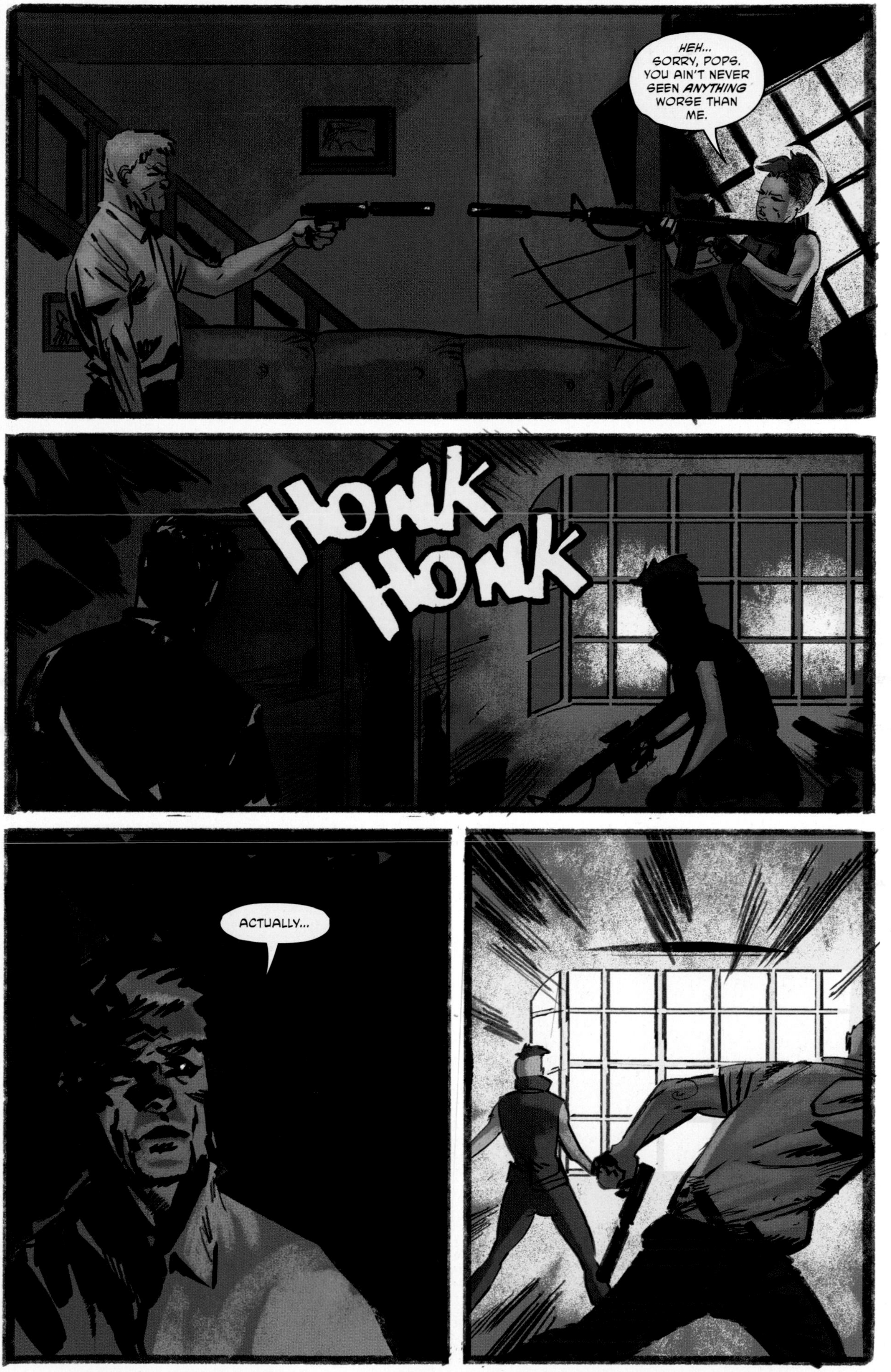
HEH... SORRY, POPS. YOU AIN'T NEVER SEEN ANYTHING WORSE THAN ME.
HONK HONK
ACTUALLY...

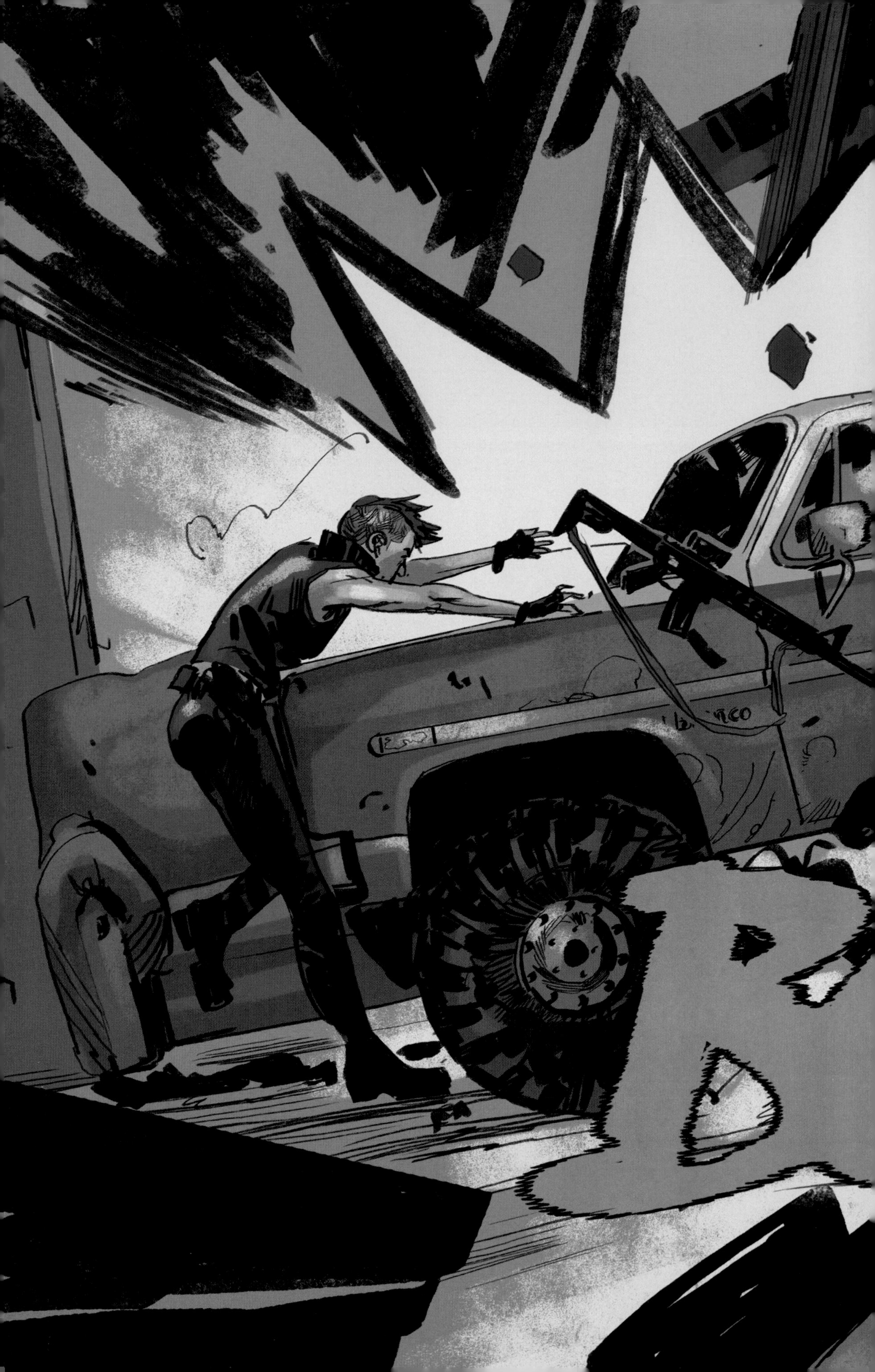

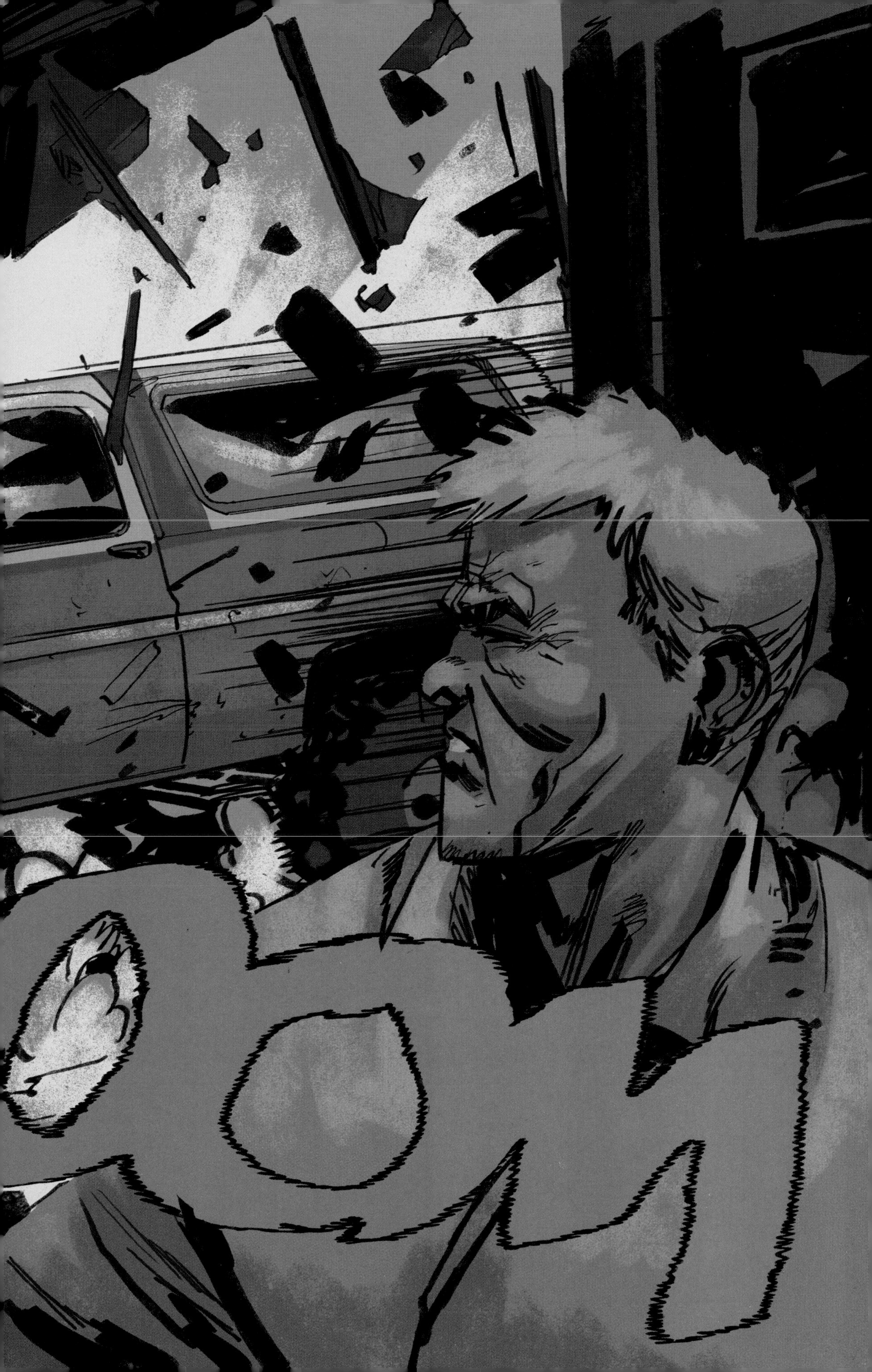

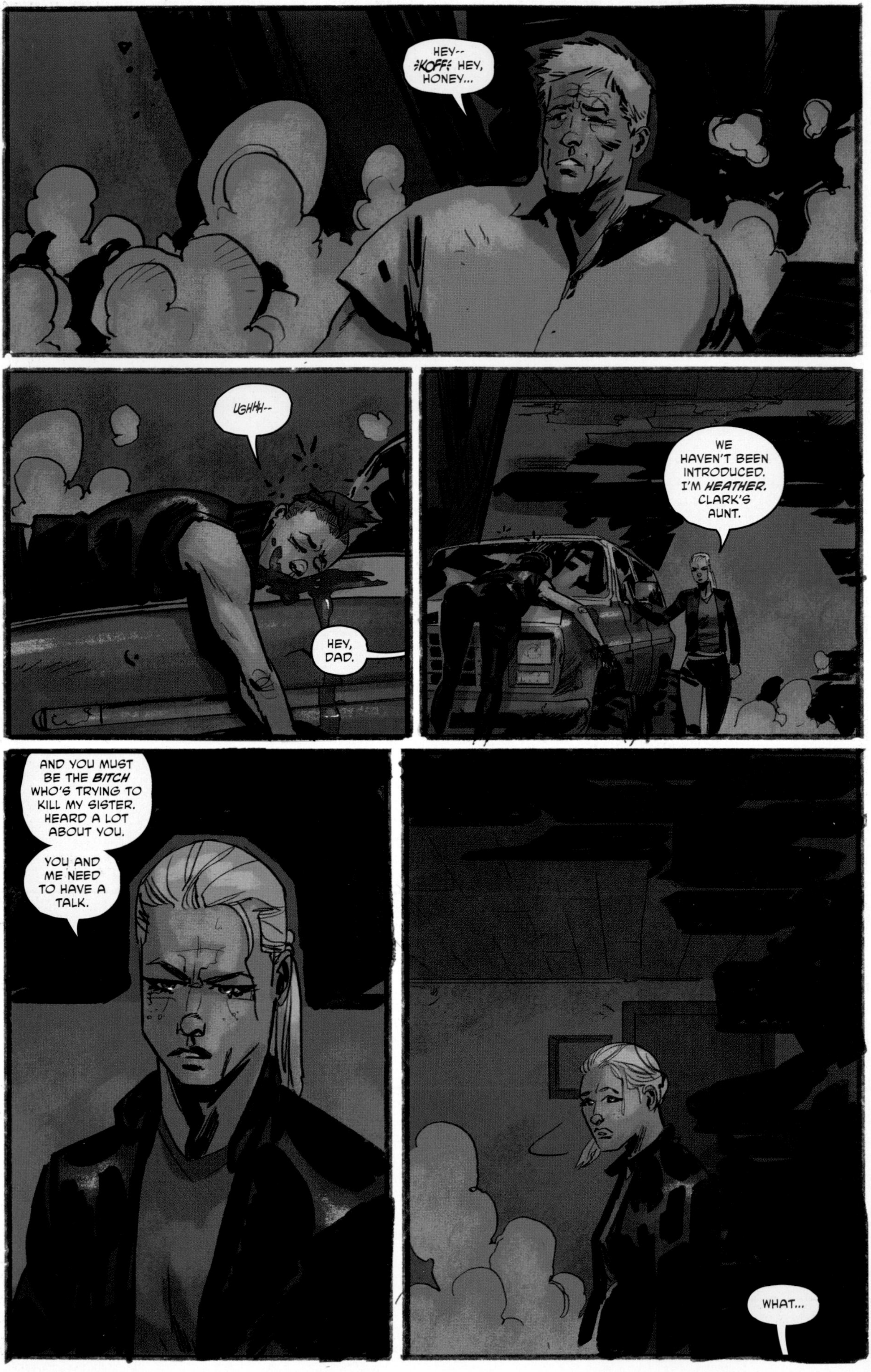
HEY-- *KOFF* HEY, HONEY...
UGHHH--
HEY, DAD.
WE HAVEN'T BEEN INTRODUCED. I'M HEATHER. CLARK'S AUNT.
AND YOU MUST BE THE BITCH WHO'S TRYING TO KILL MY SISTER. HEARD A LOT ABOUT YOU.
YOU AND ME NEED TO HAVE A TALK.
WHAT...

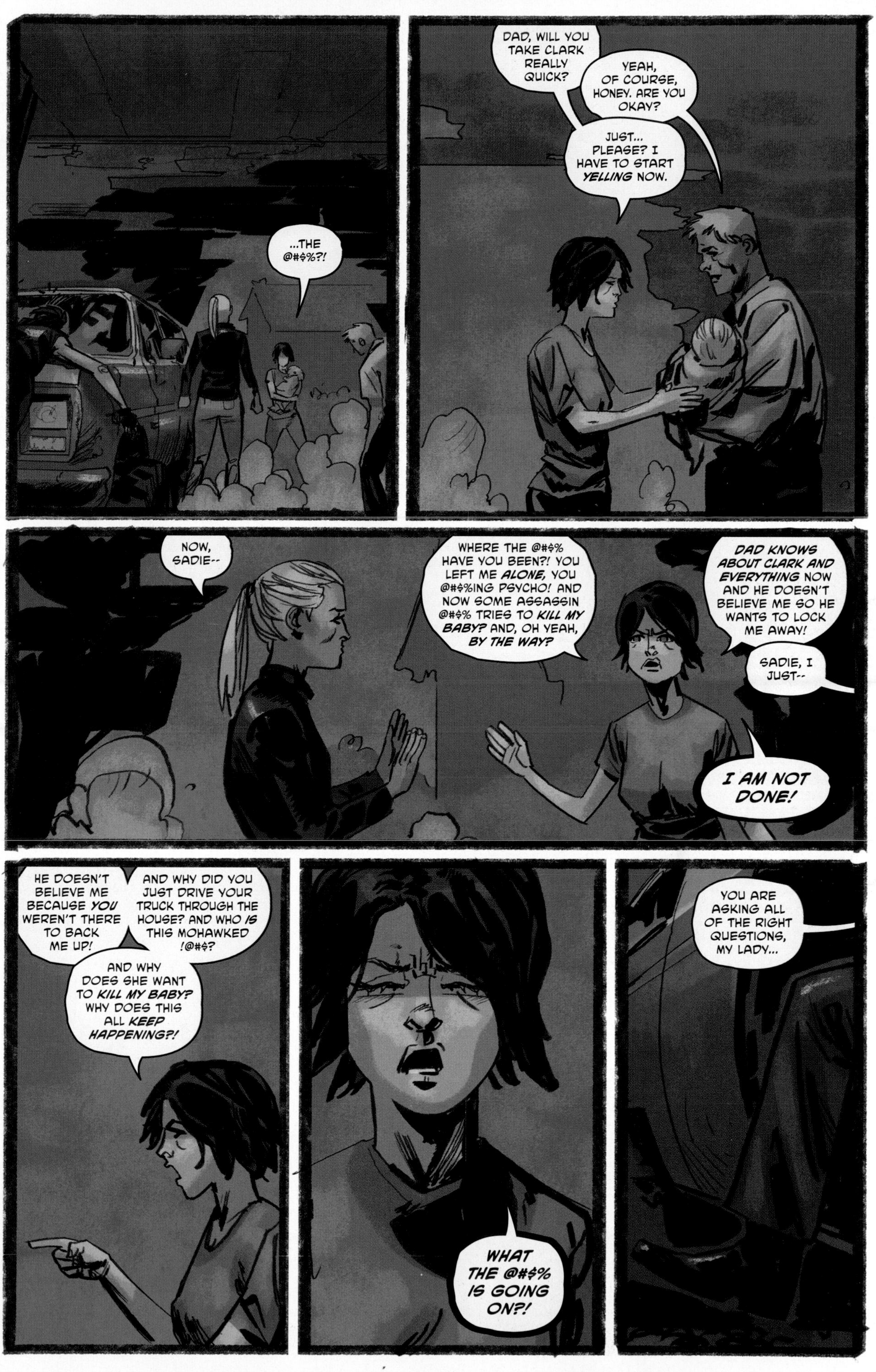
...THE @#$%?!
DAD, WILL YOU TAKE CLARK REALLY QUICK?
YEAH, OF COURSE, HONEY. ARE YOU OKAY?
JUST... PLEASE? I HAVE TO START *YELLING* NOW.
NOW, SADIE--
WHERE THE @#$% HAVE YOU BEEN?! YOU LEFT ME *ALONE,* YOU @#$%ING PSYCHO! AND NOW SOME ASSASSIN @#$% TRIES TO *KILL MY BABY?* AND, OH YEAH, *BY THE WAY?*
DAD KNOWS ABOUT CLARK AND EVERYTHING NOW AND HE DOESN'T BELIEVE ME SO HE WANTS TO LOCK ME AWAY!
SADIE, I JUST--
I AM NOT DONE!
HE DOESN'T BELIEVE ME BECAUSE *YOU* WEREN'T THERE TO BACK ME UP!
AND WHY DID YOU JUST DRIVE YOUR TRUCK THROUGH THE HOUSE? AND WHO *IS* THIS MOHAWKED !@#$?
AND WHY DOES SHE WANT TO *KILL MY BABY?* WHY DOES THIS ALL *KEEP HAPPENING?!*
WHAT THE @#$% IS GOING ON?!
YOU ARE ASKING ALL OF THE RIGHT QUESTIONS, MY LADY...

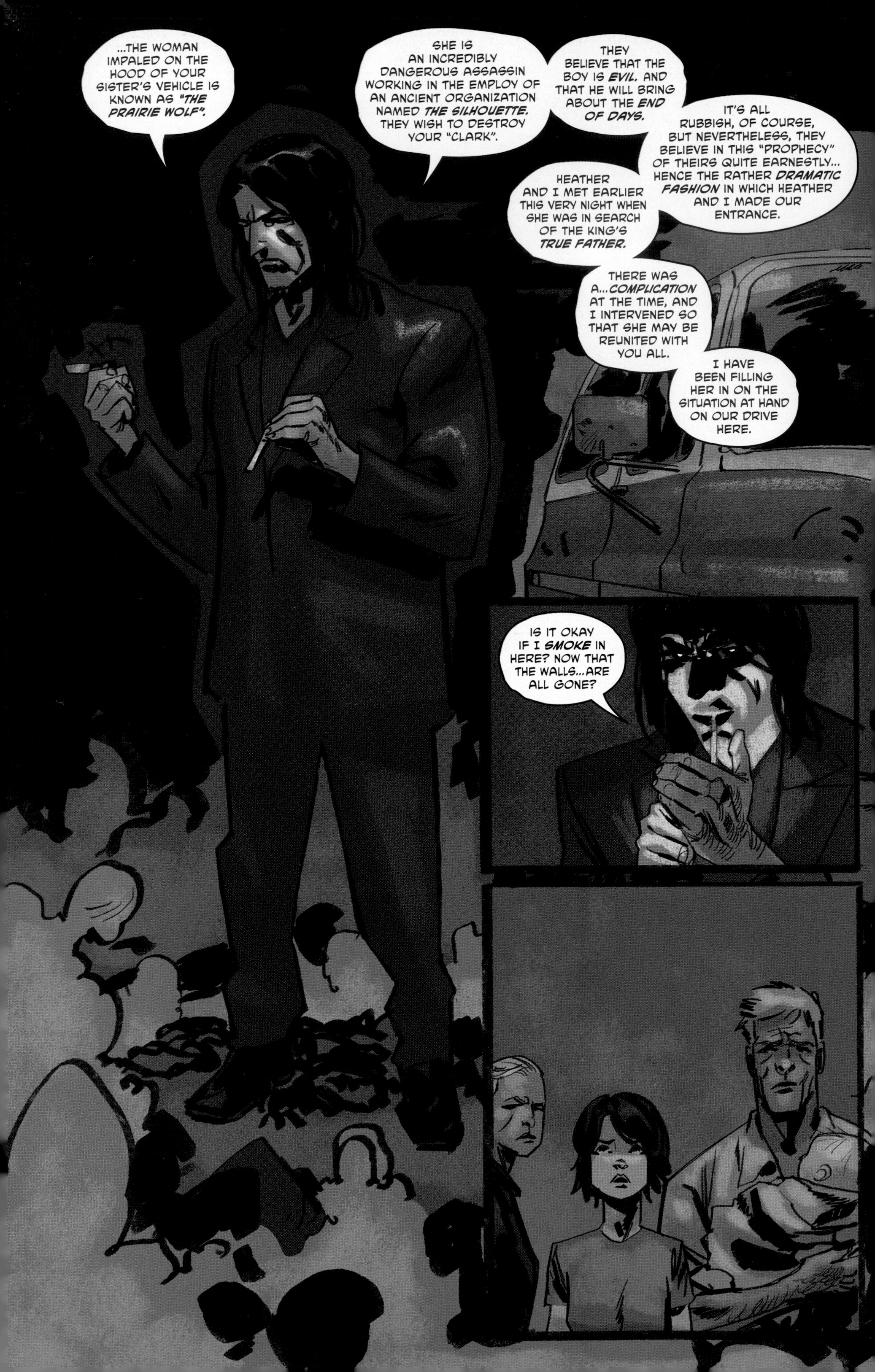
...THE WOMAN IMPALED ON THE HOOD OF YOUR SISTER'S VEHICLE IS KNOWN AS *"THE PRAIRIE WOLF"*.
SHE IS AN INCREDIBLY DANGEROUS ASSASSIN WORKING IN THE EMPLOY OF AN ANCIENT ORGANIZATION NAMED *THE SILHOUETTE.* THEY WISH TO DESTROY YOUR "CLARK".
THEY BELIEVE THAT THE BOY IS *EVIL,* AND THAT HE WILL BRING ABOUT THE *END OF DAYS.*
IT'S ALL RUBBISH, OF COURSE, BUT NEVERTHELESS, THEY BELIEVE IN THIS "PROPHECY" OF THEIRS QUITE EARNESTLY... HENCE THE RATHER *DRAMATIC FASHION* IN WHICH HEATHER AND I MADE OUR ENTRANCE.
HEATHER AND I MET EARLIER THIS VERY NIGHT WHEN SHE WAS IN SEARCH OF THE KING'S *TRUE FATHER.*
THERE WAS A...*COMPLICATION* AT THE TIME, AND I INTERVENED SO THAT SHE MAY BE REUNITED WITH YOU ALL.
I HAVE BEEN FILLING HER IN ON THE SITUATION AT HAND ON OUR DRIVE HERE.
IS IT OKAY IF I *SMOKE* IN HERE? NOW THAT THE WALLS...ARE ALL GONE?

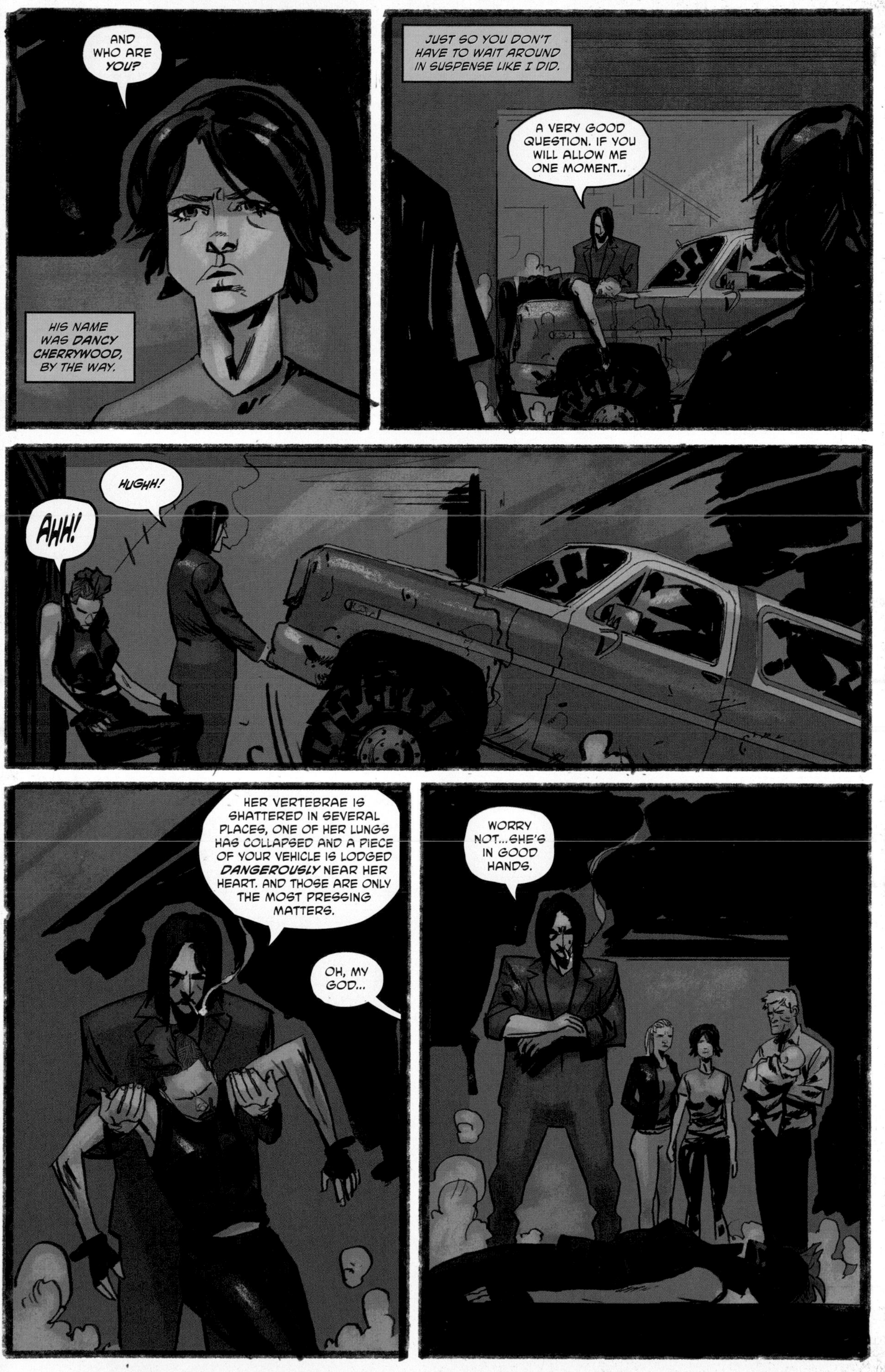

AND WHO ARE YOU?
HIS NAME WAS DANCY CHERRYWOOD, BY THE WAY.
JUST SO YOU DON'T HAVE TO WAIT AROUND IN SUSPENSE LIKE I DID.
A VERY GOOD QUESTION. IF YOU WILL ALLOW ME ONE MOMENT...
AHH!
HUGHH!
HER VERTEBRAE IS SHATTERED IN SEVERAL PLACES, ONE OF HER LUNGS HAS COLLAPSED AND A PIECE OF YOUR VEHICLE IS LODGED DANGEROUSLY NEAR HER HEART. AND THOSE ARE ONLY THE MOST PRESSING MATTERS.
OH, MY GOD...
WORRY NOT...SHE'S IN GOOD HANDS.

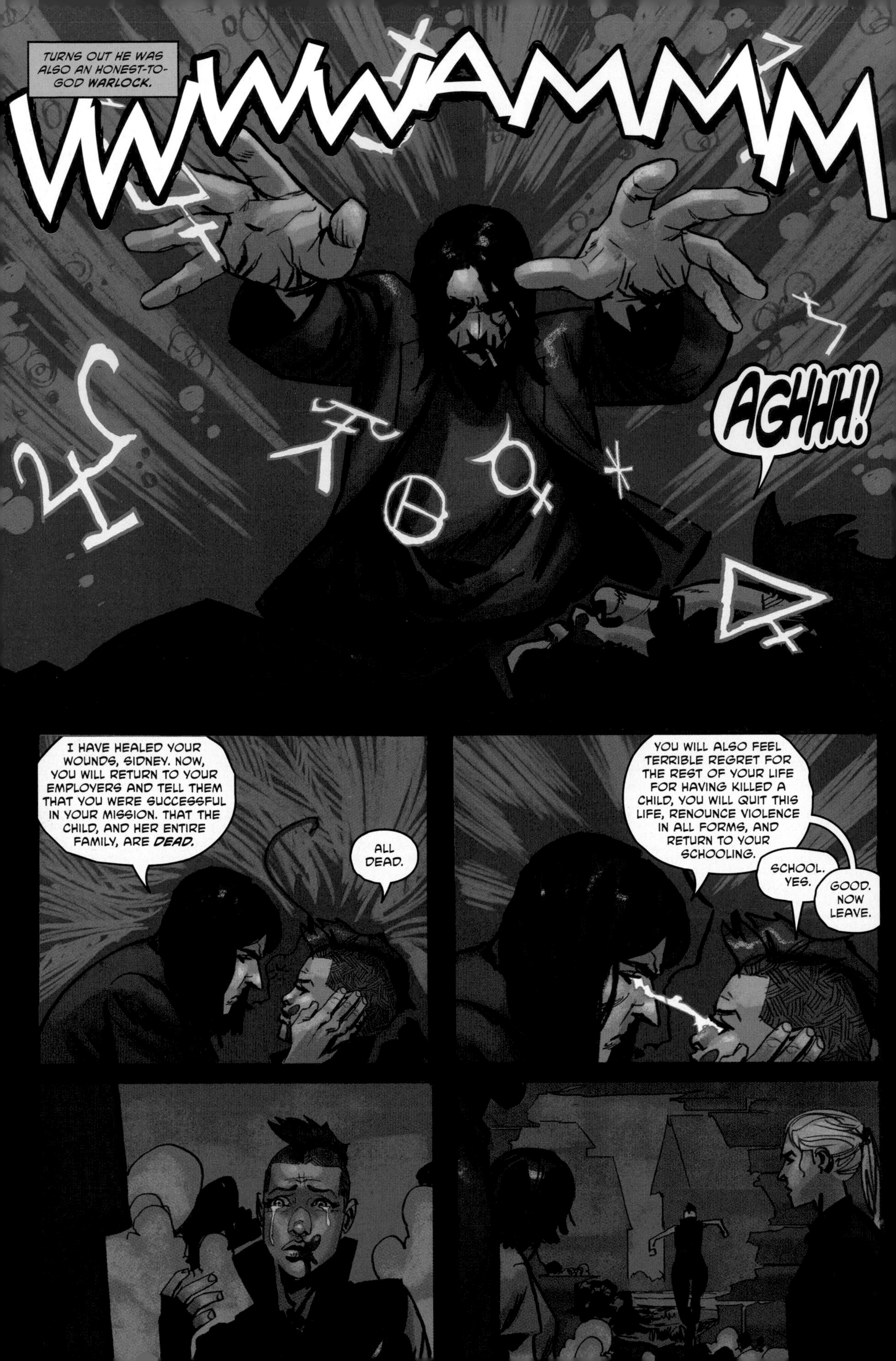

TURNS OUT HE WAS ALSO AN HONEST-TO-GOD WARLOCK.
VWWWAMMM
AGHHH!
I HAVE HEALED YOUR WOUNDS, SIDNEY. NOW, YOU WILL RETURN TO YOUR EMPLOYERS AND TELL THEM THAT YOU WERE SUCCESSFUL IN YOUR MISSION. THAT THE CHILD, AND HER ENTIRE FAMILY, ARE DEAD.
ALL DEAD.
YOU WILL ALSO FEEL TERRIBLE REGRET FOR THE REST OF YOUR LIFE FOR HAVING KILLED A CHILD, YOU WILL QUIT THIS LIFE, RENOUNCE VIOLENCE IN ALL FORMS, AND RETURN TO YOUR SCHOOLING.
SCHOOL. YES.
GOOD. NOW LEAVE.

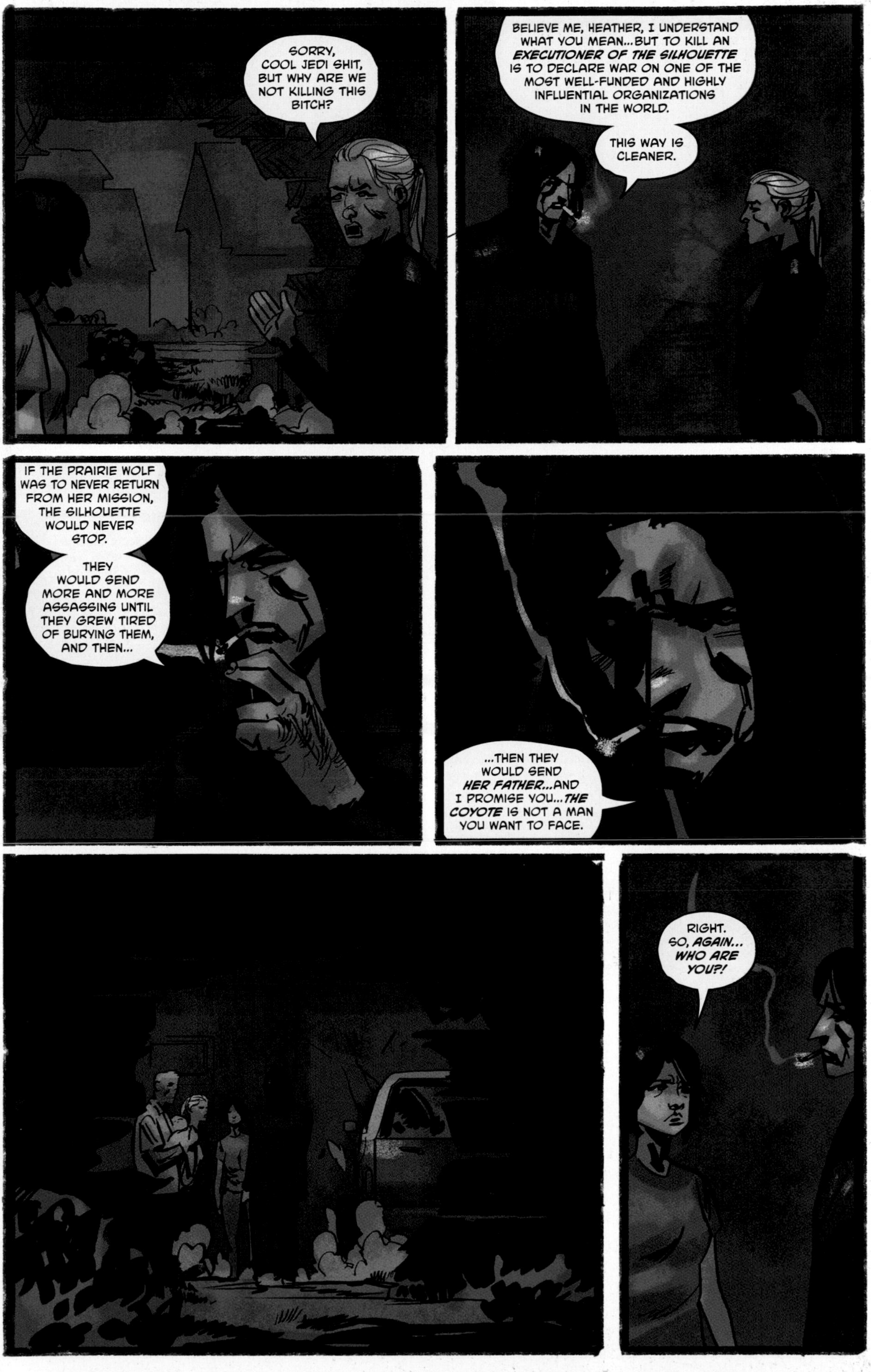
SORRY, COOL JEDI SHIT, BUT WHY ARE WE NOT KILLING THIS BITCH?
BELIEVE ME, HEATHER, I UNDERSTAND WHAT YOU MEAN...BUT TO KILL AN *EXECUTIONER OF THE SILHOUETTE* IS TO DECLARE WAR ON ONE OF THE MOST WELL-FUNDED AND HIGHLY INFLUENTIAL ORGANIZATIONS IN THE WORLD.
THIS WAY IS CLEANER.
IF THE PRAIRIE WOLF WAS TO NEVER RETURN FROM HER MISSION, THE SILHOUETTE WOULD NEVER STOP.
THEY WOULD SEND MORE AND MORE ASSASSINS UNTIL THEY GREW TIRED OF BURYING THEM, AND THEN...
...THEN THEY WOULD SEND *HER FATHER*...AND I PROMISE YOU...*THE COYOTE* IS NOT A MAN YOU WANT TO FACE.
RIGHT. SO, *AGAIN... WHO ARE YOU?!*

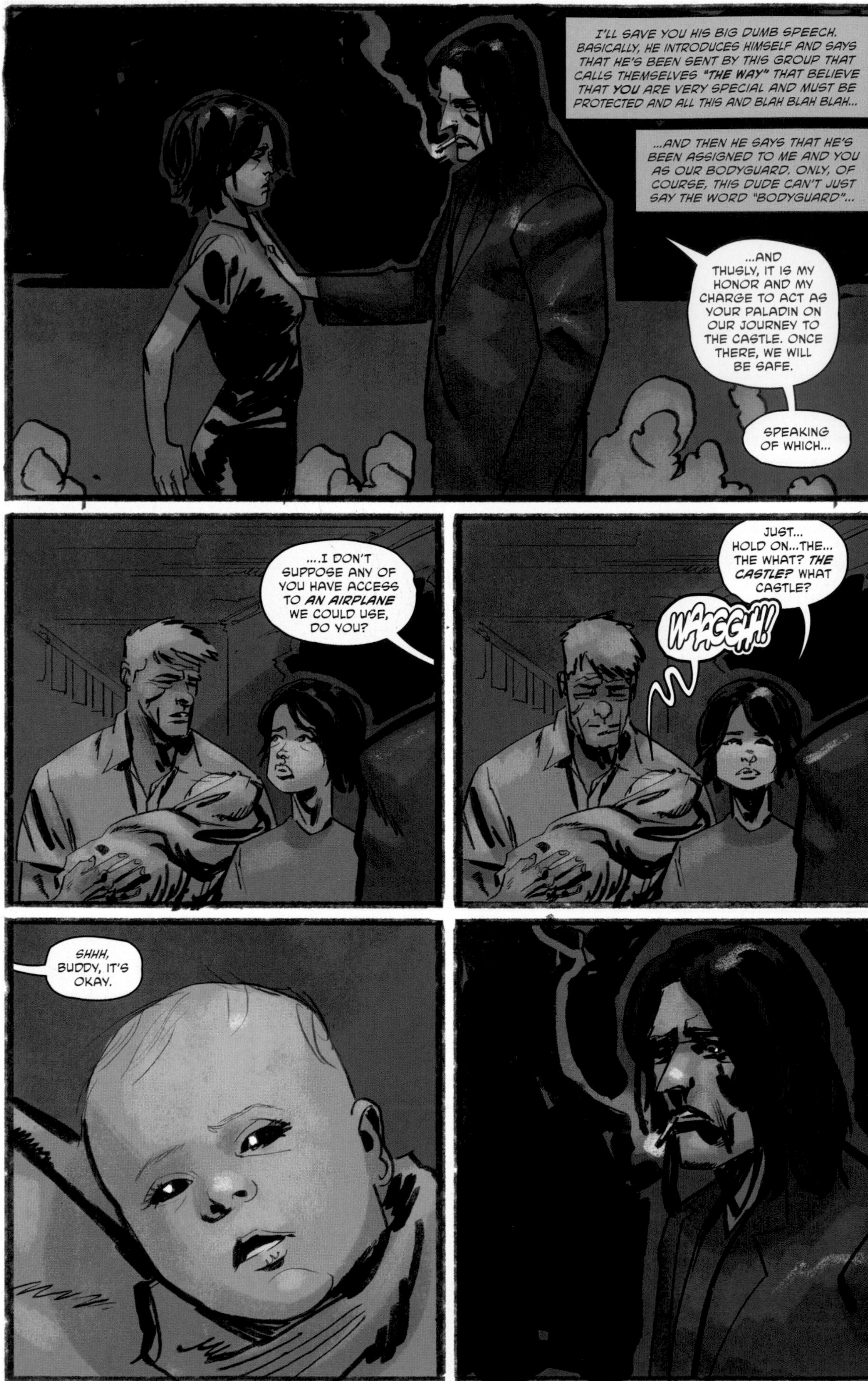
I'LL SAVE YOU HIS BIG DUMB SPEECH. BASICALLY, HE INTRODUCES HIMSELF AND SAYS THAT HE'S BEEN SENT BY THIS GROUP THAT CALLS THEMSELVES "THE WAY" THAT BELIEVE THAT YOU ARE VERY SPECIAL AND MUST BE PROTECTED AND ALL THIS AND BLAH BLAH BLAH...
...AND THEN HE SAYS THAT HE'S BEEN ASSIGNED TO ME AND YOU AS OUR BODYGUARD. ONLY, OF COURSE, THIS DUDE CAN'T JUST SAY THE WORD "BODYGUARD"...
...AND THUSLY, IT IS MY HONOR AND MY CHARGE TO ACT AS YOUR PALADIN ON OUR JOURNEY TO THE CASTLE. ONCE THERE, WE WILL BE SAFE.
SPEAKING OF WHICH...
....I DON'T SUPPOSE ANY OF YOU HAVE ACCESS TO AN AIRPLANE WE COULD USE, DO YOU?
JUST... HOLD ON...THE... THE WHAT? THE CASTLE? WHAT CASTLE?
WAAGGH!!
SHHH, BUDDY, IT'S OKAY.

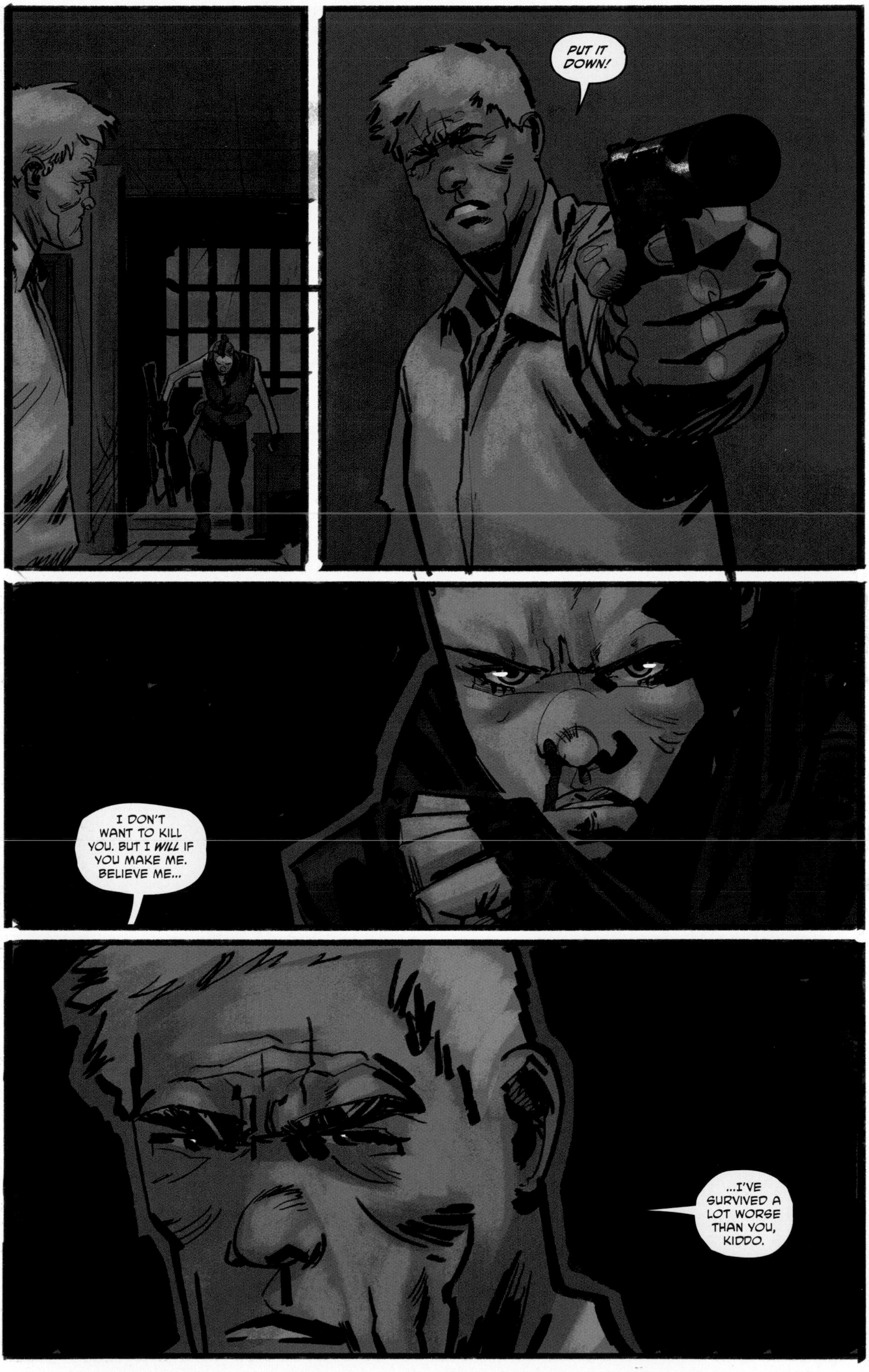
PUT IT DOWN!
I DON'T WANT TO KILL YOU. BUT I WILL IF YOU MAKE ME. BELIEVE ME...
...I'VE SURVIVED A LOT WORSE THAN YOU, KIDDO.

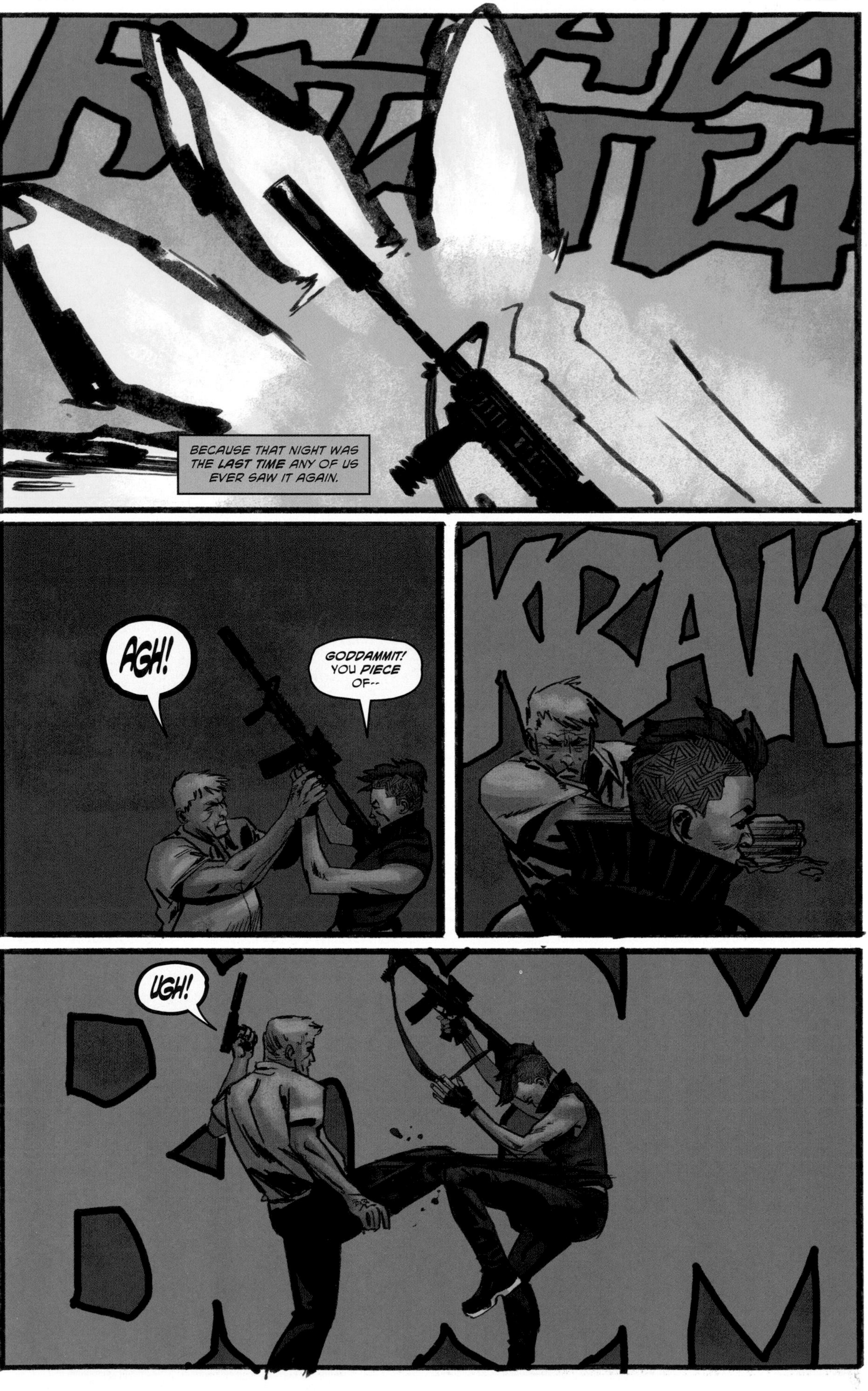
BECAUSE THAT NIGHT WAS THE **LAST TIME** ANY OF US EVER SAW IT AGAIN.
AGH!
GODDAMMIT! YOU *PIECE* OF--
KRAK
UGH!

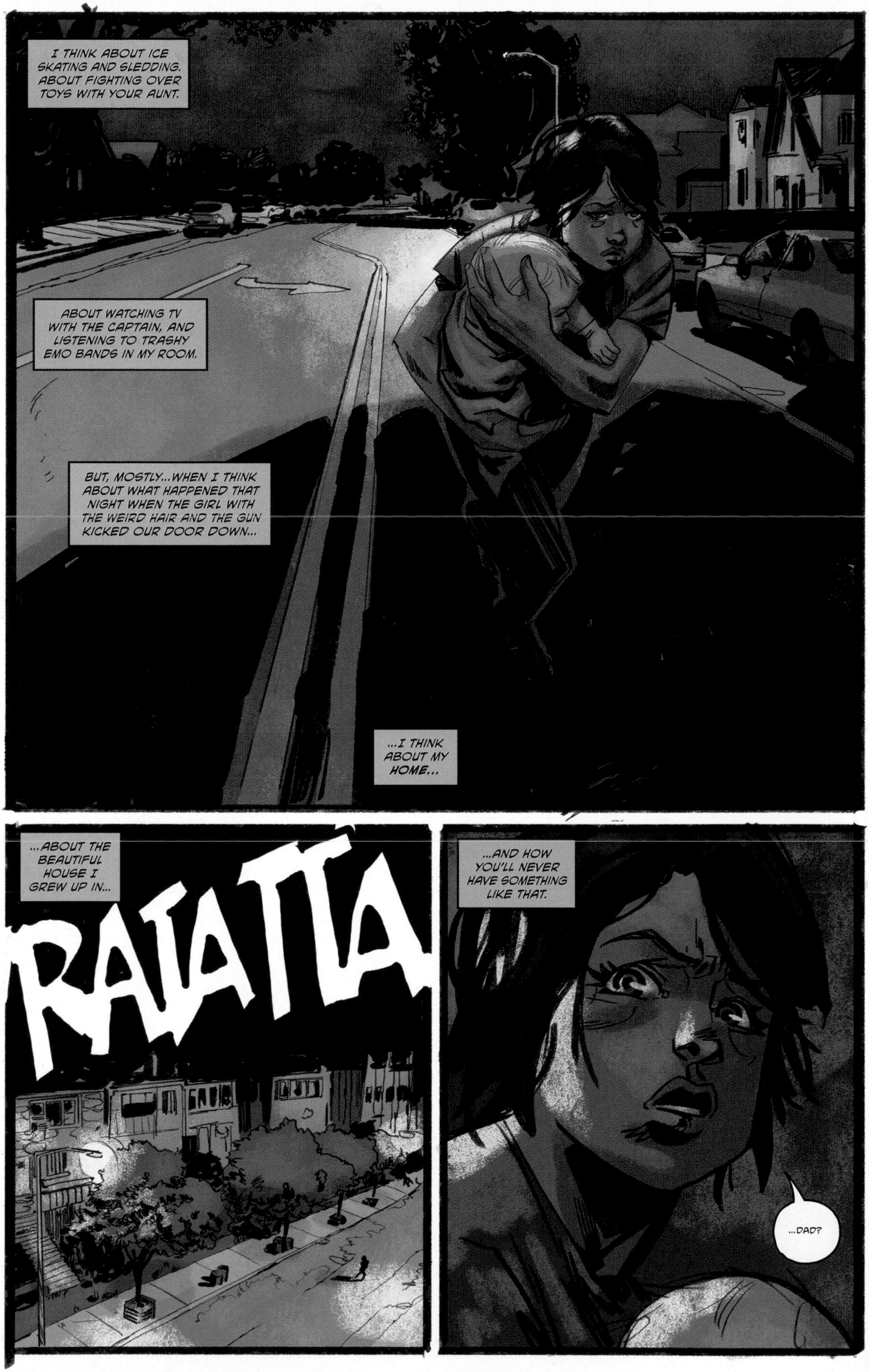
I THINK ABOUT ICE SKATING AND SLEDDING. ABOUT FIGHTING OVER TOYS WITH YOUR AUNT.
ABOUT WATCHING TV WITH THE CAPTAIN, AND LISTENING TO TRASHY EMO BANDS IN MY ROOM.
BUT, MOSTLY...WHEN I THINK ABOUT WHAT HAPPENED THAT NIGHT WHEN THE GIRL WITH THE WEIRD HAIR AND THE GUN KICKED OUR DOOR DOWN...
...I THINK ABOUT MY HOME...
...ABOUT THE BEAUTIFUL HOUSE I GREW UP IN...
RATATTA
...AND HOW YOU'LL NEVER HAVE SOMETHING LIKE THAT.
...DAD?

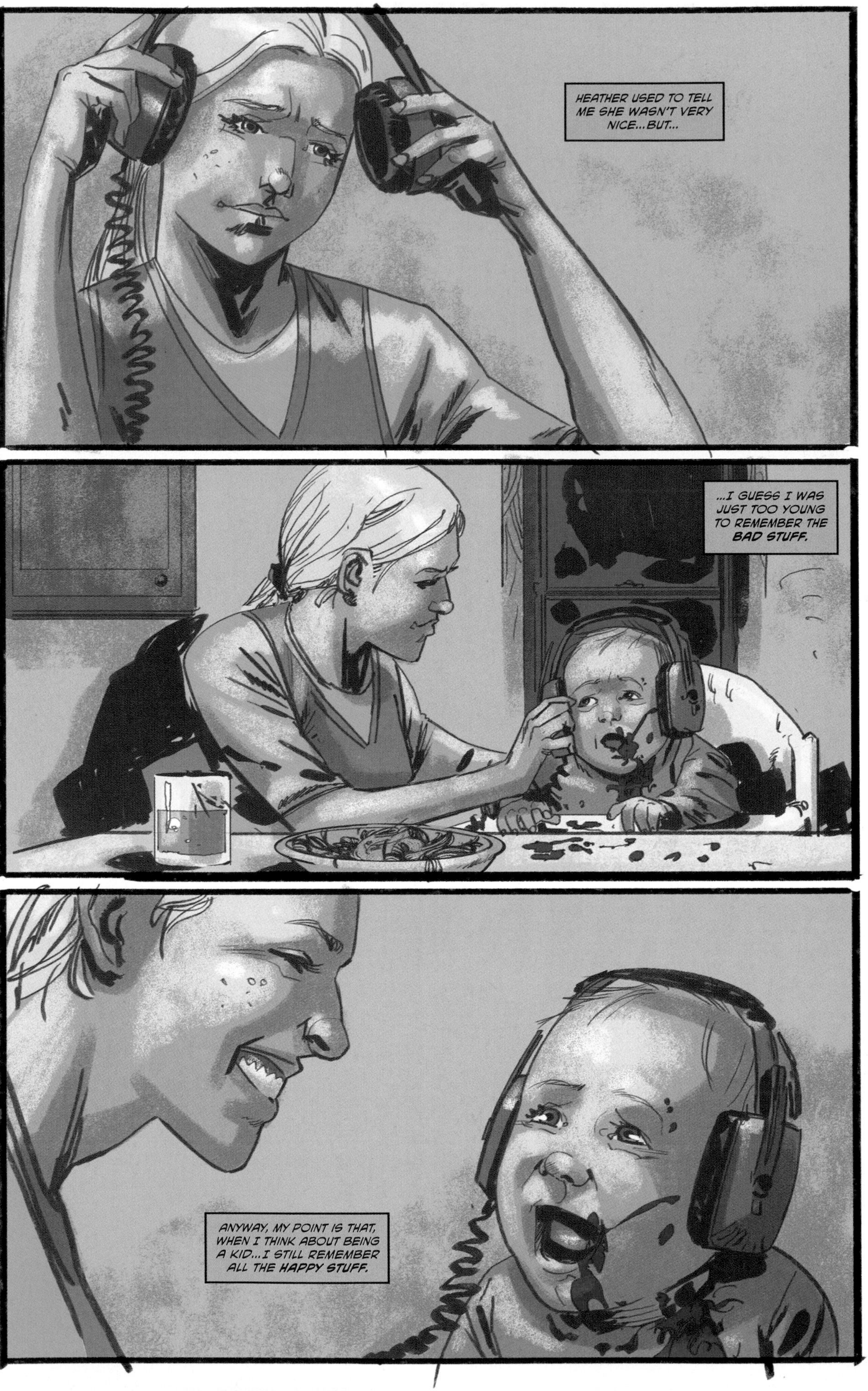
HEATHER USED TO TELL ME SHE WASN'T VERY NICE...BUT...
...I GUESS I WAS JUST TOO YOUNG TO REMEMBER THE BAD STUFF.
ANYWAY, MY POINT IS THAT, WHEN I THINK ABOUT BEING A KID...I STILL REMEMBER ALL THE HAPPY STUFF.

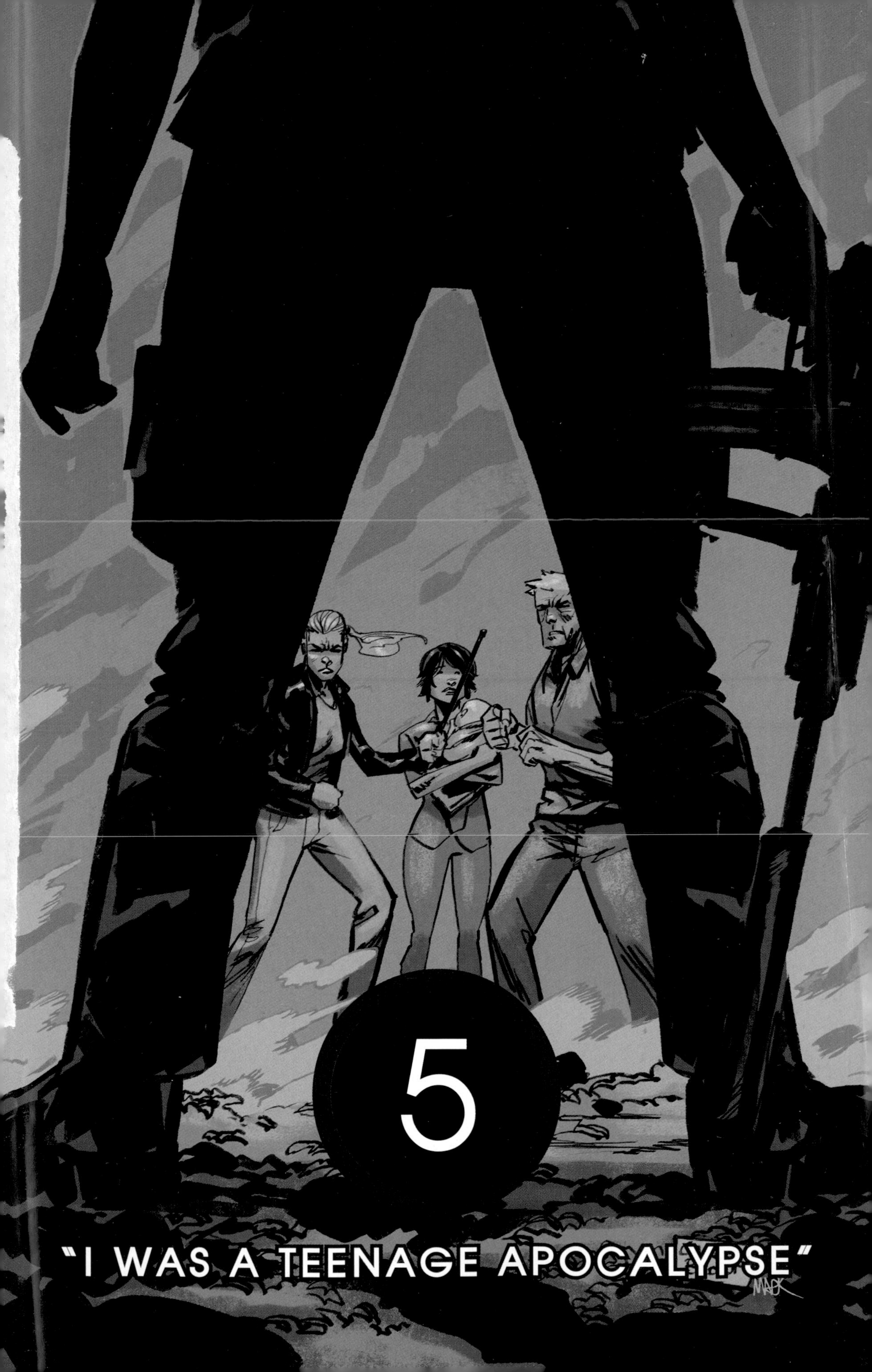
5
"I WAS A TEENAGE APOCALYPSE"
MACK

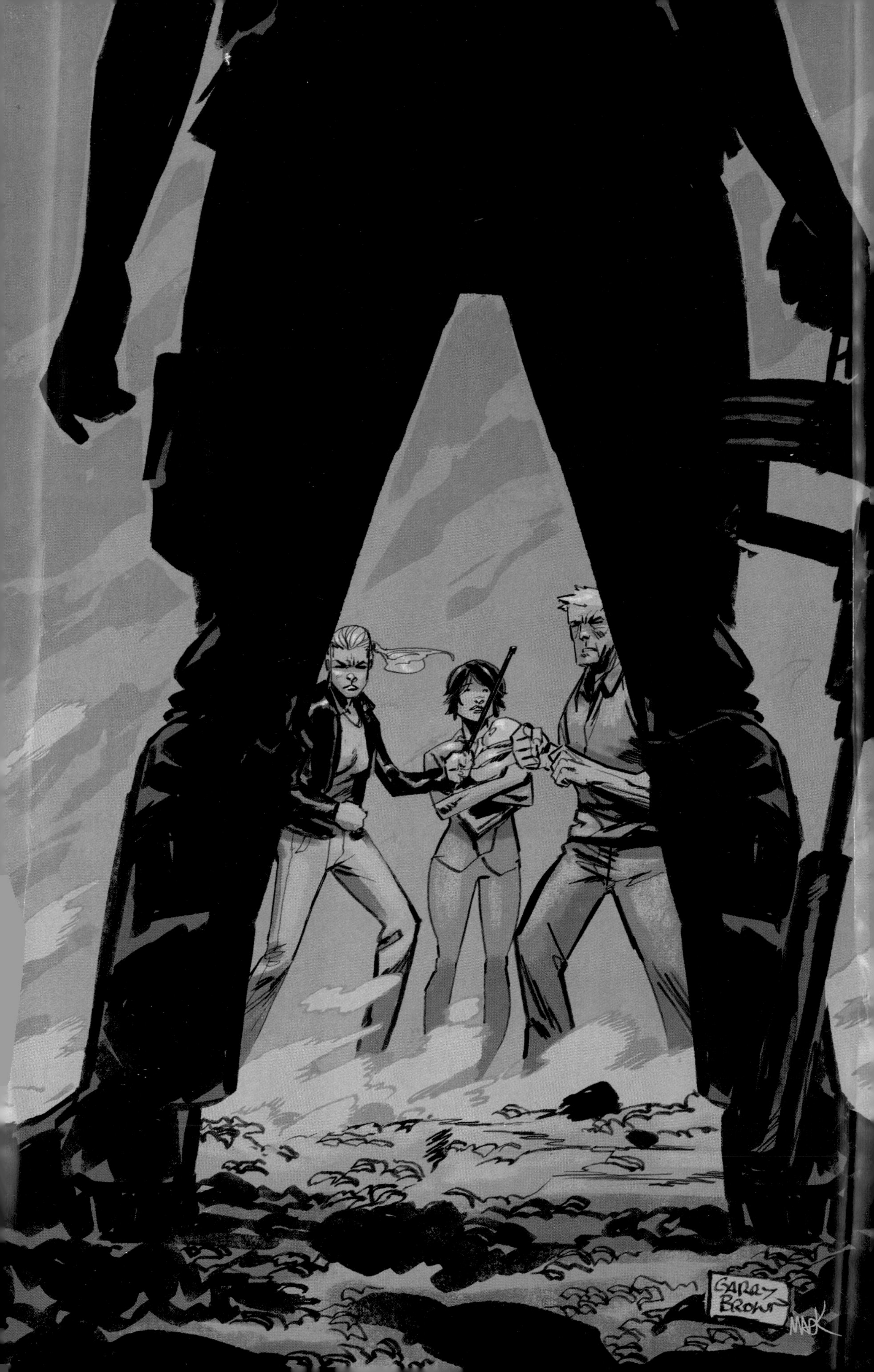
GARRY BROWN
MACK

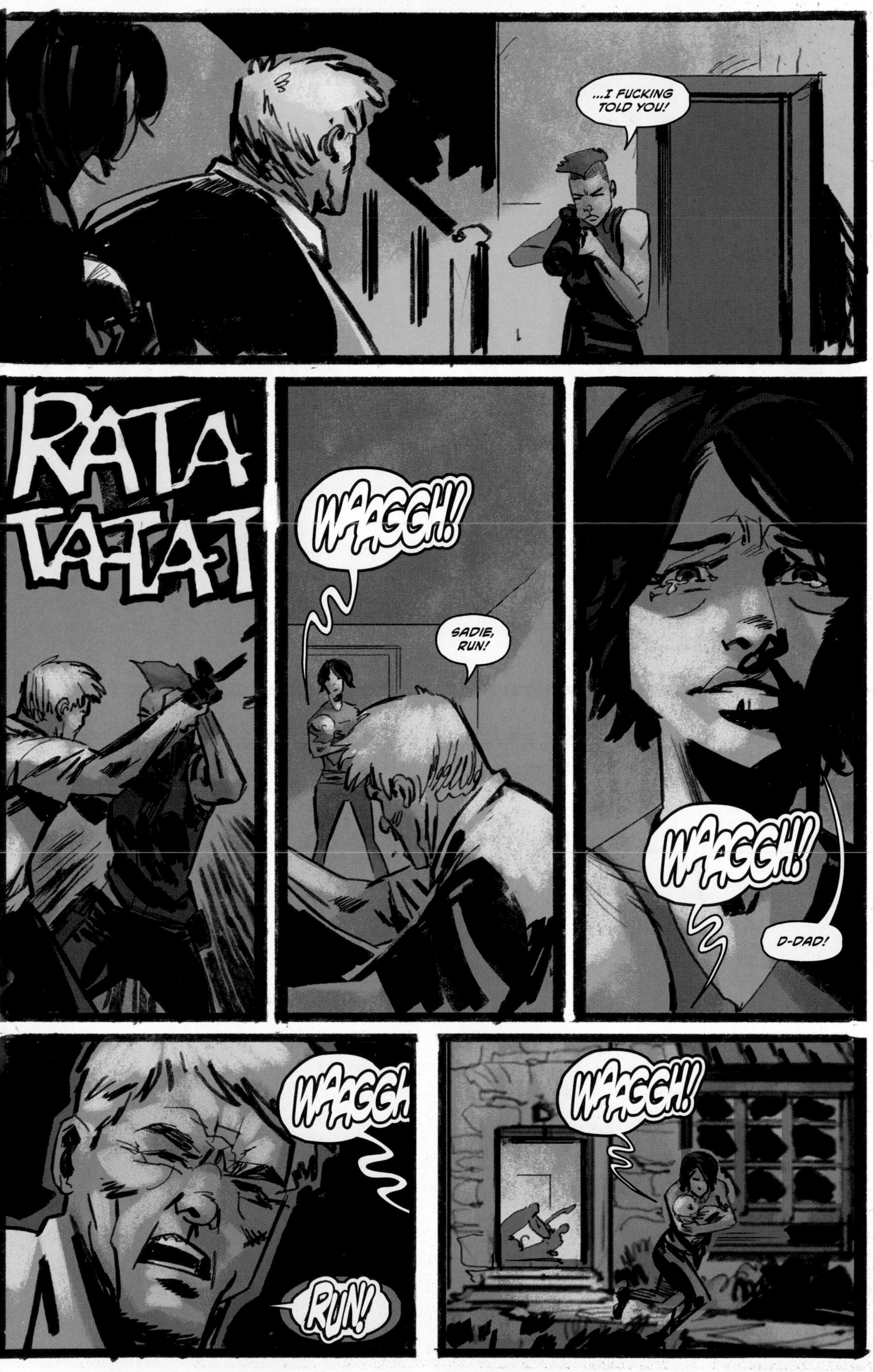
...I FUCKING TOLD YOU!
RATA TA-TA-TAT
WAAGGH!
SADIE, RUN!
WAAGGH!
D-DAD!
WAAGGH
RUN!
WAAGGH!

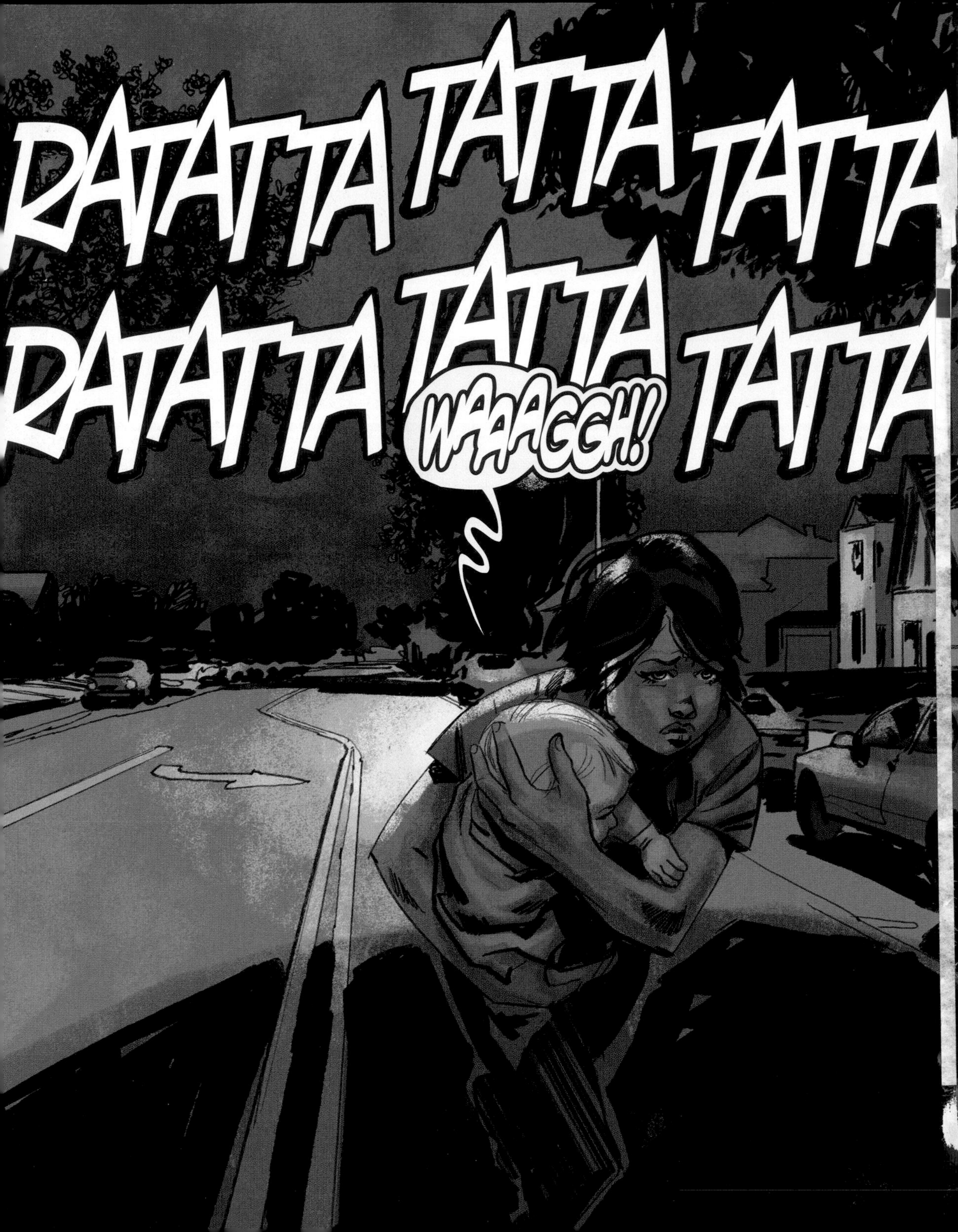
RATATTA TATTA TATTA
RATATTA TATTA TATTA
WAAAGGH!!

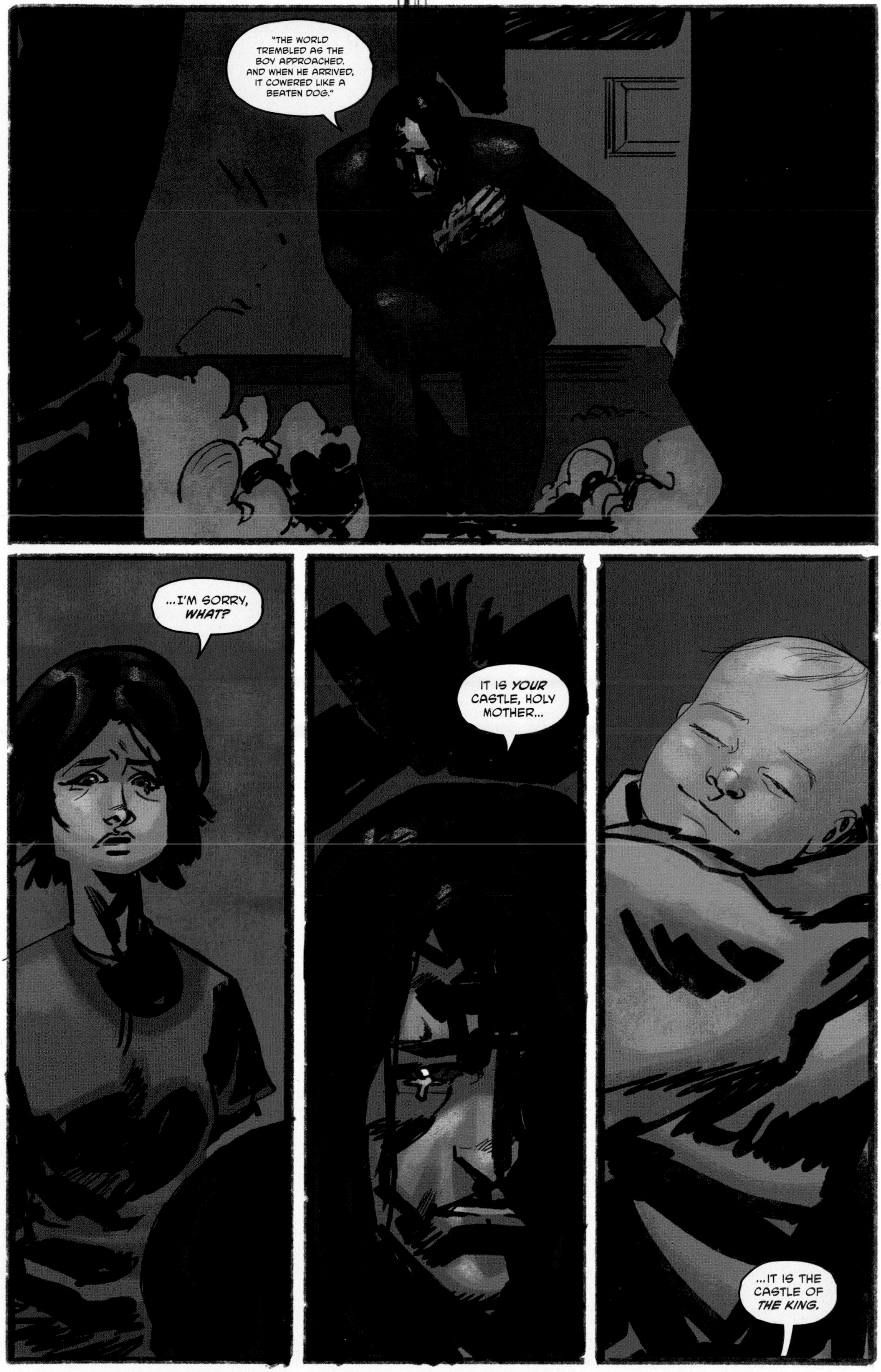
"THE WORLD TREMBLED AS THE BOY APPROACHED. AND WHEN HE ARRIVED, IT COWERED LIKE A BEATEN DOG."
...I'M SORRY, WHAT?
IT IS YOUR CASTLE, HOLY MOTHER...
...IT IS THE CASTLE OF THE KING.

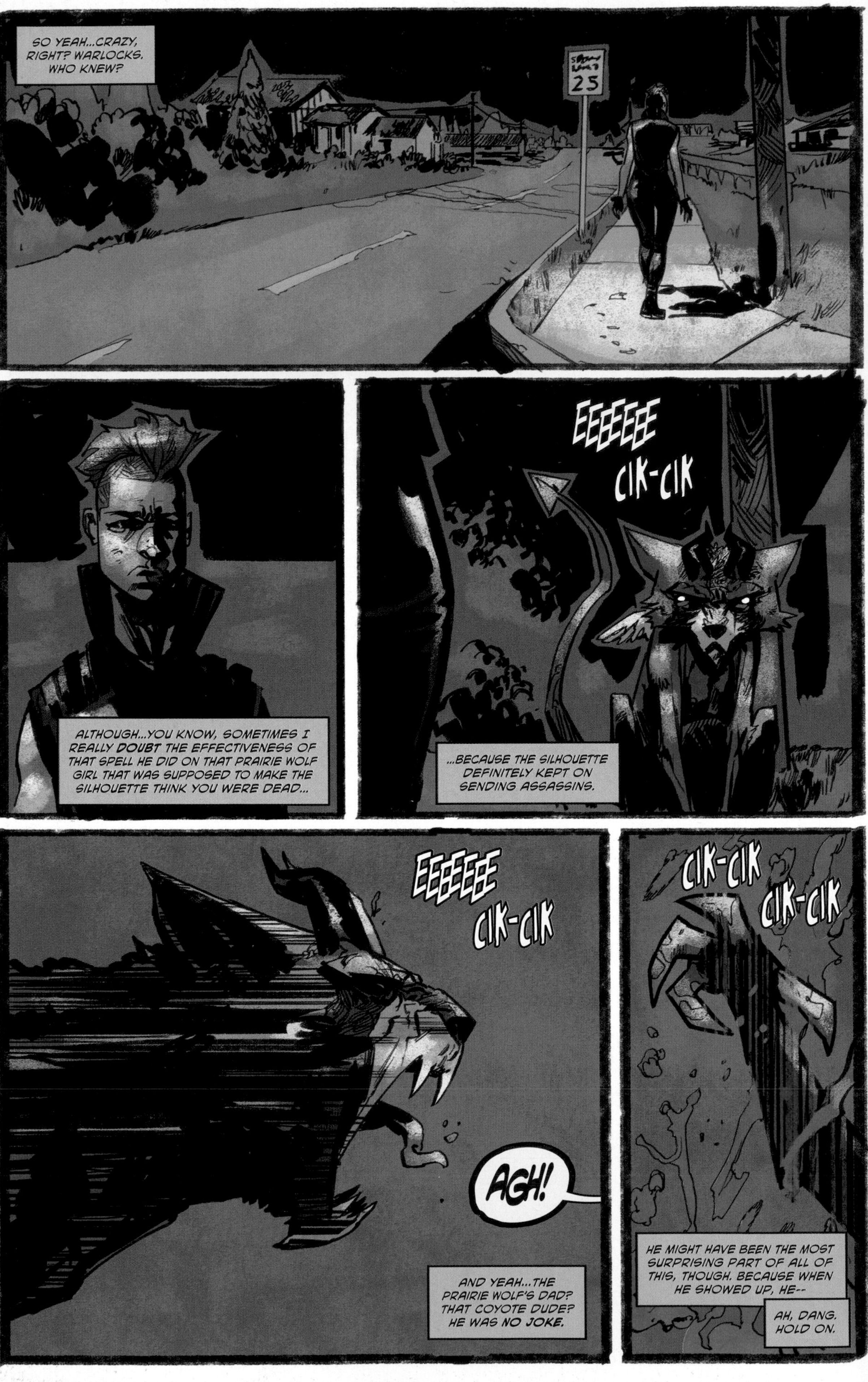
SO YEAH...CRAZY, RIGHT? WARLOCKS. WHO KNEW?
25
ALTHOUGH...YOU KNOW, SOMETIMES I REALLY DOUBT THE EFFECTIVENESS OF THAT SPELL HE DID ON THAT PRAIRIE WOLF GIRL THAT WAS SUPPOSED TO MAKE THE SILHOUETTE THINK YOU WERE DEAD...
EEEEEEE
CIK-CIK
...BECAUSE THE SILHOUETTE DEFINITELY KEPT ON SENDING ASSASSINS.
EEEEEEE
CIK-CIK
AGH!
AND YEAH...THE PRAIRIE WOLF'S DAD? THAT COYOTE DUDE? HE WAS NO JOKE.
CIK-CIK
CIK-CIK
HE MIGHT HAVE BEEN THE MOST SURPRISING PART OF ALL OF THIS, THOUGH. BECAUSE WHEN HE SHOWED UP, HE--
AH, DANG. HOLD ON.

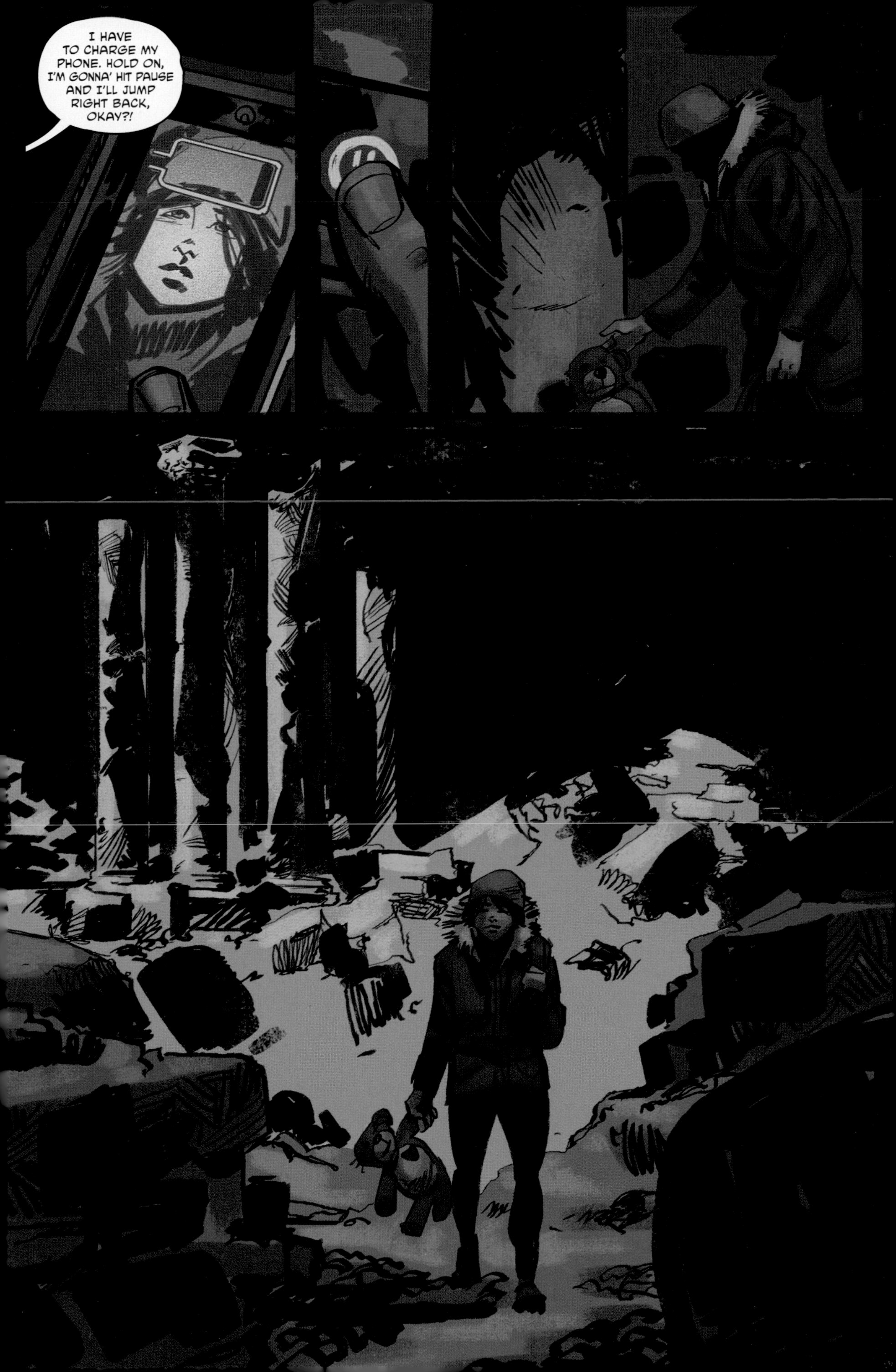
I HAVE TO CHARGE MY PHONE. HOLD ON, I'M GONNA' HIT PAUSE AND I'LL JUMP RIGHT BACK, OKAY?!

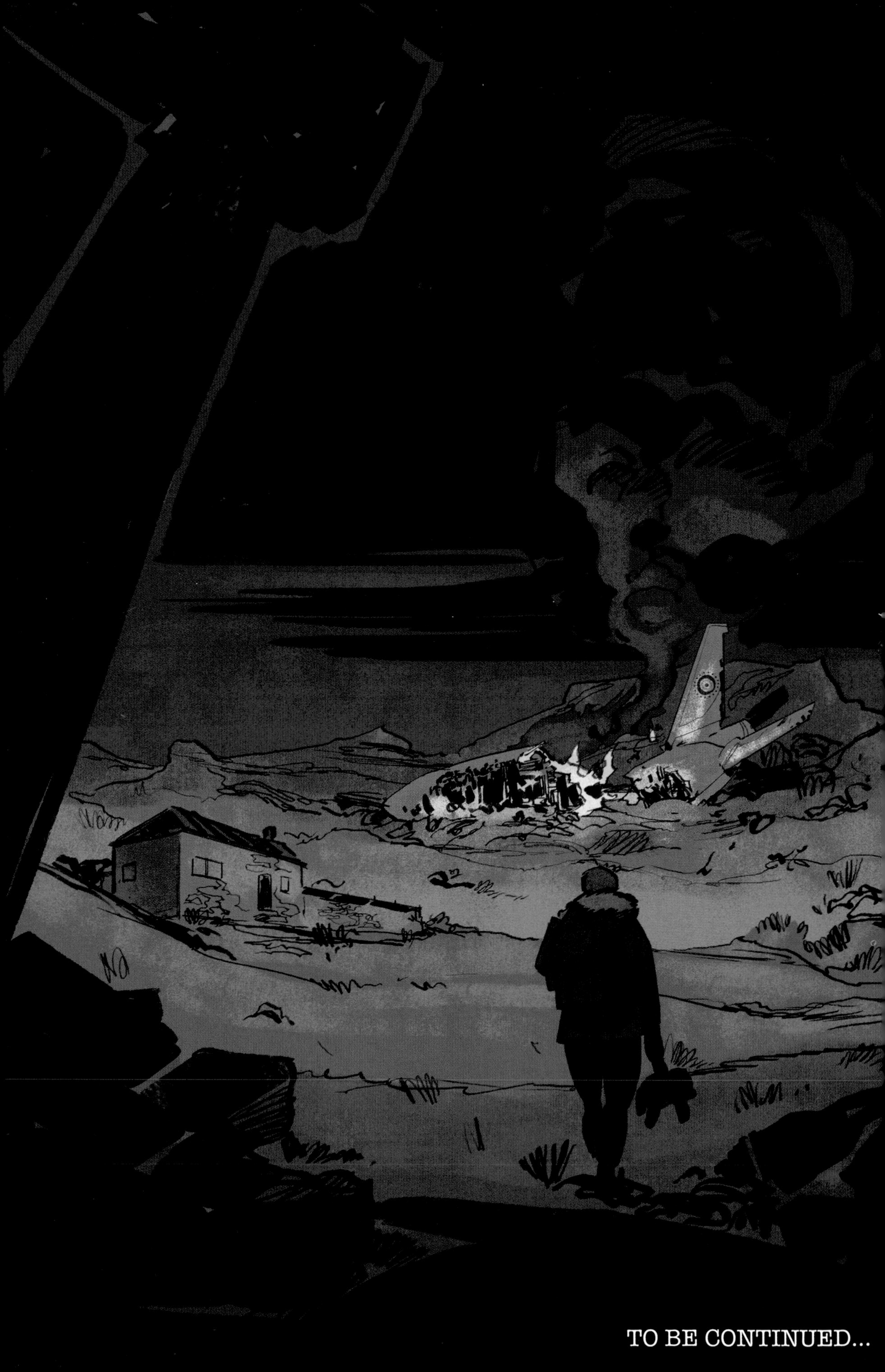
TO BE CONTINUED...

BABY+ᴇᴇTH

COVER GALLERY

Issue 1
Cover B
ELIZABETH TORQUE

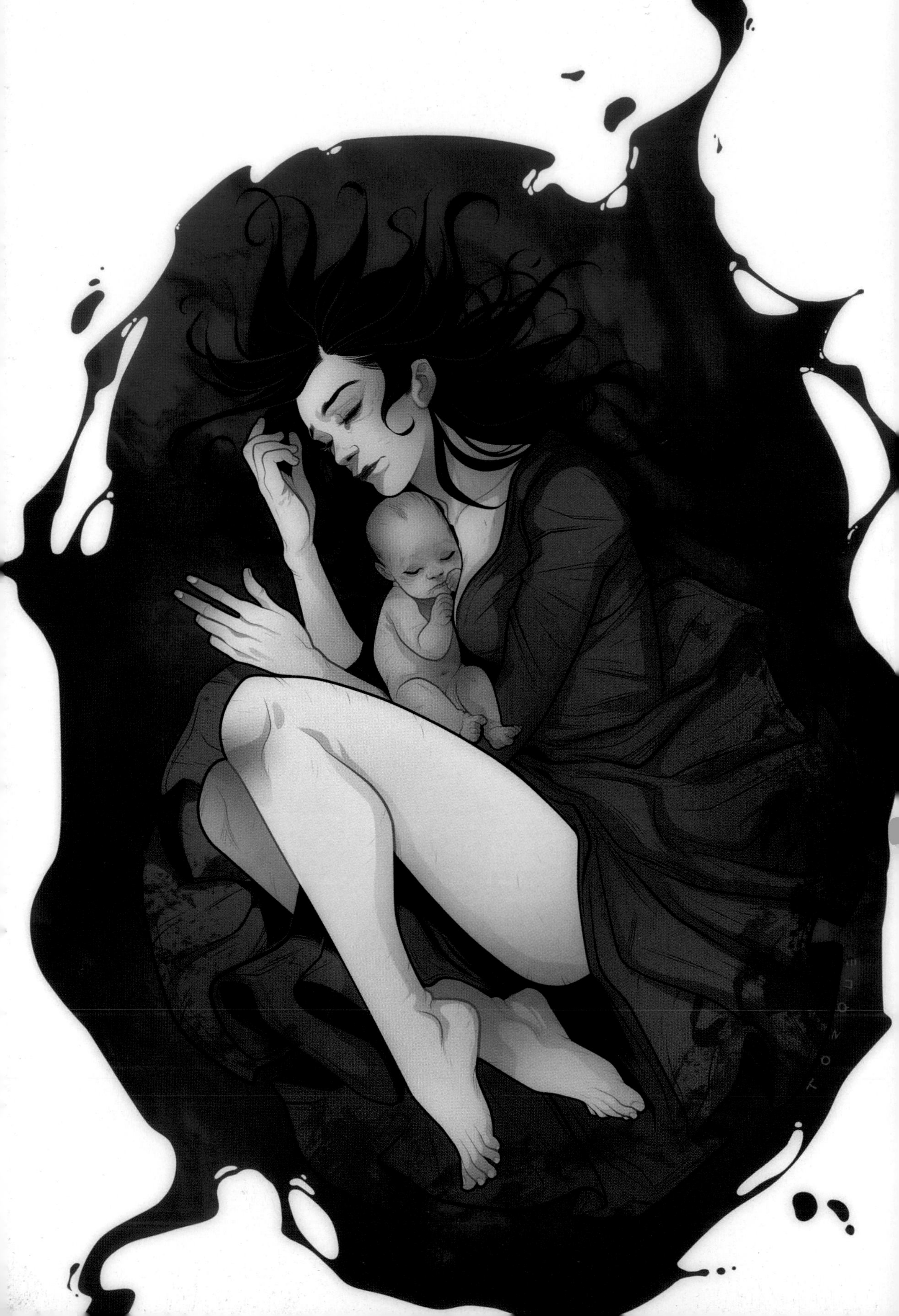
TORQUE

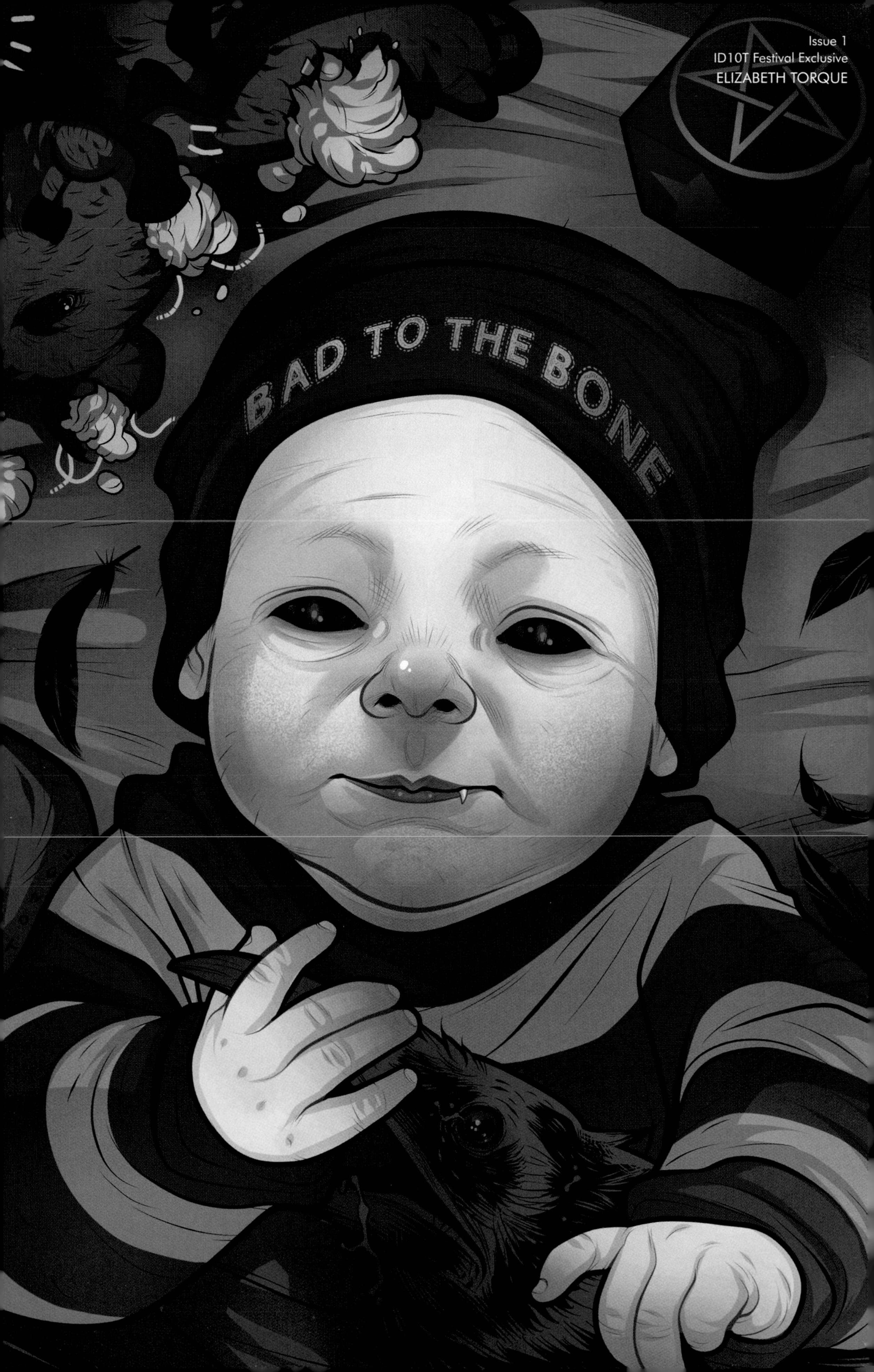
Issue 1
ID10T Festival Exclusive
ELIZABETH TORQUE
BAD TO THE BONE

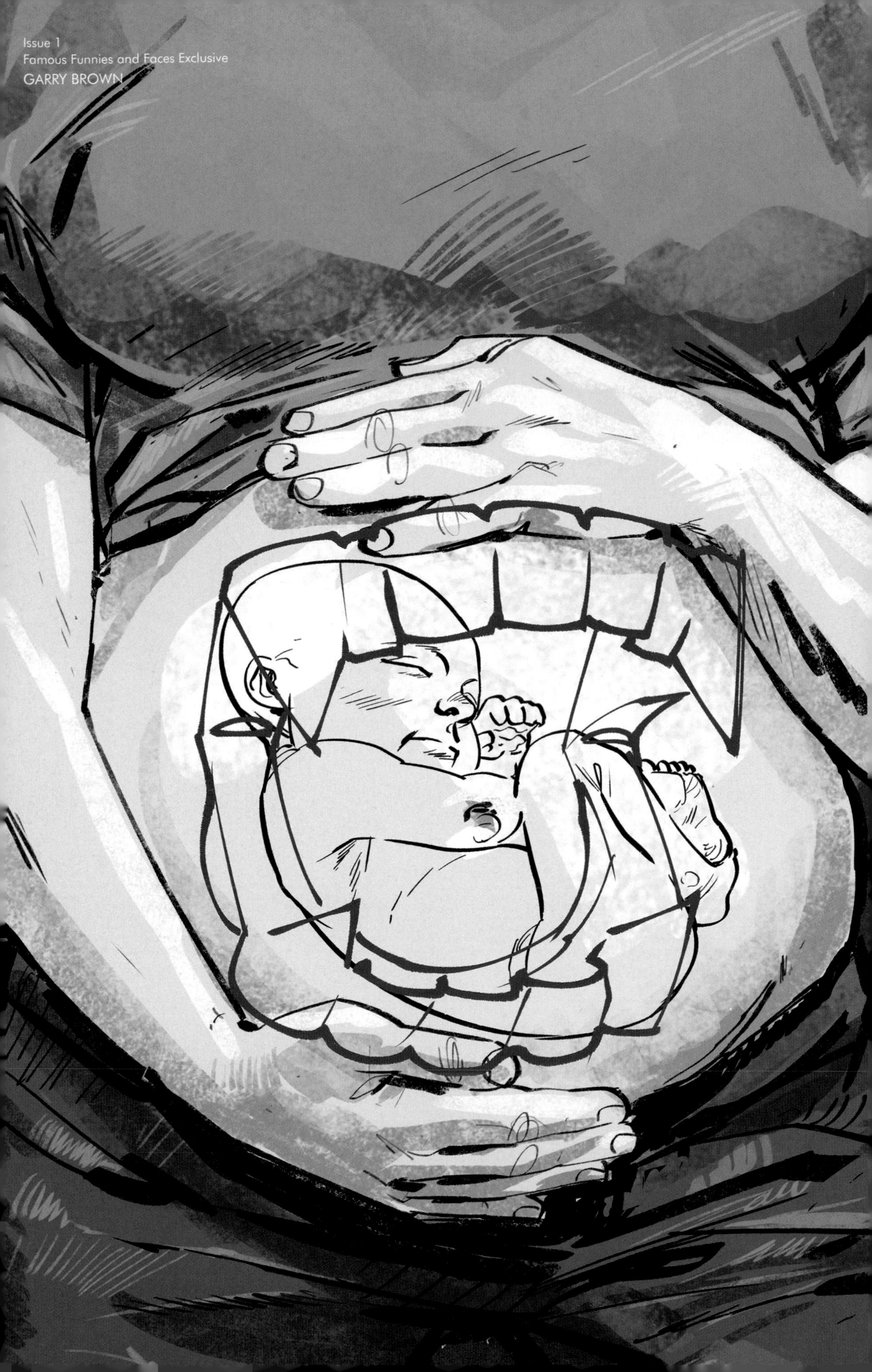
Issue 1
Famous Funnies and Faces Exclusive
GARRY BROWN

Issue 1
Jet Pack Comics / Forbidden Planet UK Exclusive
JUAN DOE

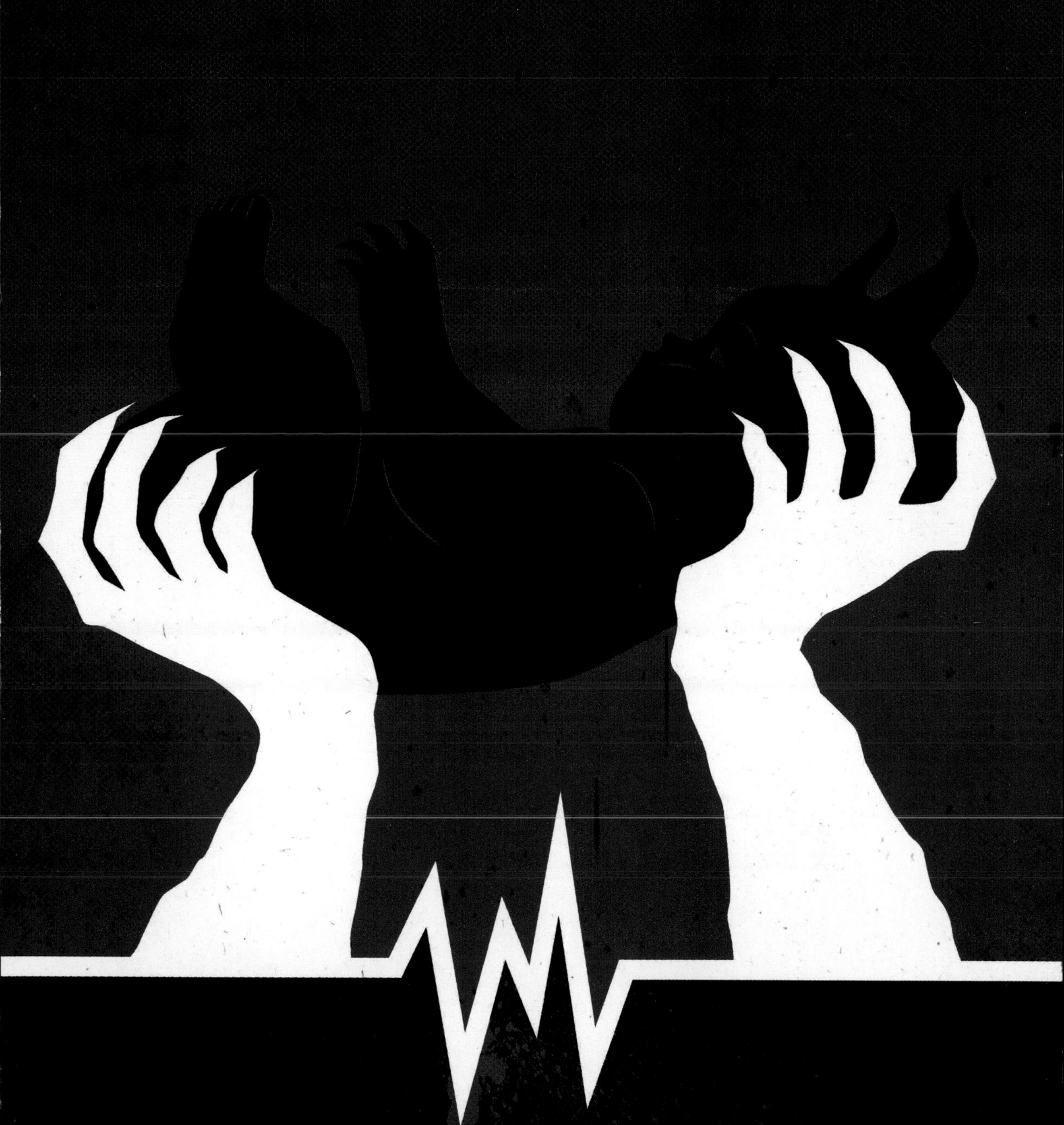
TM

Issue 1
Lenticular Cover A - Frankie's Comics
MIKE ROOTH

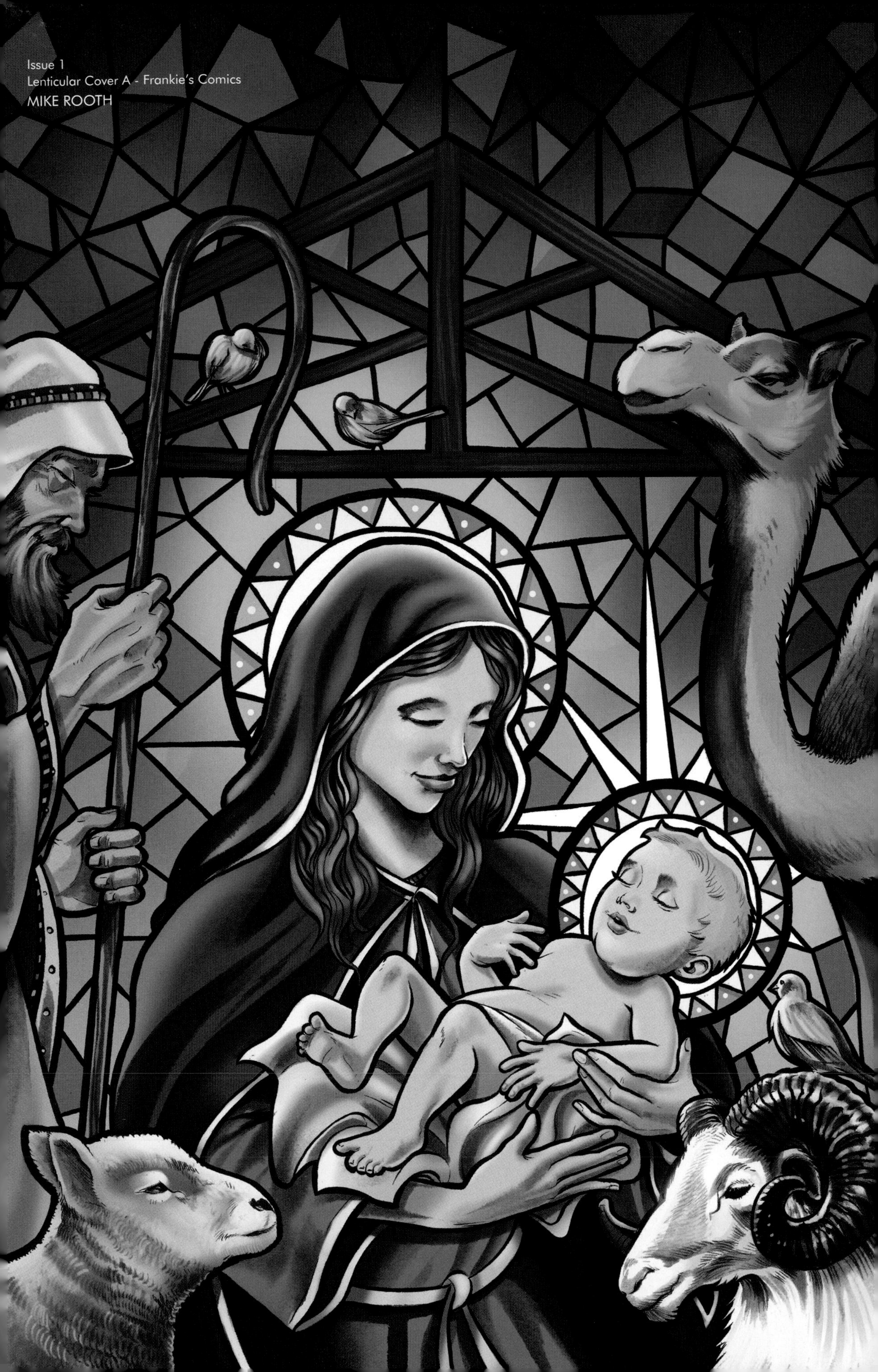

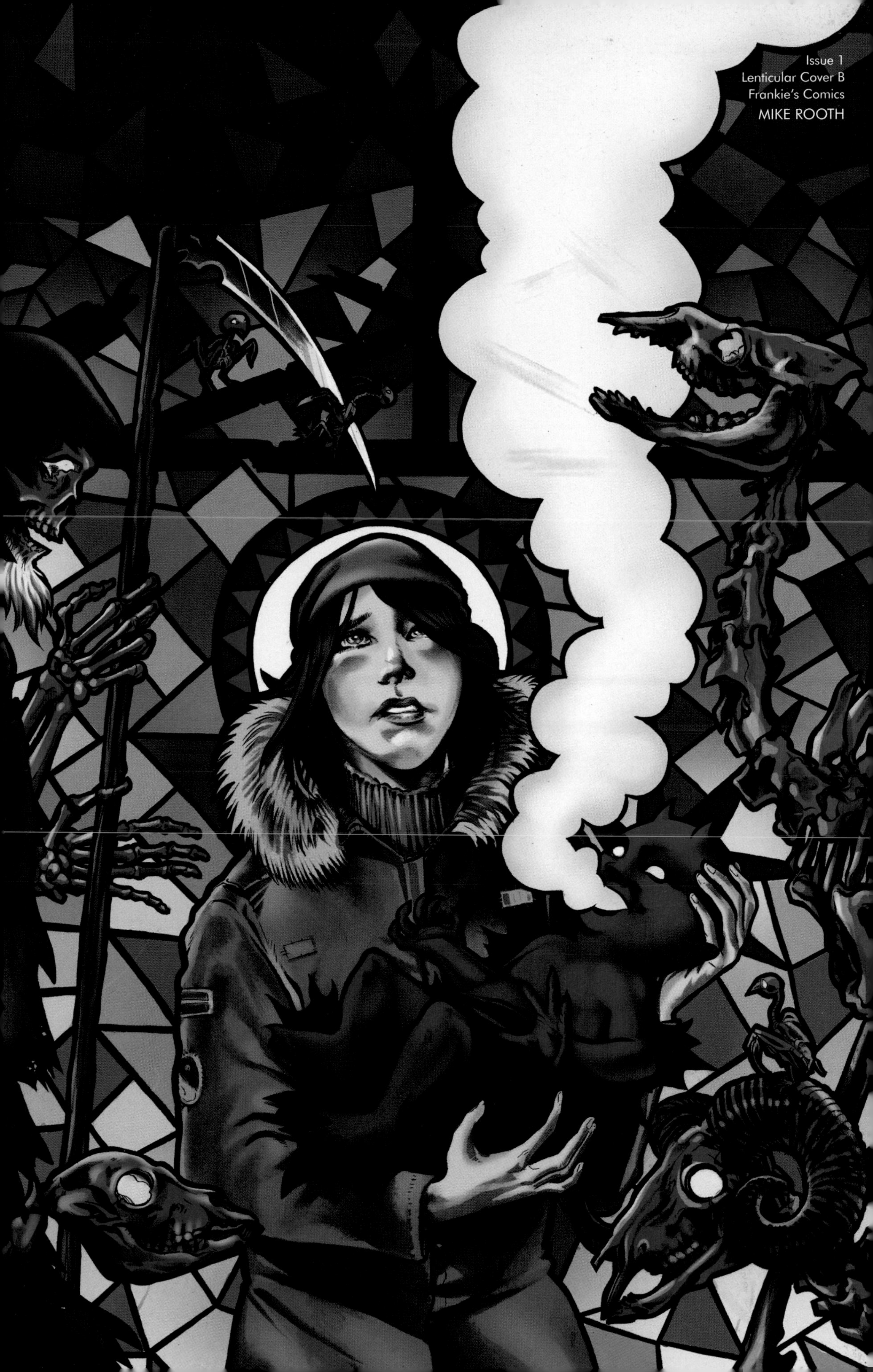
Issue 1
Lenticular Cover B
Frankie's Comics
MIKE ROOTH

Issue 1
Gotham Central Exclusive
Cover A
NAT JONES

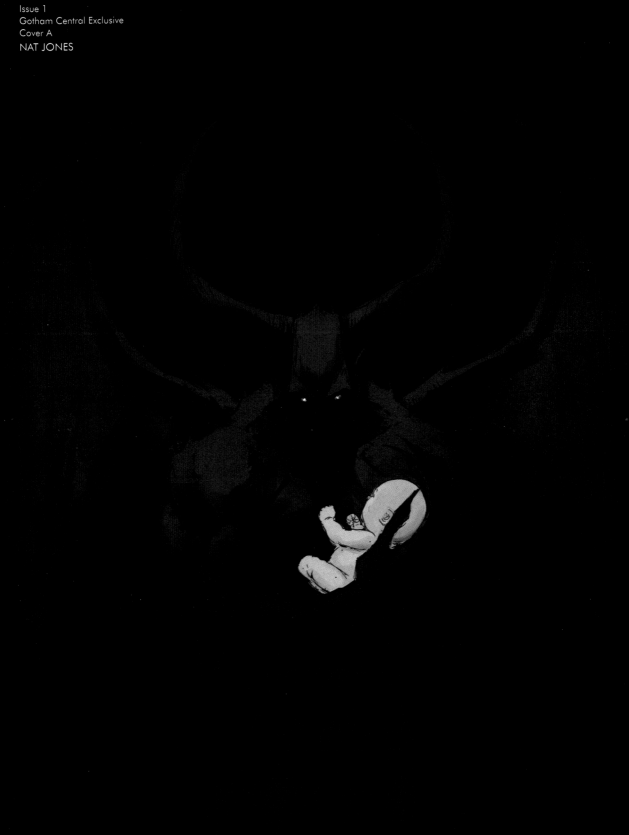

Issue 1
Gotham Central Exclusive
Cover B
NAT JONES

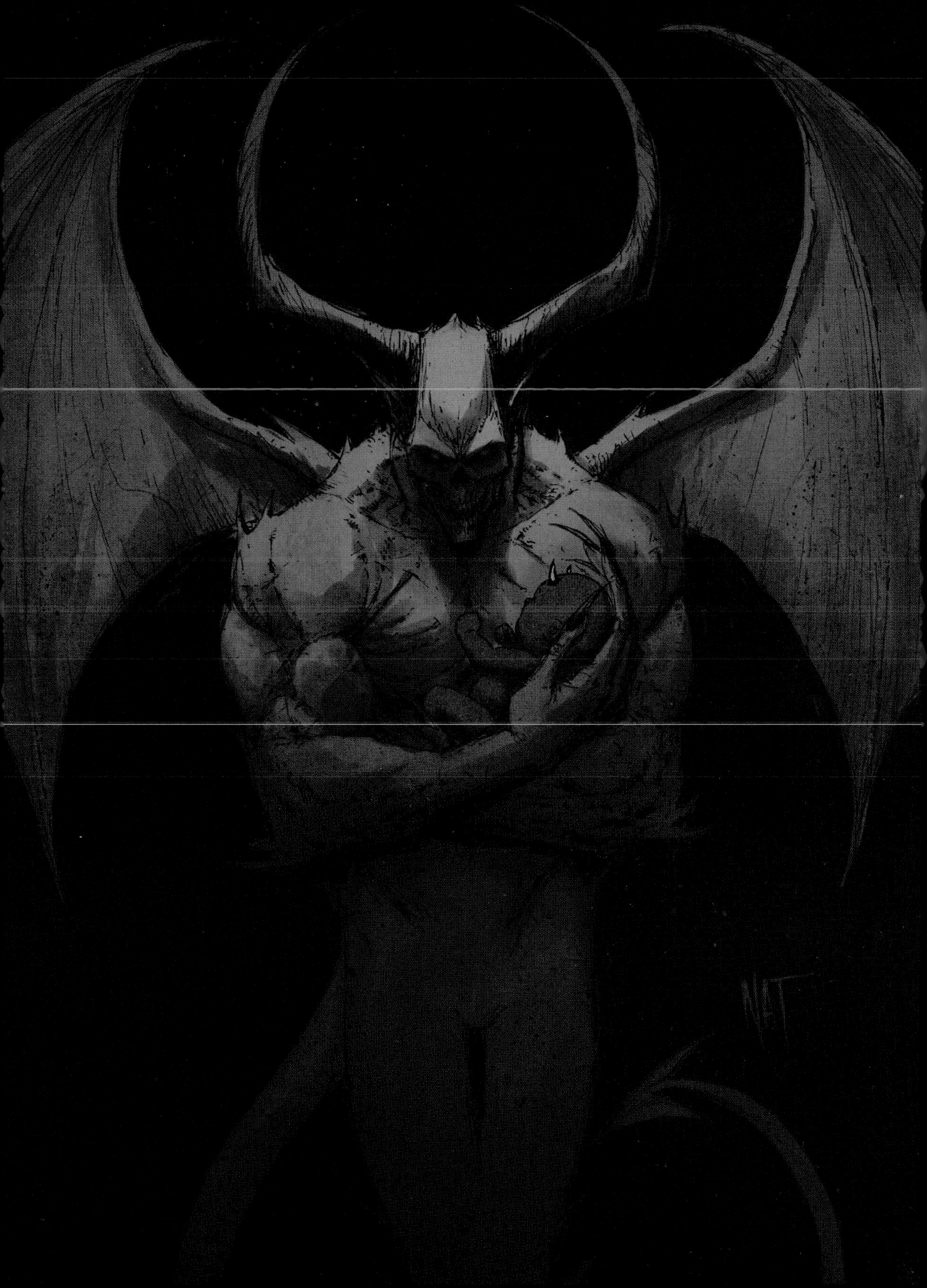

Issue 1
Gotham Central Exclusive
Cover C - Red Foil
NAT JONES

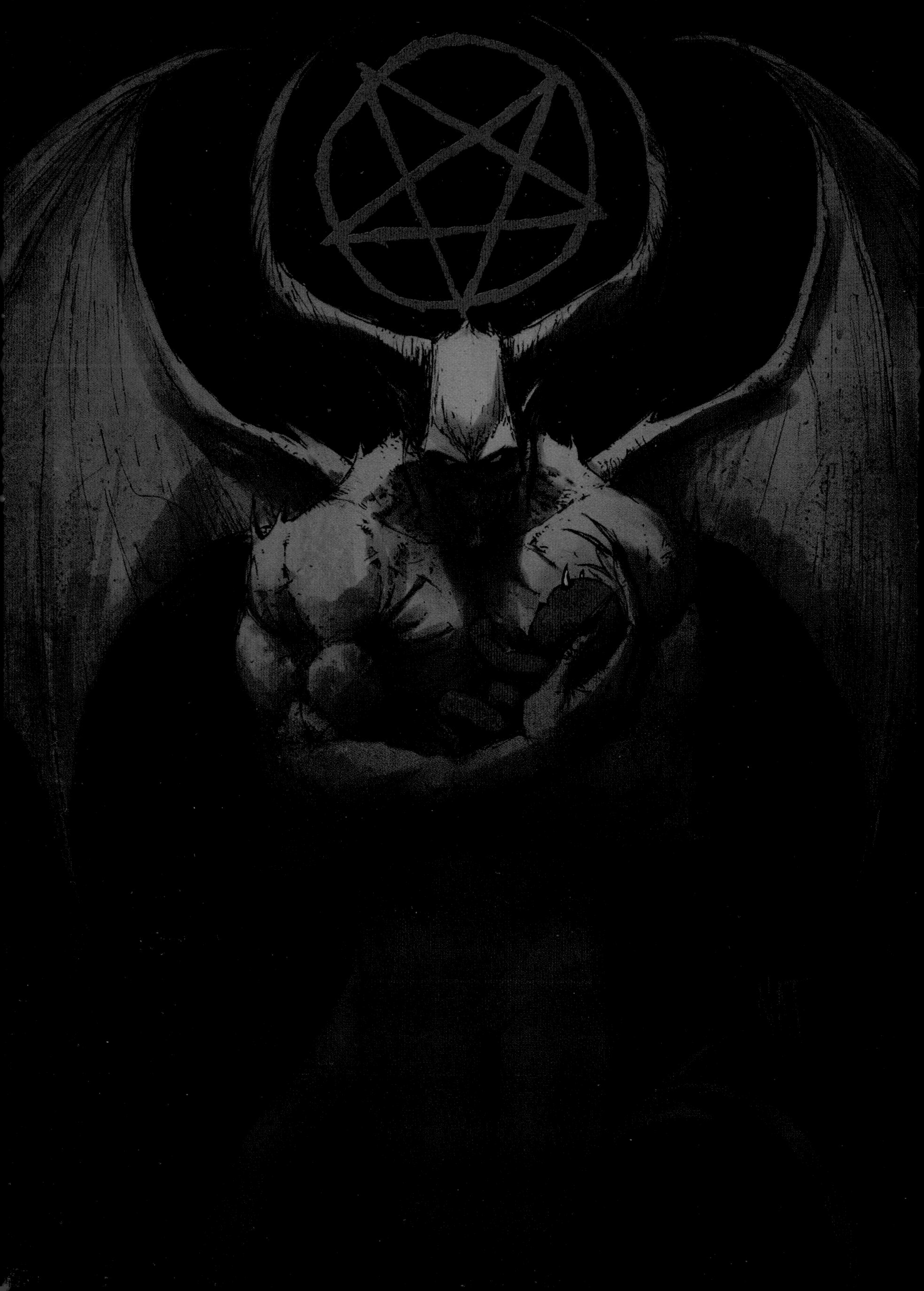

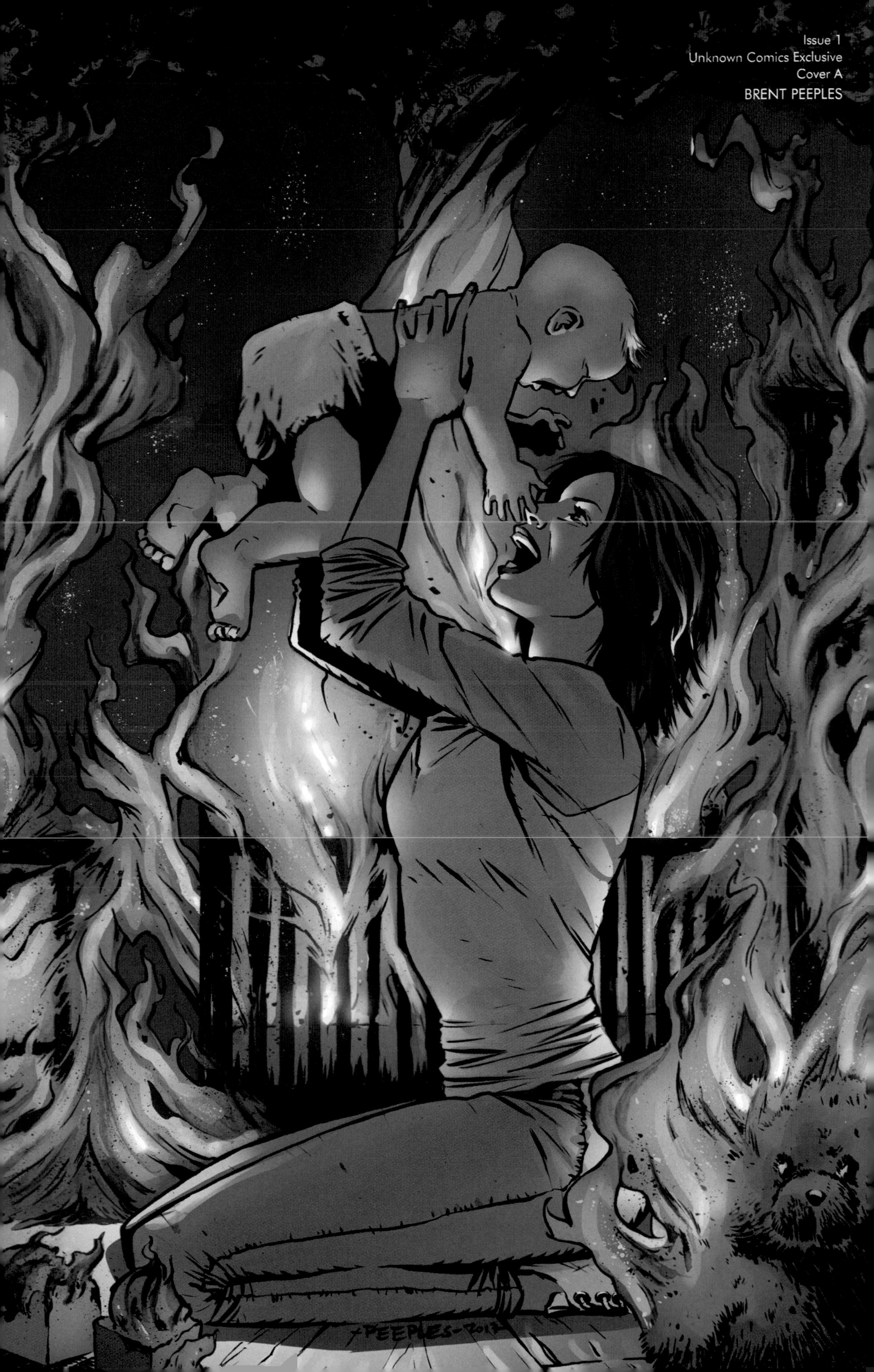
Issue 1
Unknown Comics Exclusive
Cover A
BRENT PEEPLES
PEEPLES-2012

Issue 1
Unknown Comics Exclusive
Cover B
BRENT PEEPLES

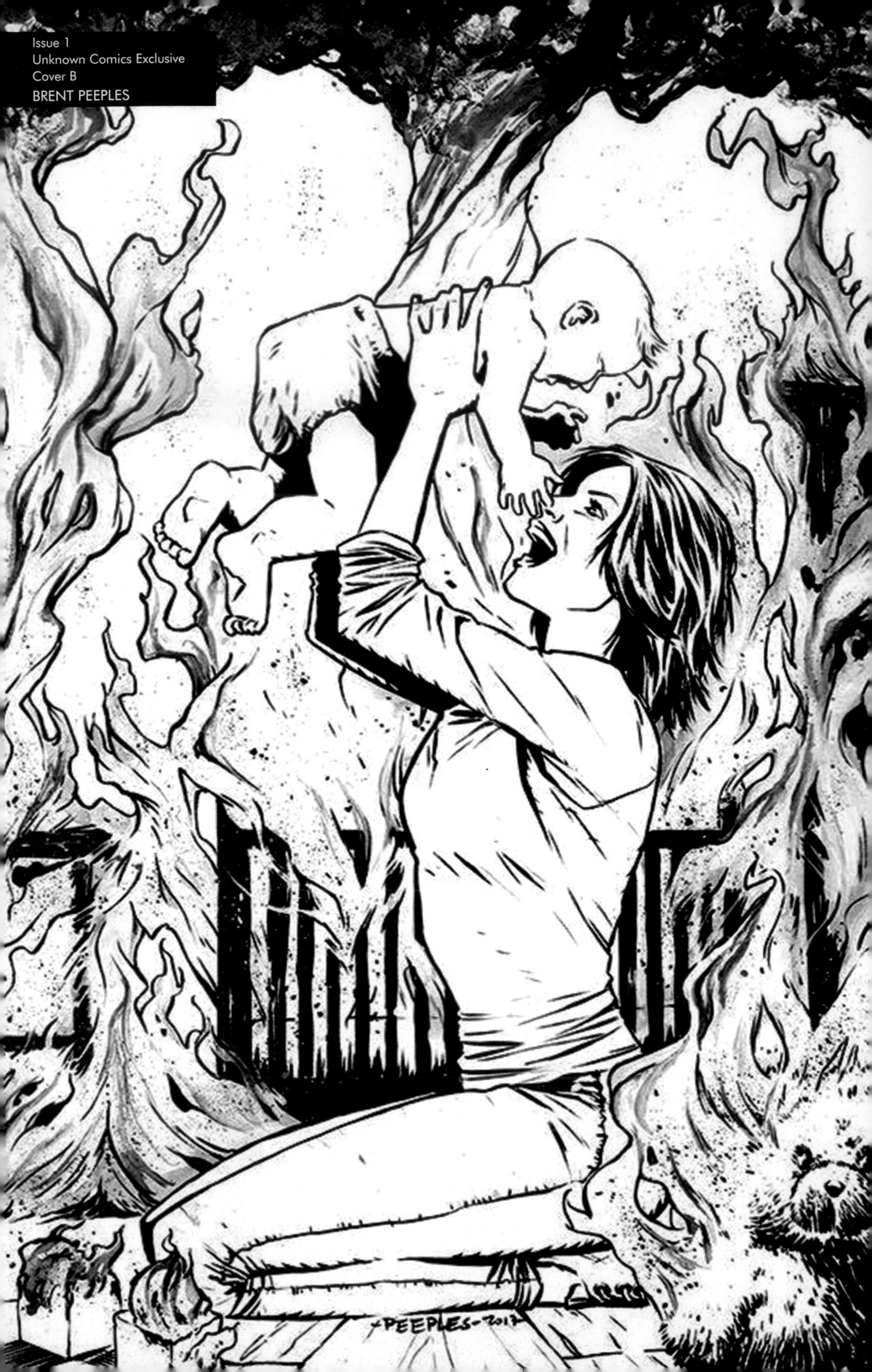

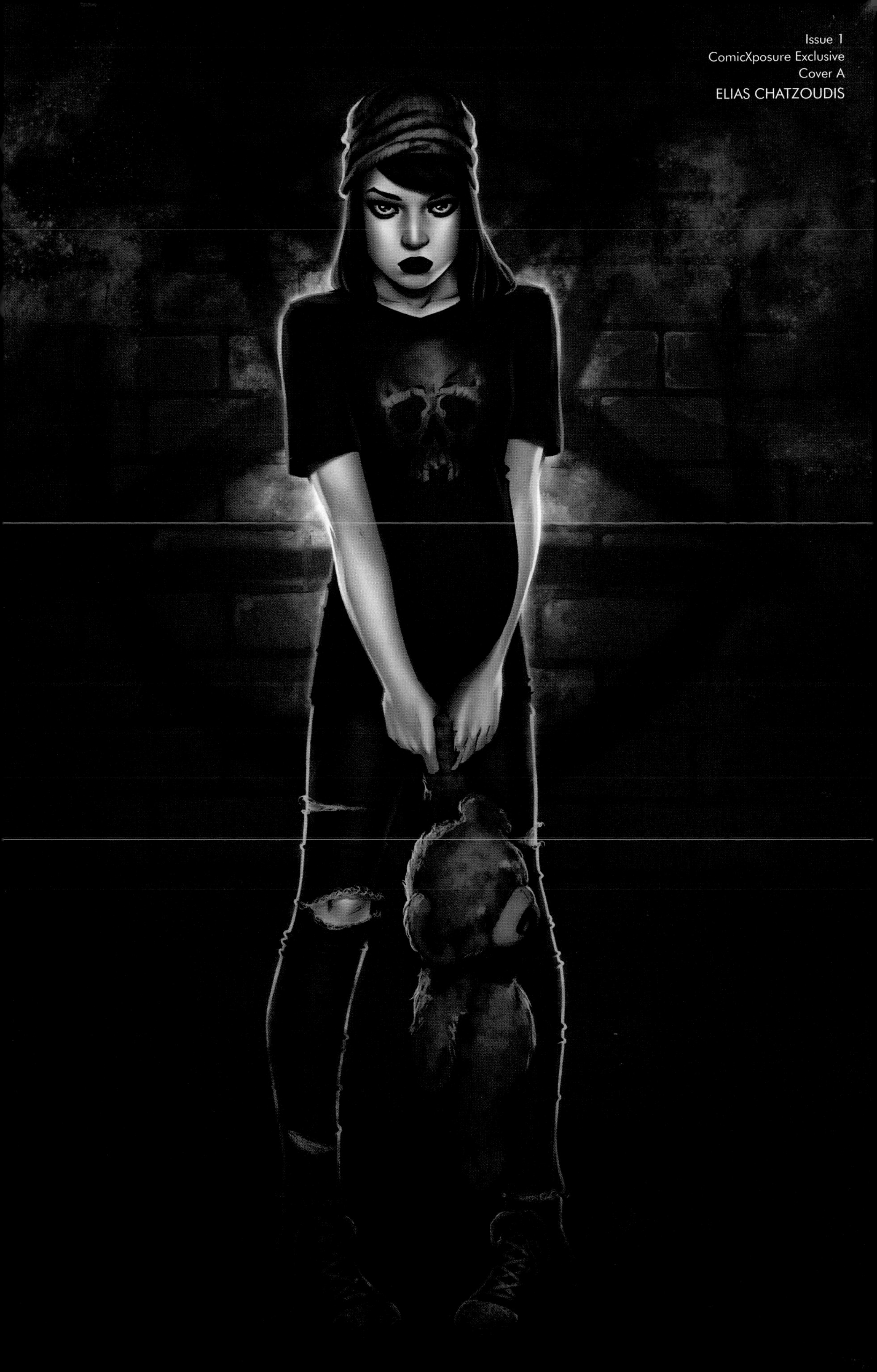

Issue 1
ComicXposure Exclusive
Cover A
ELIAS CHATZOUDIS

Issue 1
ComicXposure Exclusive
Cover B
ELIAS CHATZOUDIS

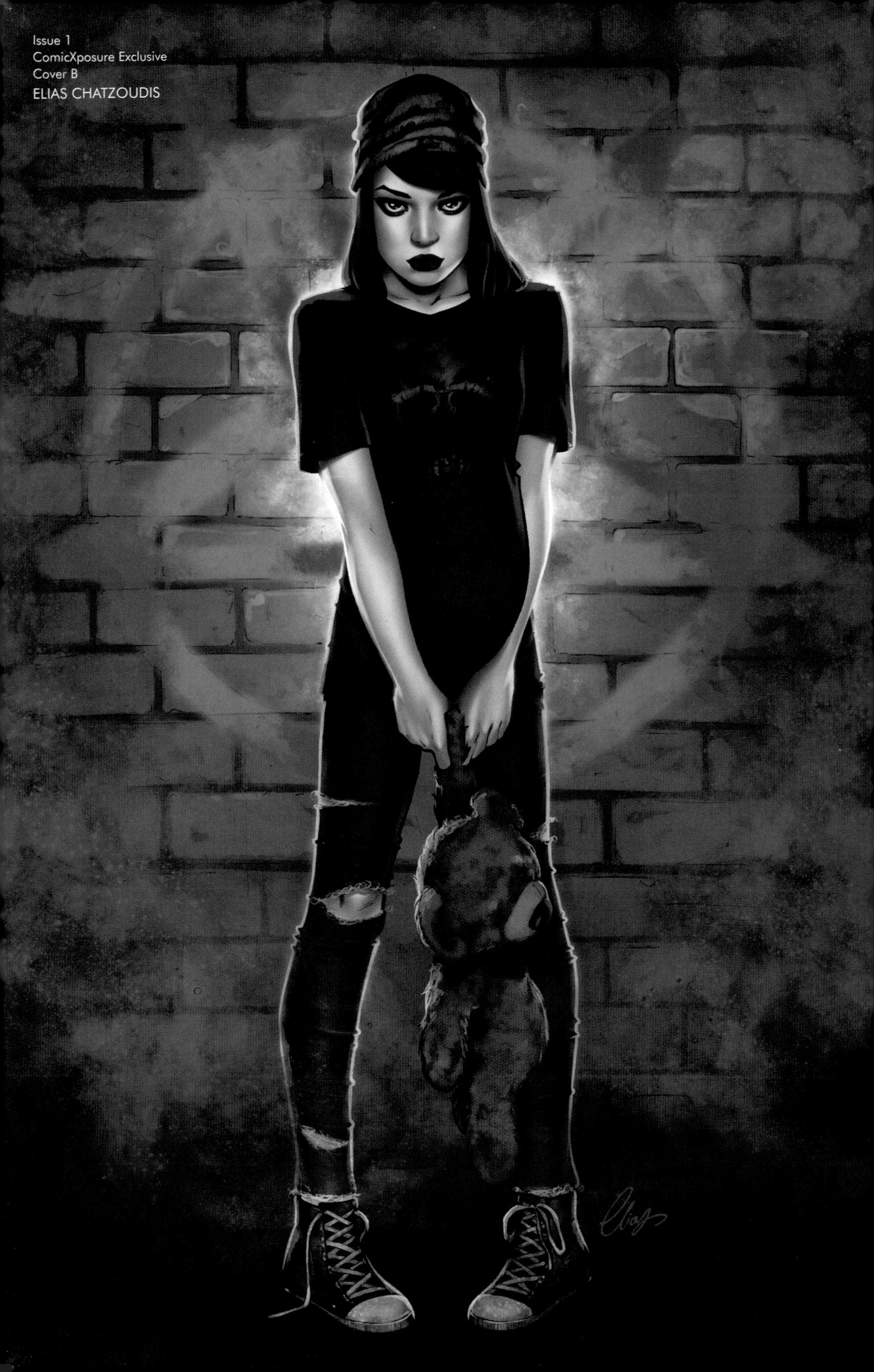

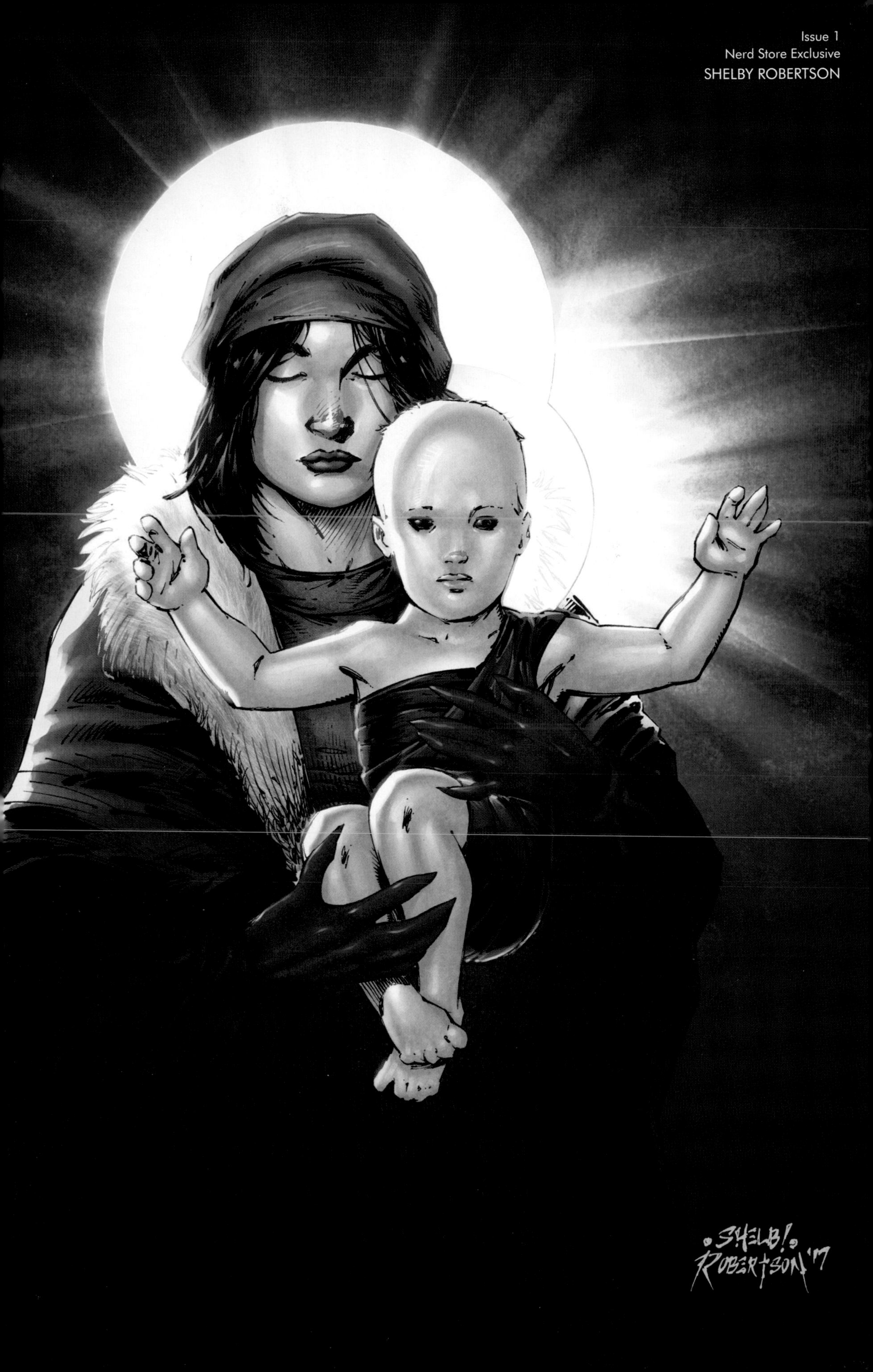
Issue 1
Nerd Store Exclusive
SHELBY ROBERTSON

Issue 1
Red Pegasus Exclusive
ARTURO TORRES

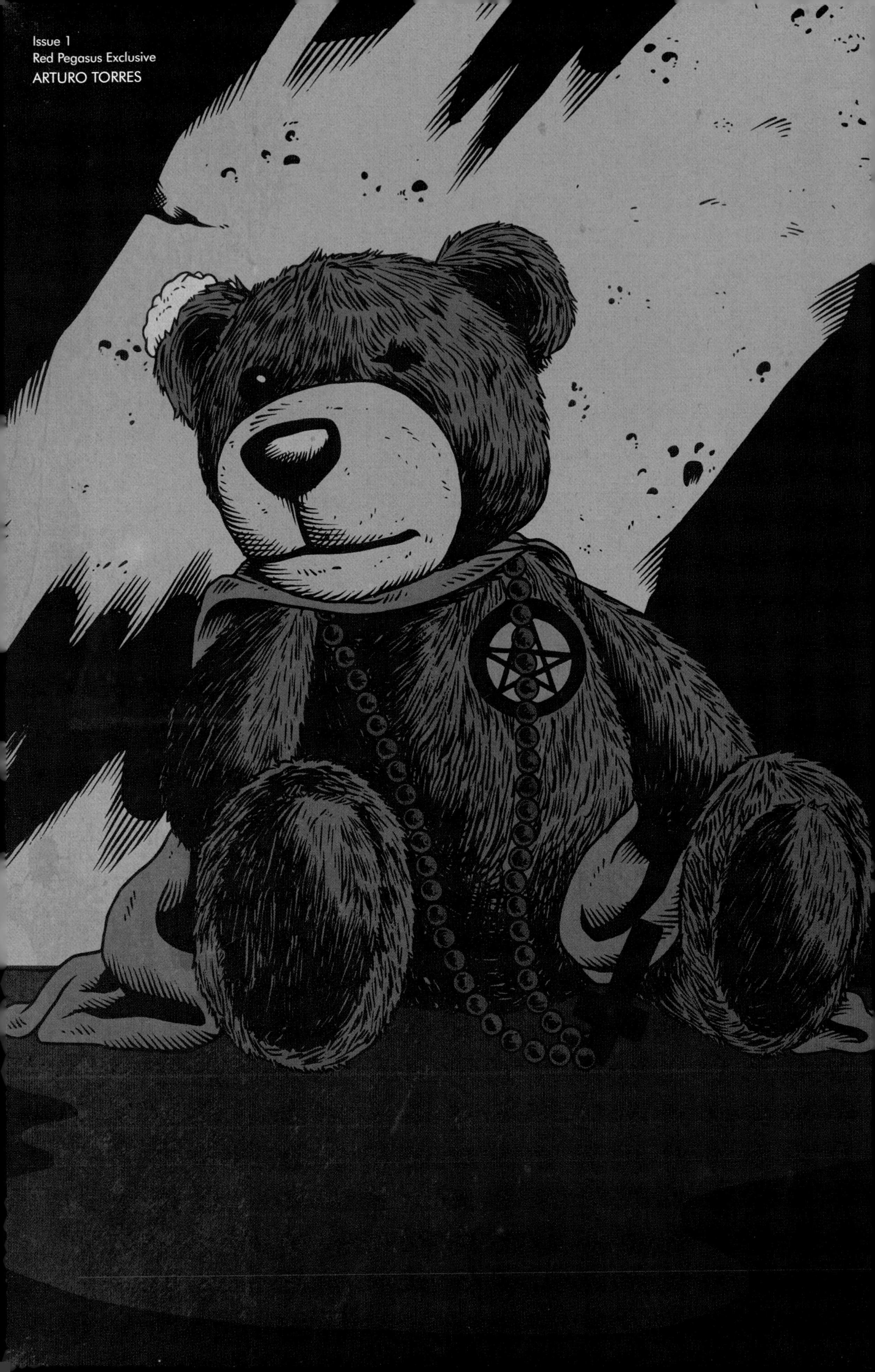

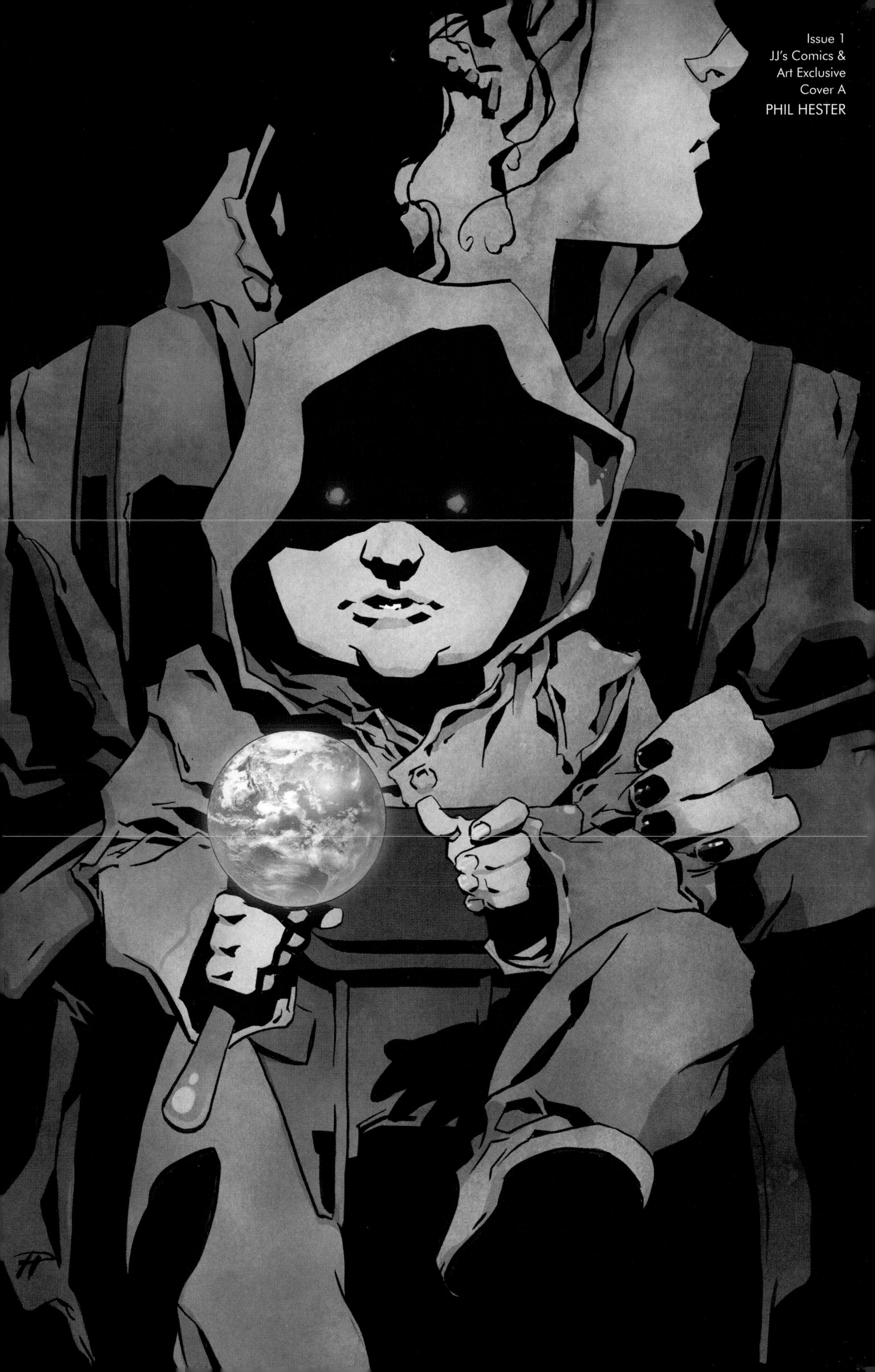
Issue 1
JJ's Comics &
Art Exclusive
Cover A
PHIL HESTER

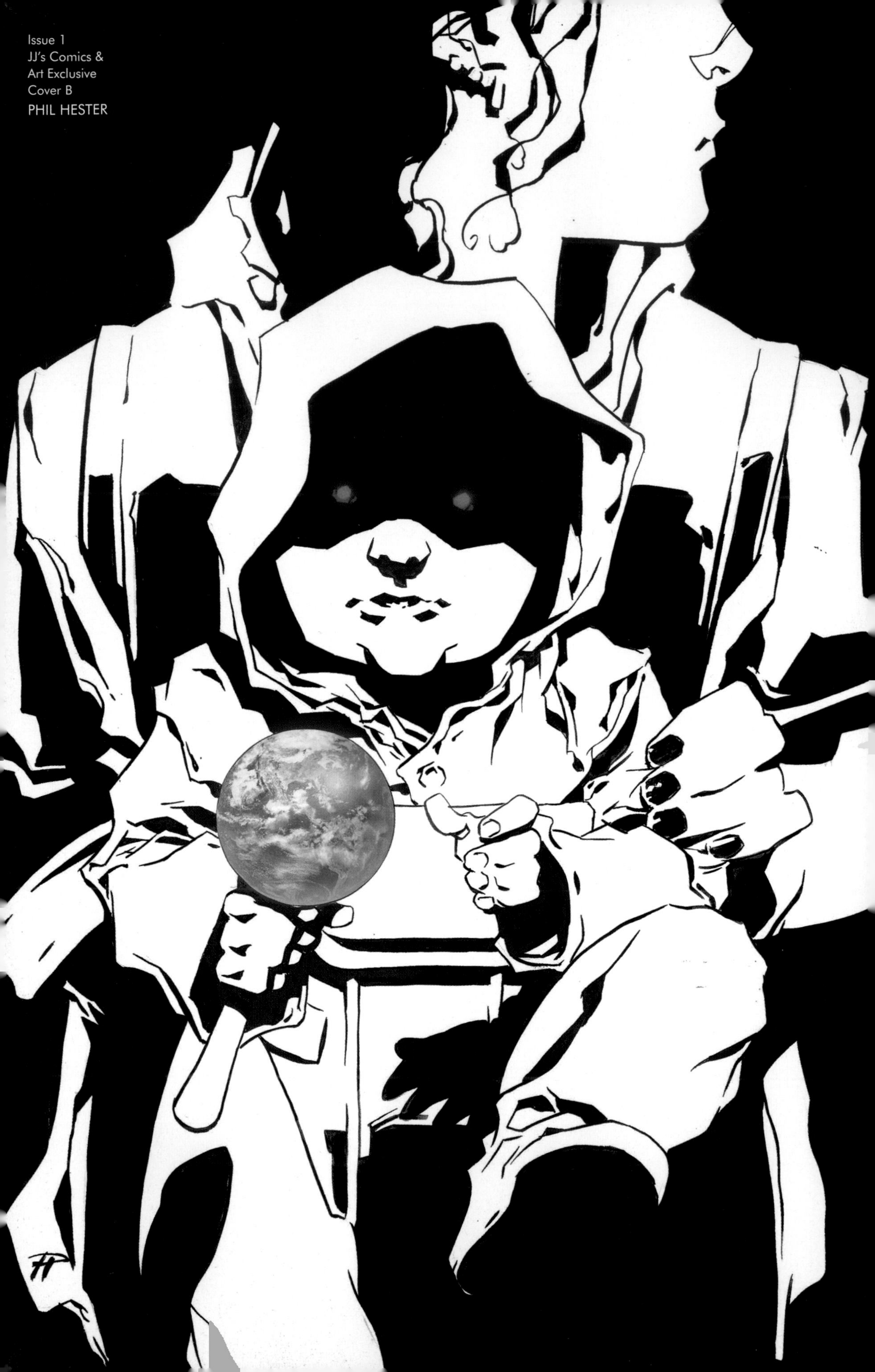
Issue 1
JJ's Comics &
Art Exclusive
Cover B
PHIL HESTER

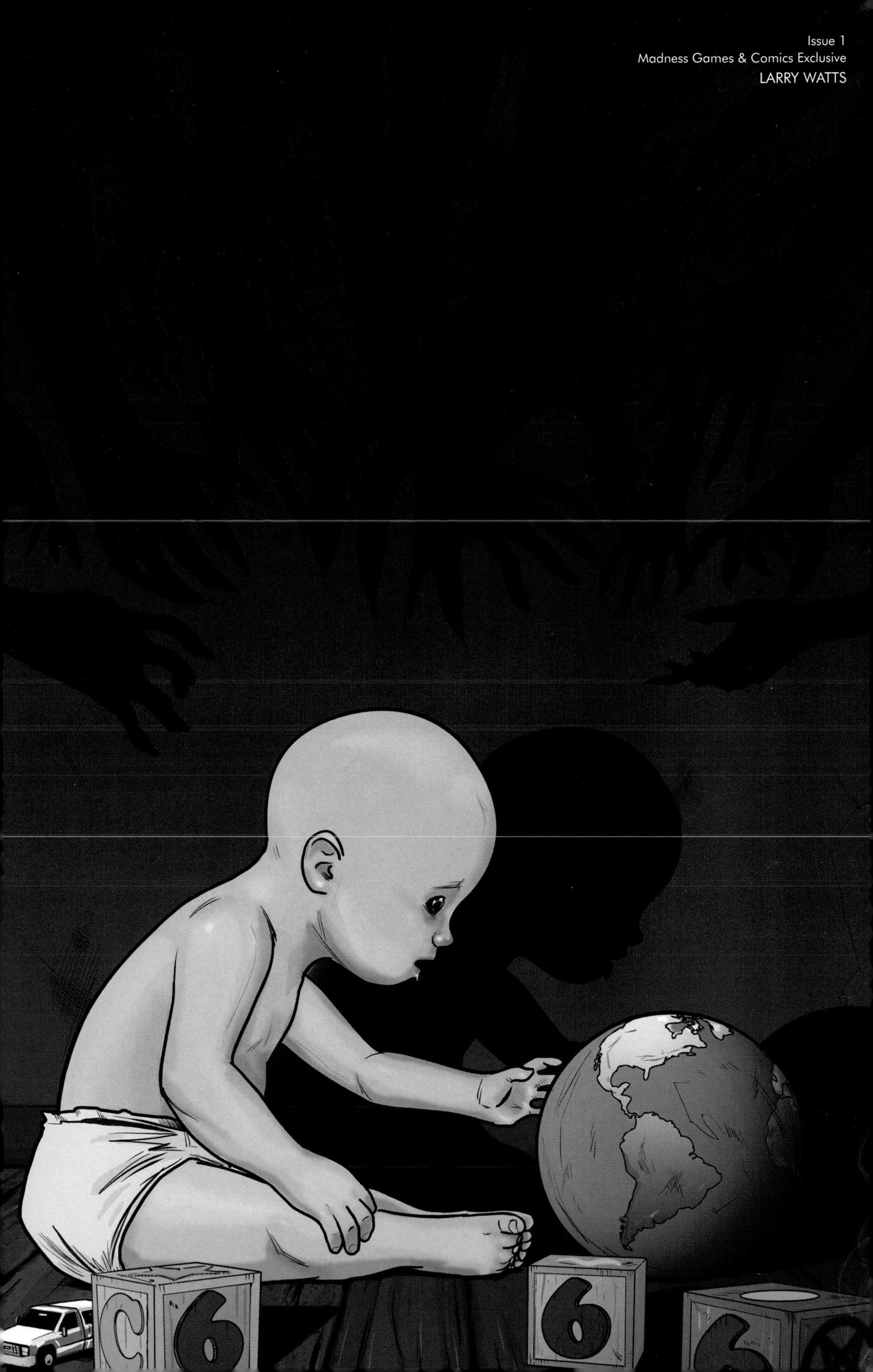
Issue 1
Madness Games & Comics Exclusive
LARRY WATTS

Issue 1
ComicMint.com Exclusive
DYLAN BURNETT

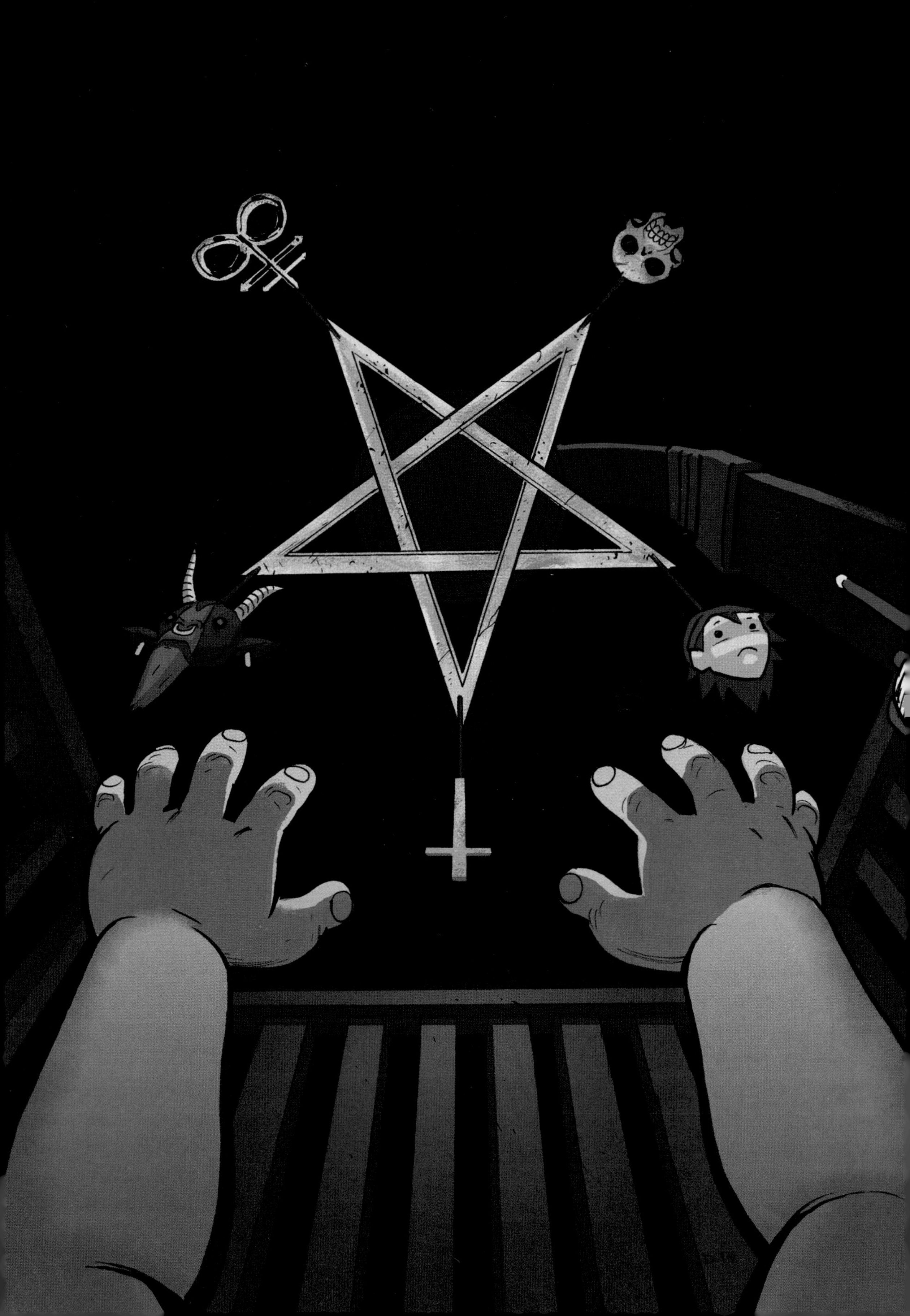

Issue 1
Collectible Comics & Games Exclusive
TOBIAS MARROW

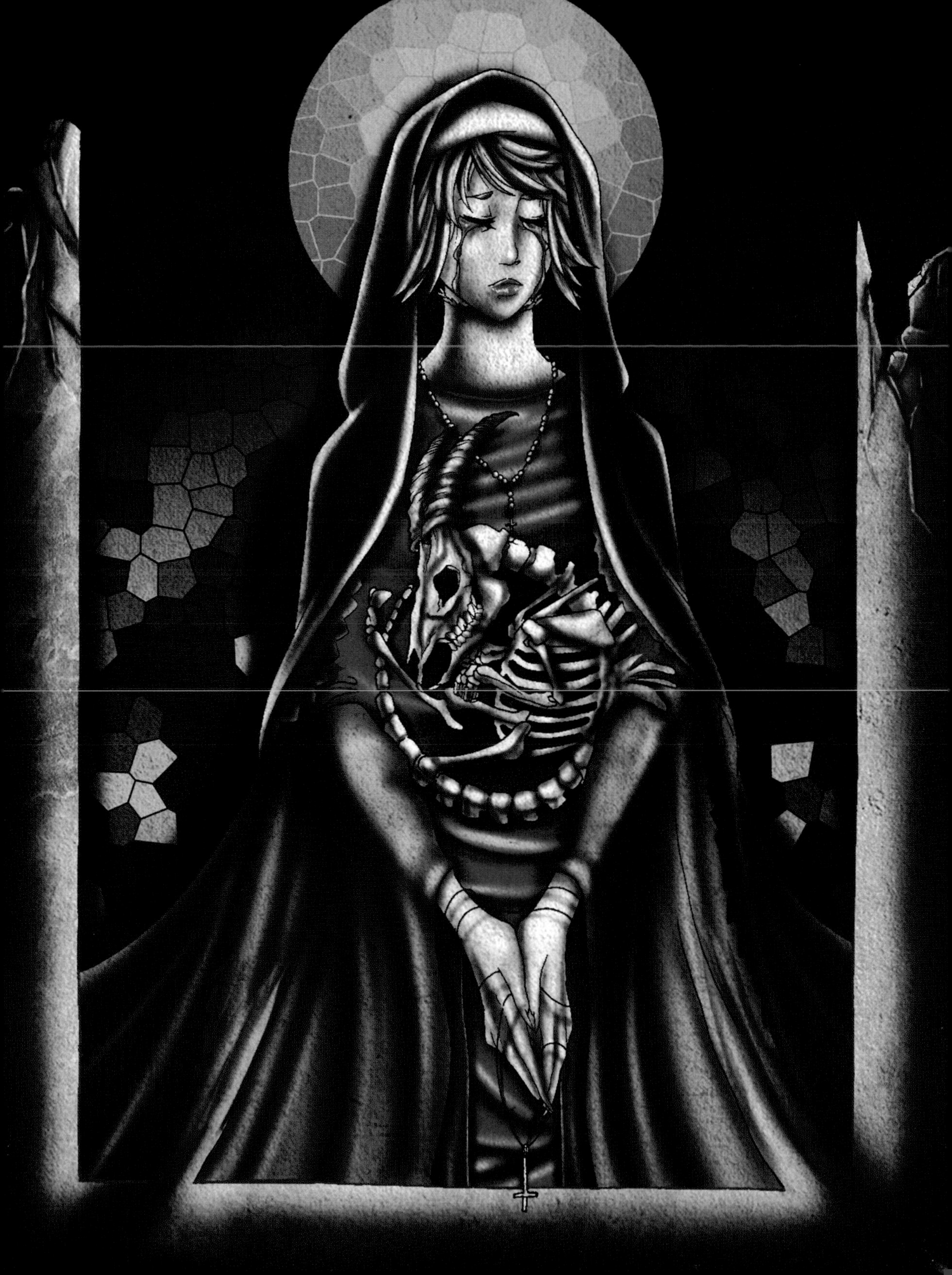

Issue 1
Midtown Comics Exclusive
FRANCESCO FRANCAVILLA

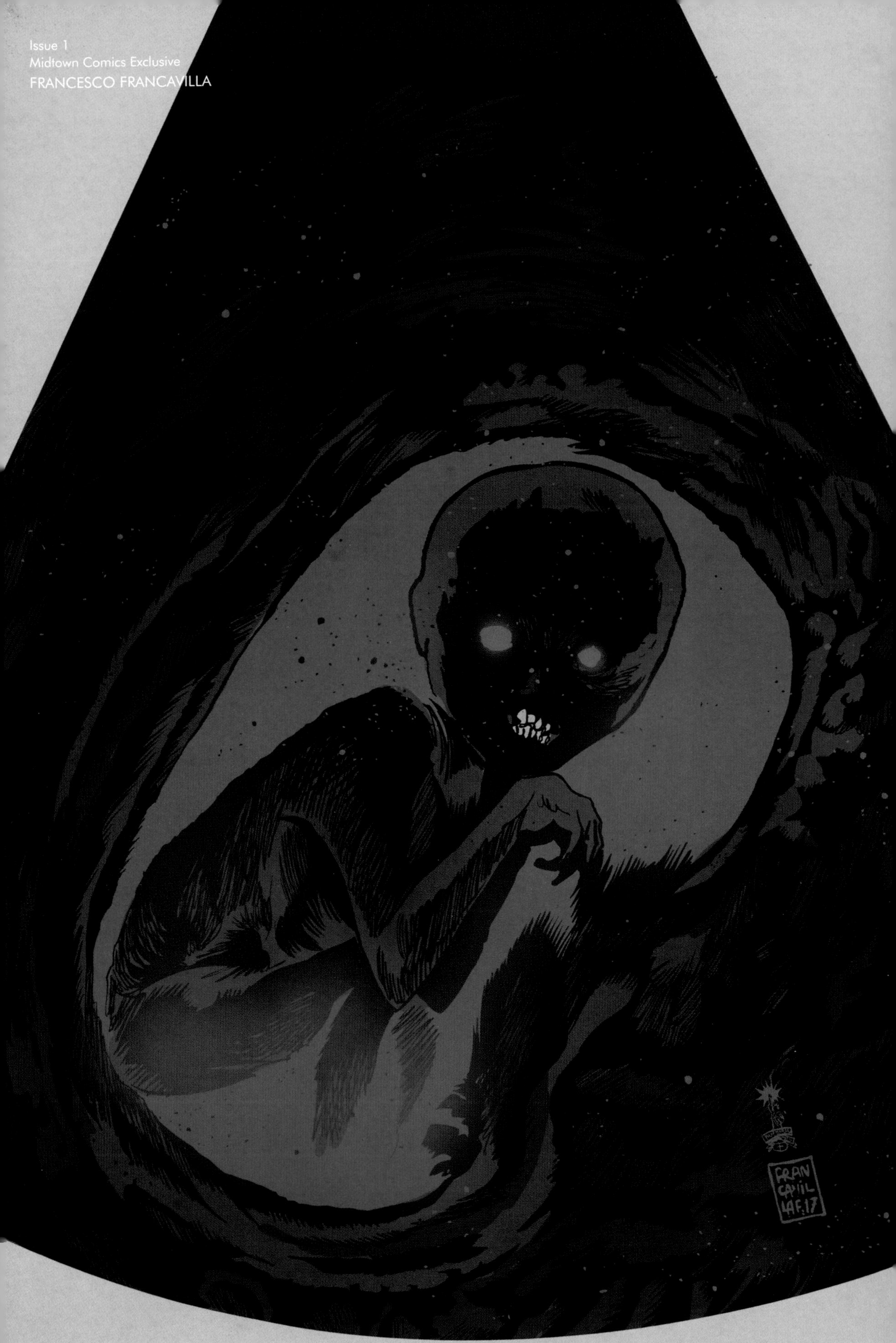

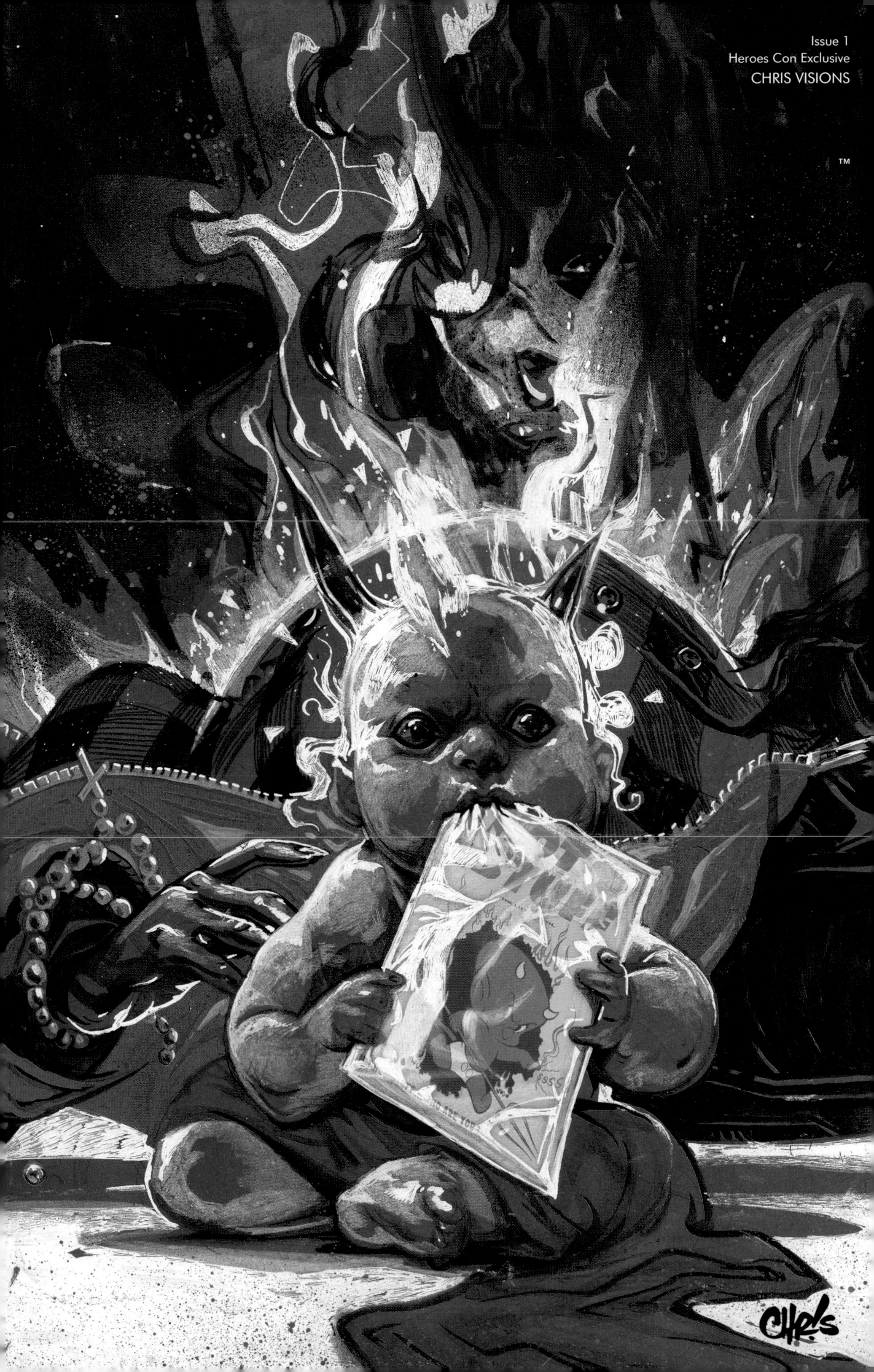
Issue 1
Heroes Con Exclusive
CHRIS VISIONS
™

Issue 1
Wade's Comic Madness Exclusive
Cover A
KARL WALLER

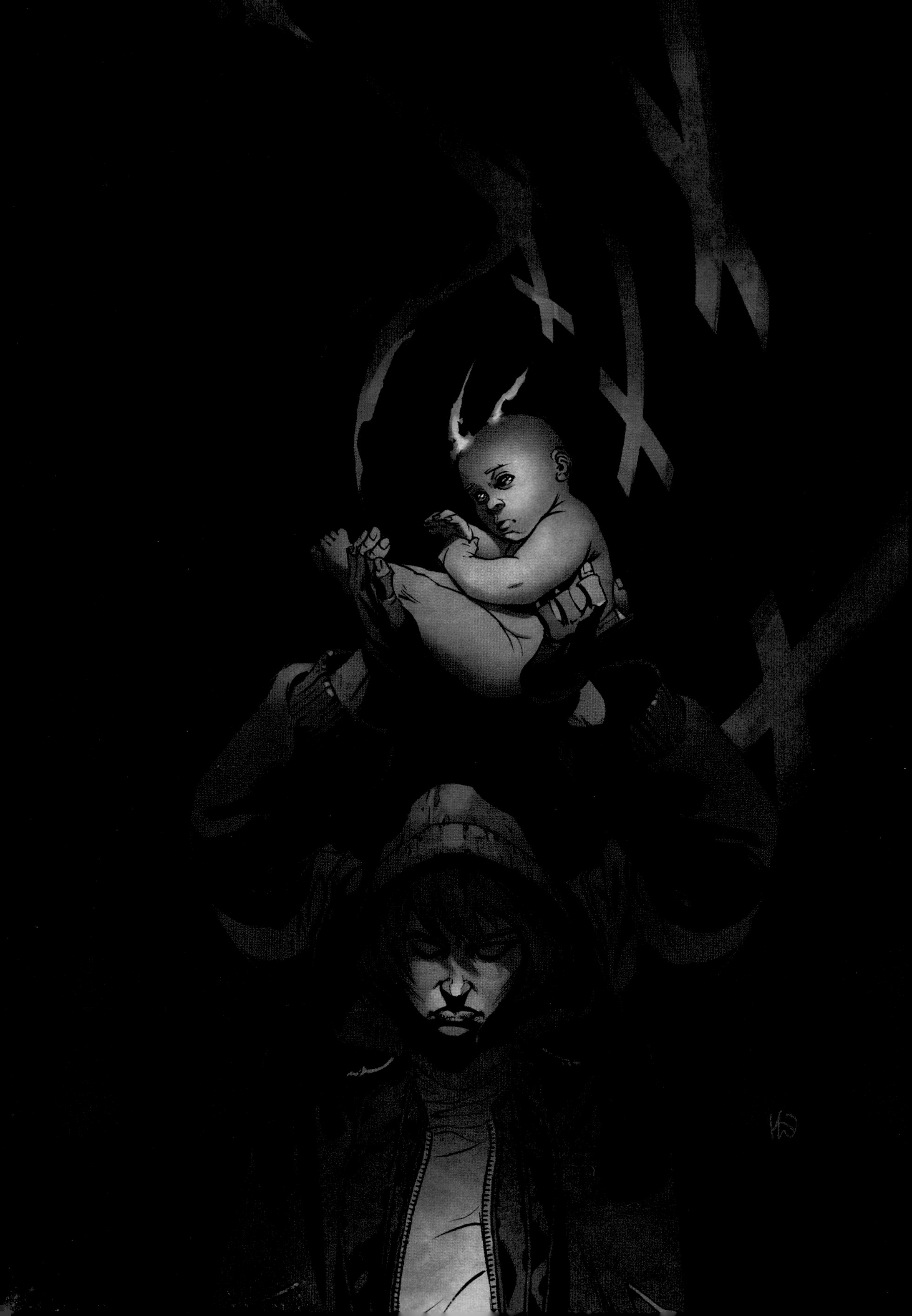

Wade's Comic Madness Exclusive
Cover B
KARL WALLER

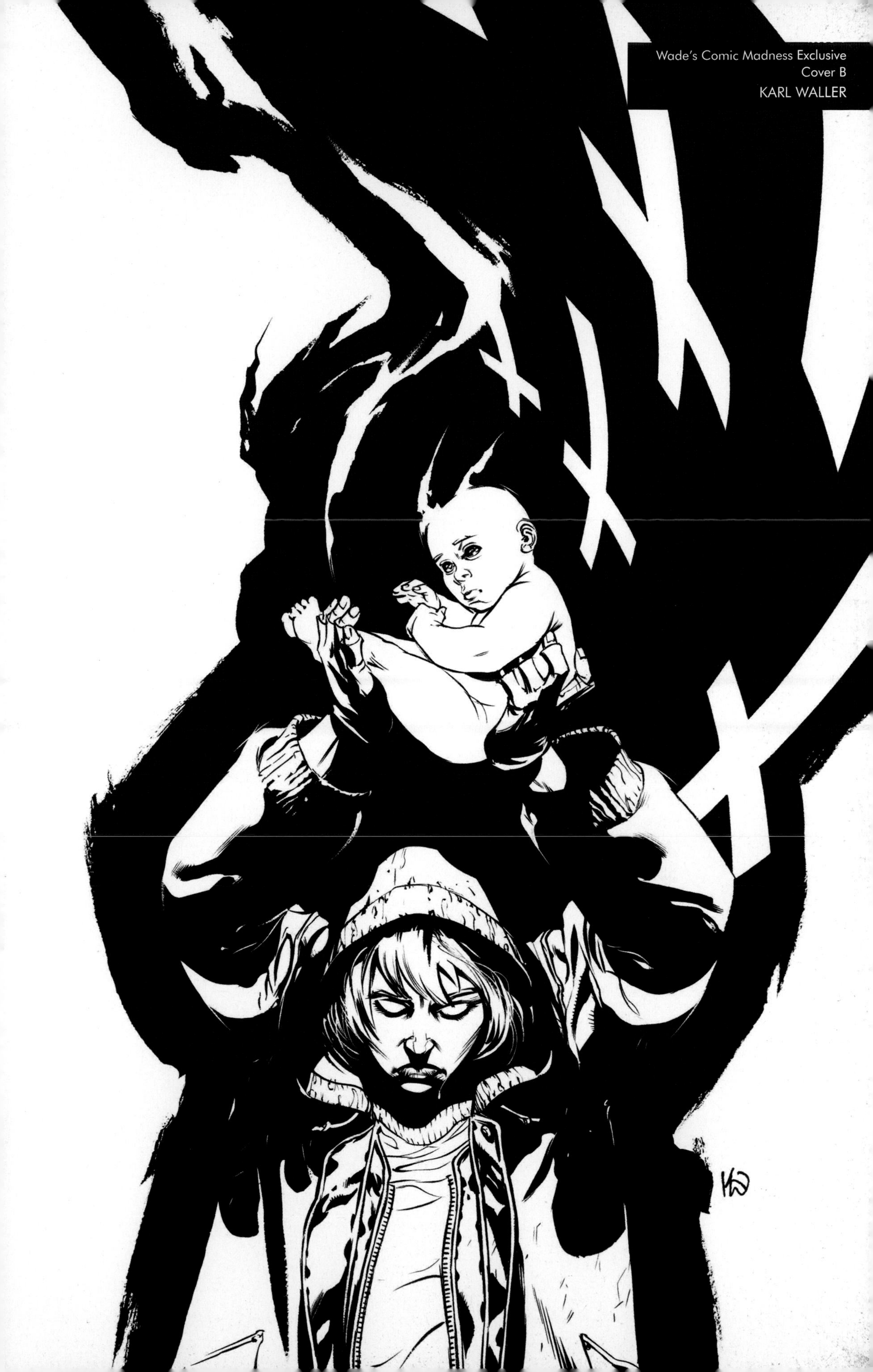

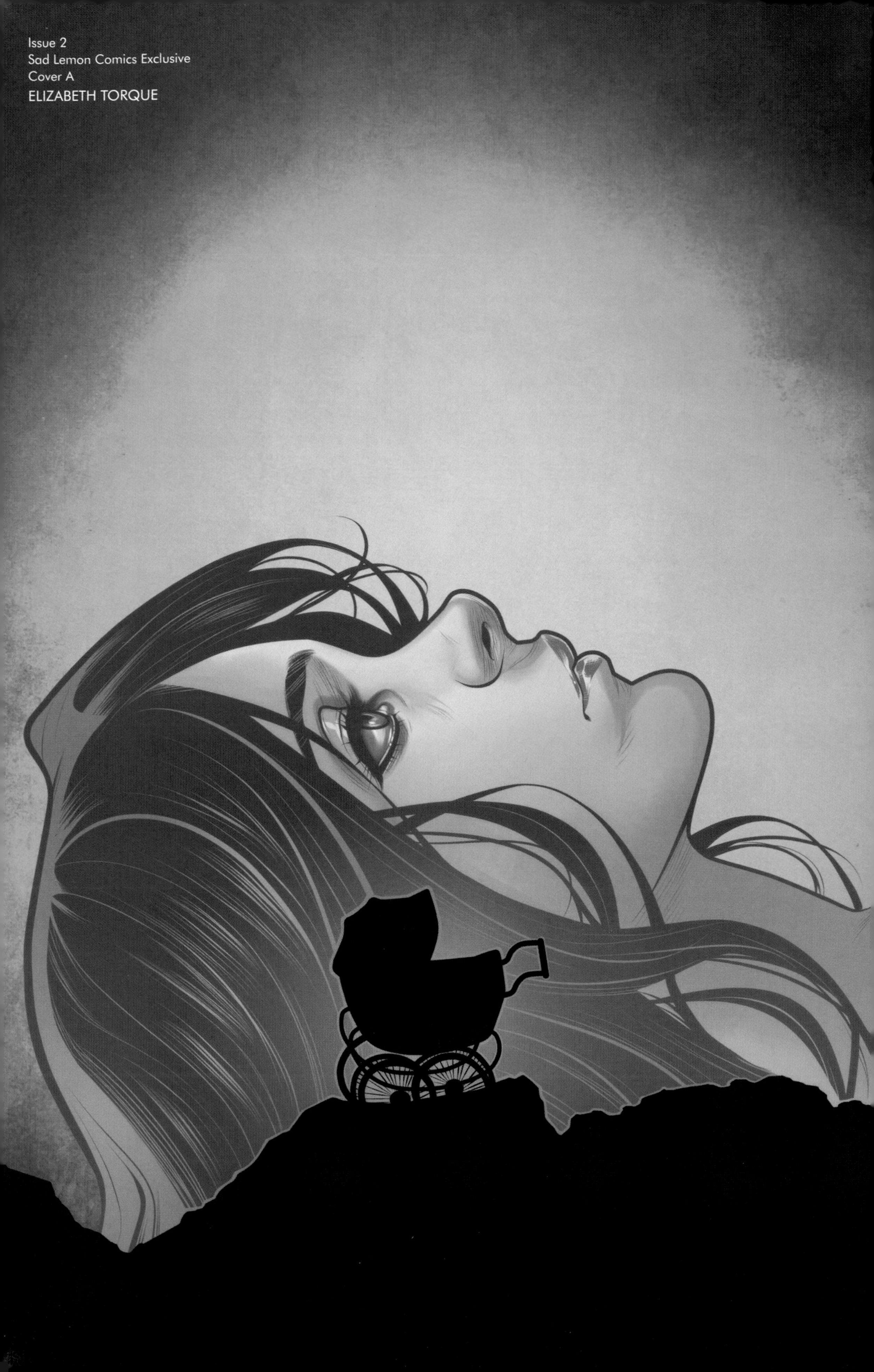

Issue 2
Sad Lemon Comics Exclusive
Cover A
ELIZABETH TORQUE

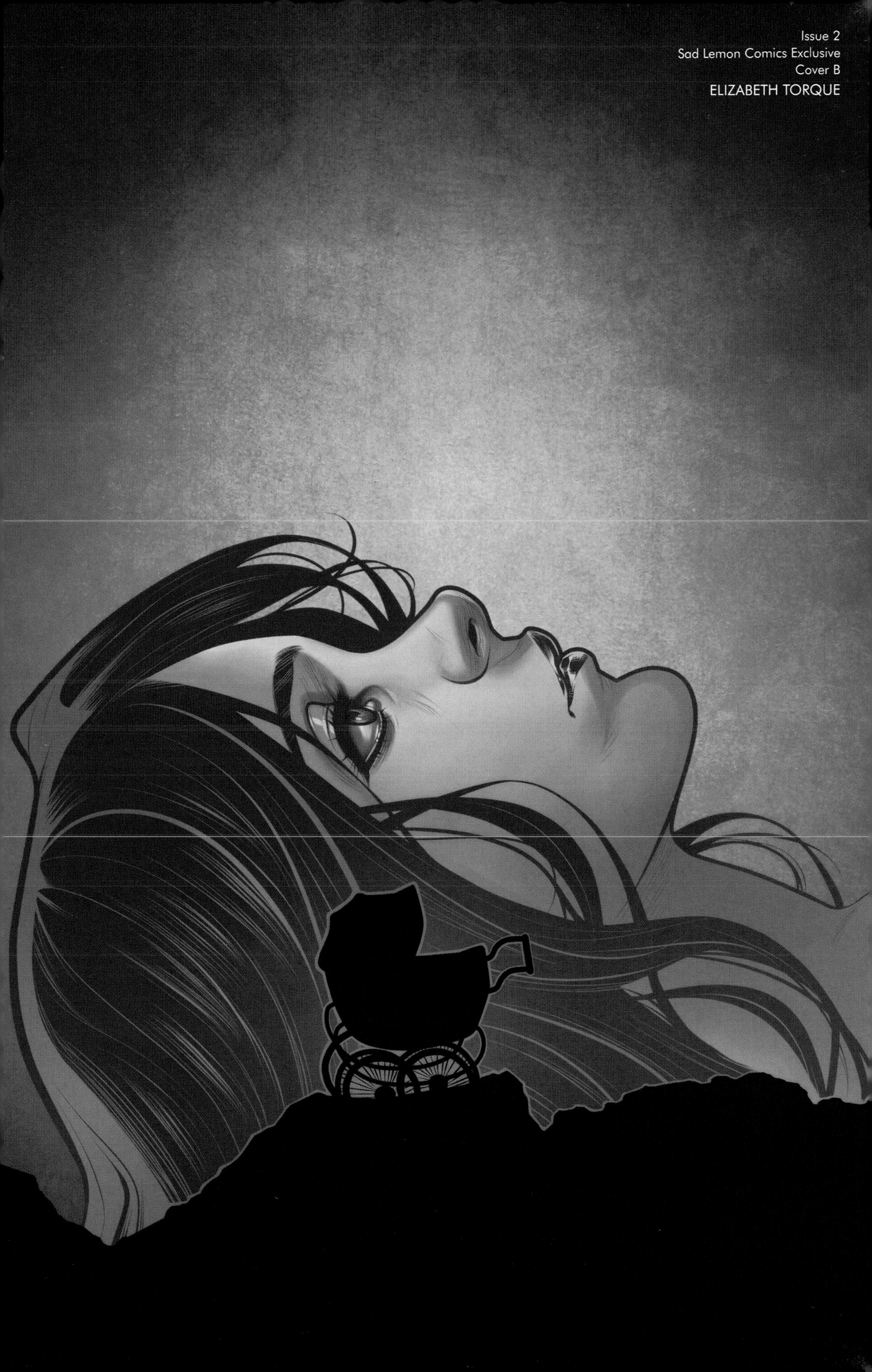
Issue 2
Sad Lemon Comics Exclusive
Cover B
ELIZABETH TORQUE

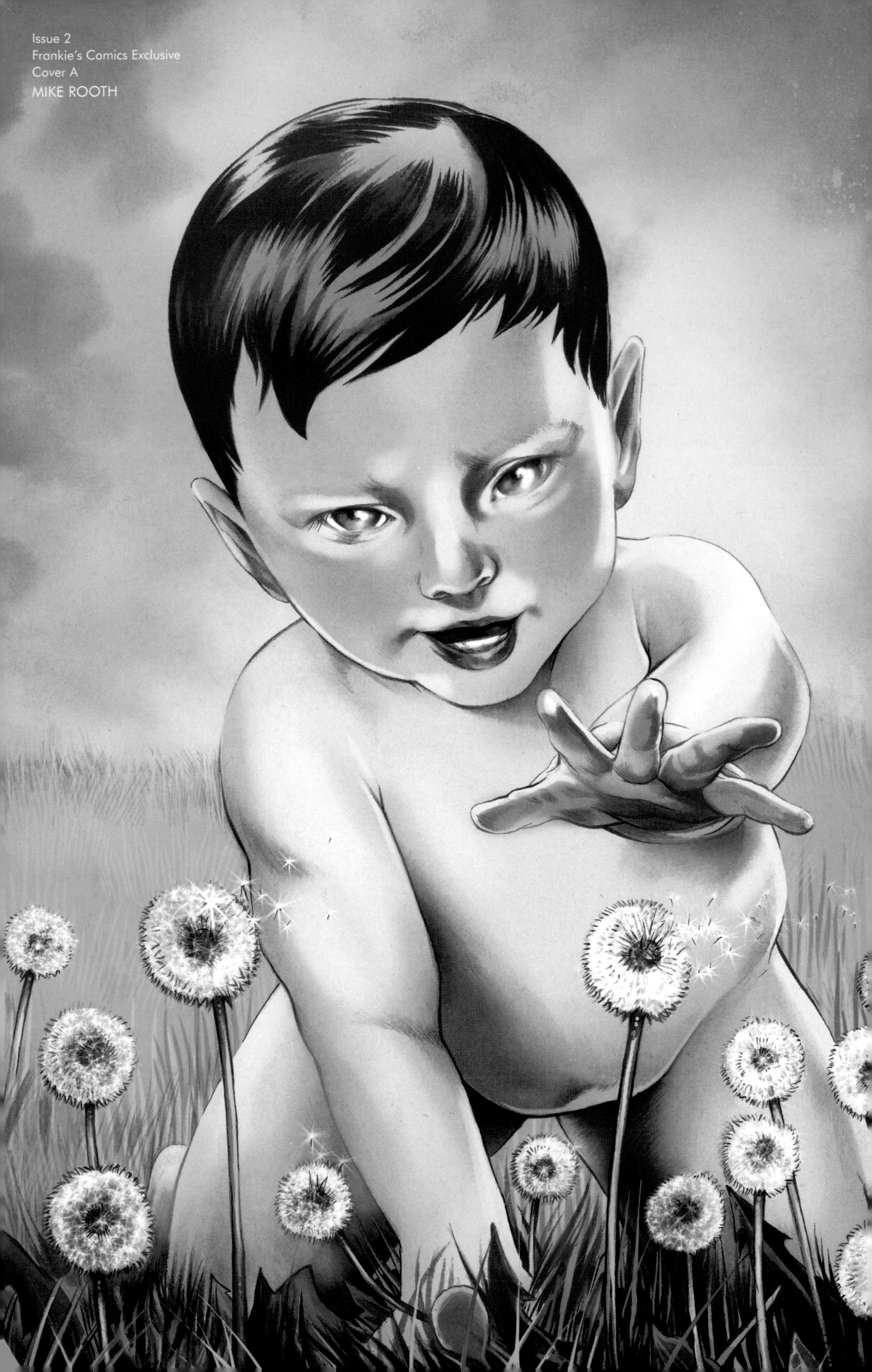

Issue 2
Frankie's Comics Exclusive
Cover A
MIKE ROOTH

Issue 2
Frankie's Comics Exclusive
Cover B - Glow in the Dark
MIKE ROOTH

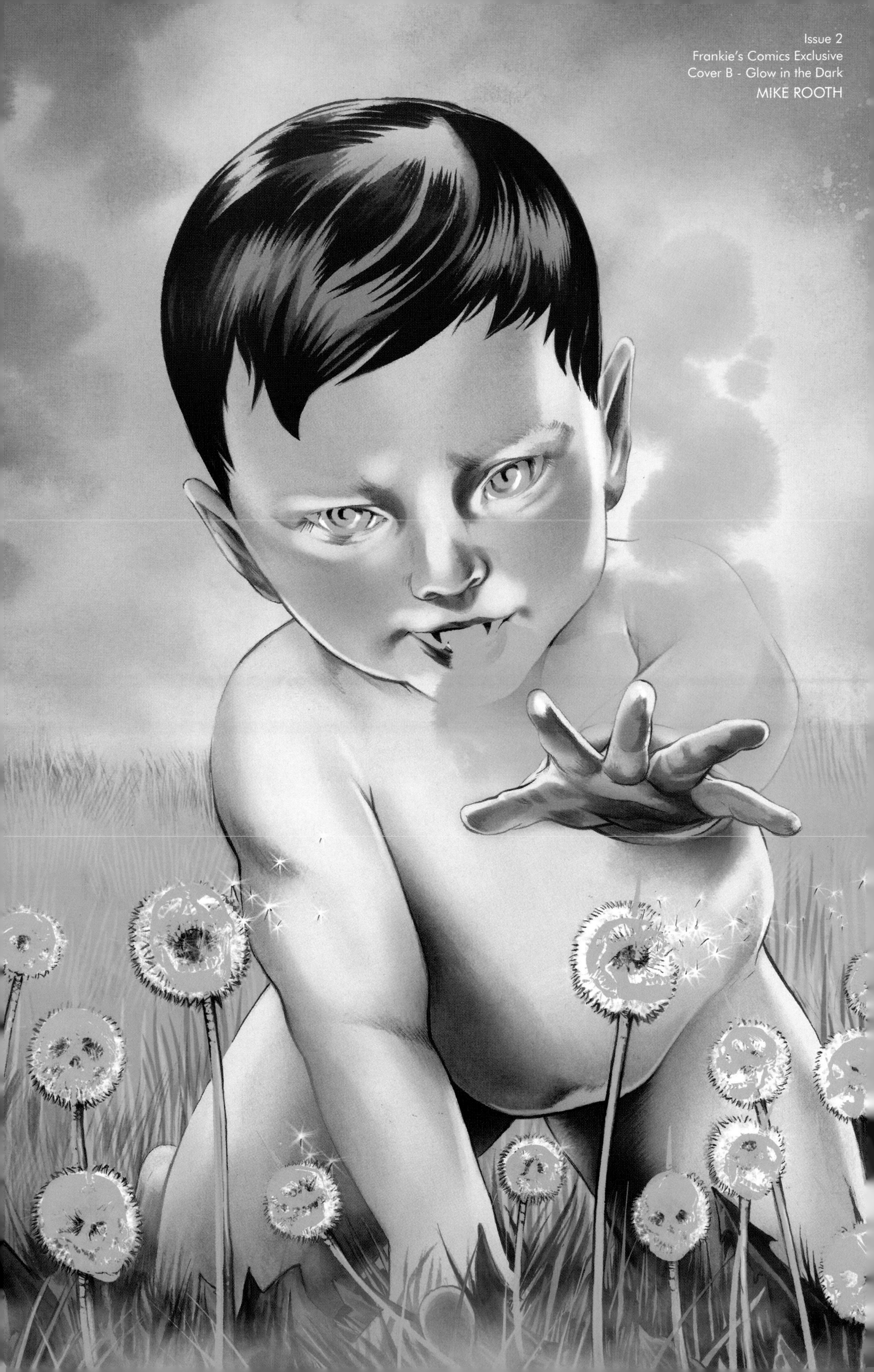

Issue 2
Jet Pack Comics / Forbidden Planet UK Exclusive
Cover A
LARRY WATTS

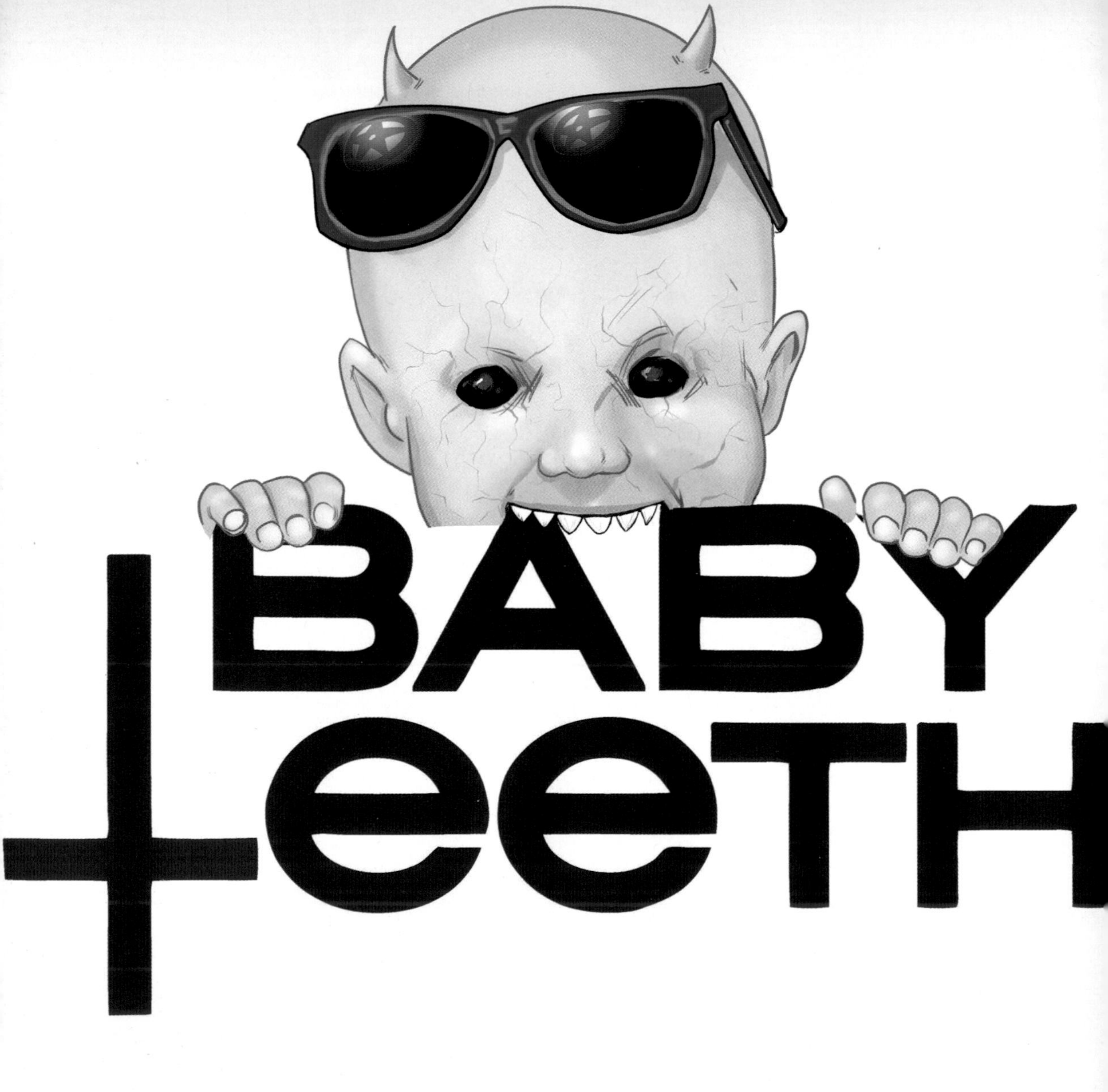
BABY
teeth

Issue 2
Jet Pack Comics / Forbidden Planet UK Exclusive
Cover B
LARRY WATTS

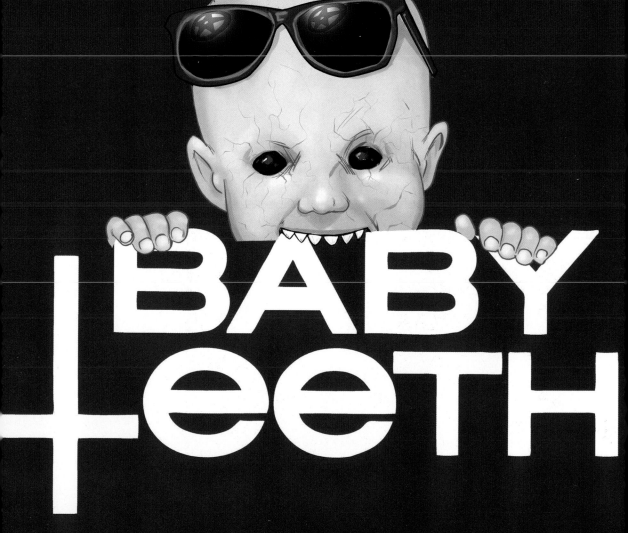

Issue 2
Gotham Central Exclusive
Cover A
NAT JONES

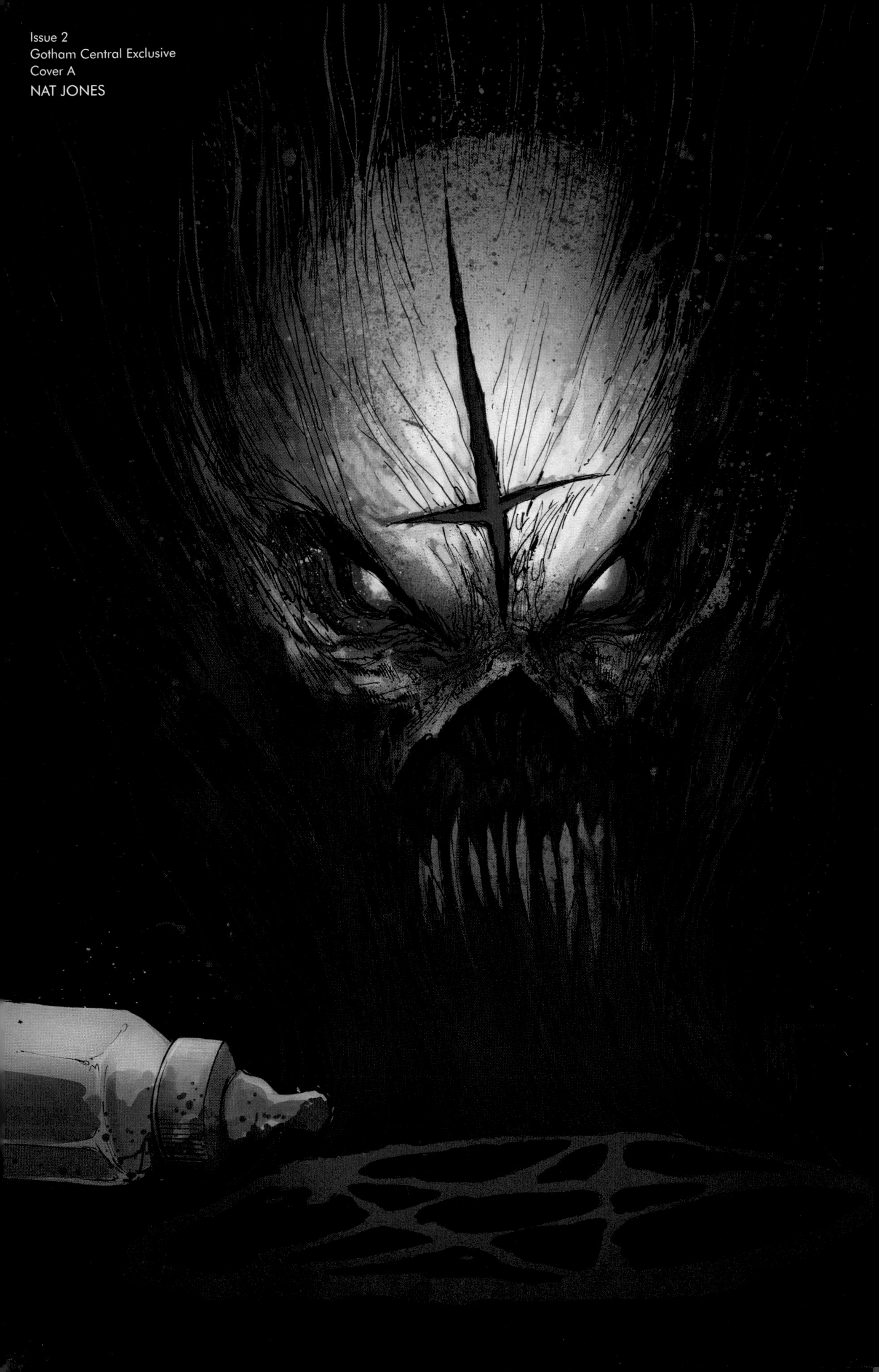

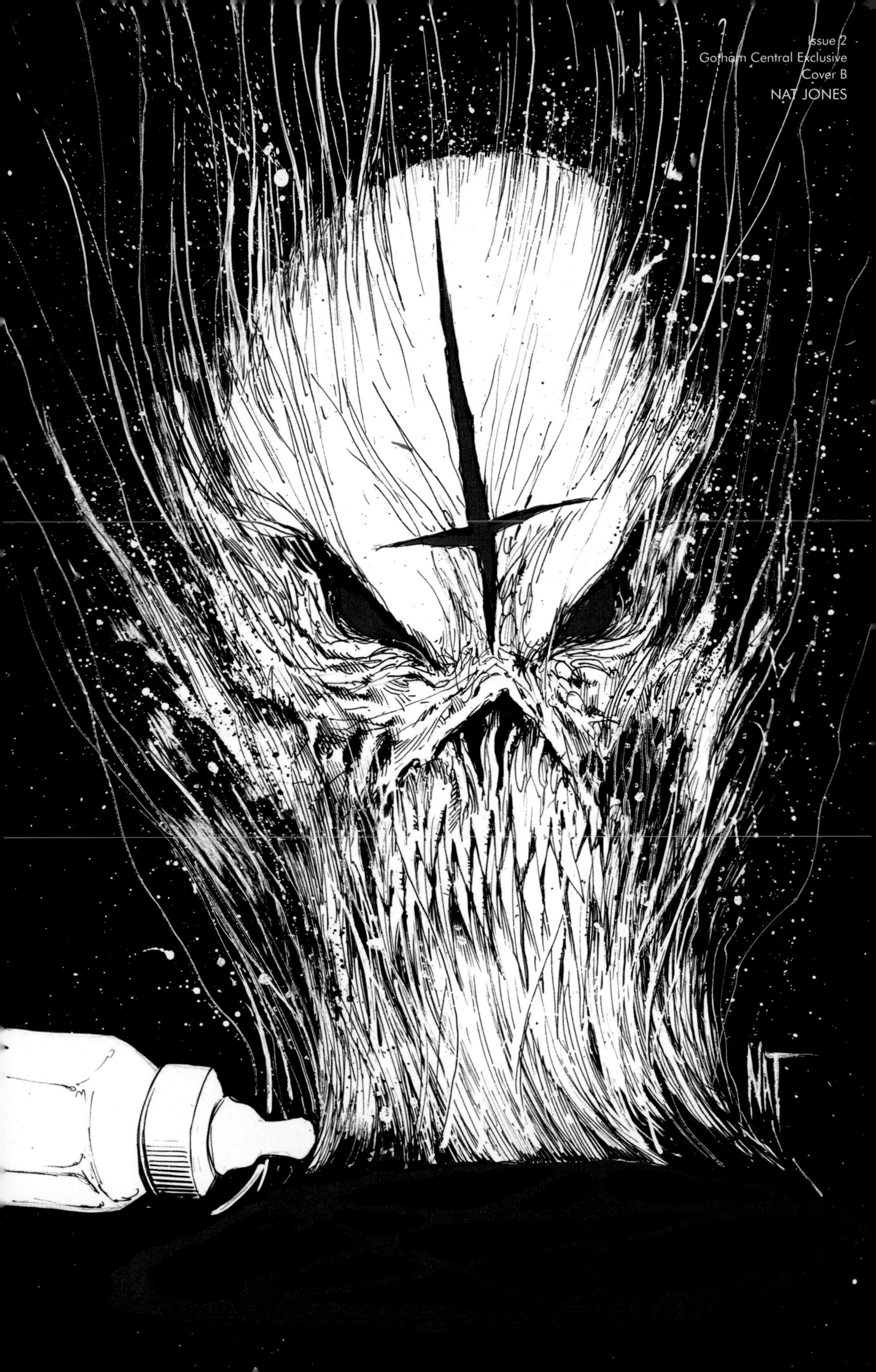
Issue 2
Gotham Central Exclusive
Cover B
NAT JONES
NAT

Issue 2
Unknown Comics Exclusive
Cover A
BRENT PEEPLES

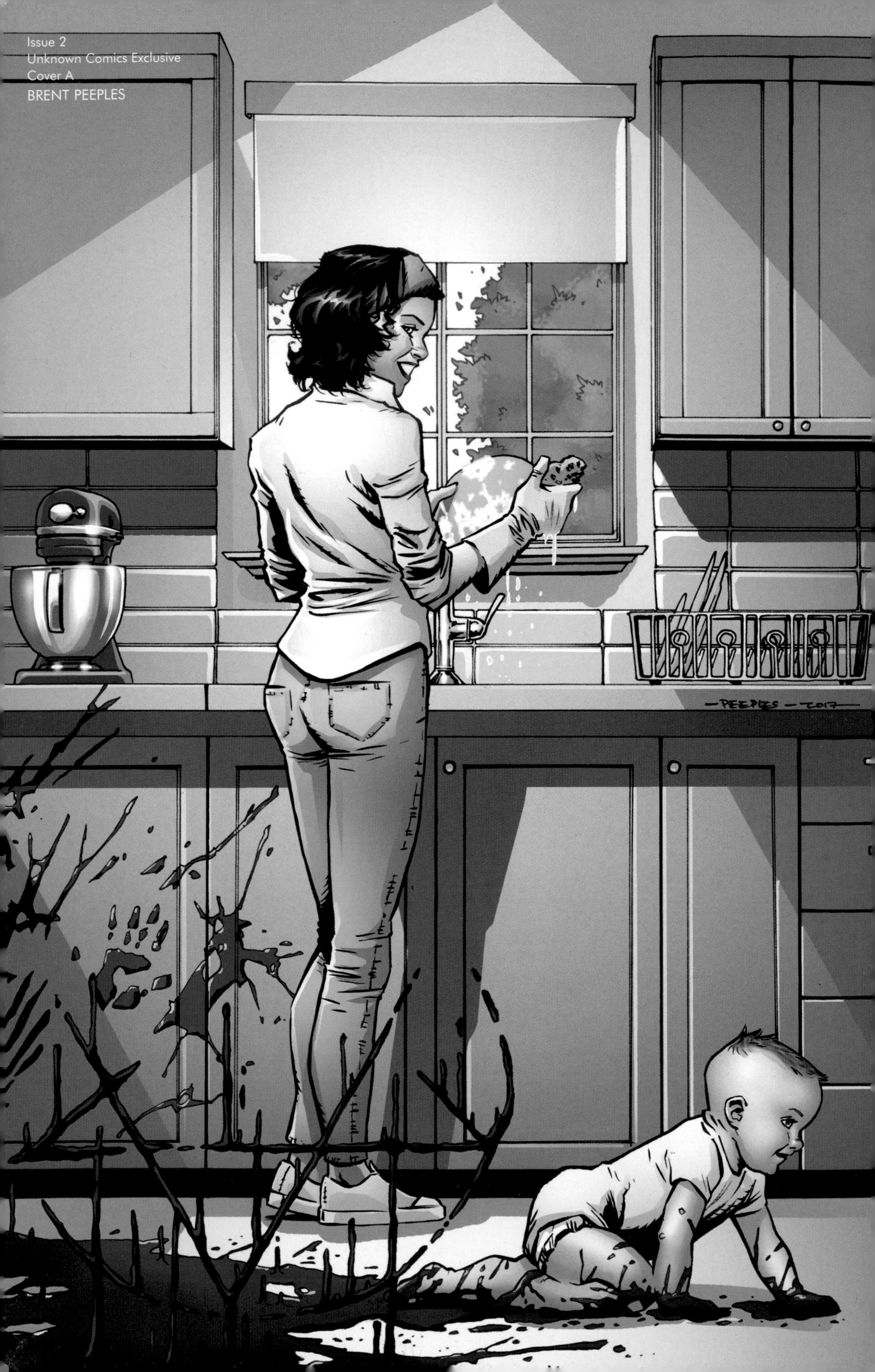
PEEPLES 2017

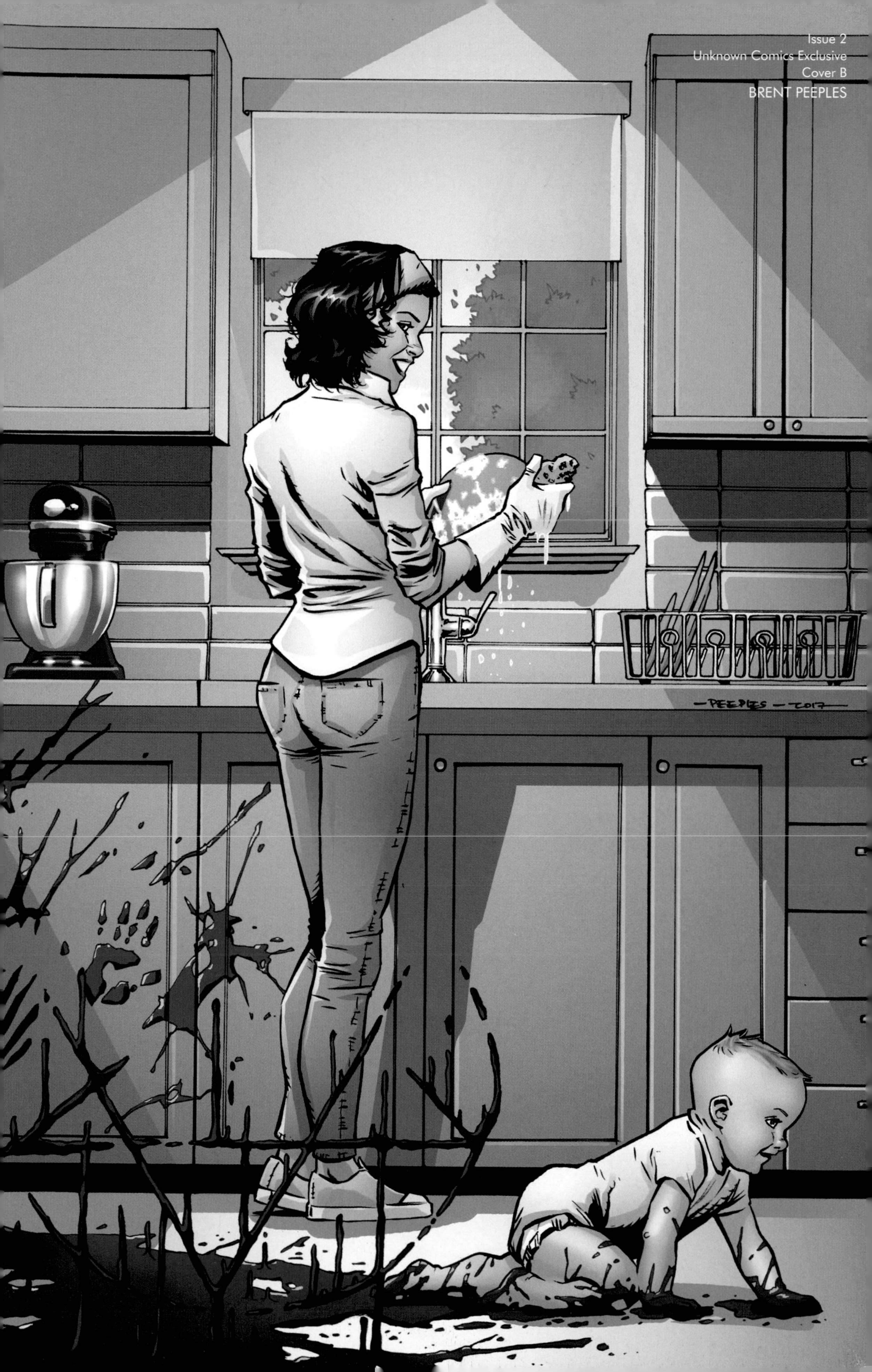
Issue 2
Unknown Comics Exclusive
Cover B
BRENT PEEPLES
PEEPLES 2017

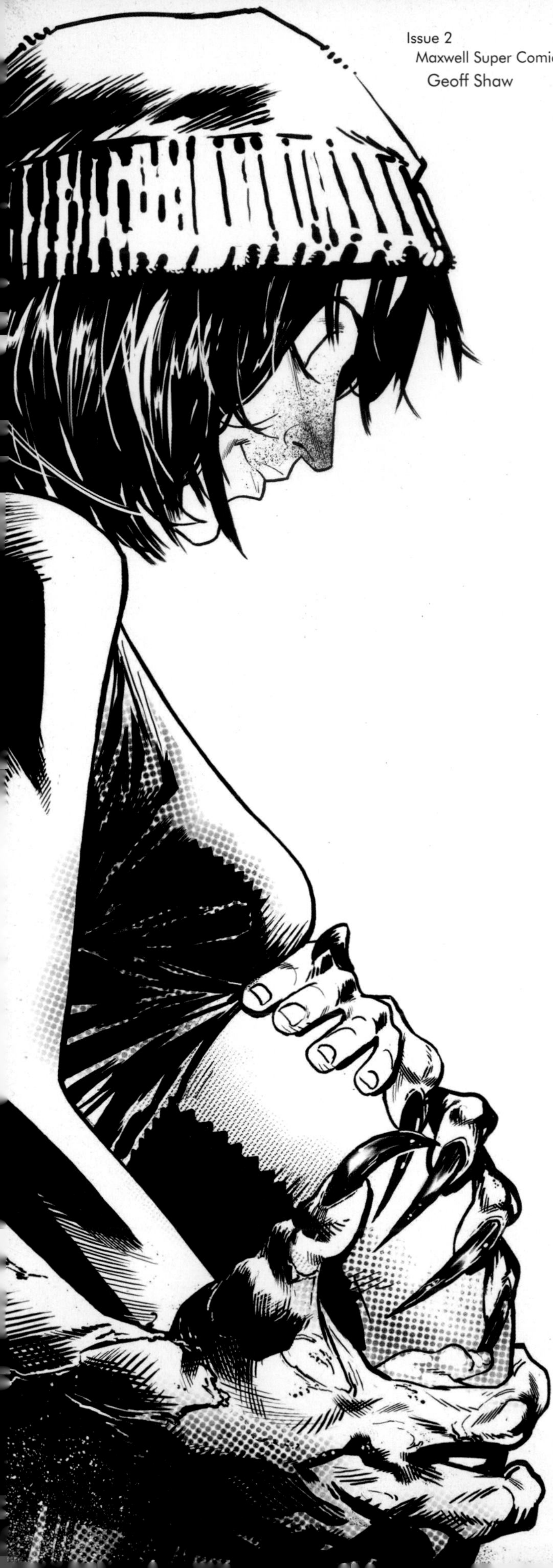

Issue 2
Maxwell Super Comics / MGA Exclusive
Geoff Shaw

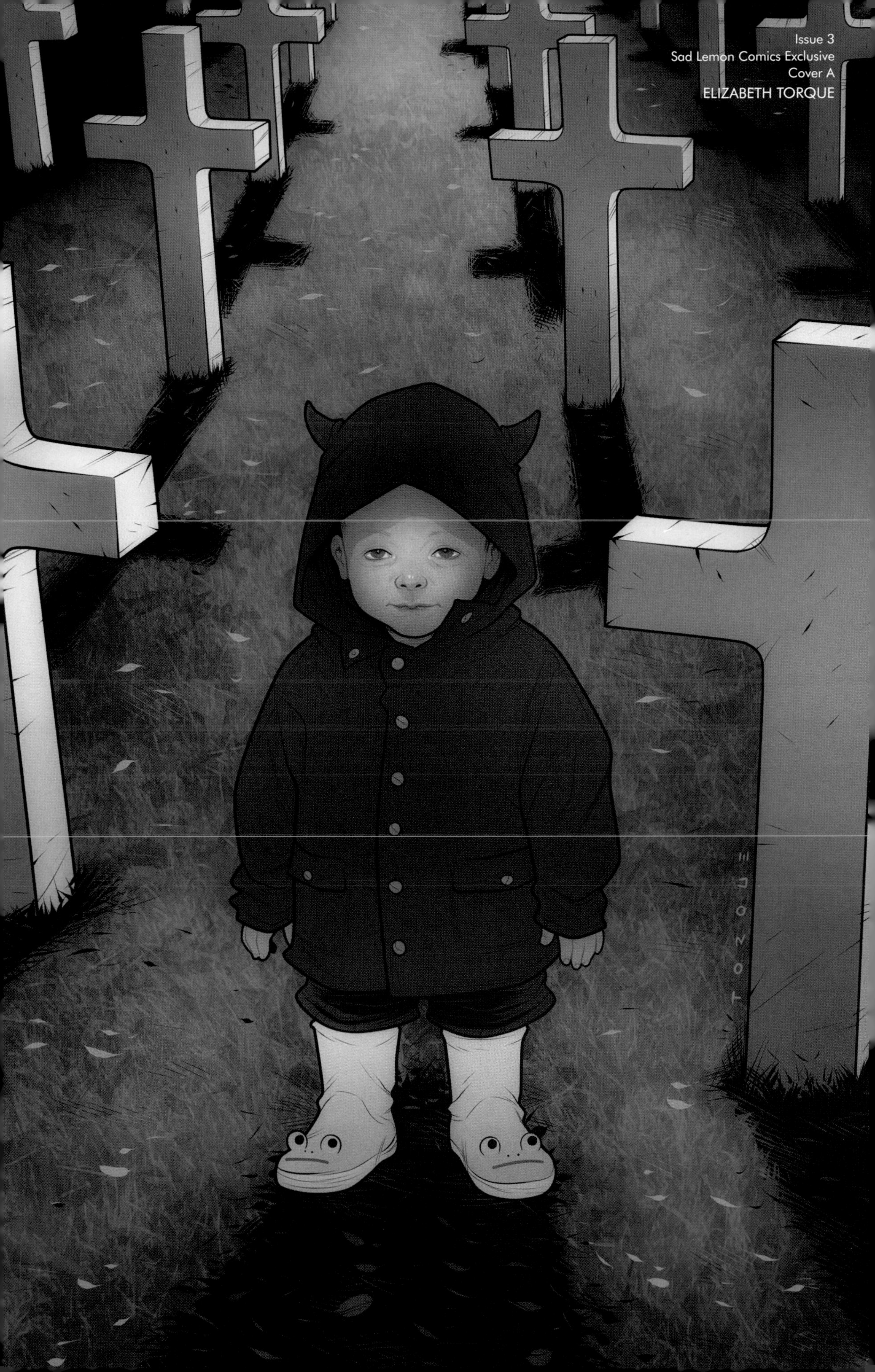
Issue 3
Sad Lemon Comics Exclusive
Cover A
ELIZABETH TORQUE
TORQUE

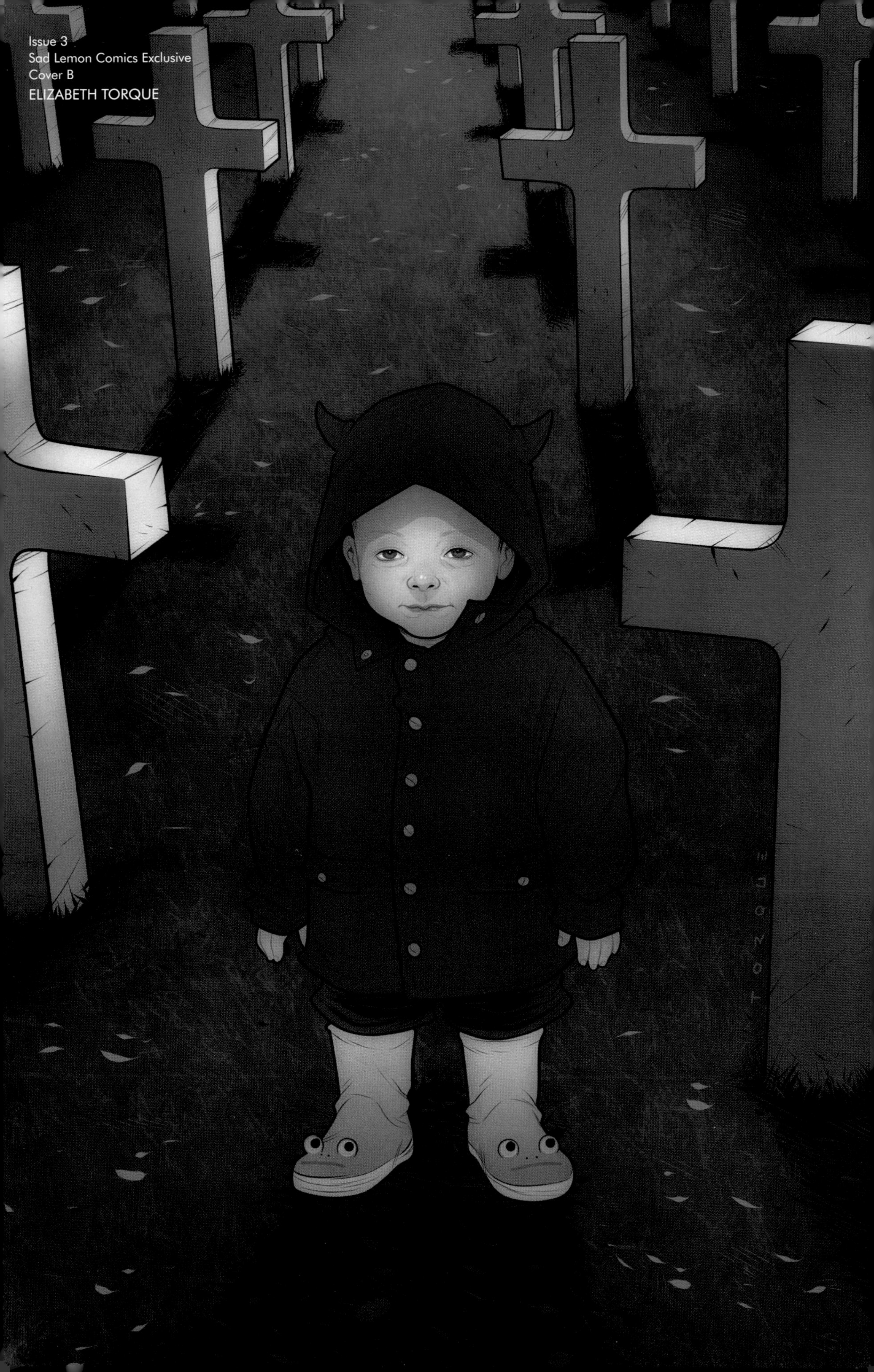
Issue 3
Sad Lemon Comics Exclusive
Cover B
ELIZABETH TORQUE
TORQUE

Issue 3
Gotham Central Exclusive
Cover A
NAT JONES

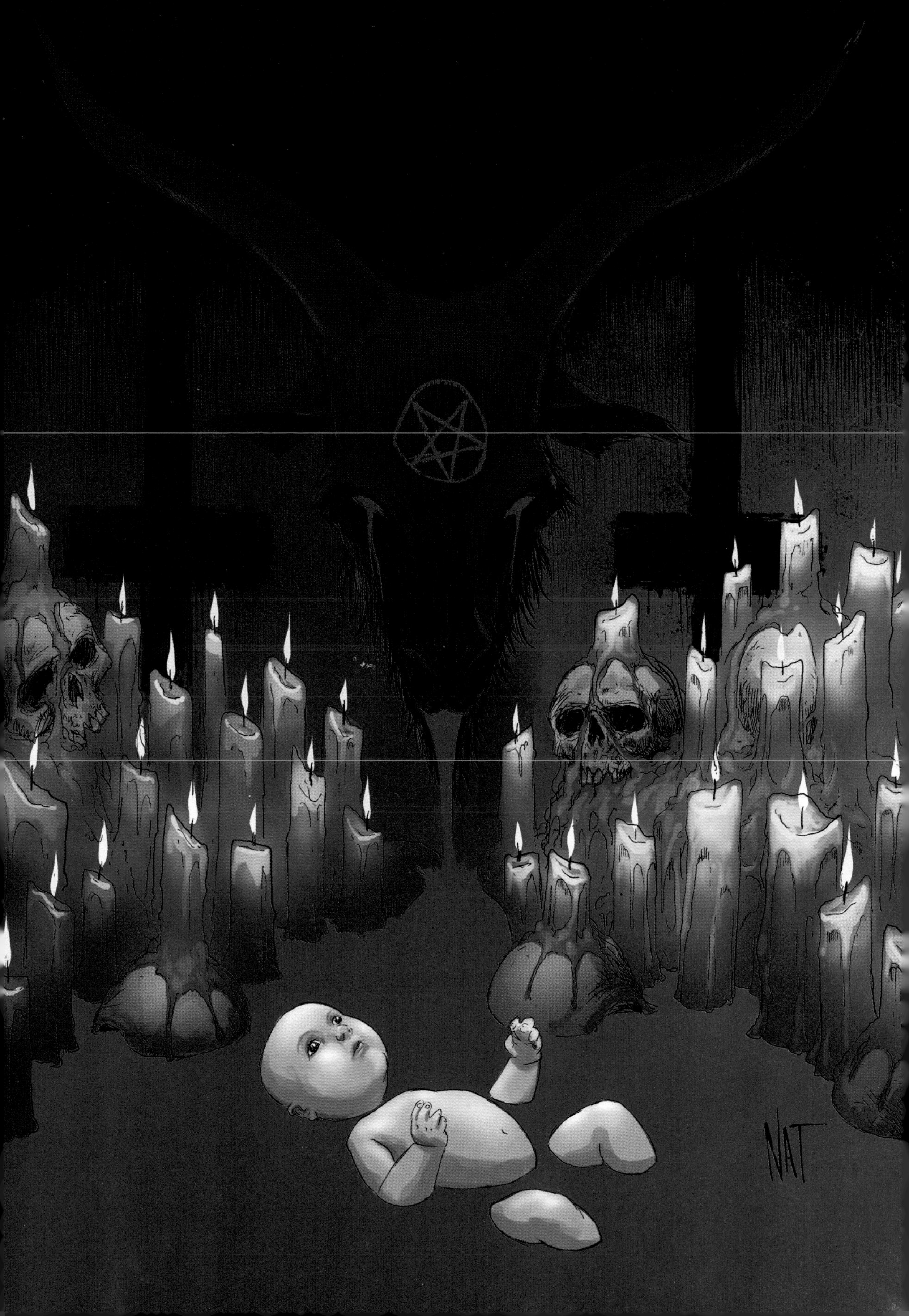
NAT

Issue 3
Gotham Central Exclusive
Cover B
NAT JONES

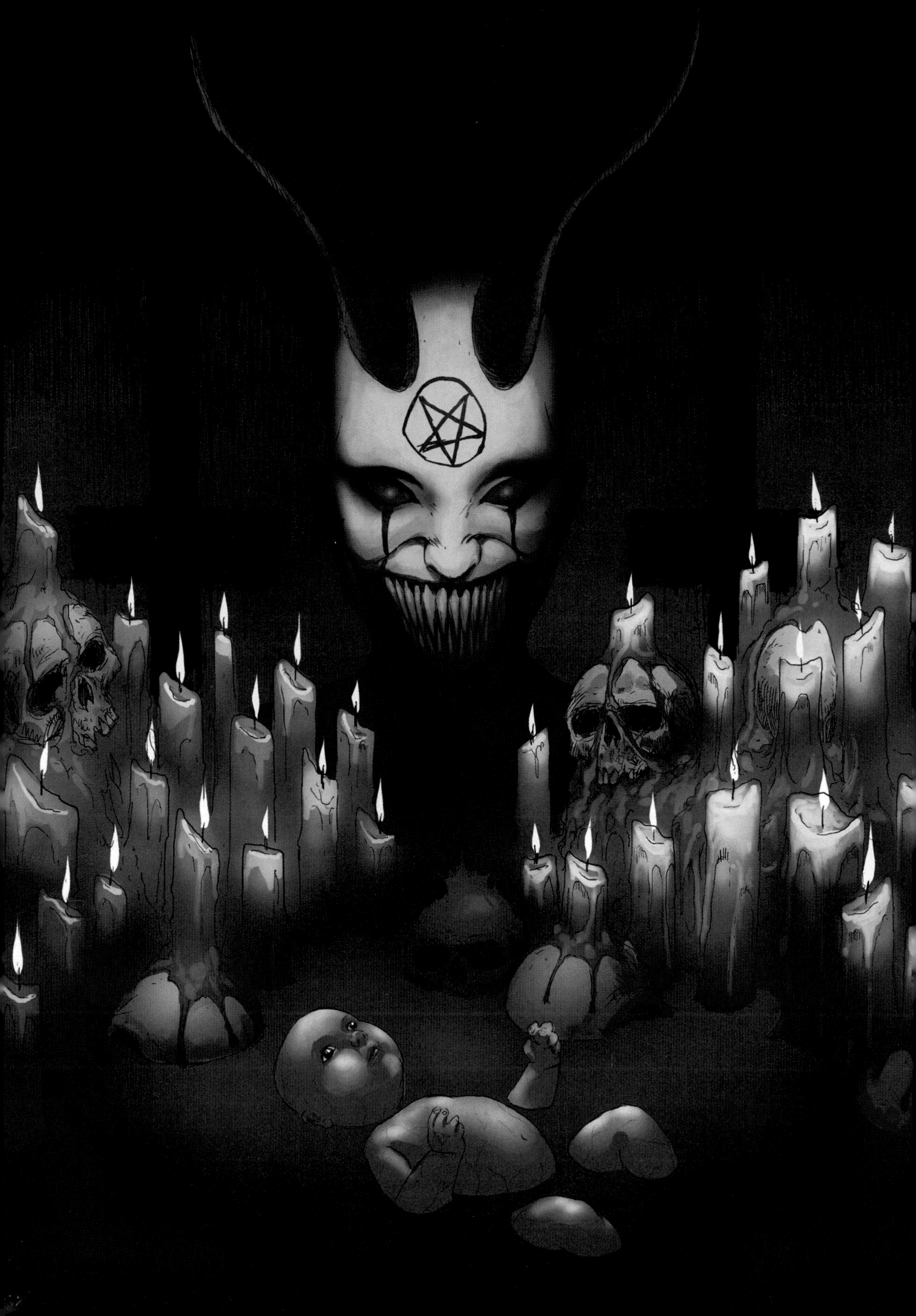

BABY-|-eeTH ™

MAKING OF ISSUE #1

AFTERSHOCK ™

BABYTEETH™ #1

PAGE 5:

Panel 1: Same shot. She ignores him. He just stands there. Getting angry.

Kevin: Sadie...

Panel 2: He snaps a finger in her face here. She jumps a bit.

SFX: SNAP!

Kevin: Hey!

Panel 3: Sadie looks up at him with a sincere smile on her face. She's pulling headphones out of her ear and looking up at him with a gentle, if not a bit nervous, smile as she puts her comic in her open backpack.

Sadie: Oh! Oh, hey Kevin, I'm sorry I was reading and I had my--sorry, whatever--what's up?

Panel 4: Kevin snatches her book bag out of her lap here. It shocks her as it's attached to her. She can't really get up very fast to follow it, so it's really awkward.

Kevin: What is all this shit? Comic books?!

Sadie: Hey...stop it!

Panel 5: Kevin is pretty much picking Sadie up from her shoulders off the ground and going through her bag looking at books. He's picked up a book out of the bag here and it's "what to expect when you're expecting". Sadie looks mortified.

Sadie: Kevin, please...just--

Kevin: The fuck? Why do you have--

Panel 6: Kevin and Sadie both look up off panel towards the parking lot with fear in their eyes. Someone or something is coming that is very scary to them both. It's a car driving right at them btw.

Kevin: --HOLY SHIT!

SFX: HONK! HONK!

script by
DONNY CATES

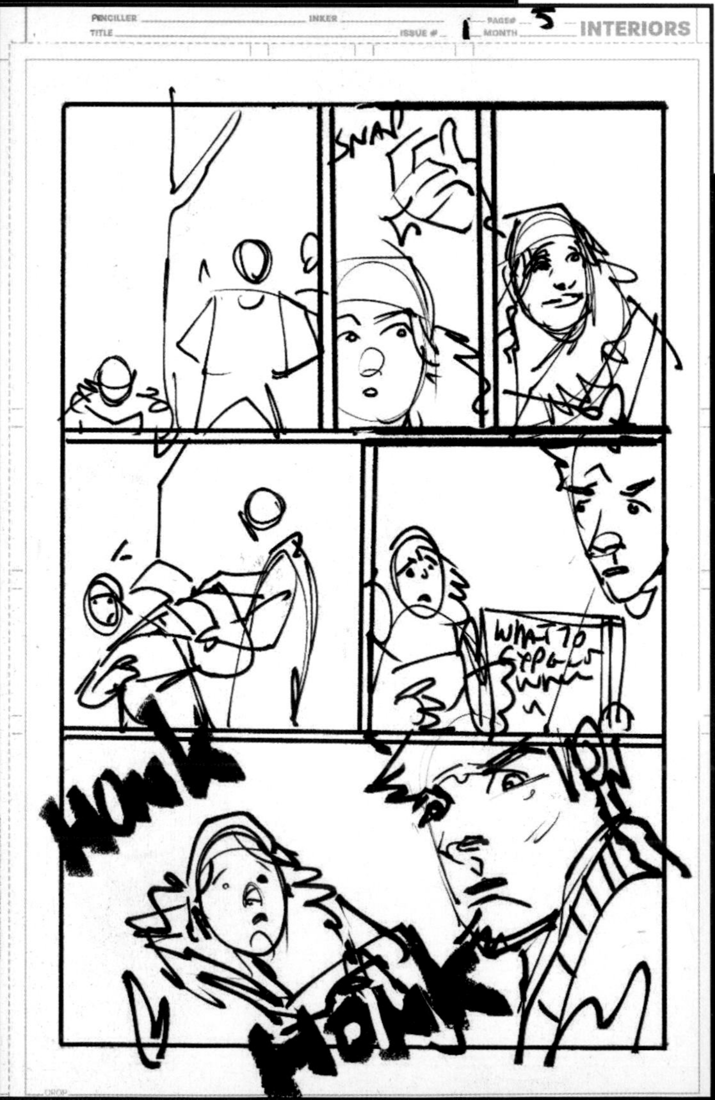
PENCILLER
INKER
PAGE#
5
TITLE
ISSUE #
1
MONTH
INTERIORS
SNAP
HONK
HONK

PAGE 5 PROCESS

layouts by
GARRY BROWN

inks by
GARRY BROWN

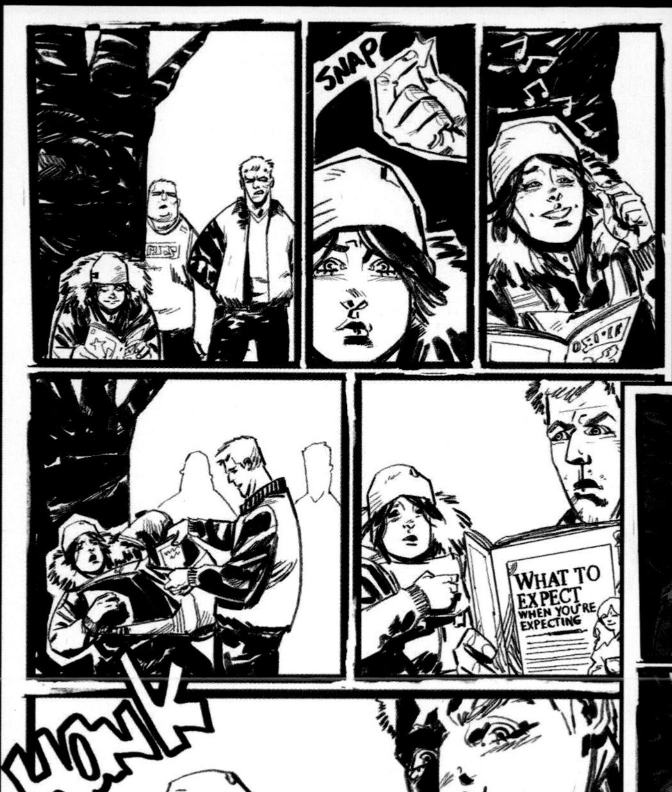
SNAP
WHAT TO EXPECT WHEN YOU'RE EXPECTING
HONK
HONK

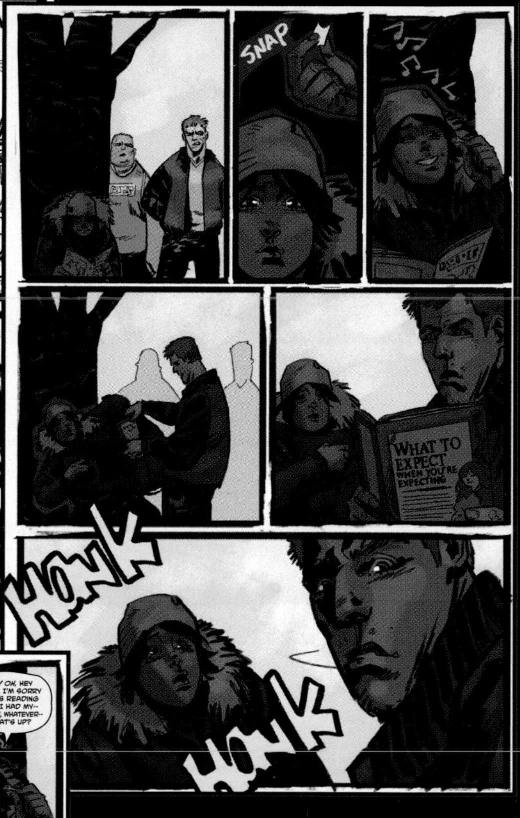
SNAP
WHAT TO EXPECT WHEN YOU'RE EXPECTING
HONK
HONK

colors by
MARK ENGLERT

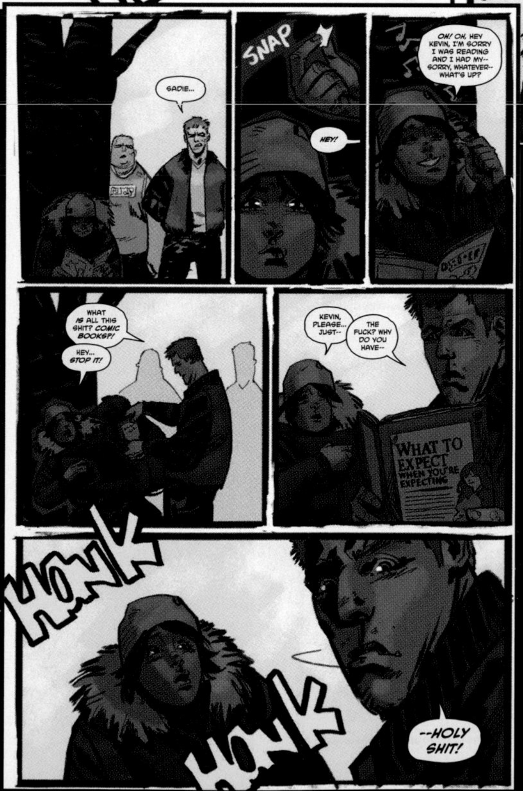
SADIE...
SNAP
HEY!
OH! OH, HEY KEVIN, I'M SORRY I WAS READING AND I HAD MY-- SORRY, WHATEVER-- WHAT'S UP?
WHAT IS ALL THIS SHIT? COMIC BOOKS?!
HEY... STOP IT!
KEVIN, PLEASE... JUST--
THE FUCK? WHY DO YOU HAVE--
WHAT TO EXPECT WHEN YOU'RE EXPECTING
HONK
HONK
--HOLY SHIT!

lettering by
TAYLOR ESPOSITO

PAGE 6 PROCESS

PAGE 6:

Panel 1: Heather has driven her 1980 Bronco up over the parking lot curb and onto the grass of the school grounds and is heading straight at Kevin (And Sadie for that matter).

Caption: All in all, everything was going really well.

Kevin: AH!!

SFX: VRRRR!

Panel 2: Heather stops maybe a foot away from hitting Kevin. Heather's not going to kill his stupid ass, but the point has been made. The bronco is stopped here. Kevin has one of his hands on the hood to show us, the audience, that the truck has stopped. He looks shocked, terrified. Sadie does not. Like this kind of shit happens all the time.

Caption: Some pregnancies are all dramatic and intense. It was never that way with you. Well, not at first...

Caption: You were simple. Easy. Calm.

SFX: VRR--

Panel 3: Biggest panel on the page. Heather has parked and is getting out of the truck. Heather is pissed the fuck off. Her eyes wide. She's a very masculine woman. Very tall and imposing. But not BIG like thick. She's thin, and dangerous, like a junkie that would cut you. She wears a leather jacket that's too big for her, but it works. She has a bit of acne on her face. She does a lot of drugs. Even though it's cold outside, we can see that she has a tank top under her leather jacket, and tattoo's covering her chest and her stomach. Garry, what those tattoos are I'll leave up to you, as you'll be the one who has to draw them all the time. Anyway, she's a fucking badass, and she just drove up on someone messing with her sister. People all around them scatter. Like a gunfighter just showed up on the school ground. She has pulled up maybe a foot away from Sadie and Kevin and the tree. She literally could have almost killed them.

Caption: (you got that from me)

Heather: Walk away from my sister.

Panel 4: Kevin smashes his hand on the hood of her car. Screaming at Heather. His friends start to back him up, but they look scared to get too close. Sadie grabs her book bag and pulls it close to her chest. Embarrassed.

Kevin: Are you fucking kidding me?!

Sadie: (small) Hey, Heather.

SFX: SLAM!

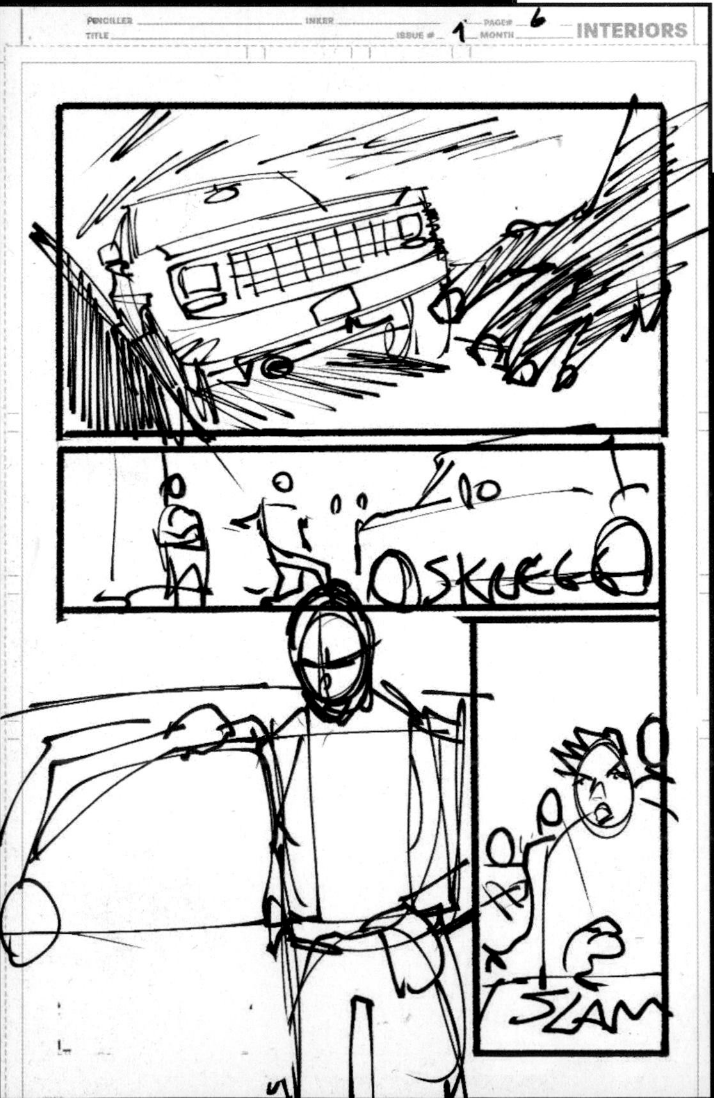
PENCILLER
INKER
TITLE
ISSUE # 1
PAGE# 6
MONTH
INTERIORS
SLAM

script by
DONNY CATES

layouts by
GARRY BROWN

inks by

GARRY BROWN

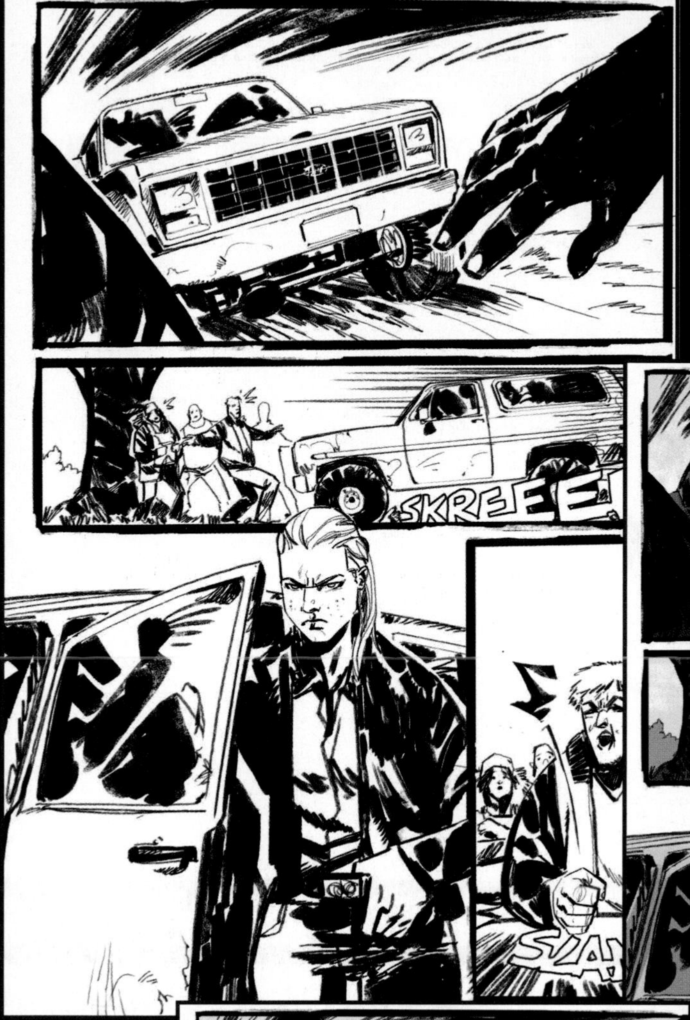
SKREEE
SLA

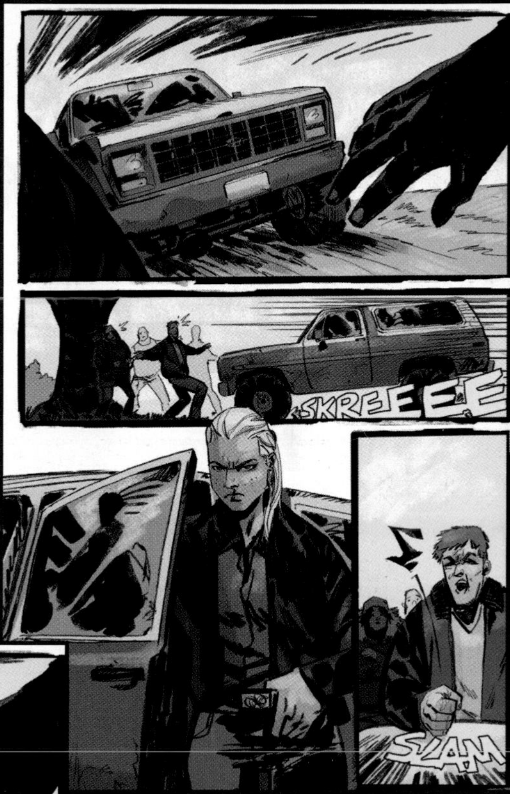
SKREEEE
SLAM

colors b

MARK ENGLER

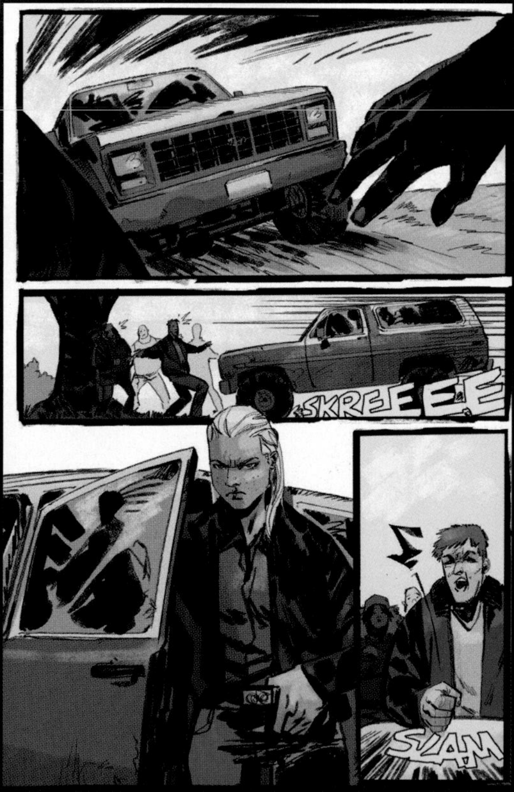
SKREEEE
SLAM

lettering by

TAYLOR ESPOSITO

ABOUT THE CREATORS OF

BABYTEETH™

DONNY CATES writer

@DonCates

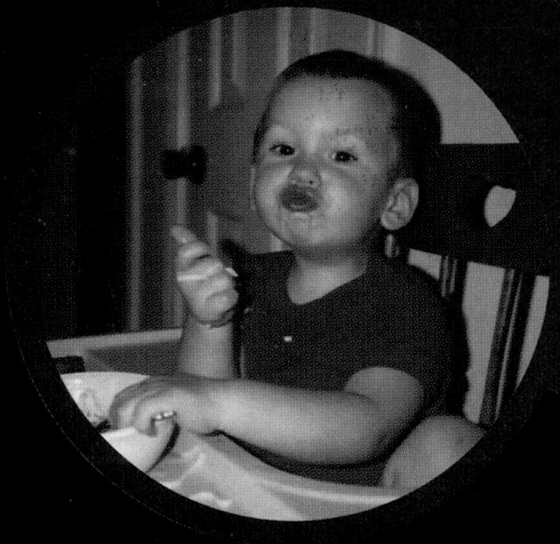

Donny Cates is a writer of comic books. You know him from such things as *God Country* and *Redneck* from Image Comics, *Buzzkill, The Ghost Fleet* and *The Paybacks* from Dark Horse Comics, *Star Trek* from IDW, *Atomahawk, The Simulationists* and *Interceptor* from Heavy Metal and now... BABYTEETH from the fine folks at AfterShock. He lives in Austin, Texas and on Twitter and he thanks you for your time.

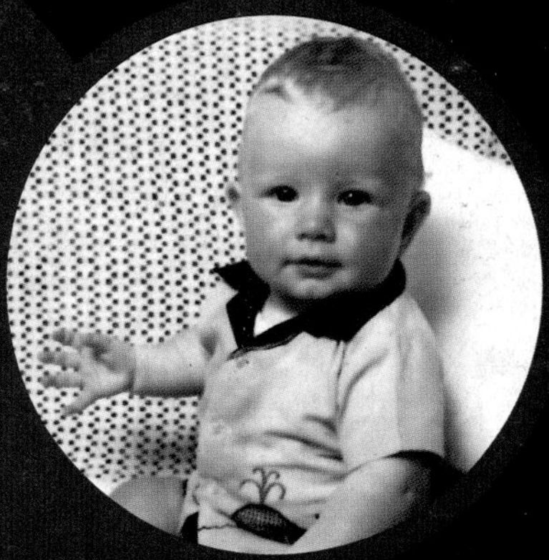

GARRY BROWN artist

@GarryBoom

Garry Brown is a Scottish comic artist working and living in LA with his wife and four cats. He is the co-creator of *Black Road* at Image and has worked on *Catwoman, Batman, Green Arrow, Iron Patriot, The Massive,* THE REVISIONIST and more. He now brings his artistic talents to BABYTEETH for AfterShock Comics.

MARK ENGLERT colorist

@markenglert

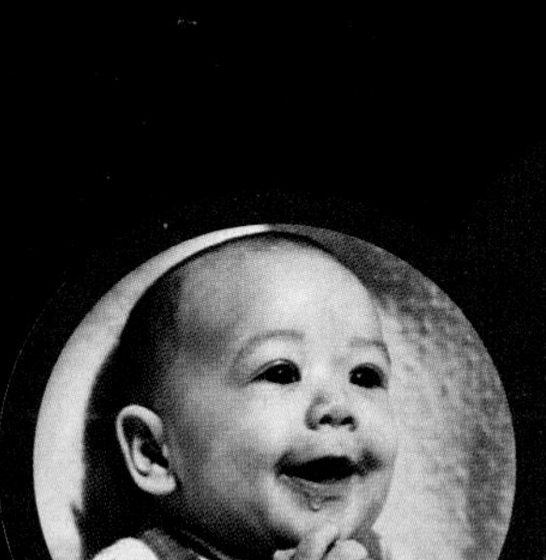

Mark Englert was born in 1979. The first movie he ever saw on opening day was *Star Trek: The Motion Picture* and he slept through the whole thing. Since then, he grew up a little, saw a lot more movies, watched way too much TV, spent countless hours reading comic books when he wasn't busy playing video games. He has been steadily working as an illustrator since 1999, coloring comics, doing concept work at Microsoft and drawing posters for almost every major movie studio. His future plans include continuing to work on comics, illustrate a lot more posters and to one day stay awake for an entire viewing of *Star Trek: The Motion Picture.*

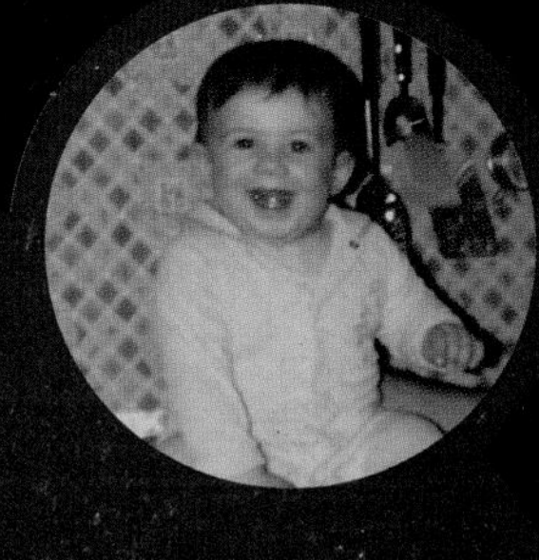

TAYLOR ESPOSITO letterer

@TaylorEspo

Taylor is a comic book lettering professional and owner of Ghost Glyph Studios. As a staff letterer at DC, he lettered titles such as *Red Hood and The Outlaws, Constantine, Bodies, CMYK, The New 52: Future's End* and *New Suicide Squad.* He's also worked on creator-owned titles such as *Interceptor, The Paybacks* (Dark Horse) and *Jade Street Protection Services* (Black Mask). He is currently working on the *Sovereign* and related books (Dynamite), *Heroine Chic, Dents, Mirror, and Firebrand* (Line Webtoon). Other publishers he has worked with include Image, Zenescope, BOOM!, and Heavy Metal.